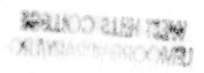

CRIME, PRISONS, AND JAILS

ISSN 1938-890X

CRIME, PRISONS, AND JAILS

Kim Masters Evans

INFORMATION PLUS® REFERENCE SERIES
Formerly Published by Information Plus, Wylie, Texas

GALE
CENGAGE Learning™

Detroit • New York • San Francisco • New Haven, Conn • Waterville, Maine • London

GALE
CENGAGE Learning™

Crime, Prisons, and Jails

Kim Masters Evans

Kepos Media, Inc., Paula Kepos and Janice Jorgensen, Series Editors

Project Editors: Kathleen J. Edgar, Elizabeth Manar, Kimberley A. McGrath

Rights Acquisition and Management: Robyn V. Young

Composition: Evi Abou-El-Seoud, Mary Beth Trimper

Manufacturing: Cynde Lentz

For product information and technology assistance, contact us at
Gale Customer Support, 1-800-877-4253.
For permission to use material from this text or product,
submit all requests online at **www.cengage.com/permissions.**
Further permissions questions can be e-mailed to
permissionrequest@cengage.com

Cover photograph: Image copyright spaxiax, 2009. Used under license from Shutterstock.com.

Gale
27500 Drake Rd.
Farmington Hills, MI 48331-3535

ISBN-13: 978-0-7876-5103-9 (set)   ISBN-10: 0-7876-5103-6 (set)
ISBN-13: 978-1-4144-4857-2   ISBN-10: 1-4144-4857-0

ISSN 1938-890X

This title is also available as an e-book.
ISBN-13: 978-1-4144-7524-0 (set)
ISBN-10: 1-4144-7524-1 (set)
Contact your Gale sales representative for ordering information.

Printed in the United States of America
1 2 3 4 5 6 7 15 14 13 12 11

TABLE OF CONTENTS

PREFACE

Crime, Prisons, and Jails is part of the *Information Plus Reference Series.* The purpose of each volume of the series is to present the latest facts on a topic of pressing concern in modern American life. These topics include the most controversial and studied social issues of the 21st century: abortion, capital punishment, care of senior citizens, education, the environment, health care, immigration, minorities, national security, social welfare, water, women, youth, and many more. Even though this series is written especially for high school and undergraduate students, it is an excellent resource for anyone in need of factual information on current affairs.

By presenting the facts, it is the intention of Gale, Cengage Learning to provide its readers with everything they need to reach an informed opinion on current issues. To that end, there is a particular emphasis in this series on the presentation of scientific studies, surveys, and statistics. These data are generally presented in the form of tables, charts, and other graphics placed within the text of each book. Every graphic is directly referred to and carefully explained in the text. The source of each graphic is presented within the graphic itself. The data used in these graphics are drawn from the most reputable and reliable sources, such as from the various branches of the U.S. government and from private organizations and associations. Every effort has been made to secure the most recent information available. Readers should bear in mind that many major studies take years to conduct and that additional years often pass before the data from these studies are made available to the public. Therefore, in many cases the most recent information available in 2011 is dated from 2008 or 2009. Older statistics are sometimes presented as well if they are landmark studies or of particular interest and no more-recent information exists.

Even though statistics are a major focus of the *Information Plus Reference Series*, they are by no means its only content. Each book also presents the widely held positions and important ideas that shape how the book's subject is discussed in the United States. These positions are explained in detail and, where possible, in the words of their proponents. Some of the other material to be found in these books includes historical background, descriptions of major events related to the subject, relevant laws and court cases, and examples of how these issues play out in American life. Some books also feature primary documents or have pro and con debate sections that provide the words and opinions of prominent Americans on both sides of a controversial topic. All material is presented in an even-handed and unbiased manner; readers will never be encouraged to accept one view of an issue over another.

HOW TO USE THIS BOOK

In general, crime has been on the decline in recent years. Some crimes, however, are increasing in number among different segments of the population. For example, violent crime has decreased since the 1990s, whereas identity theft has increased. Besides exploring crime in the United States, this volume examines the U.S. penal system as well as its inmates. Prisons and jails are an important and controversial part of the effort to control crime in the United States. Much public funding is spent on the construction of new prisons and jails and on the maintenance of old facilities, but many people question the effectiveness of prisons and jails as a deterrent to crime. Who is locked up in U.S. prisons, what crimes have they committed, and how effective is the prison system? These and other basic questions are discussed in this volume.

Crime, Prisons, and Jails consists of 10 chapters and three appendixes. Each chapter is devoted to a particular aspect of crime, prisons, and jails in the United States. For a summary of the information covered in each chapter, please see the synopses provided in the Table of Contents. Chapters generally begin with an overview of the basic facts and background information on the chapter's topic, then proceed to examine subtopics of particular interest. For example, Chapter 5, White-Collar Crime, defines various white-collar crimes and provides Federal Bureau of Investigation (FBI) statistics on the number of arrests for these types of crimes. It also provides survey and database results from the National White-Collar Crime Center, the Bureau of Justice Statistics, and the Federal Trade Commission about people who have been victimized by white-collar crimes. Next, recent cases investigated by the FBI's Financial Crime Section are described in the categories of corporate fraud, mortgage fraud, securities and commodities fraud, health care fraud, insurance fraud, mass marketing fraud, and money laundering. The chapter then addresses famous corporate crimes, which is followed by computer crimes and federal legislation that has been enacted to punish the perpetrators of these crimes. Crimes involving violation of intellectual property rights, tax fraud, and forgery and counterfeiting are also described. The chapter concludes with a look at public corruption and gives specific examples of individuals and groups that have allegedly violated the public trust. Readers can find their way through a chapter by looking for the section and subsection headings, which are clearly set off from the text. They can also refer to the book's extensive index, if they already know what they are looking for.

Statistical Information

The tables and figures featured throughout *Crime, Prisons, and Jails* will be of particular use to readers in learning about this topic. These tables and figures represent an extensive collection of the most recent and valuable statistics on prisons and jails, as well as related issues—for example, graphics cover the number of people in jail or prison in the United States; the characteristics of those incarcerated; and the amount of money the government spends on the criminal justice system. Gale, Cengage Learning believes that making this information available to readers is the most important way to fulfill the goal of this book: to help readers understand the issues and controversies surrounding crime, prisons, and jails in the United States and to reach their own conclusions.

Each table or figure has a unique identifier appearing above it for ease of identification and reference. Titles for the tables and figures explain their purpose. At the end of each table or figure, the original source of the data is provided.

To help readers understand these often complicated statistics, all tables and figures are explained in the text. References in the text direct readers to the relevant statistics. Furthermore, the contents of all tables and figures are fully indexed. Please see the opening section of the index at the back of this volume for a description of how to find tables and figures within it.

Appendixes

Besides the main body text and images, *Crime, Prisons, and Jails* has three appendixes. The first is the Important Names and Addresses directory. Here, readers will find contact information for a number of government and private organizations that can provide further information on aspects of crime and the U.S. prison and jail system. The second appendix is the Resources section, which can also assist readers in conducting their own research. In this section, the author and editors of *Crime, Prisons, and Jails* describe some of the sources that were most useful during the compilation of this book. The final appendix is the detailed index. It has been greatly expanded from previous editions and should make it even easier to find specific topics in this book.

ADVISORY BOARD CONTRIBUTIONS

The staff of Information Plus would like to extend its heartfelt appreciation to the Information Plus Advisory Board. This dedicated group of media professionals provides feedback on the series on an ongoing basis. Their comments allow the editorial staff who work on the project to make the series better and more user-friendly. The staff's top priority is to produce the highest-quality and most useful books possible, and the Information Plus Advisory Board's contributions to this process are invaluable.

The members of the Information Plus Advisory Board are:

- Kathleen R. Bonn, Librarian, Newbury Park High School, Newbury Park, California
- Madelyn Garner, Librarian, San Jacinto College, North Campus, Houston, Texas
- Anne Oxenrider, Media Specialist, Dundee High School, Dundee, Michigan
- Charles R. Rodgers, Director of Libraries, Pasco-Hernando Community College, Dade City, Florida
- James N. Zitzelsberger, Library Media Department Chairman, Oshkosh West High School, Oshkosh, Wisconsin

COMMENTS AND SUGGESTIONS

The editors of the *Information Plus Reference Series* welcome your feedback on *Crime, Prisons, and Jails*. Please direct all correspondence to:

Editors
Information Plus Reference Series
27500 Drake Rd.
Farmington Hills, MI 48331-3535

CHAPTER 1
AN OVERVIEW OF CRIME

A crime occurs when a person commits an act that is prohibited by law or fails to act where there is a legal responsibility to do so. Crime has both legal and moral components. Federal, state, and local laws define criminal behavior and specify corresponding punishments. These laws are designed to protect the public good and are based, in some part, on the moral beliefs that are held by U.S. society about the relative rightness and wrongness of various human actions. Americans consider crime to be a serious problem. They worry about the level of criminal behavior in their neighborhoods and in the country as a whole.

CATEGORIZING CRIME
Morality and Mental State

At a basic level, crime is divided into two categories based on whether the behavior violates the moral standards of a society or simply the administrative policies of its government. The Latin term *mala in se* means "morally wrong" or "inherently wrong." *Mala in se* crimes are those condemned universally as wrong or evil because the criminal action is inherently bad. These are crimes that offend the moral beliefs of people. Crimes such as murder and stealing have been considered wrong since ancient times. Some societal morals change with time. For example, slavery was once accepted as a legal practice in the United States. Eventually, it became so morally repugnant that it was considered a *mala in se* crime. In recent decades actions such as driving under the influence or using certain drugs have become *mala in se*. By contrast, other crimes are considered *mala prohibita* (wrongs prohibited). These are behaviors that are not inherently bad in themselves, but are prohibited by government policy. Many traffic laws are *mala prohibita*. For example, speeding is criminal not because it is morally evil, but because it is deemed criminal by government authorities.

Governments' decisions about how to define and punish certain crimes are based, in part, on the moral beliefs of the society in which the crimes occur. Even though *mala in se* behaviors are universally condemned as wrong, punishments for these crimes can vary significantly between societies and between governments. During the colonial period in U.S. history the death penalty was commonly meted out for crimes such as horse stealing and robbery. Over time, societal morals demanded less harsh punishments for these crimes.

An important element in how crimes are categorized and punished is called *mens rea*, which translates from Latin as "guilty mind," or more commonly, "criminal intent." The U.S. justice system seeks to determine the mental state of a perpetrator at the time the criminal act was committed and to assign punishment accordingly. Intentional criminal acts that are planned in advance are considered much more serious than unintentional criminal acts or crimes committed in the "heat of passion."

Punishment Categories

From a punishment standpoint, crimes are divided into three broad categories: felonies, misdemeanors, and infractions. Felonies are considered the most serious crimes and are punished the most severely. The word *felony* is believed to be derived from a Latin word meaning "evil doer." Crimes that inflict death or serious injury or the threat of death or serious injury are considered felonies. Many property crimes that involve large economic losses to the victim are also classified as felonies. In general, people convicted of felonies are punished with prison terms at least a year in length and are sometimes assessed a fine of many thousands of dollars. Convicted felons may also lose some of their constitutional rights, such as the right to vote in elections. In some states the loss of rights only applies while a felon is incarcerated; in other states rights can be lost permanently. The most serious felony is the intentional murder of another human being. This crime is considered so heinous that capital punishment (execution) is sometimes the penalty for committing murder.

Misdemeanors are less serious crimes than felonies. They involve less personal harm and lower economic losses than felonies. These "lesser" crimes are typically punished with jail sentences of less than one year and fines of up to a few thousand dollars. People convicted of misdemeanors do not typically lose any of their constitutional rights once their sentences are served.

States divide felonies and misdemeanors into levels or classes to indicate their relative seriousness. For example, the Virginia Department of Alcoholic Beverage Control indicates in "Punishment for Criminal Offenses" (2011, http://www.abc.state.va.us/facts/punish.html) that Virginia has six classes of felonies and four classes of misdemeanors. In both categories Class 1 crimes are the most serious and punished the most severely. Other states use a letter system in which Class A felonies or misdemeanors are considered the most serious in their category.

Finally, the least serious crimes are called infractions (or petty offenses). These include minor traffic and parking violations and violations of local ordinances. The punishment for an infraction is usually only a fine of up to a few hundred dollars.

DEFINING THE TYPES OF CRIMES

Crimes are defined and punished differently by different jurisdictions within the United States. Sorting out all the various and complicated legal definitions for particular crimes can be challenging. This section will present some general and widely used definitions for the most common crimes. The American Bar Association (ABA) is a private organization for legal professionals, such as lawyers and judges. The ABA maintains an online glossary (http://www.abanet.org/publiced/glossary.html) of legal terms that includes general definitions of various crimes. This glossary is the source for many of the crime definitions that are presented in this section.

Killing Crimes

Killing crimes are defined and punished at various levels depending on the mental state of the killer and the circumstances under which the killing took place. Criminal intent (or lack thereof) plays a major role in how these crimes are categorized. Killing with criminal intent is typically called murder. There are various degrees (or levels) of murder in criminal law. First-degree murder is the most serious charge and means the killer planned the crime and deliberately carried it out. First-degree murder is often described as deliberate killing with "malice aforethought." Malice is the desire or intent to cause great harm. Aforethought means "previously in mind." In other words, murder committed with aforethought is premeditated (considered and thought through before being committed).

Second-degree murder is a lesser charge that is applied to a killing that may or may not be intentional but is not premeditated. A person who gets into a fistfight and ultimately kills his or her opponent might be charged with second-degree murder. This crime might also be called manslaughter. There are two levels of manslaughter: voluntary manslaughter and involuntary manslaughter. Voluntary manslaughter is a killing believed to be intentional but not premeditated. It occurs on a sudden impulse, as in the fistfight example. Involuntary manslaughter is an unintentional killing that occurs as a consequence of reckless behavior or extreme negligence. The reckless behavior is typically some minor unlawful action that is not ordinarily expected to result in a death. An example is a driver who runs a red light and inadvertently strikes and kills a pedestrian crossing the street. Ordinarily, running a red light is a minor crime. The accidental taking of life elevates the crime to the level of manslaughter. Involuntary manslaughter involving extreme negligence may also be called criminally negligent homicide. Involuntary manslaughter involving recklessness, rather than negligence, is often called nonnegligent homicide.

An accidental killing that occurs as a result of a felony is a much more serious crime in the eyes of the law. Some states define a crime called felony murder. It can be charged against any willing participant in a serious felony (such as a bank robbery) if a person is inadvertently killed as a result of the felonious act. These laws apply even to criminals who are not actually in the victim's presence at the time of the accidental death (e.g., getaway drivers at bank robberies). As a result, these laws are highly controversial.

There are some homicides that are not considered criminal. These include killings performed in self-defense and accidental killings that occur during noncriminal actions. Intent and circumstances are the primary elements that influence whether criminal charges are filed and the extent of any resulting punishments.

Bodily Harm Crimes

Bodily harm crimes are crimes that are intended to cause or do cause personal injury to another person. The primary example is assault, which is an attempted or completed attack on a victim by a perpetrator who intends to inflict or recklessly inflicts bodily harm.

AGGRAVATED AND SIMPLE ASSAULT. In general, there are two levels of assault: aggravated assault and simple assault. Aggravated assault charges are typically filed if the attacker uses a deadly weapon and/or intends to inflict or does inflict serious injury to the victim. Aggravated assault can also result from reckless behavior. Simple assault is a lesser crime that does not include the more serious circumstances or consequences to the victim. Simple assault can also be charged when a person's extreme negligence causes bodily harm to another person. Some state laws define a crime called assault and battery that includes both threat (assault) and bodily attack (battery).

In most jurisdictions the penalties for assault (or assault and battery) are more severe when the victim is a public official, such as a law enforcement officer, firefighter, social worker, judge, or school teacher, who is attacked while on duty.

Sex Crimes

Sexually based offenses are crimes that involve some type of sexual activity that is deemed illegal. The most serious sexual offenses are those in which force or the threat of force is used by the perpetrator and those in which the victims are children.

RAPE. Rape, or sexual assault as it is called in some states, is a crime. In *Crime in the United States, 2009* (September 2010, http://www2.fbi.gov/ucr/cius2009/index .html), the Federal Bureau of Investigation (FBI) defines forcible rape as "the carnal knowledge of a female forcibly and against her will. Attempts or assaults to commit rape by force or threat of force are also included; however, statutory rape (without force) and other sex offenses are excluded." State laws typically classify rapes at different felony levels depending on the circumstances of the crime. For example, the Office of Code Revision Indiana Legislative Services Agency (2011, http://www.in.gov/legislative/ic/code/title 35/ar42/ch4.html) indicates that Indiana classifies rape as a Class A felony if the rape includes the threat or use of deadly force, the perpetrator has a deadly weapon (such as a firearm), the victim is seriously injured during the attack, or the victim is unknowingly drugged by the perpetrator. Otherwise, rape is a Class B felony in Indiana.

Use (or threat) of force and lack of consent are common elements that define rape when the victim is an adult with full mental and physical capacities. Statutory rape is a separately defined crime in which the victim is either younger than a legally set age of consent or the victim is an adult with a debilitating mental or physical condition. In these cases a crime occurs even if the victim consents to the sexual activity and no force or threat of force is used.

There are many other offenses besides rape that may be considered sexually based crimes under the law. Typical examples include offenses related to prostitution or pornography. Depending on the circumstances, these crimes might be deemed felonies or less serious misdemeanors.

Theft Crimes

Theft crimes cover a broad spectrum of offenses. The most serious theft crime is called robbery. In *Crime in the United States, 2009*, the FBI defines robbery as "the taking or attempting to take anything of value from the care, custody, or control of a person or persons by force or threat of force or violence and/or by putting the victim in fear." An important distinction between robbery and other theft crimes is that robbery involves an element of personal force or the threat of personal force and harm to the victim. Thus,

robberies are typically face-to-face crimes in which the victim is personally menaced by the perpetrator. This can occur on the street (e.g., a mugging or carjacking) or in a business or residence (e.g., a bank robbery or home invasion). Because of the danger to the victims posed by these personal encounters, the penalties for robbery are severe.

Burglary is a different crime from robbery. The FBI defines burglary as "the unlawful entry of a structure to commit a felony or theft." Burglary is also known as breaking and entering, although the actual act of "breaking in" is not always required. In general, any entry made without the owner's permission, for example, through an unlocked door, may legally be considered burglary.

Theft (or larceny) is a broad category that includes many different offenses. For example, California's penal code Section 484(a) (January 15, 2011, http://law.onecle .com/california/penal/484.html) defines theft as:

> Every person who shall feloniously steal, take, carry, lead, or drive away the personal property of another, or who shall fraudulently appropriate property which has been entrusted to him or her, or who shall knowingly and designedly, by any false or fraudulent representation or pretense, defraud any other person of money, labor or real or personal property, or who causes or procures others to report falsely of his or her wealth or mercantile character and by thus imposing upon any person, obtains credit and thereby fraudulently gets or obtains possession of money, or property or obtains the labor or service of another, is guilty of theft.

The FBI states in *Crime in the United States, 2009* that larceny-theft is "the unlawful taking, carrying, leading, or riding away of property from the possession or constructive possession of another," and includes offenses such as stealing bicycles, shoplifting, pocket picking, and other theft crimes in which force or violence is not used.

There are many other theft-type offenses that are defined by law. Examples include forgery, counterfeiting, fraud, identity theft, confidence games, writing bad checks, and embezzlement. In all these cases, the intent of the perpetrator is to obtain something of value through illegal means.

Theft crimes are generally classified into levels or degrees of seriousness based on the particular circumstances of the crime. These classifications often take into account the economic losses to the victim. In other words, a large-value theft is treated more severely than a low-value theft.

WHITE-COLLAR CRIMES. White-collar crimes are a subset of theft crimes. They differ from crimes such as burglary and robbery in that white-collar crimes are typically conducted without the threat or use of violence and without physical labor (e.g., breaking into a building) on the part of the perpetrator. Examples include fraud, counterfeiting, and embezzlement. White-collar crimes are discussed in detail in Chapter 5.

Alcohol and Drug Crimes

Alcohol and drugs are substances that can impair judgment and inflame passions. People under the influence of these substances may engage in reckless or violent behavior that seriously harms others. Societal concerns about alcohol and drug use have varied dramatically throughout U.S. history.

ALCOHOL CRIMES. During the late 1880s and early 1900s a Progressive movement swept the nation in which many people believed that laws could "socially engineer" Americans out of immoral and destructive behaviors—such as drinking alcohol. Some states passed laws that were intended to restrict its consumption. By 1918 alcohol was considered to be such a menace to the public good that its manufacture and sales were outlawed by Congress via the 18th Amendment to the U.S. Constitution. Prohibition, as it was called, proved to be unworkable and was abandoned at the federal level in 1933. Nevertheless, states and local jurisdictions have passed laws that criminalize certain alcohol-related actions, particularly public drunkenness and driving under the influence of alcohol.

DRUG CRIMES. The history of drug criminalization has also been checkered. Drugs such as cocaine and heroin were once common ingredients in popular products that Americans bought and consumed. Over time, growing awareness about the physical, psychological, and social harms that were associated with the use of these drugs spurred laws against them. Modern drug laws are complex and sometimes controversial as Americans continue to debate how best to control human behaviors that are considered undesirable to the public good. A detailed discussion of drug crimes is presented in Chapter 4.

Hate Crimes

Laws against some crimes, such as murder and stealing, have their roots in the ancient past. Other behaviors are deemed illegal because of social mores that have developed more recently, such as prohibitions against alcohol and drug offenses. Hate crimes are criminal offenses that are motivated by the offender's personal prejudice or bias against the victim. Even though no single, comprehensive legal definition is available for the term *hate crime*, the FBI defines it in *Hate Crime Statistics, 2009* (November 2010, http://www2.fbi.gov/ucr/hc2009/index.html) as "criminal offenses that are motivated, in whole or in part, by the offender's bias against a race, religion, sexual orientation, ethnicity/national origin, or disability and are committed against persons, property, or society."

The first federal legislation against hate crimes was passed in 1969. In 1990 Congress passed the Hate Crime Statistics Act, which required the U.S. attorney general to "acquire data ... about crimes that manifest evidence of prejudice based on race, religion, disability, sexual orientation, or ethnicity" and to publish a summary of the data. The Hate Crimes Statistics Act was amended by the Violent Crime and Law Enforcement Act of 1994 to include bias-motivated acts against disabled people. Further amendments in the Church Arsons Prevention Act of 1996 directed the FBI to track bias-related church arsons as a permanent part of its duties.

The Anti-Defamation League, an organization that fights anti-Semitism and bigotry, notes in "State Hate Crime Statutory Provisions" (http://www.adl.org/learn/hate_crimes_laws/map_frameset.html) that as of 2010, 45 states and the District of Columbia had adopted some form of statute against "bias-motivated violence and intimidation." The exceptions were Arkansas, Georgia, Indiana, South Carolina, and Wyoming.

THE CONSTITUTIONALITY OF HATE CRIME LEGISLATION. The constitutionality of hate crime legislation has been challenged on the grounds that these laws punish free thought. In 1992 the U.S. Supreme Court, in *R.A.V. v. City of St. Paul* (505 U.S. 377), found a Minnesota law outlawing certain "fighting words" to be unconstitutional. In this case, the defendant had burned a cross "inside the fenced yard of a black family."

A law limiting pure speech or symbolic speech can only be upheld if it meets the "clear and present danger" standard of *Brandenburg v. Ohio* (395 U.S. 444 [1969]). This standard means that speech may be outlawed if it incites or produces "imminent lawless action."

However, in *Wisconsin v. Mitchell* (508 U.S. 476 [1993]), the Supreme Court upheld laws that impose harsher prison sentences and greater fines for criminals who are motivated by bigotry. The court found that statutes such as the Wisconsin law do not illegally restrict free speech and are not so general as to restrict constitutional behavior.

Terrorism

Terrorism is difficult to define legally. In fact, there are many different definitions under federal and state laws. In *2009 Report on Terrorism* (April 30, 2010, http://www.nctc.gov/witsbanner/docs/2009_report_on_terrorism.pdf), the National Counterterrorism Center (NCTC) defines terrorism as "premeditated, politically motivated violence perpetrated against noncombatant targets by subnational groups or clandestine agents." This definition is taken directly from the U.S. Code at 22 USC Section 2656f(d)(2), which focuses on foreign relations.

Generally, the term *terrorism* is associated with violent actions that are perpetrated by people with a certain mind-set against other people. The perpetrators of terrorist acts typically justify their behavior as appropriate because it is waged against people they consider to be enemies for various political, social, and/or religious reasons. Thus, terrorism is the ultimate hate crime and is motivated by bias. Much modern terrorism is international in nature, meaning that it involves perpetrators and victims of different nationalities. Some horrifying acts of international terrorism have taken place, including the September 11, 2001, attacks on the United States. Such acts are criminal under U.S. law, and the perpetrators can be tried and convicted of criminal offenses. The scope of international terrorism places it squarely under the jurisdiction of federal authorities. However, capturing and trying foreign nationals can be difficult, particularly when they are in countries unfriendly to the United States. In some cases, the U.S. armed forces may become involved, as they have in the war in Afghanistan, to capture alleged terrorists for prosecution under U.S. law.

Domestic Terrorism

Terrorism is domestic when the perpetrators and the victims are citizens or residents of the same country, such as a terrorist attack that is carried out on U.S. soil by U.S. citizens or residents. The perpetrators would actually be charged with legally defined crimes, such as murder, assault, arson, and so on. The main distinction between acts of domestic terrorism and other domestic crimes hinges on motive.

The U.S. government has numerous agencies and offices that are devoted to protecting U.S. national security, including preventing, investigating, and responding to terrorist attacks. The FBI, which is a law enforcement agency within the U.S. Department of Justice, takes a lead role in domestic terrorism cases. The FBI is aided by the U.S. Department of Homeland Security (DHS), an agency that was created in 2002 in response to the September 11, 2001, terrorist attacks. The DHS works with other federal entities that are devoted to national security to gather and share information, secure the nation's borders and transportation systems, and conduct law enforcement counterterrorism activities.

It can be difficult to determine whether a particular crime is committed for social/political reasons, personal reasons (e.g., revenge), or a mixture of these motives. For example, in January 1998 Theodore Kaczynski (1942–) was sentenced to life imprisonment with no possibility of parole for his actions as the "Unabomber." Over a 17-year period Kaczynski committed 16 bombings in several states. Three people were killed and 23 were injured in the attacks. Kaczynski has given varying reasons for his crimes, including personal revenge and a deep hatred against the use of high technology in American society. In October 2002 two men dubbed "the Beltway snipers" terrorized people in the District of Columbia area with a killing spree that left 10 people dead and three people wounded. One of the perpetrators, John Allen Muhammad (1960–2009), has been described in the media as committing the killings for a mixture of personal and social/political reasons. He reportedly hoped to extract revenge on his former wife and extort money from the government to fund a terrorist training camp. These cases highlight the difficulties in branding particular crimes as terrorist incidents. However, there have been a number of crimes committed in the United States since the mid-1990s that are widely considered to be incidents of domestic terrorism.

OKLAHOMA CITY BOMBING. On April 19, 1995, one of the most deadly acts of domestic terrorism occurred in Oklahoma City, Oklahoma, when a 2-ton (1.8-t) truck bomb exploded just outside the Alfred P. Murrah Federal Building, killing 168 people and injuring more than 800. The attack was perpetrated by Timothy McVeigh (1968–2001), a 27-year-old military veteran with ties to antigovernment militia groups. McVeigh was executed by lethal injection in June 2001. Terry L. Nichols (1955–), an accomplice who helped McVeigh plan the attack and construct the bomb, was sentenced to life in prison without the possibility of parole.

OLYMPIC PARK BOMBING. On July 27, 1996, during the Olympic Games in Atlanta, Georgia, a nail-packed pipe bomb exploded in a large common area. One person was killed and over 100 people were injured. Even though authorities had no leads at the time, similar explosive devices were later used in bomb attacks on a nightclub that was favored by homosexuals and two abortion clinics. These incidents led investigators to Eric Robert Rudolph (1967–), a Christian extremist whose views combined antigovernment political sentiments with opposition to abortion and antihomosexual bigotry. Rudolph eluded capture for five years before he surrendered to authorities in May 2003. Confessing to the Olympic bombing, he said he was motivated by antigovernment and antisocialist beliefs. He was sentenced to life in prison without the possibility of parole.

ANTHRAX ATTACKS. On September 25, 2001, a letter containing a white powdery substance was handled by an assistant to the NBC News anchor Tom Brokaw (1940–). After complaining of a rash, the assistant consulted a physician and tested positive for exposure to the anthrax bacterium (*Bacillus anthracis*), an infectious agent that, if inhaled into the lungs, can lead to death. Over the next two months envelopes testing positive for anthrax were received by various U.S. news organizations and by government offices, including the offices of the U.S. Senate majority leader Tom Daschle (1947–; D-SD) and the New York governor George Pataki (1945–). As a result of exposure to anthrax that was sent via the U.S. mail system, five people died, including two postal workers who handled letters carrying the anthrax spores. Hundreds more who were exposed were placed on antibiotics as a preventive measure.

The FBI eventually traced the source of the anthrax to the U.S. Army Medical Research Institute of Infectious Diseases, a bioweapons laboratory at Fort Detrick, Maryland. At first, authorities focused on Steven Hatfill (1953–), a civilian researcher at that facility. He was later cleared of the attacks. In August 2008 Bruce Ivins (1946–2008), another researcher at the same laboratory, committed suicide before he could be arrested and charged with the crime. The FBI has expressed confidence that Ivins was the perpetrator of the 2001 anthrax attacks. However, because he will never stand trial, some doubts remain about the strength of the government's case against Ivins.

MIDWEST PIPE BOMBER. In a spree that began on May 3, 2002, 18 pipe bombs were found in rural mailboxes in Colorado, Illinois, Iowa, Nebraska, and Texas, which injured a total of five people. Four days after the first bomb exploded, the FBI arrested Lucas John Helder (1981–), a 21-year-old college student, in connection with the bombings. Helder was charged by federal prosecutors with using an explosive device to maliciously destroy property affecting interstate commerce and with using a destructive device to commit a crime of violence, which is punishable by up to life imprisonment. The pipe bombs, some of which did not detonate, were accompanied by letters that warned of excessive government control over individual behavior. In 2004 a federal judge ruled that Helder was not mentally fit to stand trial and ordered that he be held for psychological evaluation. As of February 2011, Helder remained in federal custody.

ATTACKS SINCE 2004. The NCTC maintains the online database Worldwide Incidents Tracking System (WITS; https://wits.nctc.gov/FederalDiscoverWITS/index.do?N=0), which includes statistics that have been gathered by U.S. agencies about terrorist incidents. The database shows the number, location, and type of terrorist incidents that are committed around the world each year and the number of people killed, injured, or taken hostage during these incidents. According to the NCTC, between January 2004 and February 2011 there were 29 terrorism incidents that occurred inside the United States. The NCTC explains in *2009 Report on Terrorism* that "failed or foiled" attacks in which no one is killed or injured are not included in the database.

More than half the attacks are believed to have been carried out by ecoterrorist groups. These are extremist groups that support causes, such as environmentalism or animal rights, and use criminal violence to promote their ideas and attack their perceived enemies. For example, radical animal rights activists are believed to be behind bombs that exploded outside the homes of two University of California, Santa Cruz, biomedical researchers in August 2008. Four people were wounded in the attacks. The scientists were allegedly targeted because they use animals in their research—research

that the university claims is being conducted using the highest humane standards.

The remaining incidents of domestic terrorism reported by the NCTC are attributed to perpetrators with a variety of political, religious, and social biases. Most of these events did not result in any deaths or injuries. Incidents in which the NCTC does report deaths and/or injuries are as follows:

- March 2006—nine people were injured when an Islamic extremist drove a sport-utility vehicle through a crowd of students at the University of North Carolina, Chapel Hill. The perpetrator was an Iranian-born U.S. citizen who allegedly wanted to avenge the deaths of Muslims around the world.

- May 2009—a medical doctor who was affiliated with a clinic that performed abortions was shot and killed in Wichita, Kansas, by a radical anti-abortionist.

- June 2009—one soldier was killed and another injured by an attack outside a U.S. Army recruiting office in Little Rock, Arkansas. The assailant was a U.S. citizen who said he was avenging the deaths of Muslims by the U.S. military in Iraq and Afghanistan.

- June 2009—a security guard at the U.S. Holocaust Memorial Museum in Washington, D.C., was shot and killed by a man alleged to be a white supremacist.

- November 2009—13 people were killed and 43 were injured in an armed attack at the Fort Hood Army Base in Killeen, Texas. Most of those killed or injured were soldiers. The alleged shooter was a U.S.-born major in the U.S. Army with suspected ties to Islamic extremists.

GOVERNMENT JURISDICTION AND SPENDING

As noted throughout this chapter, criminal legislation and law enforcement are carried out by federal, state, and local governments. Sometimes government entities have overlapping responsibilities. State and local governments have always played a central role in controlling crime. They operate police and law enforcement agencies, court systems, and correctional facilities, such as prisons and jails. The federal government enforces laws that fall within its jurisdiction. Examples include mail fraud, bank robbery, gun laws, counterfeiting, forgery, espionage, immigration violations, child pornography, drug trafficking, and money laundering. The federal government also operates the federal court system and has its own prisons for people convicted of federal crimes. In addition, the federal government provides funding for some state and local crime-control programs.

Figure 1.1 shows direct expenditures on criminal justice by federal, state, and local governments between 1982 and 2007. During this period local expenditures increased by more than 450%, state expenditures increased by 645%, and federal expenditures increased by more than 800%. In

FIGURE 1.1

Direct government expenditures on criminal justice, by level of government, 1982–2007

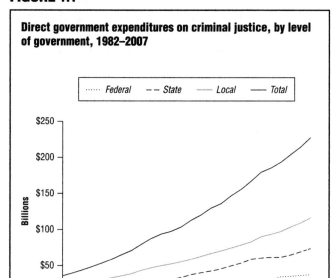

SOURCE: Adapted from Steve W. Perry, "Direct Expenditure on Criminal Justice, by Level of Government, 1982–2006," in *Justice Expenditure and Employment Extracts 2006*, U.S. Department of Justice, Office of Justice Programs, Bureau of Justice Statistics, December 15, 2008, http://bjs.ojp.usdoj.gov/content/glance/tables/expgovtab.cfm (accessed November 10, 2010), and Tracey Kyckelhahn, "Table 1. Percent Distribution of Expenditure for the Justice System by Type of Government, Fiscal Year 2007," in *Justice Expenditure and Employment Extracts 2007*, U.S. Department of Justice, Office of Justice Programs, Bureau of Justice Statistics, September 14, 2010, http://bjs.ojp.usdoj.gov/content/pub/sheets/cjee07.zip (accessed November 10, 2010)

fiscal year (FY) 2007 local governments spent $116.5 billion on criminal justice and state governments spent $79.4 billion. (See Table 1.1.) The federal government spent $41.2 billion on criminal justice in FY 2007.

Figure 1.2 provides a breakdown of criminal justice expenditures by major function (police, corrections, and judicial) for all three levels of government between 1982 and 2007. Corrections refers to the system of prisons, jails, and other facilities that are operated to house arrested and convicted individuals, and to the programs for the oversight of these and other individuals under the supervision of the criminal justice system. Between 1982 and 2007 police expenditures increased by more than 440%, corrections expenditures increased by 720%, and judicial expenditures increased by nearly 540%. In FY 2007 police expenditures totaled $103.6 billion, corrections expenditures totaled $74.2 billion, and judicial expenditures totaled $49.7 billion. (See Table 1.1.)

PUBLIC OPINION ABOUT CRIME

The Gallup Organization conducts annual polls on American concerns and viewpoints about crime. The latest results were published in November 2010 based on polling that was conducted in October 2010.

How Serious Is the Crime Problem?

In *Americans Still Perceive Crime as on the Rise* (November 18, 2010, http://www.gallup.com/poll/144827/Americans-Perceive-Crime-Rise.aspx), Jeffrey M. Jones of the Gallup Organization reviews U.S. public opinion on the

TABLE 1.1

Government expenditures on criminal justice, by level of government and activity, fiscal year 2007

Amount [Thousands of dollars]

Activity	All governments*	Federal government	State governments	Local governments
Total justice system	**$227,562,377**	**$41,244,000**	**$79,425,264**	**$116,525,835**
Direct expenditure	$227,562,377	$36,899,000	$74,325,804	$116,337,573
Intergovernmental expenditure	—	$4,345,000	$5,099,460	$188,262
Police protection	**$103,643,293**	**$21,926,978**	**$12,875,854**	**$72,658,253**
Direct expenditure	$103,643,293	$19,617,000	$11,383,130	$72,643,163
Intergovernmental expenditure	—	$2,309,978	$1,492,724	$15,090
Judicial and legal	**$49,721,257**	**$12,243,876**	**$20,051,535**	**$19,886,939**
Direct expenditure	$49,721,257	$10,954,000	$18,921,485	$19,845,772
Intergovernmental expenditure	—	$1,289,876	$1,130,050	$41,167
Corrections	**$74,197,827**	**$7,073,146**	**$46,497,875**	**$23,980,643**
Direct expenditure	$74,197,827	$6,328,000	$44,021,189	$23,848,638
Intergovernmental expenditure	—	$745,146	$2,476,686	$132,005

Notes: Local government data are estimates subject to sampling variability.
Federal government data are for the fiscal period beginning October 1, 2006 and ending September 30, 2007.
*The total lines for each criminal justice activity, and for the total justice system, exclude duplicative intergovernmental amounts. This was done to avoid the artificial inflation that would result if an intergovernmental expenditure of a government were tabulated and then counted again when the recipient government(s) expended the amount. The intergovernmental expenditure lines are not totaled for the same reason.

SOURCE: Adapted from Tracey Kyckelhahn, "Table 1. Percent Distribution of Expenditure for the Justice System by Type of Government, Fiscal Year 2007," in *Justice Expenditure and Employment Extracts 2007*, U.S. Department of Justice, Office of Justice Programs, Bureau of Justice Statistics, September 14, 2010, http://bjs.ojp.usdoj.gov/content/pub/sheets/cjee07.zip (accessed November 10, 2010)

FIGURE 1.2

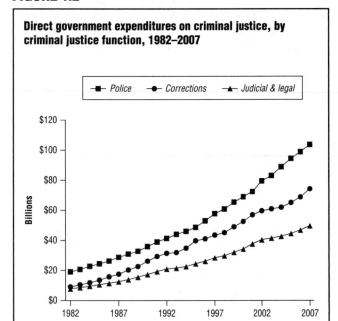

Direct government expenditures on criminal justice, by criminal justice function, 1982–2007

■ *Police* ● *Corrections* ▲ *Judicial & legal*

SOURCE: Adapted from Steve W. Perry, "Direct Expenditures by Criminal Justice Function, 1982–2006," in *Justice Expenditure and Employment Extracts 2006*, U.S. Department of Justice, Office of Justice Programs, Bureau of Justice Statistics, December 15, 2008, http://bjs.ojp.usdoj.gov/content/glance/tables/exptyptab.cfm (accessed November 10, 2010), and Tracey Kyckelhahn, "Table 1. Percent Distribution of Expenditure for the Justice System by Type of Government, Fiscal Year 2007," in *Justice Expenditure and Employment Extracts 2007*, U.S. Department of Justice, Office of Justice Programs, Bureau of Justice Statistics, September 14, 2010, http://bjs.ojp.usdoj.gov/content/pub/sheets/cjee07.zip (accessed November 10, 2010)

seriousness of crime. Figure 1.3 shows the ratings that were given by respondents during the 2010 poll when they were asked to describe the crime problem in the area where they live and in the United States overall. The national crime problem was rated as "extremely/very serious" by 60% of respondents. This value was up considerably from 42% of respondents in 2004.

Poll participants have historically expressed a far more optimistic viewpoint about crime in their own area. Only 13% of those asked in 2010 said the crime problem was "extremely/very serious" in their area. (See Figure 1.3.) This compares to 8% who gave the same viewpoint in 2004.

Is There More Crime or Less Crime in the 21st Century?

Figure 1.4 shows the results when poll participants were asked about the national level of crime and its change over the previous year. In 2010 nearly two-thirds (66%) of respondents said crime had increased in the United States in the past year, whereas 17% thought national crime had decreased. Gallup presents results for this question dating back to 1989. At that time, and throughout the early 1990s, more than 80% of respondents said crime had increased in the United States during the previous year. National crime was seen as decreasing until soon after the turn of the 21st century. Poll respondents then began saying that crime in the United States was increasing.

FIGURE 1.3

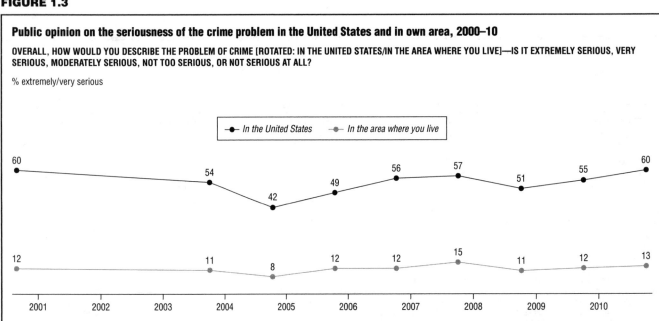

Public opinion on the seriousness of the crime problem in the United States and in own area, 2000–10

OVERALL, HOW WOULD YOU DESCRIBE THE PROBLEM OF CRIME [ROTATED: IN THE UNITED STATES/IN THE AREA WHERE YOU LIVE]—IS IT EXTREMELY SERIOUS, VERY SERIOUS, MODERATELY SERIOUS, NOT TOO SERIOUS, OR NOT SERIOUS AT ALL?

% extremely/very serious

● *In the United States* ● *In the area where you live*

SOURCE: Jeffrey M. Jones, "Overall, how would you describe the problem of crime [ROTATED: in the United States/in the area where you live]—is it extremely serious, very serious, moderately serious, not too serious, or not serious at all?" in *Americans Still Perceive Crime As on the Rise*, The Gallup Organization, November 18, 2010, http://www.gallup.com/poll/144827/Americans-Perceive-Crime-Rise.aspx (accessed November 18, 2010). Copyright © 2010 by The Gallup Organization. Reproduced by permission of The Gallup Organization.

FIGURE 1.4

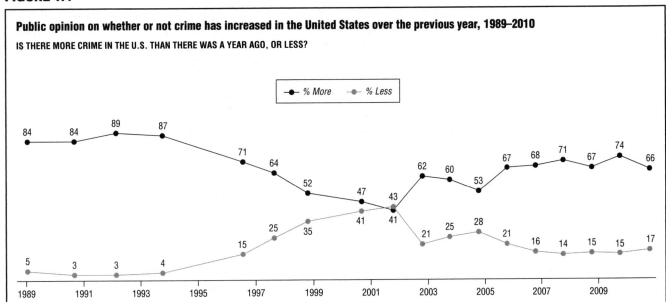

Public opinion on whether or not crime has increased in the United States over the previous year, 1989–2010

IS THERE MORE CRIME IN THE U.S. THAN THERE WAS A YEAR AGO, OR LESS?

SOURCE: Jeffrey M. Jones, "Is there more crime in the U.S. than there was a year ago, or less?" in *Americans Still Perceive Crime As on the Rise*, The Gallup Organization, November 18, 2010, http://www.gallup.com/poll/144827/Americans-Perceive-Crime-Rise.aspx (accessed November 18, 2010). Copyright © 2010 by The Gallup Organization. Reproduced by permission of The Gallup Organization.

FIGURE 1.5

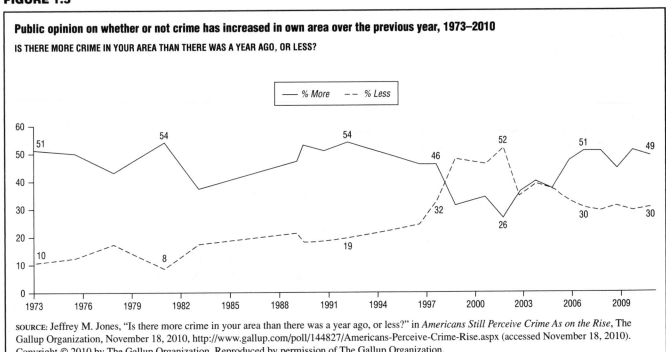

Public opinion on whether or not crime has increased in own area over the previous year, 1973–2010

IS THERE MORE CRIME IN YOUR AREA THAN THERE WAS A YEAR AGO, OR LESS?

SOURCE: Jeffrey M. Jones, "Is there more crime in your area than there was a year ago, or less?" in *Americans Still Perceive Crime As on the Rise*, The Gallup Organization, November 18, 2010, http://www.gallup.com/poll/144827/Americans-Perceive-Crime-Rise.aspx (accessed November 18, 2010). Copyright © 2010 by The Gallup Organization. Reproduced by permission of The Gallup Organization.

Gallup also asked poll participants whether they believe there is more or less crime in their area than there was the previous year. Less than half (49%) of respondents thought there was more crime in their area in 2010 than there had been the year before. (See Figure 1.5.) Three out of 10 (30%) respondents believed there was less crime in their area in 2010.

During the late 1990s and the early years of the first decade of the 21st century the percentage of poll respondents saying there was less crime in their area actually outranked the percentage saying there was more crime in their area. (See Figure 1.5.) As will be explained in Chapters 2 and 3, crime rates did fall dramatically during this period. In fact, crime rates continued to decline through the remainder of the decade. Yet, as shown in Figure 1.4 and Figure 1.5, poll respondents reported the crime situation was getting worse through 2010. Jones notes that Americans' perceptions about crime may be affected by "how things are going in the country." The crime situation was seen as improving throughout the 1990s and into the early years of the next decade. This was a time of strong economic performance for the country overall. The slump in the housing market that began in 2005 and the subsequent economic recession that began in late 2007 may have soured poll respondents' views about the crime situation. Jones states that "the current estimates of increasing crime may to some degree be inflated due to widespread dissatisfaction with the state of the U.S. today."

Crime Victims

Table 1.2 provides the percentages of poll participants indicating that they or another member in their household had been the victim of a specific crime in the 12 months leading up to Gallup's 2010 survey. The largest percentage (16%) had money or property stolen. Other categories included 14% who said their home, car, or other property had been vandalized; 11% who had been victims of a computer or Internet-based crime; and 8% who had been victims of identity theft within the previous year. Smaller percentages had a car stolen (2%), been mugged or physically assaulted (2%), had money or property stolen by an assailant using force or the threat of force (2%), or had been sexually assaulted (1%).

TABLE 1.2

Poll respondents who have been crime victims within the previous year, October 2010

[Sorted by "yes"]

	% Yes	% No
Money or property stolen from you or another member of your household	16	84
A home, car, or property owned by you or another household member vandalized	14	86
You or another household member was victim of computer/Internet crime	11	89
You or another household member was the victim of identity theft	8	91
Your house or apartment broken into	4	96
A car owned by you or another household member stolen	2	98
You or another household member mugged or physically assaulted	2	98
Money or property taken by force, with gun, knife, weapon or physical attack	2	98
You or another household member sexually assaulted	1	99

SOURCE: Jeff Jones and Lydia Saad, "Please tell me which, if any, of these incidents have happened to you or your household within the last twelve months?" in *Gallup Poll Social Series: Crime*, The Gallup Organization, November 18, 2010, http://www.gallup.com/poll/File/144782/Crime_Review_Nov_18_2010.pdf (accessed November 19, 2010). Copyright © 2010 by The Gallup Organization. Reproduced by permission of The Gallup Organization.

In *Gallup Poll Social Series: Crime* (November 18, 2010, http://www.gallup.com/poll/File/144782/Crime_Review_Nov_18_2010.pdf), the Gallup Organization presents results that were obtained for these polling questions dating back to 2000 in most cases. The results indicate few changes between 2000 and 2010 in the percentages of respondents reporting being victims of the particular crimes listed in Table 1.2. The major exception was computer or Internet-based crime. Gallup polling conducted in 2003, the first year the question was asked, found that only 6% of respondents reported that they or another household member had been the victim of a computer or Internet-based crime while using a home computer. By 2010 this value had climbed to 11%, an increase of five percentage points.

According to Lydia Saad of the Gallup Organization, in *In U.S., 11% of Households Report Computer Crimes, a New High* (December 13, 2010, http://www.gallup.com/poll/145205/New-High-Households-Report-Computer-Crimes.aspx), younger respondents were much more likely than older respondents in 2010 to say they had been victimized by a computer or Internet-based crime while using a home computer. The values by age of respondents were 11% of those aged 18 to 34 years (up from 6% in 2009), 16% of those aged 35 to 54 years (up from 11% in 2009), and 6% of those aged 55 years and older (up from 5% in 2009).

Reporting Crimes to the Police

In the October 2010 poll, Gallup asked respondents who said that they or their household had been victimized by a crime within the previous year whether or not they reported that crime to the police. As shown in Table 1.3, more than half (59%) of respondents said they reported the victimization to the police, whereas 41% said they did not report the victimization to the police. The percentage saying they had made a police

TABLE 1.3

Poll respondents who have reported to the police a crime against their household within the previous year, October 2010

[In percent]

	Crime reported	Crime not reported
2010 Oct 7–10	59	41
2009 Oct 1–4	63	37
2008 Oct 3–5	64	36
2007 Oct 4–7	69	31
2006 Oct 9–12	62	38
2005 Oct 13–16	61	39
2004 Oct 11–14	56	44
2003 Oct 6–8	65	35

SOURCE: Jeff Jones and Lydia Saad, "Crime against Household Reported to Police in the Past Year," in *Gallup Poll Social Series: Crime*, The Gallup Organization, November 18, 2010, http://www.gallup.com/poll/File/144782/Crime_Review_Nov_18_2010.pdf (accessed November 19, 2010). Copyright © 2010 by The Gallup Organization. Reproduced by permission of The Gallup Organization.

report about being victimized by a crime declined some-what from 65% in 2003.

Worry about Being Victimized by Crime

In October 2009 Gallup asked poll participants how often they worry about being victimized by particular crimes. The results were reported by Saad in *Two in Three Americans Worry about Identity Theft* (October 16, 2009, http://www.gallup.com/poll/123713/Two-in-Three-Ameri cans-Worry-About-Identity-Theft.aspx). Two-thirds (66%) worried frequently or occasionally about being a victim of identity theft. Almost half (47%) worried frequently or occasionally about their car being stolen or broken into by criminals. Nearly as many (46%) worried frequently or occasionally about their home being burglarized while they are not home. Smaller percentages admitted worrying frequently or occasionally about being a victim of terrorism (35%), having their home burglarized while they are at home (33%), getting mugged (31%), having their child harmed at school (31%), or being attacked while driving their car (23%). Nearly one-fifth (19%) of respondents worried frequently or occasionally about being sexually assaulted or being murdered, and 17% worried frequently or occasionally about becoming the victim of a hate crime. A smaller group of poll participants (4%) worried frequently or occasionally about being assaulted or killed by a coworker or other employee at their workplace.

Crime Protection Methods

In October 2007 Gallup asked Americans whether they use (or have used) various crime protection methods. The results were reported by Joseph Carroll of the Gallup Organization in *How Americans Protect Themselves from Crime* (October 26, 2007, http://www.gallupcom/poll/102 418/How-Americans-Protect-Themselves-From-Crime .aspx). Concern about crime kept nearly half (48%) of respondents from going to certain places or neighborhoods they might otherwise have visited. Nearly one-third (31%) each kept a dog for protection or had a burglar alarm installed in their home. Nearly one-quarter (23%) of those asked had bought a gun for self-protection or protection of their home, 14% carried mace or pepper spray, and 12% each carried a knife or gun for defense purposes.

CHAPTER 2
CRIME STATISTICS

The Federal Bureau of Investigation (FBI) is the primary federal government source for crime statistics. The FBI's Uniform Crime Reporting (UCR) Program gathers crime data from law enforcement agencies around the country and publishes selected data in the annual *Crime in the United States*. The most recent edition, *Crime in the United States, 2009* (http://www2.fbi.gov/ucr/cius2009/index.html), was published in September 2010. According to the FBI, in 2009 nearly 18,000 agencies participated in the program, representing 96.3% of the U.S. population. However, not every agency contributed data for every crime that was tracked by the UCR Program. In other words, the tables and figures in *Crime in the United States, 2009* provide crime statistics on only those crimes that were reported to the UCR Program and do not reflect the total number of crimes that were committed or processed by local agencies.

The FBI compiles two main sets of crime statistics: crimes reported to agencies and crimes cleared by agencies. Reported crimes do not necessarily result in arrests or convictions. Cleared offenses are of two types. The first type of cleared offenses consists of crimes for which agencies report that at least one person has been arrested, charged, and turned over to the court for prosecution. This does not necessarily mean the person arrested was guilty or convicted of the crime. The second type of cleared offenses includes those cleared by "extraordinary means," that is, offenses for which there can be no arrest. Such cases include, for example, a murder-suicide, when the perpetrator is known to be deceased.

The FBI collects data for dozens of specifically defined crimes. Some of these crimes are categorized as violent crimes or property crimes. In *Crime in the United States, 2009*, the FBI defines violent crimes as those that "involve force or threat of force." These crimes include murder and nonnegligent manslaughter, forcible rape, robbery, and aggravated assault. According to the FBI, murder and nonnegligent manslaughter is "the willful (nonnegligent) killing of one human being by another." The murder statistics do not include suicides, accidents, or justifiable homicides by either citizens or law enforcement officers. The FBI considers four crimes to be property crimes: burglary, larceny-theft, motor vehicle theft, and arson. The FBI explains that "the object of the theft-type offenses is the taking of money or property, but there is no force or threat of force against the victims."

REPORTED CRIMES

Table 2.1 lists the number of certain crimes that were reported by law enforcement agencies between 1990 and 2009 and the rates of these crimes per 100,000 inhabitants. In 2009 just over 1.3 million violent crimes were reported, including 15,241 murders and nonnegligent manslaughters, 88,097 forcible rapes, 408,217 robberies, and 806,843 aggravated assaults. The overall rate for violent crime in 2009 was 429.4 per 100,000 inhabitants. The rates for different types of violent crime varied. For example, the rate for murder and nonnegligent manslaughter was 5 per 100,000 inhabitants; for forcible rape, 28.7 per 100,000; for robbery, 133 per 100,000; and for aggravated assault, 262.8 per 100,000. All these rates are down dramatically from rates dating back to 1990.

Murder and Nonnegligent Manslaughter

The total number of reported murders and nonnegligent manslaughters in 2009 was 15,241 for a rate of 5 per 100,000 inhabitants. (See Table 2.1.) During the early 1990s the murder rate was much higher at more than 9 murders per 100,000 inhabitants. The rate began dropping during the mid-1990s and has ranged between 5 and 6 murders per 100,000 inhabitants since 1997. It should be noted that Table 2.1 does not include the thousands of people who were killed as a result of the September 11, 2001, terrorist attacks against the United States.

TABLE 2.1

Violent crimes and property crimes by volume and rate per 100,000 inhabitants, 1990–2009

Year	Population[a]	Violent crime	Violent crime rate	Murder and nonnegligent manslaughter	Murder and nonnegligent manslaughter rate	Forcible rape	Forcible rape rate	Robbery	Robbery rate	Aggravated assault	Aggravated assault rate	Property crime	Property crime rate	Burglary	Burglary rate	Larceny-theft	Larceny-theft rate	Motor vehicle theft	Motor vehicle theft rate
1990	249,464,396	1,820,127	729.6	23,438	9.4	102,555	41.1	639,271	256.3	1,054,863	422.9	12,655,486	5,073.1	3,073,909	1,232.2	7,945,670	3,185.1	1,635,907	655.8
1991	252,153,092	1,911,767	758.2	24,703	9.8	106,593	42.3	687,732	272.7	1,092,739	433.4	12,961,116	5,140.2	3,157,150	1,252.1	8,142,228	3,229.1	1,661,738	659.0
1992	255,029,699	1,932,274	757.7	23,760	9.3	109,062	42.8	672,478	263.7	1,126,974	441.9	12,505,917	4,903.7	2,979,884	1,168.4	7,915,199	3,103.6	1,610,834	631.6
1993	257,782,608	1,926,017	747.1	24,526	9.5	106,014	41.1	659,870	256.0	1,135,607	440.5	12,218,777	4,740.0	2,834,808	1,099.7	7,820,909	3,033.9	1,563,060	606.3
1994	260,327,021	1,857,670	713.6	23,326	9.0	102,216	39.3	618,949	237.8	1,113,179	427.6	12,131,873	4,660.2	2,712,774	1,042.1	7,879,812	3,026.9	1,539,287	591.3
1995	262,803,276	1,798,792	684.5	21,606	8.2	97,470	37.1	580,509	220.9	1,099,207	418.3	12,063,935	4,590.5	2,593,784	987.0	7,997,710	3,043.2	1,472,441	560.3
1996	265,228,572	1,688,540	636.6	19,645	7.4	96,252	36.3	535,594	201.9	1,037,049	391.0	11,805,323	4,451.0	2,506,400	945.0	7,904,685	2,980.3	1,394,238	525.7
1997	267,783,607	1,636,096	611.0	18,208	6.8	96,153	35.9	498,534	186.2	1,023,201	382.1	11,558,475	4,316.3	2,460,526	918.8	7,743,760	2,891.8	1,354,189	505.7
1998	270,248,003	1,533,887	567.6	16,974	6.3	93,144	34.5	447,186	165.5	976,583	361.4	10,951,827	4,052.5	2,332,735	863.2	7,376,311	2,729.5	1,242,781	459.9
1999	272,690,813	1,426,044	523.0	15,522	5.7	89,411	32.8	409,371	150.1	911,740	334.3	10,208,334	3,743.6	2,100,739	770.4	6,955,520	2,550.7	1,152,075	422.5
2000	281,421,906	1,425,486	506.5	15,586	5.5	90,178	32.0	408,016	145.0	911,706	324.0	10,182,584	3,618.3	2,050,992	728.8	6,971,590	2,477.3	1,160,002	412.2
2001[b]	285,317,559	1,439,480	504.5	16,037	5.6	90,863	31.8	423,557	148.5	909,023	318.6	10,437,189	3,658.1	2,116,531	741.8	7,092,267	2,485.7	1,228,391	430.5
2002	287,973,924	1,423,677	494.4	16,229	5.6	95,235	33.1	420,806	146.1	891,407	309.5	10,455,277	3,630.6	2,151,252	747.0	7,057,379	2,450.7	1,246,646	432.9
2003	290,788,976	1,383,676	475.8	16,528	5.7	93,883	32.3	414,235	142.5	859,030	295.4	10,442,862	3,591.2	2,154,834	741.0	7,026,802	2,416.5	1,261,226	433.7
2004	293,656,842	1,360,088	463.2	16,148	5.5	95,089	32.4	401,470	136.7	847,381	288.6	10,319,386	3,514.1	2,144,446	730.3	6,937,089	2,362.3	1,237,851	421.5
2005	296,507,061	1,390,745	469.0	16,740	5.6	94,347	31.8	417,438	140.8	862,220	290.8	10,174,754	3,431.5	2,155,448	726.9	6,783,447	2,287.8	1,235,859	416.8
2006[c]	298,754,819	1,435,951	480.6	17,318	5.8	94,782	31.7	449,803	150.6	874,048	292.6	10,031,359	3,357.7	2,196,304	735.2	6,636,615	2,221.4	1,198,440	401.1
2007[c]	301,290,332	1,421,990	472.0	17,157	5.7	91,874	30.5	447,155	148.4	865,804	287.4	9,872,815	3,276.8	2,187,277	726.0	6,587,040	2,186.3	1,098,498	364.6
2008[c]	304,374,846	1,392,629	457.5	16,442	5.4	90,479	29.7	443,574	145.7	842,134	276.7	9,775,149	3,211.5	2,228,474	732.1	6,588,046	2,164.5	958,629	315.0
2009	307,006,550	1,318,398	429.4	15,241	5.0	88,097	28.7	408,217	133.0	806,843	262.8	9,320,971	3,036.1	2,199,125	716.3	6,327,230	2,060.9	794,616	258.8

[a]Populations are U.S. Census Bureau provisional estimates as of July 1 for each year except 1990 and 2000, which are decennial census counts.
[b]The murder and nonnegligent homicides that occurred as a result of the events of September 11, 2001, are not included in this table.
[c]The crime figures have been adjusted.
Notes: Although arson data are included in the trend and clearance tables, sufficient data are not available to estimate totals for this offense. Therefore, no arson data are published in this table.

SOURCE: "Table 1. Crime in the United States, by Volume and Rate per 100,000 Inhabitants, 1990–2009," in *Crime in the United States, 2009*, U.S. Department of Justice, Federal Bureau of Investigation, September 2010, http://www2.fbi.gov/ucr/cius2009/data/documents/09tbl01.xls (accessed September 30, 2010)

The FBI collects detailed homicide data in the UCR Program's Supplementary Homicide Report (SHR). SHR data include the age, sex, and race of the offenders and victims, the relationship between the offenders and victims, the circumstances surrounding the murders, and the types of weapons used in the murders. It should be noted that not all these statistics are reported by all agencies for every reported murder, offender, and victim.

MURDER OFFENDERS AND VICTIMS. As shown in Table 2.2, SHR data for 2009 include age, sex, and race data for 15,760 murder offenders. These data are reported by the FBI in *Crime in the United States, 2009*. Because offender data are based on reported crimes rather than on actual arrests, SHR tables classify the age, sex, or race of some offenders as "unknown." SHR categorizations for 2009 murder offenders by sex are:

- Male offenders—10,391 (65.9% of the total)
- Female offenders—1,197 (7.6%)
- Unknown—4,172 (26.5%)

SHR categorizations for 2009 murder offenders by race are:

- African-American offenders—5,890 (37.4% of the total)
- White offenders—5,286 (33.5%)
- Other offenders—245 (1.6%)
- Unknown—4,339 (27.5%)

The ages of 4,991 murder offenders (31.7% of the total) are listed as unknown. (See Table 2.2.) Offenders for which ages are known fall mostly within the range of 17 to 34 years old.

SHR data for 2009 murder victims include age, sex, and race data for 13,636 victims. (See Table 2.3.) The vast majority of these murder victims (10,496 or 77% of the total) were male, whereas 3,122 (22.9%) were female. Another 18 victims (0.1%) were of unknown sex. Whites accounted for 6,568 (48.2%) of the victims, and African-Americans accounted for 6,556 (48.1%) of the victims. Another 360 victims (2.6%) were of other races, and 152 victims (1.1%) were of unknown race.

The vast majority of murder victims (12,095 or 88.7% of the total) were aged 18 years and older. (See Table 2.3.) Only 1,348 victims (9.9% of the total) were under the age of 18 years. Ages were reported as unknown for 193 victims (1.4%). Overall, young adults between the ages of 20 and 34 years accounted for the largest numbers of murder victims in 2009.

TABLE 2.2

Murder offenders where age, sex, and race are known, 2009

Age	Total	Sex			Race			
		Male	Female	Unknown	White	Black	Other	Unknown
Total	**15,760**	**10,391**	**1,197**	**4,172**	**5,286**	**5,890**	**245**	**4,339**
Percent distribution[a]	100.0	65.9	7.6	26.5	33.5	37.4	1.6	27.5
Under 18[b]	923	850	73	0	353	539	27	4
Under 22[b]	3,541	3,258	280	3	1,348	2,098	68	27
18 and over[b]	9,846	8,728	1,097	21	4,794	4,731	215	106
Infant (under 1)	0	0	0	0	0	0	0	0
1 to 4	0	0	0	0	0	0	0	0
5 to 8	1	1	0	0	0	1	0	0
9 to 12	10	9	1	0	5	5	0	0
13 to 16	465	422	43	0	186	264	13	2
17 to 19	1,765	1,642	123	0	638	1,077	36	14
20 to 24	2,682	2,425	253	4	1,119	1,484	54	25
25 to 29	1,794	1,592	195	7	781	957	38	18
30 to 34	1,123	971	152	0	577	517	18	11
35 to 39	800	685	113	2	481	287	20	12
40 to 44	602	496	105	1	341	234	21	6
45 to 49	562	480	78	4	365	176	11	10
50 to 54	402	351	51	0	256	130	10	6
55 to 59	215	185	29	1	142	60	11	2
60 to 64	145	130	14	1	99	40	4	2
65 to 69	72	66	6	0	54	16	2	0
70 to 74	42	37	5	0	34	7	1	0
75 and over	89	86	2	1	69	15	3	2
Unknown	4,991	813	27	4,151	139	620	3	4,229

[a]Because of rounding, the percentages may not add to 100.0.
[b]Does not include unknown ages.

SOURCE: Expanded Homicide Data Table 3. Murder Offenders, by Age, Sex, and Race, 2009, in *Crime in the United States, 2009*, U.S. Department of Justice, Federal Bureau of Investigation, September 2010, http://www2.fbi.gov/ucr/cius2009/offenses/expanded_information/data/documents/09shrtbl03.xls (accessed November 7, 2010)

TABLE 2.3

Murder victims where age, sex, and race are known, 2009

Age	Total	Sex			Race			
		Male	Female	Unknown	White	Black	Other	Unknown
Total	13,636	10,496	3,122	18	6,568	6,556	360	152
Percent distribution[a]	100.0	77.0	22.9	0.1	48.2	48.1	2.6	1.1
Under 18[b]	1,348	913	435	0	654	639	44	11
Under 22[b]	3,304	2,603	701	0	1,381	1,813	79	31
18 and over[b]	12,095	9,459	2,632	4	5,821	5,847	313	114
Infant (under 1)	193	102	91	0	106	72	9	6
1 to 4	298	158	140	0	159	129	9	1
5 to 8	72	34	38	0	40	27	4	1
9 to 12	71	36	35	0	43	23	5	0
13 to 16	400	319	81	0	190	199	9	2
17 to 19	1,246	1,068	178	0	476	738	22	10
20 to 24	2,426	2,081	344	1	931	1,407	64	24
25 to 29	1,941	1,605	335	1	789	1,097	39	16
30 to 34	1,534	1,216	318	0	645	845	25	19
35 to 39	1,205	950	255	0	573	583	40	9
40 to 44	1,006	734	271	1	543	419	34	10
45 to 49	926	642	284	0	559	337	23	7
50 to 54	701	519	181	1	423	242	27	9
55 to 59	455	309	146	0	286	144	21	4
60 to 64	312	216	96	0	210	88	11	3
65 to 69	227	152	75	0	165	57	4	1
70 to 74	134	85	49	0	104	26	1	3
75 and over	296	146	150	0	233	53	10	0
Unknown	193	124	55	14	93	70	3	27

[a]Because of rounding, the percentages may not add to 100.0.
[b]Does not include unknown ages.

SOURCE: "Expanded Homicide Data Table 2. Murder Victims, by Age, Sex, and Race, 2009," in *Crime in the United States, 2009*, U.S. Department of Justice, Federal Bureau of Investigation, September 2010, http://www2.fbi.gov/ucr/cius2009/offenses/expanded_information/data/documents/09shrtbl02.xls (accessed November 7, 2010)

MURDER CIRCUMSTANCES. Table 2.4 describes the circumstances for 13,636 of the total murders reported in 2009. Of the reported murders, 14.8% (2,020) were associated with known felonies, mostly robberies and narcotic drug law violations. Nearly half (49.3% or 6,728) of the reported murders occurred due to other circumstances, mainly arguments and brawls between people. Juvenile gang killings accounted for 715 (5.4%) of the reported murders, and 180 (1.3%) of the murders were attributed to gangland killings, including organized crime syndicates.

The FBI reports in *Crime in the United States, 2009* that the relationship between the murder offender and victim was unknown in 5,986 (43.9%) of the 13,636 murders. (See Table 2.4.) Of the 7,650 murders in which the relationship could be ascertained, the vast majority (5,974 or 78.1%) were committed by someone known to the victim. The three most common relationships were those in which the victim was the offender's:

- Acquaintance—2,941 (38.4%)

- Wife—609 (8%)

- Girlfriend—472 (6.2%)

Overall, 1,855 of the victims were murdered by family members. Strangers (people unknown to the victims) accounted for 1,676 of the murders.

MURDER WEAPONS. Table 2.5 shows the weapons used in 13,636 of the murders that were committed during 2009. Nearly two-thirds (9,146 or 67.1% of the total) of these murders involved firearms, primarily handguns. Knives or other cutting instruments were used in 1,825 (13.4%) murders in 2009. Murderers used their hands, fists, and feet as weapons in 800 (5.9%) murders. Blunt objects, such as clubs and hammers, were used in 611 (4.5%) murders.

Firearms were used in 1,452 (71.9%) of the 2,020 murders that occurred during the commission of other felonies. (See Table 2.5.) Murder by firearm was most common during robberies (632) and narcotic drug crimes (422). Firearms were used in 4,209 (62.6%) of the 6,728 murders that were not related to the commission of other felonies. These include murders that occurred during arguments, brawls, and other circumstances.

Forcible Rape

Rape is a crime of violence in which the victim may suffer serious physical injury and long-term psychological pain. In *Crime in the United States, 2009*, the FBI defines forcible rape as "the carnal knowledge of a female forcibly and against her will." The FBI includes assaults and attempts to commit rape by force or threat of force, but statutory rape and other sex offenses are not included.

TABLE 2.4

Murder victims where relationship to offender and circumstances are known, 2009

Circumstances	Total murder victims	Husband	Wife	Mother	Father	Son	Daughter	Brother	Sister	Other family	Acquaintance	Friend	Boyfriend	Girlfriend	Neighbor	Employee	Employer	Stranger	Unknown
Total	13,636	141	609	131	116	247	201	94	35	281	2,941	404	138	472	132	12	20	1,676	5,986
Felony type total:	2,020	7	20	13	5	17	8	2	3	34	503	63	4	17	23	1	7	489	804
Rape	24	0	0	0	0	0	1	0	0	1	3	2	0	1	0	0	0	7	9
Robbery	849	1	0	1	1	0	0	1	0	18	176	13	3	1	6	1	4	306	317
Burglary	105	0	2	1	0	0	0	0	1	2	22	1	0	4	4	0	0	29	39
Larceny-theft	13	0	1	0	0	0	0	0	0	0	6	1	0	0	0	0	0	4	1
Motor vehicle theft	23	0	0	1	0	0	0	0	0	0	8	2	0	1	0	0	0	2	9
Arson	38	0	1	0	1	0	0	0	0	5	7	0	0	0	1	0	0	7	16
Prostitution and commercialized vice	6	0	0	0	0	0	0	0	0	0	2	0	0	1	0	0	0	0	3
Other sex offenses	10	0	0	0	0	1	0	0	0	0	2	1	0	1	1	0	0	1	3
Narcotic drug laws	487	1	0	0	0	1	0	0	0	1	183	26	1	2	4	0	0	51	217
Gambling	5	0	0	0	0	0	0	0	0	0	2	0	0	0	0	0	0	2	1
Other—not specified	460	5	16	10	3	15	7	1	2	7	92	17	0	6	7	0	3	80	189
Suspected felony type	56	2	4	0	0	2	0	1	1	0	7	0	0	4	0	0	0	3	32
Other than felony type total:	6,728	115	491	101	84	181	161	73	25	191	1,925	282	115	379	87	6	8	842	1,662
Romantic triangle	87	1	6	1	1	0	0	0	0	1	43	3	2	10	2	0	1	10	7
Child killed by babysitter	28	0	0	0	0	0	0	1	0	2	25	0	0	0	0	0	0	0	0
Brawl due to influence of alcohol	116	1	4	1	2	0	2	2	0	4	45	7	3	0	4	0	0	23	18
Brawl due to influence of narcotics	93	0	0	0	1	4	0	0	0	2	32	2	0	2	0	0	0	17	32
Argument over money or property	203	1	3	4	3	1	0	7	0	5	116	7	1	2	11	2	3	23	14
Other arguments	3,334	69	315	55	51	30	13	54	9	103	1,052	202	90	277	54	4	1	366	589
Gangland killings	180	0	0	0	0	0	0	0	0	0	37	10	0	0	0	0	0	56	77
Juvenile gang killings	715	0	0	0	0	0	0	0	0	0	163	4	0	0	0	0	0	128	420
Institutional killings	10	0	0	0	0	0	0	0	0	1	7	0	0	0	0	0	0	1	1
Sniper attack	1	0	0	0	0	0	0	0	0	0	1	0	0	0	0	0	0	0	0
Other—not specified	1,961	43	162	41	26	146	146	9	16	73	404	47	19	88	16	0	3	218	504
Unknown	4,832	17	94	17	27	47	32	18	6	56	506	59	19	72	22	5	5	342	3,488

Notes: Relationship is that of victim to offender. The relationship categories of husband and wife include both common-law and ex-spouses. The categories of mother, father, sister, brother, son, and daughter include stepparents, stepchildren, and stepsiblings. The category of acquaintance includes homosexual relationships and the composite category of other known to victim.

SOURCE: "Expanded Homicide Data Table 10. Murder Circumstances, by Relationship, 2009," in *Crime in the United States, 2009*, U.S. Department of Justice, Federal Bureau of Investigation, September 2010, http://www.fbi.gov/ucr/cius2009/offenses/expanded_information/data/documents/09shrtbl10.xls (accessed November 7, 2010)

TABLE 2.5

Murder victims where murder weapon and circumstances are known, 2009

Circumstances	Total murder victims	Total firearms	Handguns	Rifles	Shotguns	Other guns or type not stated	Knives or cutting instruments	Blunt objects (clubs, hammers, etc.)	Personal weapons (hands, fists, feet, etc.)	Poison	Pushed or thrown out window	Explosives	Fire	Narcotics	Drowning	Strangulation	Asphyxiation	Other
Total	**13,636**	**9,146**	**6,452**	**348**	**418**	**1,928**	**1,825**	**611**	**800**	**6**	**1**	**2**	**99**	**45**	**8**	**121**	**77**	**895**
Felony type total:	2,020	1,452	1,037	52	60	303	200	103	76	1	0	0	45	11	0	20	16	96
Rape	24	0	0	0	0	0	8	7	7	0	0	0	0	0	0	6	1	0
Robbery	849	632	497	27	17	91	72	68	32	0	0	0	2	0	0	3	6	34
Burglary	105	62	39	2	6	15	26	5	6	0	0	0	2	0	0	2	0	2
Larceny-theft	13	10	7	0	1	2	2	0	1	0	0	0	0	0	0	0	0	0
Motor vehicle theft	23	8	3	0	2	3	4	7	0	0	0	0	0	0	0	1	1	2
Arson	38	4	4	0	0	0	3	3	1	0	0	0	24	0	0	0	0	3
Prostitution and commercialized vice	6	2	2	0	0	0	1	0	1	0	0	0	0	0	0	1	0	1
Other sex offenses	10	0	0	0	0	0	3	2	2	0	0	0	0	0	0	0	1	4
Narcotic drug laws	487	422	299	7	11	105	27	9	6	0	0	0	4	8	0	0	2	9
Gambling	5	5	5	0	0	0	0	0	0	0	0	0	0	0	0	0	0	0
Other—not specified	460	307	181	16	23	87	54	9	20	1	0	0	13	3	0	7	5	41
Suspected felony type	56	36	26	0	1	9	9	4	1	0	0	0	0	1	0	1	0	4
Other than felony type total:	6,728	4,209	3,066	215	231	697	1,158	286	558	5	1	0	20	28	8	70	41	344
Romantic triangle	87	54	39	3	8	4	18	8	3	0	0	0	1	0	0	1	0	2
Child killed by babysitter	28	2	2	0	0	0	0	2	16	0	0	0	0	0	0	1	0	7
Brawl due to influence of alcohol	116	47	38	2	1	6	33	9	19	0	0	0	1	0	0	2	0	5
Brawl due to influence of narcotics	93	67	53	5	1	8	8	4	5	0	0	0	0	3	0	0	2	4
Argument over money or property	203	118	89	10	9	10	43	10	17	0	0	0	1	0	1	6	2	5
Other arguments	3,334	1,989	1,418	94	119	358	746	147	233	3	1	0	6	3	1	38	15	152
Gangland killings	180	159	105	7	3	44	15	3	1	0	0	0	0	0	0	1	0	2
Juvenile gang killings	715	665	547	20	16	82	28	8	6	0	0	0	0	0	0	1	0	7
Institutional killings	10	1	0	0	0	1	2	2	2	0	0	0	0	0	0	1	1	1
Sniper attack	1	1	0	1	0	0	0	0	0	0	0	0	0	0	0	0	0	0
Other—not specified	1,961	1,106	775	73	74	184	265	93	256	2	0	0	11	22	6	20	21	159
Unknown	4,832	3,449	2,323	81	126	919	458	218	165	0	0	2	34	5	0	30	20	451

SOURCE: "Expanded Homicide Data Table 11. Murder Circumstances, by Weapon, 2009," in *Crime in the United States, 2009*, U.S. Department of Justice, Federal Bureau of Investigation, September 2010, http://www2 .fbi.gov/ucr/cius2009/offenses/expanded_information/data/documents/09shrtbl11.xls (accessed November 7, 2010)

Rape is a very intimate crime, and rape victims may be unwilling, afraid, or ashamed to discuss it. As a result, many rapes are likely not reported to law enforcement authorities. In 2009, 88,097 forcible rapes were reported to law enforcement agencies for a rate of 28.7 forcible rapes per 100,000 inhabitants. (See Table 2.1.) The FBI indicates that the rape rate in 2009 was 56.6 per 100,000 female inhabitants.

As shown in Table 2.1, forcible rape rates have declined dramatically since the early 1990s, when rates of more than 40 rapes per 100,000 inhabitants were recorded. The FBI notes that 93% of forcible rapes recorded by law enforcement agencies in 2009 were rapes by force and 7% were attempted rapes.

Robbery

According to the FBI, in *Crime in the United States, 2009*, robbery is defined as "the taking or attempting to take anything of value from the care, custody, or control of a person or persons by force or threat of force or violence and/or by putting the victim in fear." The robbery rate peaked in 1991 at 272.7 per 100,000 inhabitants. (See Table 2.1.) Over the following decade it declined dramatically, and between 2000 and 2009 the rate stayed below 150 robberies per 100,000 inhabitants.

Figure 2.1 shows the locations of robberies that were reported in 2009. Nearly 43% of these robberies occurred on the street or highway, 16.9% occurred at residences, 16.6% occurred at miscellaneous locations, and 13.7% occurred at commercial houses (i.e., nonresidential structures that are used for businesses other than gas stations, banks, or convenience stores). Robberies at convenience stores accounted for 5.4% of the total, while gas or service station locations accounted for 2.4% and banks 2.2% of the total.

Aggravated Assault

Aggravated assault is defined by the FBI in *Crime in the United States, 2009* as "an unlawful attack by one person upon another for the purpose of inflicting severe or aggravated bodily injury." The agency further notes that aggravated assault typically involves "the use of a weapon or by other means likely to produce death or great bodily harm." Attempted aggravated assaults that involve weapons or the threat to use weapons are included in this category. However, an aggravated assault that occurs during a robbery is categorized as a robbery.

In 2009, 806,843 aggravated assaults were reported to law enforcement agencies nationwide for a rate of 262.8 aggravated assaults per 100,000 inhabitants. (See Table 2.1.) During the early to mid-1990s the rate was more than 400 aggravated assaults per 100,000 inhabitants. The rate has declined dramatically since then, falling more

FIGURE 2.1

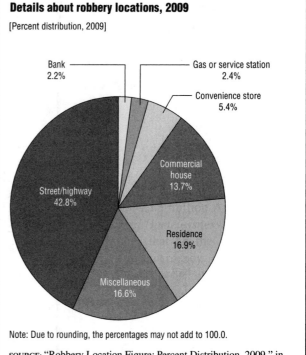

Details about robbery locations, 2009

[Percent distribution, 2009]

Bank 2.2%
Gas or service station 2.4%
Convenience store 5.4%
Commercial house 13.7%
Street/highway 42.8%
Residence 16.9%
Miscellaneous 16.6%

Note: Due to rounding, the percentages may not add to 100.0.

SOURCE: "Robbery Location Figure: Percent Distribution, 2009," in *Crime in the United States, 2009*, U.S. Department of Justice, Federal Bureau of Investigation, September 2010, http://www2.fbi.gov/ucr/cius2009/offenses/violent_crime/robbery.html (accessed September 29, 2010)

than 40% from the peak of 441.9 aggravated assaults per 100,000 inhabitants in 1992.

WEAPONS INVOLVED IN AGGRAVATED ASSAULTS. Table 2.6 lists the weapons involved in 702,471 of the aggravated assaults that occurred in 2009. In 27% (189,462) of these aggravated assaults the perpetrators used their hands, fists, and feet as weapons. Firearms were involved in 20.9% (146,650) of these crimes, and knives or other cutting instruments were involved in 18.7% (131,393) of aggravated assaults in 2009. The remaining one-third (33.4% or 234,966) of these crimes involved other weapons.

Violent Crime and Property Crime

As noted earlier, the FBI includes four crimes in the category of violent crime: forcible rape, murder and non-negligent manslaughter, aggravated assault, and robbery. A crime that includes more than one of these violent acts is counted only once under the most serious offense committed. According to the FBI, in *Crime in the United States, 2009*, the hierarchy is murder and nonnegligent homicide, forcible rape, robbery, and aggravated assault. Thus, a forcible rape in which the victim is also robbed would be counted as a forcible rape, not as a forcible rape and a robbery. In 2009, 1.3 million violent crimes were reported by law enforcement agencies for a rate of 429.4

TABLE 2.6

Details about selected offenses, 2009

Population group	Forcible rape		Robbery				Aggravated assault				Burglary			Motor vehicle theft			Arson			Number of agencies	2009 estimated population
	Rape by force	Assault to rape-attempts	Fire-arm	Knife or cutting instrument	Other weapon	Strong-arm	Fire-arm	Knife or cutting instrument	Other weapon	Hands, fists, feet, etc.	Forcible entry	Unlawful entry	Attempted forcible entry	Autos	Trucks and buses	Other vehicles	Structure	Mobile	Other		
Total all agencies 2009	71,161	5,415	149,493	26,817	30,388	144,085	146,650	131,393	234,966	189,462	1,200,235	640,593	127,113	519,117	124,129	78,144	23,643	14,992	14,802	14,266	270,511,477

SOURCE: Adapted from "Table 15. Crime Trends: Additional Information about Selected Offenses, by Population Group, 2008–2009," in *Crime in the United States, 2009*, U.S. Department of Justice, Federal Bureau of Investigation, September 2010, http://www2.fbi.gov/ucr/cius2009/data/documents/09tbl15.xls (accessed October 2, 2010)

FIGURE 2.2

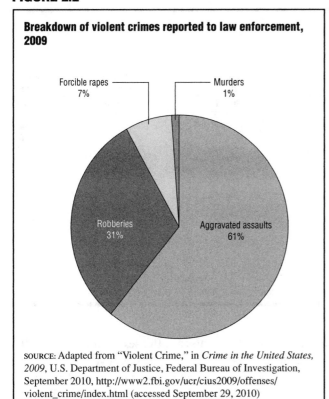

Breakdown of violent crimes reported to law enforcement, 2009

Forcible rapes 7%

Murders 1%

Robberies 31%

Aggravated assaults 61%

SOURCE: Adapted from "Violent Crime," in *Crime in the United States, 2009*, U.S. Department of Justice, Federal Bureau of Investigation, September 2010, http://www2.fbi.gov/ucr/cius2009/offenses/violent_crime/index.html (accessed September 29, 2010)

per 100,000 inhabitants. (See Table 2.1.) As shown in Figure 2.2, the breakdown of reported violent crimes by percentage is:

- Murder and nonnegligent homicide—1% of reported violent crimes
- Forcible rape—7% of reported violent crimes
- Robbery—31% of reported violent crimes
- Aggravated assault—61% of reported violent crimes

The FBI includes four crimes in the category of property crime: larceny-theft, burglary, arson, and motor vehicle theft. In 2009, 9.3 million of these property crimes were reported for a rate of 3,036.1 per 100,000 inhabitants. (See Table 2.1.) According to the FBI, the hierarchy for property crimes is burglary, larceny-theft, and motor vehicle theft; arson is not included in the hierarchy. The property crime hierarchy lies below the violent crime hierarchy, meaning that a violent crime that includes one or more property crimes is counted only under the appropriate violent crime. The following four sections describe the statistics for individual property crimes.

Burglary

According to the FBI, in *Crime in the United States, 2009*, burglary is defined as "the unlawful entry of a structure to commit a felony or theft." Unlawful entry includes both forcible and nonforcible entry (e.g., entering a home through an unlocked door without the owner's permission). The FBI's definition of structure includes houses, apartments, offices, barns, stables, and so on, but does not include automobiles. Attempted forcible entries are included in the burglary category.

Nearly 2.2 million burglaries were reported in 2009 for a rate of 716.3 per 100,000 inhabitants. (See Table 2.1.) This rate is down dramatically from the early 1990s, when the rate was more than 1,000 burglaries per 100,000 inhabitants. According to the FBI, 61% of the burglaries in 2009 involved forcible entry. Nearly a third (32.6%) were nonforcible unlawful entries, and 6.5% were attempted forcible entries.

A separate data set by the FBI covering 1.9 million burglaries in 2009 indicates that the vast majority of these burglaries (nearly 1.4 million) occurred at residences. The remainder were at nonresidences, such as stores or offices. The time of day in which the burglaries occurred could not be identified in 21.9% of the cases. Nighttime burglaries accounted for 31.8% of the total, whereas daytime burglaries accounted for 46.3% of the total.

Larceny-Theft

Larceny-theft is defined by the FBI in *Crime in the United States, 2009* as "the unlawful taking, carrying, leading, or riding away of property from the possession or constructive possession of another." Larceny-theft does not involve the use of force, violence, or fraud. Examples of fraud-based crimes are embezzlement, forgery, and passing bad checks. Larceny-theft does include offenses such as shoplifting, pocket picking, purse snatching, stealing items from motor vehicles, and stealing bicycles. Attempted larceny-thefts are also included.

In 2009 law enforcement agencies reported 6.3 million larceny-thefts for a rate of 2,060.9 per 100,000 inhabitants. (See Table 2.1.) This rate is down from a peak of 3,229.1 larceny-thefts per 100,000 inhabitants in 1991. According to the FBI, the total value of property lost by victims to larceny-theft during 2009 was nearly $5.5 billion.

Table 2.7 provides details about more than 5.4 million of the larceny-thefts that occurred in 2009. Thefts from motor vehicles (excluding accessories) accounted for nearly 1.5 million of the offenses. This was, by far, the largest category among the specifically identified larceny-theft crimes. It accounted for 27.3% of the total. Shoplifting crimes and thefts from buildings made up 18.1% and 11.1%, respectively, of the total.

As shown in Table 2.7, the average loss to victims due to larceny-thefts in 2009 was $864. A breakdown by average value is as follows:

TABLE 2.7

Details about larceny-theft crimes, 2009

[14,066 agencies; 2009 estimated population 267,639,320]

Classification		Number of offenses 2009	Percent distribution*	Average value
Larceny-theft (except motor vehicle theft):	Total	5,462,598	100.0	$864
Larceny-theft by type:	Pocket-picking	22,952	0.4	504
	Purse-snatching	26,281	0.5	445
	Shoplifting	990,636	18.1	181
	From motor vehicles (except accessories)	1,488,948	27.3	742
	Motor vehicle accessories	494,083	9.0	530
	Bicycles	183,028	3.4	318
	From buildings	606,913	11.1	1,234
	From coin-operated machines	22,482	0.4	364
	All others	1,627,275	29.8	1,433
Larceny-theft by value:	Over $200	2,442,404	44.7	1,862
	$50 to $200	1,244,467	22.8	110
	Under $50	1,775,727	32.5	18

*Because of rounding, the percentages may not add to 100.0.

SOURCE: Adapted from "Table 23. Offense Analysis: Number and Percent Change, 2008–2009," in *Crime in the United States, 2009*, U.S. Department of Justice, Federal Bureau of Investigation, September 2010, http://www2.fbi.gov/ucr/cius2009/data/documents/09tbl23.xls (accessed October 2, 2010)

- Value over $200—44.7% of total larceny-thefts

- Value of $50 to $200—22.8% of total larceny-thefts

- Value less than $50—32.5% of total larceny-thefts

Motor Vehicle Theft

The FBI defines motor vehicle theft in *Crime in the United States, 2009* as "the theft or attempted theft of a motor vehicle." Included in the definition of motor vehicles are cars, trucks, sport-utility vehicles, buses, motorcycles and motor scooters, snowmobiles, and all-terrain vehicles. Other types of motorized vehicles (e.g., boats, tractors, and construction equipment) are not included.

In 2009, 794,616 cases of motor vehicle theft were reported in the United States for a rate of 258.8 motor vehicle thefts per 100,000 inhabitants. (See Table 2.1.) This rate is down considerably from the early 1990s, when the rate was more than 650 motor vehicle thefts per 100,000 inhabitants. According to the FBI, the total value of the stolen motor vehicles in 2009 was $5.2 billion.

Arson

Arson is defined by the FBI in *Crime in the United States, 2009* as "any willful or malicious burning or attempting to burn, with or without intent to defraud, a dwelling house, public building, motor vehicle or aircraft, personal property of another, etc." Arson statistics do not include fires that have been classified as suspicious or of unknown origin.

The FBI notes that incomplete statistics are available for arson crimes due to limited reporting by law enforcement agencies. Reports from law enforcement agencies indicate that 58,871 arson offenses occurred in 2009. Approximately 44.5% of these arsons involved buildings, such as residences or other structures. Another 28.4% involved mobile property, such as cars, and 27.1% of the arsons involved miscellaneous types of property, such as crops or fences.

GUNS AND CRIME

The FBI reports that firearms were used in 67.1% of the murders, 42.6% of the robberies, and 20.9% of the aggravated assaults reported in 2009. (See Figure 2.3.) The agency does not, however, specify the number of total offenses or the number of reporting agencies that were involved in calculating these percentages.

In *Key Facts at a Glance* (January 31, 2011, http://bjs.ojp.usdoj.gov/content/glance/guncrime.cfm), the FBI indicates that the number of violent crimes (murders, robberies, and aggravated assaults) that were committed with firearms skyrocketed during the early 1990s, reaching nearly 600,000 per year in 1993. Since then the number has dropped dramatically, dipping below 400,000 per year during the late 1990s and the first decade of the 21st century. This is similar to the levels that were recorded during the 1970s and 1980s.

Background Checks for Firearms

In 1993 Congress passed the Brady Handgun Violence Prevention Act. The law requires federal firearms licensees to perform a criminal history background check on customers before selling them firearms. The licensing of firearms dealers is handled by the Bureau of Alcohol, Tobacco, Firearms, and Explosives, a division of the U.S. Department of Justice (DOJ). The types of people who are prohibited from buying firearms under the Brady

FIGURE 2.3

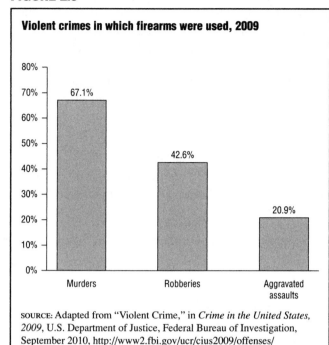

Violent crimes in which firearms were used, 2009

SOURCE: Adapted from "Violent Crime," in *Crime in the United States, 2009*, U.S. Department of Justice, Federal Bureau of Investigation, September 2010, http://www2.fbi.gov/ucr/cius2009/offenses/violent_crime/index.html (accessed September 29, 2010)

Act and similar state laws include convicted felons, people under indictment for felony offenses, people who have been convicted of misdemeanor domestic violence, and people subject to a restraining order due to harassment, stalking, or threatening of an intimate partner or child.

The DOJ reports in *Background Checks for Firearm Transfers, 2009—Statistical Tables* (October 2010, http://bjs.ojp.usdoj.gov/content/pub/html/bcft/2009/bcft09st.pdf) that 10.8 million applications for firearm transfers or permits were subject to background checks in 2009 under the Brady Act and similar state laws. Only 1.4% of the applications were denied. The most common reason for denial was a felony conviction or indictment of the applicant.

HATE CRIMES

As noted in Chapter 1, hate crimes are crimes that are motivated by the offender's personal prejudice or bias against the victim. The FBI includes hate crimes in the UCR Program. The UCR Program's first publication on hate crimes was *Hate Crime Statistics, 1990: A Resource Book*, which compiled hate crime data from 11 states that had collected the information under state authority in 1990. The UCR Program continued to work with agencies that were already investigating hate crimes and collecting related information to develop a more uniform method of nationwide data collection. *Hate Crime Statistics, 1992* offered the first data reported by law enforcement agencies across the country that participated in UCR hate crime data collection. In the Violent Crime and Law Enforcement Act

of 1994, Congress added hate-motivated crimes against disabled people to the list of bias crimes; the FBI began gathering data on hate crimes against this population on January 1, 1997.

Data on hate crimes are likely incomplete because many incidents may not be reported or cannot be verified as hate crimes. Some victims may not report hate crimes due to fear that the criminal justice system is biased against the group to which the victim belongs and that law enforcement authorities will not be responsive. Attacks against homosexuals may not be reported because the victims do not want to reveal their sexual orientation to others. In addition, proving that an offender acted from bias can be a long, tedious process, requiring much investigation. Until a law enforcement investigator can find enough evidence in a particular case to be sure the offender's actions came, at least in part, from bias, the crime is not counted as a hate crime.

Hate Crime Statistics

As of February 2011, the most recent UCR Program–based report on hate crimes was *Hate Crime Statistics, 2009* (November 2010, http://www2.fbi.gov/ucr/hc2009/index.html). It covers crimes that were motivated by offender bias against the race, ethnicity or national origin, sexual orientation, religion, or disability of the victim. The UCR Program notes that in 2009, 2,034 law enforcement agencies reported 6,604 hate crime incidents involving 7,789 specific offenses. Almost all the incidents (6,598) were due to a single bias on behalf of the offender:

- Racial bias—48.5%
- Religious bias—19.7%
- Sexual-orientation bias—18.5%
- Ethnicity/national origin bias—11.8%
- Disability bias—1.5%

Of the 7,789 offenses reported in 2009, 61.5% were crimes against people. Another 38.1% were crimes against property. The FBI explains that "the remainder were crimes against society."

The following is a breakdown of the hate crime offenses that were committed against people in 2009:

- Intimidation—45%
- Simple assault—35.3%
- Aggravated assault—19.1%
- Murder and forcible rape—0.4%

THE DECLINE OF CRIME

Between 2000 and 2009 both the number of crimes reported each year and the crime rate decreased for all the crimes that are monitored by the DOJ under the UCR

Program. (See Table 2.1.) The UCR Program relies on information from law enforcement agencies. The DOJ also conducts an annual victimization survey in which a random group of U.S. inhabitants is quizzed about their experiences with crime during the previous year. Because not all crimes are reported to law enforcement, the victimization surveys provide information about the true extent of crime in the United States.

Violent Crime Decreases

Figure 2.4 includes data from the UCR Program and victimization surveys dating back to 1973. It shows four measures of serious violent crime: homicide, rape, robbery, and aggravated assault.

"Estimated total violent crime" is based on the number of homicides committed against people aged 12 years and older as reported by law enforcement agencies plus the number of rapes, robberies, and aggravated assaults tallied in victimization surveys regardless of whether or not these crimes were reported to law enforcement agencies by victims. "Violent victimizations reported to police" includes homicides committed against people aged 12 years and

older as reported by law enforcement agencies plus the number of rapes, robberies, and aggravated assaults tallied in victimization surveys that the victims claim were reported to law enforcement agencies. "Violent crimes recorded by police in uniform crime reports" is based on UCR Program records, but includes only homicides, forcible rapes, robberies (excluding commercial robberies), and aggravated assaults committed against people aged 12 years and older.

Figure 2.4 indicates that the total estimated number of serious violent crimes hovered between 3 million and just over 4 million offenses per year from the early 1970s through the early 1990s. The number peaked at nearly 4.2 million offenses in 1993 and then began a steady decline that lasted until 2002. From 2003 to 2007 the total estimated number of violent crimes hovered between 1.6 million and 1.8 million per year.

A similar pattern is evident in Figure 2.5, which shows the violent crime rate per 100,000 inhabitants between 1960 and 2009 based on UCR records. The violent crime rate more than quadrupled between 1960 and 1991 from 160.9 to 758.1 violent crimes per 100,000

FIGURE 2.4

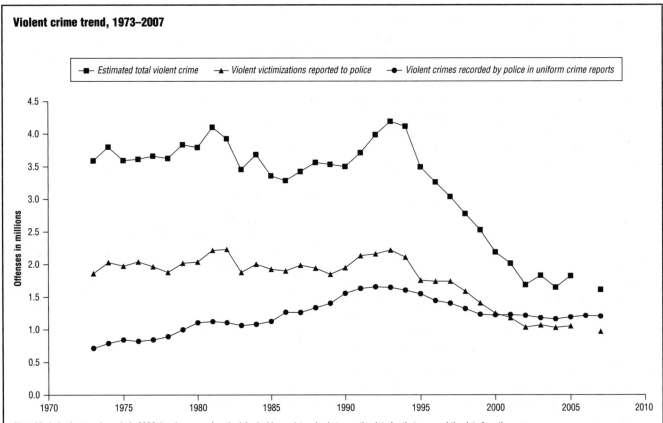

Violent crime trend, 1973–2007

Note: Victimization trends exclude 2006 data because of methodological inconsistencies between the data for that year and the data for other years.

SOURCE: Adapted from Cathy Maston and Patsy Klaus, "Four Measures of Serious Violent Crime, Violent Crimes including Homicide," in *Violent Crime: Key Facts at a Glance*, U.S. Department of Justice, Office of Justice Programs, Bureau of Justice Statistics, September 18, 2006, http://bjs.ojp.usdoj.gov/content/glance/tables/4meastab.cfm (accessed November 10, 2010)

FIGURE 2.5

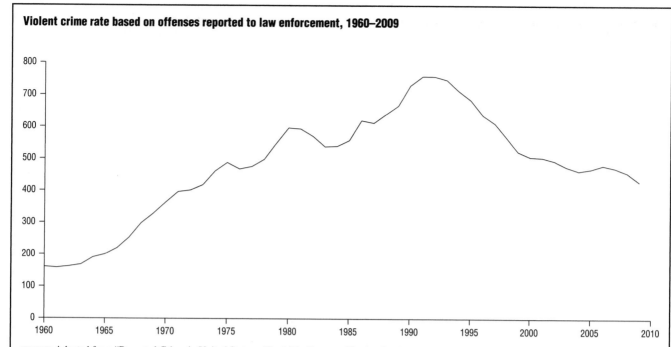

Violent crime rate based on offenses reported to law enforcement, 1960–2009

SOURCE: Adapted from "Reported Crime in United States—Total," in *Bureau of Justice Statistics—Data Online*, U.S. Department of Justice, Office of Justice Programs, Bureau of Justice Statistics, August 27, 2009, http://bjs.ojp.usdoj.gov/dataonline/Search/Crime/State/RunCrimeStatebyState.cfm (accessed October 23, 2010), and "Table 1. Crime in the United States, by Volume and Rate per 100,000 Inhabitants, 1990–2009," in *Crime in the United States, 2009*, U.S. Department of Justice, Federal Bureau of Investigation, September 2010, http://www2.fbi.gov/ucr/cius2009/data/documents/09tbl01.xls (accessed September 30, 2010)

inhabitants and then began to decline. In 2009 the rate was 429.4 violent crimes per 100,000 population. (See Table 2.1.)

Figure 2.6 shows the murder and nonnegligent manslaughter rate per 100,000 population between 1960 and 2009. The rate peaked at 10.2 offenses per 100,000 population in 1980 and remained above 8 offenses per 100,000 population into the mid-1990s before beginning to decline. By 1999 the rate had dropped below 6 offenses per 100,000 population, a level not seen since the mid-1960s. Between 1999 and 2009 the murder and nonnegligent manslaughter rate hovered between 5 and 6 offenses per 100,000 population. (See Table 2.1.) In 2009 the rate was 5 offenses per 100,000 population.

Figure 2.7 shows the forcible rape rate per 100,000 population between 1960 and 2009. The rate peaked at 42.8 forcible rapes per 100,000 population in 1992 and then began a general decline. In 2000 the rate dropped below 33 forcible rapes per 100,000 population. (See Table 2.1.) In 2009 the forcible rape rate was 28.7 per 100,000 population.

Figure 2.8 shows the robbery rate per 100,000 population between 1960 and 2009. The rate was above 200 robberies per 100,000 population much of the time from the mid-1970s through the mid-1990s. In 2000 the rate dropped below 150 robberies per 100,000 population.

(See Table 2.1.) In 2009 the rate was 133 robberies per 100,000 population.

Figure 2.9 shows the aggravated assault rate per 100,000 population between 1960 and 2009. During the early 1960s the rate was less than 100 aggravated assaults per 100,000 population. The rate skyrocketed over the following decades, reaching 441.9 aggravated assaults per 100,000 population in 1992. (See Table 2.1.) The rate then began a dramatic decrease, dropping to 262.8 aggravated assaults per 100,000 population in 2009.

Property Crime Decreases

Figure 2.10 shows the number of property crimes (burglary, larceny-theft, and motor vehicle theft) per 100,000 population between 1960 and 2009. The rate was around 5,000 property crimes per 100,000 population from the late 1970s through the early 1990s. Its highest point was 5,353.3 property crimes per 100,000 population in 1980. The rate remained above 4,000 through the 1990s before beginning a steady decline. In 2009 the property crime rate was 3,036.1 per 100,000 population. (See Table 2.1.)

As shown in Figure 2.8, the burglary rate per 100,000 population soared from 1960 through 1980. The rate peaked at 1,684.1 burglaries per 100,000 population in 1980. Since then it has declined dramatically. By 1999 the rate was below 800 burglaries per 100,000 population.

FIGURE 2.6

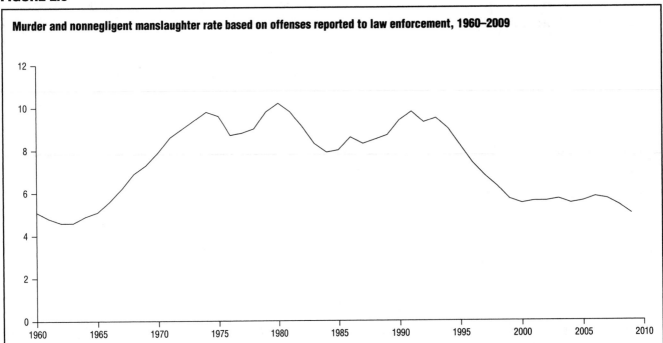

Murder and nonnegligent manslaughter rate based on offenses reported to law enforcement, 1960–2009

SOURCE: Adapted from "Reported Crime in United States—Total," in *Bureau of Justice Statistics—Data Online*, U.S. Department of Justice, Office of Justice Programs, Bureau of Justice Statistics, October 23, 2010, http://bjs.ojp.usdoj.gov/dataonline/Search/Crime/State/RunCrimeStatebyState.cfm (accessed October 23, 2010), and "Table 1. Crime in the United States, by Volume and Rate per 100,000 Inhabitants, 1990–2009," in *Crime in the United States, 2009*, U.S. Department of Justice, Federal Bureau of Investigation, September 2010, http://www2.fbi.gov/ucr/cius2009/data/documents/09tbl01.xls (accessed September 30, 2010)

FIGURE 2.7

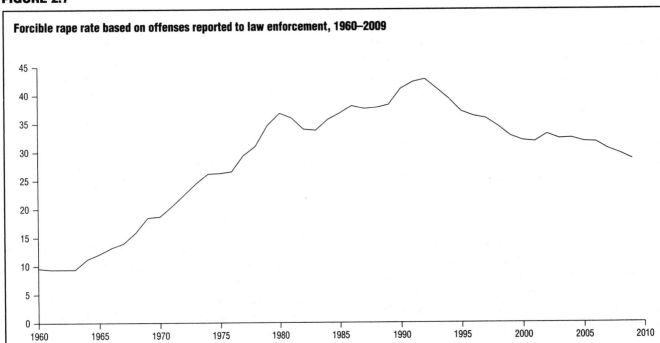

Forcible rape rate based on offenses reported to law enforcement, 1960–2009

SOURCE: Adapted from "Reported Crime in United States—Total," in *Bureau of Justice Statistics—Data Online*, U.S. Department of Justice, Office of Justice Programs, Bureau of Justice Statistics, October 23, 2010, http://bjs.ojp.usdoj.gov/dataonline/Search/Crime/State/RunCrimeStatebyState.cfm (accessed October 23, 2010), and "Table 1. Crime in the United States, by Volume and Rate per 100,000 Inhabitants, 1990–2009," in *Crime in the United States, 2009*, U.S. Department of Justice, Federal Bureau of Investigation, September 2010, http://www2.fbi.gov/ucr/cius2009/data/documents/09tbl01.xls (accessed September 30, 2010)

FIGURE 2.8

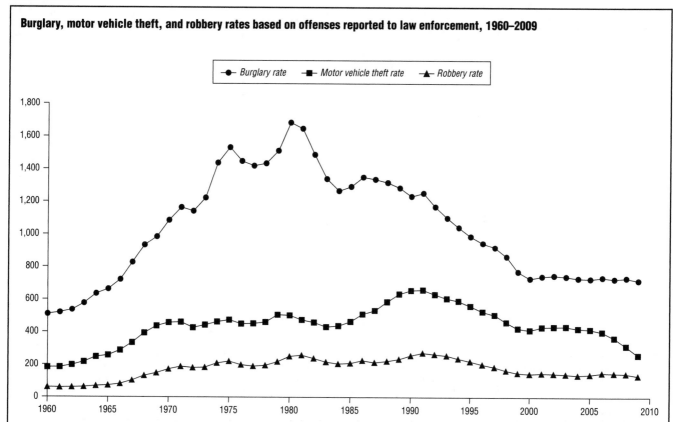

Burglary, motor vehicle theft, and robbery rates based on offenses reported to law enforcement, 1960–2009

SOURCE: Adapted from "Reported Crime in United States—Total," in *Bureau of Justice Statistics—Data Online*, U.S. Department of Justice, Office of Justice Programs, Bureau of Justice Statistics, October 23, 2010, http://bjs.ojp.usdoj.gov/dataonline/Search/Crime/State/RunCrimeStatebyState.cfm (accessed October 23, 2010), and "Table 1. Crime in the United States, by Volume and Rate per 100,000 Inhabitants, 1990–2009," in *Crime in the United States, 2009*, U.S. Department of Justice, Federal Bureau of Investigation, September 2010, http://www2.fbi.gov/ucr/cius2009/data/documents/09tbl01.xls (accessed September 30, 2010)

(See Table 2.1.) Between 2000 and 2009 the rate leveled off at around 730 to 750 burglaries per 100,000 population. The burglary rate has not been this low since the mid-1960s. In 2009 the rate was 716.3 burglaries per 100,000 population.

Figure 2.8 also shows the motor vehicle theft rate per 100,000 population between 1960 and 2009. The rate peaked during the early 1990s in excess of 600 thefts per 100,000 population. It has declined dramatically since that time, dropping to 258.8 thefts per 100,000 population in 2009. (See Table 2.1.)

Figure 2.11 shows the larceny-theft rate per 100,000 population between 1960 and 2009. The rate climbed from just over 1,000 in 1960 to more than 3,000 during the 1980s and 1990s before beginning to decrease. By 2009 the larceny-theft rate had dropped to 2,060.9 per 100,000 population. (See Table 2.1.)

WHY DID CRIME RISE AND FALL?

According to Arthur J. Lurigio, in "Crime and Communities: Prevalence, Impact, and Programs" (Lawrence B. Joseph, ed., *Crime, Communities, and Public Policy*, 1995),

the national crime rate fell from 1900 until the Prohibition era (1920–1933). Crime spiked during Prohibition and then fell and leveled off until World War II (1939–1945). Crime dropped dramatically during the war because many young men were away. Following the war, a baby boom occurred, meaning that there was a dramatic increase in births. The baby boom lasted from the late 1940s into the 1960s, resulting in a huge surge of teenagers and young adults in the population from the 1960s through the 1980s.

Figure 2.5 and Figure 2.10 show historical crime rates for violent crimes and property crimes, respectively, between 1960 and 2009. In both categories a huge increase occurred from 1960 through the 1980s and 1990s. A variety of social, economic, and even environmental reasons have been proposed to explain this increase:

- Huge influx in youth due to the baby boom

- Decrease in high-paying blue-collar manufacturing jobs for low-skilled workers

- Growth of ghettos and low-income housing projects in the inner cities

- Breakdown of the traditional family structure

FIGURE 2.9

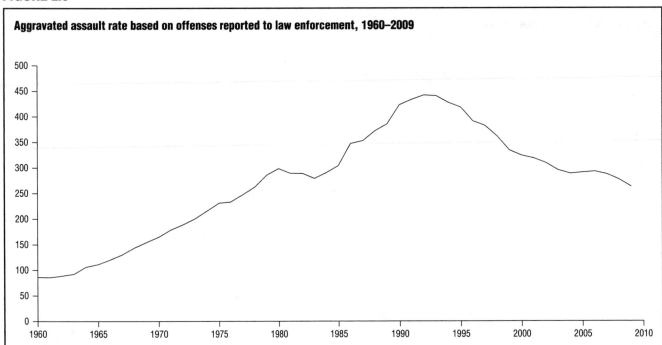

Aggravated assault rate based on offenses reported to law enforcement, 1960–2009

SOURCE: Adapted from "Reported Crime in United States—Total," in *Bureau of Justice Statistics—Data Online*, U.S. Department of Justice, Office of Justice Programs, Bureau of Justice Statistics, October 23, 2010, http://bjs.ojp.usdoj.gov/dataonline/Search/Crime/State/RunCrimeStatebyState.cfm (accessed October 23, 2010), and "Table 1. Crime in the United States, by Volume and Rate per 100,000 Inhabitants, 1990–2009," in *Crime in the United States, 2009*, U.S. Department of Justice, Federal Bureau of Investigation, September 2010, http://www2.fbi.gov/ucr/cius2009/data/documents/09tbl01.xls (accessed September 30, 2010)

FIGURE 2.10

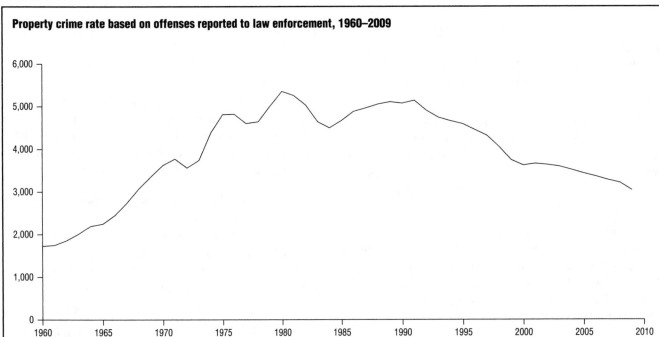

Property crime rate based on offenses reported to law enforcement, 1960–2009

SOURCE: Adapted from "Reported Crime in United States—Total," in *Bureau of Justice Statistics—Data Online*, U.S. Department of Justice, Office of Justice Programs, Bureau of Justice Statistics, October 23, 2010, http://bjs.ojp.usdoj.gov/dataonline/Search/Crime/State/RunCrimeStatebyState.cfm (accessed October 23, 2010), and "Table 1. Crime in the United States, by Volume and Rate per 100,000 Inhabitants, 1990–2009," in *Crime in the United States, 2009*, U.S. Department of Justice, Federal Bureau of Investigation, September 2010, http://www2.fbi.gov/ucr/cius2009/data/documents/09tbl01.xls (accessed September 30, 2010)

FIGURE 2.11

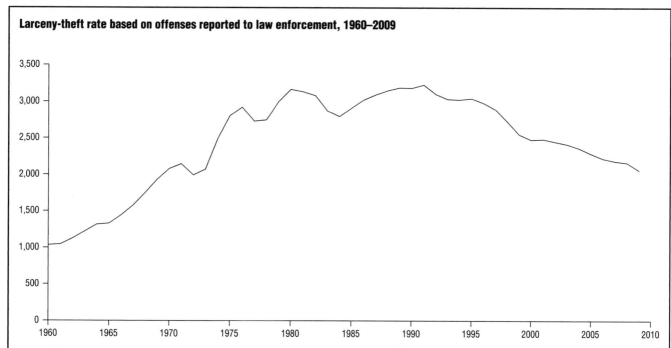

Larceny-theft rate based on offenses reported to law enforcement, 1960–2009

SOURCE: Adapted from "Reported Crime in United States—Total," in *Bureau of Justice Statistics—Data Online*, U.S. Department of Justice, Office of Justice Programs, Bureau of Justice Statistics, October 23, 2010, http://bjs.ojp.usdoj.gov/dataonline/Search/Crime/State/RunCrimeStatebyState.cfm (accessed October 23, 2010), and "Table 1. Crime in the United States, by Volume and Rate per 100,000 Inhabitants, 1990–2009," in *Crime in the United States, 2009*, U.S. Department of Justice, Federal Bureau of Investigation, September 2010, http://www2.fbi.gov/ucr/cius2009/data/documents/09tbl01.xls (accessed September 30, 2010)

- New drug culture, particularly heroin and cocaine during the 1970s and crack cocaine during the 1980s

- Growth of youth gangs

- Easy availability of firearms

- Better crime-tracking methods

- Exposure of infants and children to lead in paint and gasoline before the late 1970s (lead exposure has been linked to a range of developmental and behavioral issues, including inattention, irritability, aggressiveness, and violent behavior)

During the early 1990s the crime rate began a dramatic and sustained decline. (See Figure 2.5 and Figure 2.10.) Many of the conditions that had been blamed for the crime surge continued into the 1990s and the first decade of the 21st century, even as the crime rate decreased. The breakdown of the traditional family, the growth of youth gangs, and the loss of high-paying blue-collar jobs continued to occur even as the crime rate plummeted. Likewise, crime-tracking methods continued to improve over time. Sociologists and criminologists have struggled to explain why the crime rate increased and then decreased. Some of the reasons suggested for the decrease are:

- A strong economy during the 1990s provided many job opportunities

- Tougher sentencing rules took hard-core criminals off the streets and kept them behind bars for longer periods of time

- Tougher gun control laws made firearms less accessible to criminals

- The U.S. population aged as baby boomers became older and less prone to criminal behavior

- Some ghettos and low-income housing projects that had been hotbeds for crime in the inner cities were dismantled

- There were more police officers per capita

- Policing methods improved

- People increased their crime prevention efforts, such as the use of security systems and neighborhood watch programs

- The crack cocaine epidemic subsided

- The national legalization of abortion in 1973 prevented unwanted babies from being born and potentially growing up to become criminals

- Lead exposure in infants and children decreased dramatically after the 1970s

It remains to be seen whether these explanations for the crime decline will hold up to future scrutiny.

CHAPTER 3
CRIME VICTIMS

As described in Chapter 2, the Federal Bureau of Investigation (FBI) operates the Uniform Crime Reports (UCR) Program, which compiles national crime data that are submitted by thousands of law enforcement agencies from around the country. The UCR Program provides data on the types of crimes that are reported to law enforcement agencies. It also includes some data on the victims of these crimes. Another, more detailed examination of crime victims is conducted by the Bureau of Justice Statistics (BJS), an agency within the U.S. Department of Justice (DOJ). This program is called the National Crime Victimization Survey (NCVS).

THE NATIONAL CRIME VICTIMIZATION SURVEY

Since 1972 the BJS has conducted an annual survey that measures the levels of victimization resulting from criminal activity in the United States. The survey was previously known as the National Crime Survey, but was renamed in 1991 to emphasize the measurement of victimization that is experienced by U.S. residents and households. Each year the NCVS collects data from thousands of households on the frequency, characteristics, and consequences of criminal victimization in the United States. As of February 2011, the most recent survey data were reported by Jennifer L. Truman and Michael R. Rand of the BJS in *Criminal Victimization, 2009* (October 2010, http://bjs.ojp.usdoj.gov/content/pub/pdf/cv09.pdf). The BJS states in the press release "Violent and Property Crime Rates Declined in 2009, Continuing the Trend Observed in the Last Ten Years" (October 13, 2010, http://bjs.ojp .usdoj.gov/content/pub/press/cv09pr.cfm) that "38,728 households and 68,665 individuals age 12 or older were interviewed twice during the year for the [2009] NCVS."

The BJS uses NCVS data to create detailed tables of criminal victimization information. As of February 2011, the most recently published detailed data set was reported by Cathy T. Maston of the BJS in *Criminal Victimization in the United States, 2007—Statistical Tables* (March 2, 2010, http://bjs.ojp.usdoj.gov/index.cfm?ty=pbdetail &iid=1743).

The NCVS measures the levels of criminal victimization of people and households for the following crimes: rape and sexual assault, robbery, aggravated and simple assault, purse snatching and pocket picking (which are called personal crimes), household burglary, motor vehicle theft, and other thefts (which are called household crimes). Murder and other killing crimes are not counted in the NCVS because the data are gathered only through interviews with victims. The BJS uses NCVS data to calculate victimization rates as follows:

- Personal crimes—number of victims per 1,000 U.S. residents aged 12 years and older

- Household crimes—number of incidents per 1,000 U.S. households

According to the BJS, in *Survey Methodology for Criminal Victimization in the United States, 2007* (April 2, 2010, http://bjs.ojp.usdoj.gov/content/pub/pdf/cvus/cvus07mt .pdf), neither the interviewers nor the victims classify events as specific crimes during the interviews. A computer program later performs crime classification based on victim answers to specific detailed questions about the nature of each event. For events that include more than one crime (e.g., rape and burglary), only the most serious crime is counted using the following hierarchy: rape, sexual assault, robbery, assault, burglary, motor vehicle theft, and theft.

Comparing NCVS and UCR Data

The NCVS was created because of a concern that the FBI's UCR Program did not fully portray the true volume of crime in the United States. The UCR provides data on crimes that are reported to law enforcement authorities, but not all crimes are reported by victims.

Some observers believe the NCVS is a better indicator than the UCR of the volume of crime in the United States. Nonetheless, like all surveys, the NCVS is subject to error. The accuracy of the survey data depends on people's truthful and complete reporting of incidents and events that have happened to them. Also, the NCVS and the UCR sometimes define and track crimes differently. As noted in Chapter 2, the FBI defines rape for UCR purposes as "the carnal knowledge of a female forcibly and against her will." Assaults and attempts to commit rape by force or threat of force are included in this category. By contrast, the BJS explains in "Crime Characteristics and Trends" (February 1, 2011, http://bjs.ojp.usdoj.gov/index.cfm?ty=tp&tid=93) that the NCVS counts as rape victims both female and male victims who have been subjected to "forced sexual intercourse." The NCVS also counts verbal threats of rape as attempted rape. In addition, the UCR Program counts crimes committed against babies and children (i.e., people less than 12 years old), whereas the NCVS only counts crimes against people aged 12 years and older. Thus, direct comparisons between UCR and NCVS data are difficult.

The NCVS and the UCR are generally considered the primary sources of statistical information on crime in the United States. Like all reporting systems, both have their shortcomings, but each provides valuable insights into crime in the United States.

Comparing Old and New NCVS Data

Beginning in 1979 the NCVS underwent a thorough, decade-long redesign. The new design was intended to improve the survey's ability to measure both victimization and difficult-to-measure crimes, such as rape, sexual assault, and domestic violence. Improvements included the introduction of "short cues" or techniques to jog respondents' memories of events. As anticipated, the redesign resulted in an increased number of crimes counted by the survey. Therefore, pre-1993 raw data cannot be directly compared to the later raw data. The DOJ does, however, provide graphs in which pre-1993 raw data have been adjusted to make them comparable with data collected in later years.

In 2006 the methodology of the NCVS was changed to reflect new population data collected by the U.S. Census Bureau and to increase the use of computers during the interviewing process. These changes are described at length by Michael Rand and Shannan Catalano of the BJS in *Criminal Victimization, 2006* (December 2007, http://bjs.ojp.usdoj.gov/content/pub/pdf/cv06.pdf). According to Rand and Catalano, these changes mean that 2006 NCVS victimization rates are not directly comparable to rates that were calculated for previous years. Truman and Rand explain in *Criminal Victimization, 2009* that NCVS data collected to 2006 are also not directly comparable to NCVS data that were collected between 2007 and 2009.

CRIME VICTIMIZATIONS IN 2009

According to the NCVS, more than 4.3 million U.S. residents aged 12 years and older and nearly 15.6 million households were victimized by crime in 2009. (See Table 3.1.)

Victims of Violent Crimes

As shown in Table 3.1, approximately 4.3 million U.S. residents were victims of violent crime in 2009 for a victimization rate of 17.1 per 1,000 population aged 12 years and older. The NCVS considers rape/sexual assault, robbery, and aggravated and simple assault to be serious violent crimes. Nearly 1.5 million U.S. residents aged 12 years and older were victims of these serious violent crimes in 2009. This is a victimization rate of 5.8 serious violent crimes per 1,000 population aged 12 years and older. The victimization rates for individual serious violent crimes were as follows:

- Rape/sexual assault—0.5 per 1,000 population aged 12 years and older

- Robbery—2.1 per 1,000 population aged 12 years and older

- Aggravated assault—3.2 per 1,000 population aged 12 years and older

- Simple assault—11.3 per 1,000 population aged 12 years and older

TABLE 3.1

Criminal victimization, numbers and rates, by type of crime, 2009

Type of crime	Number of victimizations 2009	Rates[a] 2009
All crimes	**20,057,180**	~
Violent crime[b]	4,343,450	17.1
Serious violent crime[c]	1,483,040	5.8
Rape/sexual assault	125,910	0.5
Robbery	533,790	2.1
Assault	3,683,750	14.5
Aggravated	823,340	3.2
Simple	2,860,410	11.3
Personal theft[d]	133,210	0.5
Property crime	15,580,510	127.4
Household burglary	3,134,920	25.6
Motor vehicle theft	735,770	6.0
Theft	11,709,830	95.7

Note: Detail may not sum to total because of rounding. Total population age 12 or older was 252,242,520 in 2008 and 254,105,610 in 2009. Total number of households was 121,141,060 in 2008 and 122,327,660 in 2009.
~Not applicable.
[a]Victimization rates are per 1,000 persons age 12 or older or per 1,000 households.
[b]Excludes murder because the NCVS (National Crime Victimization Survey) is based on interviews with victims and therefore cannot measure murder.
[c]Includes rape/sexual assault, robbery, and aggravated assault.
[d]Includes pocket picking, completed purse snatching, and attempted purse snatching.

SOURCE: Adapted from Jennifer L. Truman and Michael R. Rand, "Table 1. Criminal Victimization, Numbers, Rates, and Percent Change, by Type of Crime, 2008 and 2009," in *Criminal Victimization, 2009*, U.S. Department of Justice, Office of Justice Programs, Bureau of Justice Statistics, October 2010, http://bjs.ojp.usdoj.gov/content/pub/pdf/cv09.pdf (accessed October 23, 2010)

Victims of Personal Theft Crimes

Personal theft crimes are crimes such as pocket picking and attempted and completed purse snatching. In 2009, 133,210 U.S. residents were victims of such crimes. (See Table 3.1.) The personal theft victimization rate was 0.5 per 1,000 population aged 12 years and older.

Victims of Property Crimes

The NCVS counts household burglaries (forced and unforced), motor vehicle thefts, and other thefts (excluding purse snatching and pocket picking) as property crimes. According to NCVS data, nearly 15.6 million U.S. households were victimized by these crimes in 2009. (See Table 3.1.) This is a victimization rate of 127.4 property crimes per 1,000 households in 2009. The most common self-reported property crime was theft (other than motor vehicle theft). Thefts made up 11.7 million of the total victimizations, followed by 3.1 million household burglaries, and 735,770 motor vehicle thefts. The victimization rates for individual property crimes were as follows:

- Motor vehicle theft—6 per 1,000 households
- Household burglary—25.6 per 1,000 households
- Theft—95.7 per 1,000 households

VICTIM DEMOGRAPHICS

The BJS characterizes the demographic qualities of the crime victims that are represented in the NCVS. Victims are characterized by sex, race, Hispanic origin, age, and household income and size. In addition, some information is provided about victim-offender relationships and weapons used against the victims.

Crime Victims by Sex

In 2009 male respondents to the NCVS experienced a victimization rate of 18.4 violent crimes per 1,000 people aged 12 years and older. (See Table 3.2.) Violent crimes include rape/sexual assault, robbery, and aggravated and simple assault. The rate for females was slightly lower at 15.8 violent crimes per 1,000 people aged 12 years and older. The breakdown for crimes of violence indicates that the highest victimization rates in 2009 were for simple assault. The simple assault rates for males and females were 11.3 and 11.2, respectively, per 1,000 people aged 12 years and older.

Crime Victims by Race

Table 3.2 shows violent crime rates based on the race of the victim. Overall, people of two or more races reported the highest violent victimization rate (42.1 per 1,000 people

TABLE 3.2

Violent crime victimization rates, by gender, race, Hispanic origin, and age of victim, 2009

Demographic characteristics of victim	Population	Total	Violent victimizations per 1,000 persons age 12 or older				
			Rape/sexual assault	Robbery	Total assault	Aggravated assault	Simple assault
Gender							
Male	124,041,190	18.4	0.2^	2.7	15.6	4.3	11.3
Female	130,064,420	15.8	0.8	1.6	13.5	2.3	11.2
Race							
White	206,331,920	15.8	0.4	1.6	13.7	2.7	11.0
Black	31,046,560	26.8	1.2	5.6	19.9	6.8	13.0
Other race*	13,982,530	9.8	—^	0.5^	9.3	1.9^	7.4
Two or more races	2,744,600	42.1	—^	5.2^	36.9	9.3^	27.5
Hispanic origin							
Hispanic	35,375,280	18.1	0.5^	3.4	14.2	3.2	11.0
Non-Hispanic	218,238,010	17.0	0.5	1.9	14.6	3.3	11.3
Age							
12–15	16,230,740	36.8	0.9^	3.1	32.8	6.9	25.9
16–19	17,203,070	30.3	0.6^	5.2	24.6	5.3	19.3
20–24	20,620,150	28.1	0.8^	3.5	23.8	7.5	16.3
25–34	41,073,240	21.5	0.8^	2.8	17.9	4.5	13.4
35–49	64,323,190	16.1	0.4^	2.0	13.7	2.6	11.1
50–64	56,651,170	10.7	0.3^	1.1	9.3	1.9	7.5
65 or older	38,004,060	3.2	0.2^	0.4^	2.5	0.3^	2.2

Note: Violent crimes measured by the National Crime Victimization Survey include rape, sexual assault, robbery, aggravated assault, and simple assault. Because the NCVS interviews persons about their victimizations, murder and manslaughter cannot be included.
—Rounds to less than 0.05 violent victimizations per 1,000 persons age 12 or older.
^Based on 10 or fewer sample cases.
*Includes American Indians, Alaska Natives, Asians, Native Hawaiians, and other Pacific Islanders.

SOURCE: Jennifer L. Truman and Michael R. Rand, "Table 5. Rates of Violent Crime, by Gender, Race, Hispanic Origin, and Age of Victim, 2009," in *Criminal Victimization, 2009*, U.S. Department of Justice, Office of Justice Programs, Bureau of Justice Statistics, October 2010, http://bjs.ojp.usdoj.gov/content/pub/pdf/cv09.pdf (accessed October 23, 2010)

aged 12 years and older) in 2009, followed by African-Americans (26.8 per 1,000 people), whites (15.8 per 1,000 people), and victims identified as "other race" (9.8 per 1,000 people).

For all race categories, the victimization rates for simple assault were higher than for all other violent crimes. Victims of two or more races had higher victimization rates than people in all other race categories for simple assault (27.5 per 1,000 people aged 12 years and older), aggravated assault (9.3 per 1,000 people), and robbery (5.2 per 1,000 people). (See Table 3.2.) However, people of two or more races experienced a lower rate of rape/sexual assault victimization than did whites or African-Americans.

Crime Victims by Hispanic Origin

As shown in Table 3.2, there was little difference reported in 2009 between violent victimization rates for Hispanics (18.1 per 1,000 people aged 12 years and older) and non-Hispanics (17 per 1,000 people). Non-Hispanics were slightly more likely than Hispanics to be victimized by aggravated and simple assault. However, Hispanics had a higher robbery victimization rate (3.4 per 1,000 people aged 12 years and older) than did non-Hispanics (1.9 per 1,000 people). The rates for rape/sexual assault were equivalent for both Hispanics and non-Hispanics at 0.5 per 1,000 people aged 12 years and older.

Crime Victims by Age

Table 3.2 provides a breakdown by age group of violent crime victimization rates in 2009. The youngest respondents (aged 12 to 15 years) had the highest rate at 36.8 violent victimizations per 1,000 people aged 12 years and older. In contrast, people aged 65 years and older had the lowest rate at 3.2 violent victimizations per 1,000 people aged 12 years and older. Victims aged 12 to 15

years had the highest rates of any age group for simple assault (25.9 per 1,000 people aged 12 years and older) and rape/sexual assault (0.9 per 1,000 people). People aged 20 to 24 years reported the highest aggravated assault victimization rate (7.5 per 1,000 people aged 12 years and older), and people aged 16 to 19 years reported the highest robbery victimization rate (5.2 per 1,000 people).

Crime Victims by Household Income and Size

Table 3.3 provides a breakdown by annual household income of households that were victimized by property crimes (e.g., burglary, motor vehicle theft, and other thefts) in 2009. NCVS data indicate that individuals from low-income households experienced a much higher victimization rate than did individuals from high-income households. The property crime victimization rate for people from households making less than $7,500 per year was 201.1 per 1,000 households. In contrast, people from households with annual incomes of $75,000 or more had a rate of 124.9 victimizations per 1,000 households.

The highest property crime victimization rates per crime category in 2009 were as follows:

- Burglary—46.3 victimizations per 1,000 households for households with annual incomes of $7,500 to $14,999

- Motor vehicle theft—10.2 per 1,000 households for households with annual incomes of $35,000 to $49,999

- Other theft—150.7 per 1,000 households for households with annual incomes of less than $7,500

Table 3.3 also indicates that households containing six or more inhabitants were far more likely than smaller households to experience property crime in 2009. The

TABLE 3.3

Property crime victimization rates, by household income and size, 2009

Characteristics of household	Number of households	Victimizations per 1,000 households			
		Total	Burglary	Motor vehicle theft	Theft
Household income					
Less than $7,500	4,062,990	201.1	44.4	6.0	150.7
$7,500–$14,999	6,770,380	157.0	46.3	8.3	102.4
$15,000–$24,999	10,188,470	141.6	35.3	6.5	99.8
$25,000–$34,999	10,326,980	134.1	32.3	6.5	95.3
$35,000–$49,999	13,868,310	139.7	26.7	10.2	102.8
$50,000–$74,999	14,818,560	120.0	19.3	4.5	96.2
$75,000 or more	23,765,460	124.9	15.1	4.2	105.6
Number of persons in household					
1	35,316,700	91.8	26.8	3.7	61.3
2 or 3	60,992,130	118.6	22.8	5.7	90.1
4 or 5	22,414,460	184.6	26.7	8.6	149.4
6 or more	3,604,360	267.5	55.4	17.1	195.0

SOURCE: Jennifer L. Truman and Michael R. Rand, "Table 6. Property Crime Rates, by Household Income and Household Size, 2009," in *Criminal Victimization, 2009*, U.S. Department of Justice, Office of Justice Programs, Bureau of Justice Statistics, October 2010, http://bjs.ojp.usdoj.gov/content/pub/pdf/cv09.pdf (accessed October 23, 2010)

victimization rate for households containing six or more people was 267.5 per 1,000 households, compared with only 91.8 per 1,000 households for households containing one person. The largest households experienced, by far, the highest property crime victimization rates per individual crime: burglaries (55.4 per 1,000 households), motor vehicle thefts (17.1 per 1,000 households), and other thefts (195.0 per 1,000 households).

Victim-Offender Relationships

The NCVS indicates that females who experienced violent personal crimes in 2009 were more often victimized by relatives and people well known to them than by casual acquaintances and strangers. (See Table 3.4.) By contrast, male victims of violent personal crimes in 2009 were more likely to have been victimized by casual acquaintances and strangers than by relatives and people well known to them.

Female victims reported that 68% of victimizations in 2009 were by nonstrangers: 33% by friends or acquaintances, 26% by intimate partners (current or former spouses, boyfriends, or girlfriends), and 9% by other relatives. Overall, 31% of female victimizations in 2009 were by strangers. The offender relationship was unknown in 2% of the violent crimes that were reported by female victims to the NCVS in 2009.

Nonstrangers accounted for 79% of the offenders who raped/sexually assaulted female victims, 70% of the offenders who committed simple assault against female victims,

and 65% of the offenders who committed aggravated assault against female victims in 2009. Concerning robbery, 48% of the offenders were strangers to the female victims and 46% were nonstrangers.

Nonstranger rapes/sexual assaults against female victims were attributed almost evenly to intimate partners (41%) and friends or acquaintances (39%). The breakdown of aggravated assaults by nonstrangers was 40% by friends or acquaintances, 18% by intimate partners, and 7% by other relatives. Nonstranger simple assaults were attributed to friends or acquaintances (33%), intimate partners (28%), and other relatives (10%). Female victims attributed nonstranger robberies in 2009 to intimate partners (20%), friends or acquaintances (15%), and other relatives (11%).

Male victims reported that offenders were strangers in 52% of the victimizations in 2009; nonstrangers were blamed in 45% of the victimizations. The relationship of the offender to male victims was unknown in 3% of the victimizations. Friends or acquaintances were responsible for just over one-third (34%) of the violent victimizations that were reported by male respondents in 2009.

In 2009 strangers accounted for 74% of the offenders who raped/sexually assaulted male victims and 63% of the offenders who robbed male victims. The breakdown between strangers and nonstrangers in assault cases was much closer. Just over half (52%) of the offenders who committed aggravated assault against male victims in 2009 were strangers, compared with 47% who were nonstrangers. Likewise, 49% of simple assaults against male victims were

TABLE 3.4

Relationship between crime victim and offender, by gender of victim, 2009

Relationship to victim	Violent crime		Rape/sexual assault		Robbery		Aggravated assault		Simple assault	
	Number	Percent	Number	Percent	Number	Percent	Number	Percent	Number	Percent
Male victims										
Total	2,283,200	100%	19,820	100%^	329,070	100%	529,550	100%	1,404,760	100%
Nonstranger	1,029,710	45%	5,090	26%^	108,130	33%	247,800	47%	668,690	48%
Intimate partner*	117,210	5	—	—^	—	—^	33,150	6^	84,050	6
Other relative	130,530	6	—	—^	22,380	7^	—	—^	108,150	8
Friend/acquaintance	781,980	34	5,090	26^	85,750	26	214,640	41	476,490	34
Stranger	1,180,000	52%	14,720	74%^	205,800	63%	275,920	52%	683,560	49%
Relationship unknown	73,490	3%	—	—%^	15,140	5%^	5,840	1%^	52,510	4%
Female victims										
Total	2,060,250	100%	106,100	100%	204,720	100%	293,790	100%	1,455,650	100%
Nonstranger	1,390,720	68%	84,240	79%	94,890	46%	189,610	65%	1,021,980	70%
Intimate partner*	538,090	26	43,200	41	41,590	20	52,350	18	400,950	28
Other relative	181,670	9	—	—^	21,710	11^	19,850	7^	140,110	10
Friend/acquaintance	670,960	33	41,040	39	31,590	15^	117,410	40	480,920	33
Stranger	633,850	31%	21,860	21%^	97,250	48%	104,180	36%	410,550	28%
Relationship unknown	35,690	2%^	—	—%^	12,570	6%^	—	—%^	23,110	2%^

Note: Percentages may not sum to 100% because of rounding.
^Based on 10 or fewer sample cases.
—Rounds to less than 0.5 percent.
*Defined as current or former spouses, boyfriends, or girlfriends.

SOURCE: Jennifer L. Truman and Michael R. Rand, "Table 7. Relationship between Victim and Offender, by Gender of Victim, 2009," in *Criminal Victimization, 2009*, U.S. Department of Justice, Office of Justice Programs, Bureau of Justice Statistics, October 2010, http://bjs.ojp.usdoj.gov/content/pub/pdf/cv09.pdf (accessed October 23, 2010)

TABLE 3.5

Use of weapons during violent crimes, by type of weapon, 2009

Presence of offender's weapon	Violent crime		Rape/sexual assault		Robbery		Simple and aggravated assault	
	Number	Percent	Number	Percent	Number	Percent	Number	Percent
Total	4,130,140	100%	125,910	100%	516,060	100%	3,488,160	100%
No weapon	2,999,560	73%	106,660	85%	244,880	48%	2,648,020	76%
Weapon	904,820	22%	12,970	10%^	241,910	47%	649,940	19%
Firearm	326,090	8		—^	142,780	28	183,310	5
Knife	235,380	6	10,480	8^	48,470	9	176,430	5
Other	281,420	7	2,490	2^	39,200	8	239,740	7
Type not ascertained	61,930	2		—^	11,470	2^	50,470	1
Don't know	225,760	6%	6,280	5%^	29,270	6%^	190,200	6%

Note: Percentage may not sum to 100% because of rounding. If the offender was armed with more than one weapon, the crime was classified based on the most serious weapon present.
^Based on 10 or fewer sample cases.
—Rounds to less than 0.5 percent.

SOURCE: Jennifer L. Truman and Michael R. Rand, "Table 9. Presence of Weapons in Violent Incidents, by Type, 2009," in *Criminal Victimization, 2009*, U.S. Department of Justice, Office of Justice Programs, Bureau of Justice Statistics, October 2010, http://bjs.ojp.usdoj.gov/content/pub/pdf/cv09.pdf (accessed October 23, 2010)

attributed to strangers, compared with 48% that were attributed to nonstrangers.

Nonstranger rapes/sexual assaults against male victims were attributed entirely to friends or acquaintances (26%). The breakdown of aggravated assaults by nonstrangers was 41% by friends or acquaintances and 6% by intimate partners. Nonstranger simple assaults were attributed to friends or acquaintances (34%), other relatives (8%), and intimate partners (6%). Male victims attributed nonstranger robberies in 2009 to friends or acquaintances (26%) and other relatives (7%).

Offender Use of Weapons during Victimizations

As shown in Table 3.5, victims reported that weapons were not used by offenders during 73% of violent crime victimizations in 2009. Weapons were used in 22% of the victimizations. Victims reported not knowing whether or not weapons were used in 6% of violent crime victimizations in 2009.

Overall, weapons were not used in 85% of rapes/sexual assaults, 76% of simple and aggravated assaults, and 48% of robberies in 2009. In contrast, weapons were used in 10% of rapes/sexual assaults, 19% of simple and aggravated assaults, and 47% of robberies. Firearms were, by far, the most common weapon used by robbers; 28% of robbery victimizations reportedly involved firearm use in 2009. Firearms were involved in far fewer rapes/sexual assaults (less than 0.5%) and simple and aggravated assaults (5%). Knives were reportedly used by offenders in 9% of robberies, 8% of rapes/sexual assaults, and 5% of simple and aggravated assaults. Victims said the offenders used other weapons in 8% of robberies, 7% of simple and aggravated assaults, and 2% of rapes/sexual assaults.

TABLE 3.6

Firearm use in violent crimes, 2000 and 2009

Firearm use in crime	2000	2009
Incidents	428,670	326,090
Victimizations	533,470	352,810
Rate per 1,000 persons age 12 or older	2.4	1.4
Percent of all violent incidents	7.0%	7.9%

SOURCE: Jennifer L. Truman and Michael R. Rand, "Table 10. Firearm Use in Violent Crime, 2000 and 2009," in *Criminal Victimization, 2009*, U.S. Department of Justice, Office of Justice Programs, Bureau of Justice Statistics, October 2010, http://bjs.ojp.usdoj.gov/content/pub/pdf/cv09.pdf (accessed October 23, 2010)

Table 3.6 compares firearm usage data from the 2000 and 2009 NCVS. In 2009, 7.9% of all violent incidents involved firearms, compared with 7% in 2000. The victimization rate for crimes including firearm use declined from 2.4 per 1,000 people aged 12 years and older in 2000 to 1.4 per 1,000 people aged 12 years and older in 2009.

REPORTING VICTIMIZATIONS TO THE POLICE

Less than half (48.6%) of all violent crime victimizations compiled in the 2009 NCVS were reported by the victims to the police. (See Table 3.7.) The reporting rate was highest for victims of robbery (68.4%), followed by aggravated assault (58.2%), rape/sexual assault (55.4%), and simple assault (41.9%).

Only 39.4% of all property crime victimizations tallied in the 2009 NCVS were reported to the police. (See Table 3.7.) Motor vehicle theft was, by far, the most reported crime by victims. Nearly 85% of motor vehicle thefts were reported to the police, compared with 57.3% of burglaries and 31.8% of other thefts.

TABLE 3.7

Percent of violent and property crimes reported to police, 2009

Type of crime	Percent reported
Violent crime	48.6%
Rape/sexual assault	55.4
Robbery	68.4
Aggravated assault	58.2
Simple assault	41.9
Property crime	39.4%
Burglary	57.3
Motor vehicle theft	84.6
Theft	31.8

SOURCE: Jennifer L. Truman and Michael R. Rand, "Table 11. Percent of Violent and Property Crimes Reported to the Police, 2009," in *Criminal Victimization, 2009*, U.S. Department of Justice, Office of Justice Programs, Bureau of Justice Statistics, October 2010, http://bjs.ojp.usdoj.gov/content/pub/pdf/cv09.pdf (accessed October 23, 2010)

TABLE 3.8

Percent of violent and property crimes reported to police, by gender, race, and Hispanic origin of victim, 2009

Characteristics of victims	Violent	Property
Total	**48.6%**	**39.4%**
Male	**44.5%**	**40.2%**
White	43.2	40.8
Black	52.8	41.7
Other race*	38.6	30.7
Hispanic	46.2	36.7
Non-Hispanic	44.2	40.9
Female	**53.2%**	**38.7%**
White	52.1	38.6
Black	58.7	39.2
Other race*	56.4	40.1
Hispanic	48.7	34.5
Non-Hispanic	54.0	39.4

Note: Total includes estimates for persons identifying with two or more races, not shown separately. Racial categories displayed are for persons who identified with one race.
*Includes American Indians, Alaska Natives, Asians, Native Hawaiians, and other Pacific Islanders.

SOURCE: Jennifer L. Truman and Michael R. Rand, "Table 12. Percent of Crimes Reported to the Police, by Gender, Race, and Hispanic Origin, 2009," in *Criminal Victimization, 2009*, U.S. Department of Justice, Office of Justice Programs, Bureau of Justice Statistics, October 2010, http://bjs.ojp.usdoj.gov/content/pub/pdf/cv09.pdf (accessed October 23, 2010)

As shown in Table 3.8, the reporting rates for female and male victims of violent crime in 2009 were 53.2% and 44.5%, respectively. African-American female victims (58.7%) had the highest reporting rate of violent crimes, whereas white male victims (43.2%) had the lowest reporting rate. Non-Hispanic female victims reported 54% of violent crimes committed against them in 2009, compared with 48.7% for Hispanic females. Hispanic male victims (46.2%) had a slightly higher reporting rate of violent crimes than did non-Hispanic male victims (44.2%).

Overall, male victims reported more property crimes to the police than did female victims. The highest reporting rates of property crimes by race and gender were

FIGURE 3.1

Percent of violent and property crimes reported to police, 2000–2009

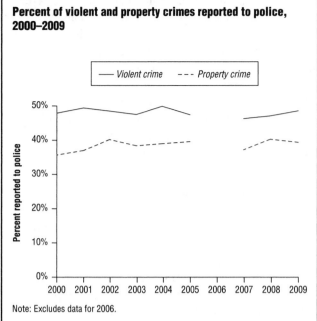

Note: Excludes data for 2006.

SOURCE: Jennifer L. Truman and Michael R. Rand, "Figure 3. Reporting of Violent Crime Has Remained Stable since 2000," in *Criminal Victimization, 2009*, U.S. Department of Justice, Office of Justice Programs, Bureau of Justice Statistics, October 2010, http://bjs.ojp.usdoj.gov/content/pub/pdf/cv09.pdf (accessed October 23, 2010)

41.7% by African-American male victims, 40.8% by white male victims, and 40.1% by female victims of other races. (See Table 3.8.) Men and women of non-Hispanic origin reported slightly higher percentages of property crime victimizations to the police than did men and women of Hispanic origin.

Figure 3.1 shows that the percentage of victims reporting violent and property crimes to the police remained relatively stable between 2000 and 2009. Approximately half of all violent victimizations were consistently reported to the police each year by victims, compared with about 40% of property crime victimizations.

Reasons Victims Do and Do Not Report Victimizations

In *Criminal Victimization, 2009*, Truman and Rand do not provide the reasons given by victims for reporting or not reporting victimizations to the police. Such data are collected by the NCVS and are released in detailed data reports. However, as of February 2011, a detailed data report for the 2009 NCVS had not been published.

In *Criminal Victimization in the United States, 2007—Statistical Tables*, Maston does provide data collected on this subject as part of the 2007 NCVS. Interviewers asked crime victims who had not reported their victimizations to the police why they chose not to do so. The largest single reason given for not reporting a personal crime (attempted or completed rape/sexual assault, robbery, aggravated or simple assault, purse snatching, and pocket picking) was that the victim considered the incident to be a private or personal matter. Nearly one-fifth (20.4%) of those asked in 2007 gave this reason. Other oft-cited reasons were that the stolen object was recovered or the offender was unsuccessful in the crime (17.1%) or the victim reported the crime to an official other than the police (15.1%). Other reasons given were that the police "would not want to be bothered" (9%), it was too inconvenient or time consuming to report the crime (5.8%), and fear of reprisal (4.8%). Just over 5% of the respondents said the victimization was "not important enough" to report to the police.

The breakdown of reasons for not reporting property crimes (attempted or completed burglary, motor vehicle theft, and other theft) was slightly different. More than a quarter (25.8%) of the victims said they did not report the crime because the object was recovered or the offender was unsuccessful. Another 14.8% said the police "would not want to be bothered," 8.6% said there was "lack of proof" for the property crime, and 7.5% said they reported the crime to an official other than the police. Approximately 4% of the respondents said the property victimization was "not important enough" to report to the police.

The top-five reasons given by victims who did report personal victimizations to the police in 2007 were as follows:

- To stop or prevent the incident from occurring— 26.6%

- To prevent further crimes by the offender against the victim—18.4%

- "Because it was a crime"—13.7%

- To prevent further crime by the offender against anyone else—8.4%

- To punish the offender—7.6%

The top-five reasons given by victims for reporting property crimes to the police in 2007 were as follows:

- To recover property—24.4%

- "Because it was a crime"—21.2%

- To stop or prevent the incident from occurring— 11.4%

- To prevent further crimes by the offender against the victim—9.1%

- To improve police surveillance—6.4%

TRENDS IN VICTIMIZATION, 1973 TO 2009

In *Criminal Victimization, 2009*, Truman and Rand provide victimization trend data from 2000 to 2009, excluding 2006. As stated earlier, the NCVS underwent a major methodology change in 2006 rendering data collected in that year incompatible with data collected in earlier and later years.

FIGURE 3.2

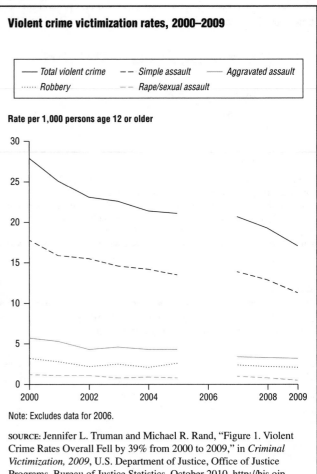

Violent crime victimization rates, 2000–2009

Rate per 1,000 persons age 12 or older

Note: Excludes data for 2006.

SOURCE: Jennifer L. Truman and Michael R. Rand, "Figure 1. Violent Crime Rates Overall Fell by 39% from 2000 to 2009," in *Criminal Victimization, 2009*, U.S. Department of Justice, Office of Justice Programs, Bureau of Justice Statistics, October 2010, http://bjs.ojp .usdoj.gov/content/pub/pdf/cv09.pdf (accessed October 23, 2010)

Figure 3.2 shows NCVS-based victimization rates for violent crimes (excluding murder) between 2000 and 2009. The rate of total violent crime fell by 38.7%, from 27.9 victimizations per 1,000 people aged 12 years and older in 2000 to 17.1 victimizations per 1,000 people aged 12 years and older in 2009. (See Table 3.9.) As shown in Figure 3.3, property crime rates also fell dramatically, from 178.1 victimizations per 1,000 households in 2000 to 127.4 victimizations per 1,000 households in 2009, a 28.5% decline. (See Table 3.9.)

According to Table 3.9, the rates of personal theft (pocket picking and attempted and completed purse snatching) decreased by 56.6% between 2000 and 2009, from 1.2 victimizations per 1,000 people aged 12 years and older to 0.5 victimizations per 1,000 people aged 12 years and older.

The BJS provides violent crime rates dating back to 1973 in *Key Facts at a Glance: Violent Crime Trends* (September 2, 2009, http://bjs.ojp.usdoj.gov/content/ glance/tables/viortrdtab.cfm). Note that the crime rates are based on NCVS data for most violent crimes, but do incorporate murder data from the UCR Program. As shown in

TABLE 3.9

Criminal victimization rates, by type of crime, 2000 and 2009

Type of crime	Victimization rates[a]		
	2000	2009	Percent change 2000–2009[b]
Violent crime[c]	27.9	17.1	−38.7%
Rape/sexual assault	1.2	0.5	−56.9
Robbery	3.2	2.1	−34.9
Assault	23.5	14.5	−38.3
Aggravated	5.7	3.2	−43.1
Simple	17.8	11.3	−36.8
Personal theft[d]	1.2	0.5	−56.6%
Property crime	178.1	127.4	−28.5%
Household burglary	31.8	25.6	−19.4
Motor vehicle theft	8.6	6.0	−30.5
Theft	137.7	95.7	−30.5

Note: The total population age 12 or older was 226,804,610 in 2000 and 254,105,610 in 2009. The total number of households in 2000 was 108,352,960 and 122,327,660 in 2009.

[a]Victimization rates are per 1,000 persons age 12 or older for violent crime or per 1,000 households for property crime.
[b]Differences between the annual rates shown do not take into account changes that may have occurred during interim years. Percent change calculated on unrounded estimates.
[c]Excludes murder because the NCVS (National Crime Victimization Survey) is based on interviews with victims and therefore cannot measure murder.
[d]Includes pocket picking, completed purse snatching, and attempted purse snatching.

SOURCE: Jennifer L. Truman and Michael R. Rand, "Table 2. Rates of Criminal Victimization and Percent Change, by Type of Crime, 2000 and 2009," in *Criminal Victimization, 2009*, U.S. Department of Justice, Office of Justice Programs, Bureau of Justice Statistics, October 2010, http://bjs.ojp .usdoj.gov/content/pub/pdf/cv09.pdf (accessed October 23, 2010)

FIGURE 3.3

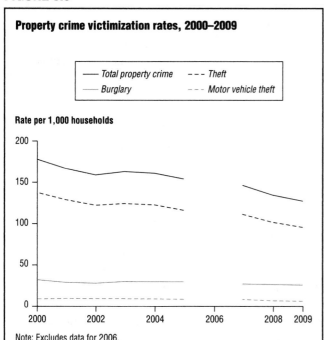

Property crime victimization rates, 2000–2009

Rate per 1,000 households

Note: Excludes data for 2006.

SOURCE: Jennifer L. Truman and Michael R. Rand, "Figure 2. Property Crime Rates Overall Fell by 29% from 2000 to 2009," in *Criminal Victimization, 2009*, U.S. Department of Justice, Office of Justice Programs, Bureau of Justice Statistics, October 2010, http://bjs.ojp .usdoj.gov/content/pub/pdf/cv09.pdf (accessed October 23, 2010)

Figure 3.4, the total violent crime rate hovered between 42 and 52 victimizations per 1,000 people from 1973 through the early 1990s. During the mid-1990s the rate began to plummet, dropping below 20 victimizations per 1,000 people toward the end of the first decade of the 21st century.

Figure 3.5 indicates that the rape victimization rate per 1,000 people zigzagged up and down from 1973 through the early 1990s, but showed a general downward trend over time. The rate declined dramatically from 2.2 victimizations per 1,000 people in 1991 to between 0.3 and 0.6 victimizations per 1,000 people from 2003 to 2009. A similar pattern is seen in the robbery rate per 1,000 people. (See Figure 3.6.) The robbery rate rose and fell from 1973 through the mid-1990s before beginning a sustained decline. In 1994 the robbery rate was 6.3 victimizations per 1,000 people; by 2009 it had dropped to 2.1 victimizations per 1,000 people.

Figure 3.7 shows NCVS-based crime rates for simple assault and aggravated assault. The rates for both crimes were relatively steady or increased slightly from 1973 through the mid-1990s. The simple assault rate peaked at 31.5 per 1,000 people in 1994 and then plummeted to 11.3 per 1,000 people in 2009. The aggravated assault rate declined from 12 per 1,000 people in 1993 to 3.2 per 1,000 people in 2009.

As shown in Figure 3.8, total property crime victimization rates fell dramatically between 1973 and 2009. After a slight increase from 1973 (519.9 per 1,000 households) to 1975 (553.6 per 1,000 households), the rates dropped more or less consistently through 2009, when the total property crime rate was 127.4 per 1,000 households. The rates of all property crime types on which the NCVS collects data fell significantly between 1973 and 2009. The burglary rate fell from 110 per 1,000 households in 1973 to just 25.6 per 1,000 households in 2009; the theft rate fell from 390.8 per 1,000 households to 95.7 per 1,000 households; and the motor vehicle theft rate fell from 19.1 per 1,000 households to 6 per 1,000 households.

CONSEQUENCES OF VICTIMIZATION

Crime victims suffer a number of consequences from being victimized, including physical injuries, economic losses, and mental distress. The economic costs borne by crime victims include direct costs, such as the value of items that have been stolen, and indirect costs, such as the expenses of the criminal justice system, which must be shared by the entire society.

Truman and Rand do not include data on victim consequences in *Criminal Victimization, 2009*; however, such data are compiled by Maston in *Criminal Victimization in the United States, 2007—Statistical Tables*. In 2007 over a third (35.7%) of all robbery victims sustained some type of physical injury due to the crime.

FIGURE 3.4

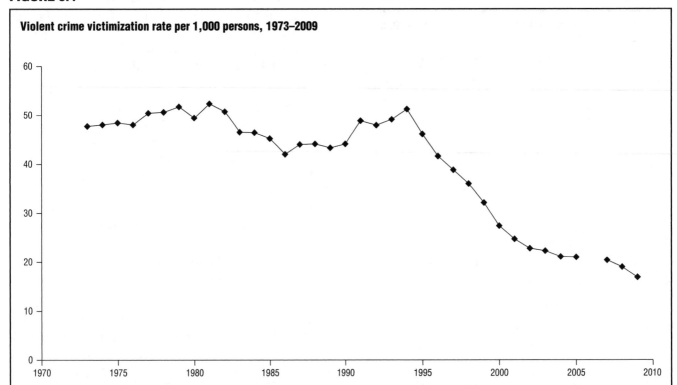

Violent crime victimization rate per 1,000 persons, 1973–2009

Note: 1973–91 data adjusted to make data comparable to data after the redesign. Estimates for 1993 and beyond are based on collection year while earlier estimates are based on data year. Estimates for 1996 and beyond are based on collection year while earlier estimates are based on data year. Victimization rate trends exclude National Crime Victimization Survey estimates for 2006 because of methodological inconsistencies between the data for that year and the data for other years.

SOURCE: Adapted from Michael Rand, "National Crime Victimization Survey, Violent Crime Trends, 1973–2008, Adjusted Violent Victimization Rates, Number of Victimizations per 1,000 Population Age 12 or Older," in *Key Facts at a Glance: Violent Crime Trends*, U.S. Department of Justice, Office of Justice Programs, Bureau of Justice Statistics, September 2, 2009, http://bjs.ojp.usdoj.gov/content/glance/tables/viortrdtab.cfm (accessed October 23, 2010)

Approximately 22.6% of all assault victims sustained physical injuries. There were significant differences between victims of different income groups. More than half (59.6%) of robbery victims with annual incomes of less than $7,500 suffered physical injuries, compared with 16% of victims with annual incomes of $50,000 to $74,999 and 36.3% of victims with annual incomes of $75,000 or more. Likewise, 34.9% of victims in the lowest income group sustained physical injuries during assaults, compared with 17.3% of victims with annual incomes of $50,000 to $74,999 and 16.9% of victims with annual incomes of $75,000 or more.

Over 596,000 victims of violent crimes received medical care in 2007 due to their injuries. Most of the victims had been subjected to simple assault (286,610), aggravated assault (174,700), or robbery (103,280).

In 2007, 94.3% of the property crime victims and 17.8% of the personal crime victims suffered economic losses. The gross loss for all crime victims was estimated at $18.1 billion. Property crimes accounted for the vast majority ($16.1 billion) of this total. The highest mean (average) dollar loss was $6,286 due to motor vehicle theft.

VICTIMS' RIGHTS

For many years victims received little consideration in justice proceedings; to some it seemed that victims were victimized again by the very system to which they had turned for help. In *Final Report of the President's Task Force on Victims of Crime* (December 1982, http://www.ojp.gov/ovc/publications/presdntstskforcrprt/87299.pdf), Lois Haight Herrington observes that "somewhere along the way, the system began to serve lawyers and judges and defendants, treating the victim with institutionalized disinterest."

The report describes a number of problems that were commonly cited by crime victims. For example, police questioning seemed to accuse rape victims of enticing their attacker or participating willingly in the act. Assault victims found that hospitals were more concerned about whether they could pay for treatment than about helping them recover from the incident. In their efforts to make sure that each defendant received a fair trial, judges and lawyers appeared to be more concerned about the accused offenders than the victims. Crime victims were not informed of court dates, sentencing hearings, or probation or parole hearings concerning their cases. They were not informed when their attacker escaped or was released from

FIGURE 3.5

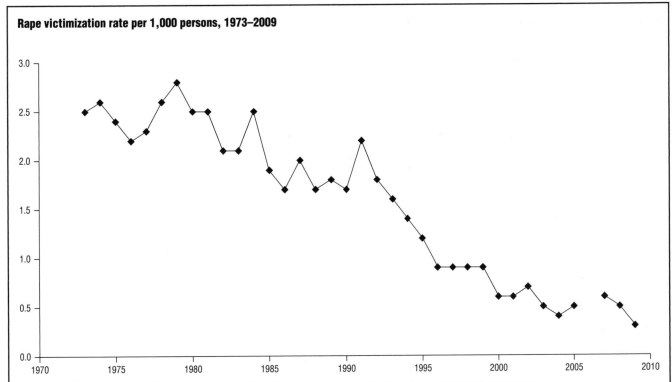

Rape victimization rate per 1,000 persons, 1973–2009

Note: Victimization trends exclude 2006 data because of methodological inconsistencies between the data for that year and the data for other years.

SOURCE: Adapted from Michael Rand, "National Crime Victimization Survey, Violent Crime Trends, 1973–2008, Adjusted Violent Victimization Rates, Number of Victimizations per 1,000 Population Age 12 or Older," in *Key Facts at a Glance: Violent Crime Trends*, U.S. Department of Justice, Office of Justice Programs, Bureau of Justice Statistics, September 2, 2009, http://bjs.ojp.usdoj.gov/content/glance/tables/viortrdtab.cfm (accessed October 23, 2010)

prison. Also, victims participating in a trial were sometimes kept outside the courtroom without ever being called to the witness stand.

The Crime Victims' Rights Movement

Attempts to improve the situation for crime victims had actually been ongoing since the 1960s. In 1965 California established the first crime victim compensation program. A growing victims' rights movement spurred the creation of victim assistance and compensation programs around the country. In 1975 the National Organization for Victim Assistance (NOVA; http://www.trynova.org/) was formed in Virginia. That same year the attorney Frank Carrington (1936–1992) published *The Victims*, a book that highlighted the problematic treatment of crime victims by the criminal justice system. He founded the Crime Victims' Legal Advocacy Institute, later renamed the Victims' Assistance Legal Organization (VALOR; http://www.valor-national.org/), and is widely considered to be the father of the victims' rights movement in the United States.

In 1976 a California probation officer named James Rowland introduced the first victim impact statements. These written statements provided the judiciary with information about the specific and often devastating impact of

crimes on victims—a viewpoint that had not previously been considered by the criminal justice system.

By the early 1980s a number of programs had been developed at the state and local levels on behalf of crime victims. In 1981 President Ronald Reagan (1911–2004) proclaimed the first-ever National Victims' Rights Week. In 1982 he spearheaded passage of the federal Victim and Witness Protection Act, which was designed to protect and assist victims and witnesses of federal crimes. The law permits victim impact statements in sentencing hearings to provide judges with information concerning financial, psychological, and/or physical harm that is suffered by victims. The law also provides for restitution (monetary compensation) to victims and prevents victims and/or witnesses from being intimidated by threatening verbal harassment. The law establishes penalties for acts of retaliation by defendants against those who testify against them.

Also in 1982 Reagan appointed the Task Force on Victims of Crime, which included Herrington, Carrington, and a number of other well-known victims' advocates. The group's aforementioned report *Final Report of the President's Task Force on Victims of Crime* presented dozens of recommendations to reform state and federal criminal justice systems to better protect victims' rights.

FIGURE 3.6

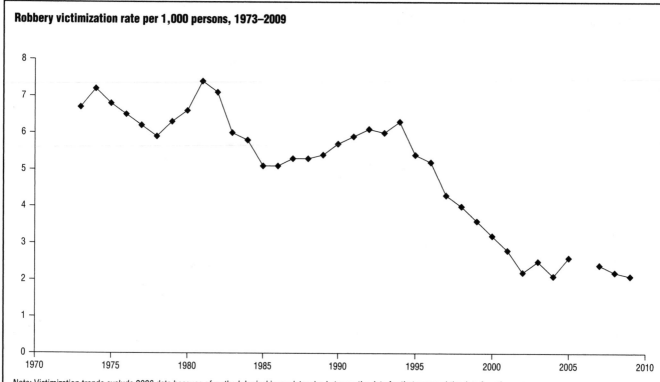

Robbery victimization rate per 1,000 persons, 1973–2009

Note: Victimization trends exclude 2006 data because of methodological inconsistencies between the data for that year and the data for other years.

SOURCE: Adapted from Michael Rand, "National Crime Victimization Survey, Violent Crime Trends, 1973–2008, Adjusted Violent Victimization Rates, Number of Victimizations per 1,000 Population Age 12 or Older," in *Key Facts at a Glance: Violent Crime Trends*, U.S. Department of Justice, Office of Justice Programs, Bureau of Justice Statistics, September 2, 2009, http://bjs.ojp.usdoj.gov/content/glance/tables/viortrdtab.cfm (accessed October 23, 2010)

The report was also generally critical of state crime victim compensation funds by noting that many of them were underfunded and poorly administrated.

In 1983 the DOJ created the Office for Victims of Crime (OVC; http://www.ojp.usdoj.gov/ovc/) to implement the task force's recommendations. The following year Congress passed the Victims of Crime Act (VOCA). The act established the Crime Victims Fund to be funded by money from federal criminal fines, penalties, and forfeited bonds. The fund supports federal and state programs for victim services and compensation.

Since the 1980s the federal and state governments, the judicial system, and private groups have all reflected an increased awareness of victims' concerns. Numerous crime laws passed at the federal and state levels have included provisions that pertain specifically to victims and their rights during criminal proceedings. Some states have passed constitutional amendments to ensure that victims' rights are preserved and protected in their criminal justice systems. Diverse organizations have begun offering services to victims of crime. These organizations include domestic violence shelters, rape crisis centers, and child abuse programs. Law enforcement agencies, hospitals, and social services agencies also provide victims' services. The types of services provided include crisis intervention, counseling, emergency shelter and transportation, and legal services.

VICTIM IMPACT STATEMENTS IN CAPITAL CASES. As noted earlier, the first use of victim impact statements was in California in 1976. Over the following decade this practice became widespread across the nation. In 1987 the U.S. Supreme Court ruled 5–4 in *Booth v. Maryland* (482 U.S. 496) that victim impact statements were unconstitutional when used in the sentencing phase of capital trials (i.e., those involving the death penalty). The court noted that "the admission of the family members' emotionally charged opinions and characterizations of the crimes could serve no other purpose than to inflame the jury and divert it from deciding the case on the relevant evidence concerning the crime and the defendant." Two years later the court narrowly reaffirmed this decision with a 5–4 ruling in *South Carolina v. Gathers* (490 U.S. 805).

The Supreme Court changed course in 1991, when it ruled 7–2 in *Payne v. Tennessee* (501 U.S. 808) that victim impact statements in capital cases are constitutional. The court concluded, "We are now of the view that a State may properly conclude that for the jury to assess meaningfully the defendant's moral culpability and blameworthiness, it

FIGURE 3.7

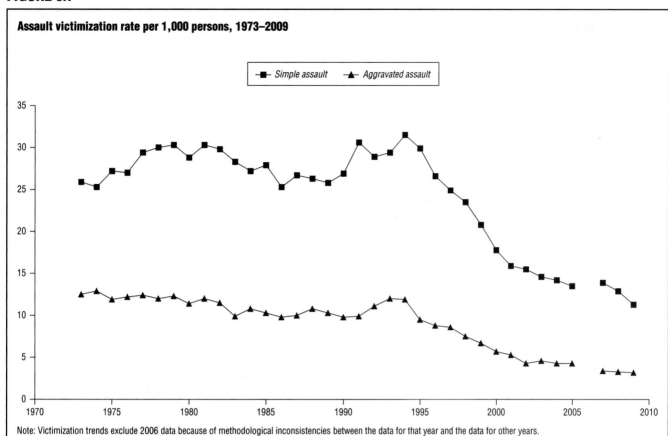

Assault victimization rate per 1,000 persons, 1973–2009

Note: Victimization trends exclude 2006 data because of methodological inconsistencies between the data for that year and the data for other years.

SOURCE: Adapted from Michael Rand, "National Crime Victimization Survey, Violent Crime Trends, 1973–2008, Adjusted Violent Victimization Rates, Number of Victimizations per 1,000 Population Age 12 or Older," in *Key Facts at a Glance: Violent Crime Trends*, U.S. Department of Justice, Office of Justice Programs, Bureau of Justice Statistics, September 2, 2009, http://bjs.ojp.usdoj.gov/content/glance/tables/viortrdtab.cfm (accessed October 23, 2010)

should have before it at the sentencing phase evidence of the specific harm caused by the defendant."

Crime Victims Organizations

Table 3.10 lists several of the national crime victims organizations. One of the organizations that is listed is the National Center for Victims of Crime (2010, http://www.ncvc.org/ncvc/main.aspx?dbID=DB_About189), which calls itself "the nation's leading resource and advocacy organization for crime victims and those who serve them." The organization operates the online database VictimLaw (http://www.victimlaw.info/victimlaw/start.do), which is funded by the OVC and serves as a clearinghouse of information regarding victims' rights at the federal, state, and tribal levels.

Victims' Participation at Sentencing

According to the National Center for Victims of Crime, every state allows courts to consider or ask for information from victims concerning the effects of the offense on their lives. Most states permit victim input at sentencing and most allow written victim impact statements. Even though impact statements are typically used at sentencing and

parole hearings, they can also be used at bail hearings, pretrial release hearings, and plea-bargaining hearings.

Several state legislatures have developed strong victims' rights legislation. For example, Section 1191.1 of the California Penal Code (http://www.leginfo.ca.gov/cgi-bin/displaycode?section=pen&group=01001-02000&file=1191-1210.5) states: "The victim ... or the next of kin ... have the right to appear, personally or by counsel, at the sentencing proceeding and to reasonably express his, her, or their views concerning the crime, the person responsible, and the need for restitution. The court in imposing sentence shall consider the statements of victims, parents or guardians, and next of kin ... and shall state on the record its conclusion concerning whether the person would pose a threat to public safety if granted probation."

Victim Compensation

Victim compensation programs pay money from a public fund to help victims with expenses incurred because of a violent crime. As noted earlier, the federal government maintains the Crime Victims Fund, which is administered by the OVC. The fund supports victim compensation and victim assistance grant programs that

FIGURE 3.8

Property crime victimization rates per 1,000 households, 1973–2009

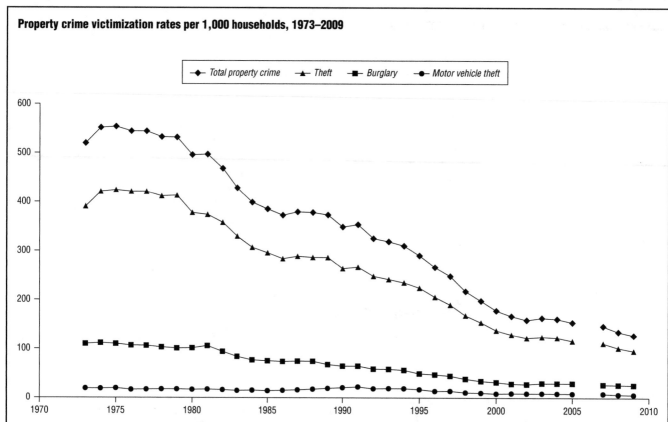

Note: 1973–91 data adjusted to make data comparable to data after the redesign. Estimates for 1993 and beyond are based on collection year while earlier estimates are based on data year. Due to changes in methodology, the 2006 Natioal Crime Victimization rates are not comparable to previous years and cannot be used for yearly trend comparisons.

SOURCE: Adapted from Cathy Maston and Patsy Klaus, "National Crime Victimization Survey Property Crime Trends, 1973–2008," in *Key Facts: Property Crime*, U.S. Department of Justice, Office of Justice Programs, Bureau of Justice Statistics, September 2, 2009, http://bjs.ojp.usdoj.gov/content/glance/tables/proptrdtab.cfm (accessed October 23, 2010), and Jennifer L. Truman and Michael R. Rand, "Table 1. Criminal Victimization, Numbers, Rates, and Percent Change, by Type of Crime, 2008 and 2009," in *Criminal Victimization, 2009*, U.S. Department of Justice, Office of Justice Programs, Bureau of Justice Statistics, October 2010, http://bjs.ojp.usdoj.gov/content/pub/pdf/cv09.pdf (accessed October 23, 2010)

TABLE 3.10

National organizations for crime victims

Childhelp USA National Child Abuse Hotline	1–800–422–4453	www.childhelp.org
Child Welfare Information Gateway	1–800–394–3366	www.childwelfare.gov
Mothers Against Drunk Driving (MADD)	1–877–623–3435	www.madd.org
National Center for Missing & Exploited Children (NCMEC)	1–800–843–5678	www.missingkids.com
National Center for Victims of Crime (NCVC)	1–800–394–2255	www.ncvc.org
National Clearinghouse for Alcohol and Drug Information	1–800–729–6686	http://ncadi.samhsa.gov
National Criminal Justice Reference Service (NCJRS)	1–800–851–3420	www.ncjrs.gov
National Domestic Violence Hotline	1–800–799–7233	www.ndvh.org
National Fraud Information Hotline	202–835–3323	www.fraud.org
National Human Trafficking Resource Center (NHTRC)	1–888–3737–888	http://nhtrc.polarisproject.org
National Organization for Victim Assistance (NOVA)	1–800–879–6682	www.trynova.org
National Resource Center on Domestic Violence	1–800–537–2238	www.nrcdv.org
National White Collar Crime Center (NW3C)	1–800–221–4424	www.nw3c.org
Parents of Murdered Children (POMC)	1–888–818–7662	www.pomc.org
Rape, Abuse & Incest National Network (RAINN)	1–800–656–4673	www.rainn.org

SOURCE: Adapted from "National Victim Organizations Stand Ready to Assist You," in *What You Can Do If You Are a Victim of Crime*, U.S. Department of Justice, Office of Justice Programs, Office for Victims of Crime, April 2010, http://www.ojp.usdoj.gov/ovc/publications/infores/whatyoucando_2010/WhatUCanDo_508.pdf (accessed October 25, 2010)

are overseen by the states. Victim compensation grant programs cover medical treatment and physical therapy costs, counseling fees, lost wages, funeral and burial expenses, and loss of support to dependents of homicide victims. Victim assistance grant programs cover the costs of crisis intervention, counseling, emergency shelter, and criminal

FIGURE 3.9

Deposits to Crime Victims Fund, fiscal years 1985–2009

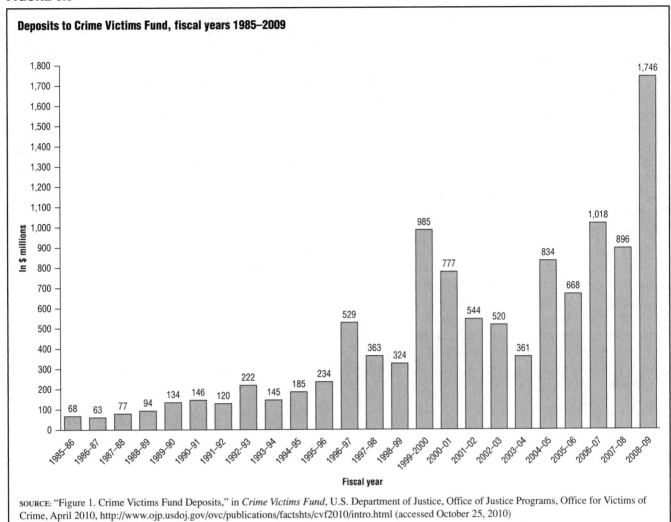

SOURCE: "Figure 1. Crime Victims Fund Deposits," in *Crime Victims Fund*, U.S. Department of Justice, Office of Justice Programs, Office for Victims of Crime, April 2010, http://www.ojp.usdoj.gov/ovc/publications/factshts/cvf2010/intro.html (accessed October 25, 2010)

justice advocacy. Deposits to the Crime Victims Fund come from fines, penalty assessments, and bond forfeitures that are collected from convicted federal criminal offenders. In 2001 legislation was passed allowing the fund to receive gifts, donations, and bequests from private entities.

Figure 3.9 shows the annual total deposits to the Crime Victims Fund made between fiscal years 1985 and 2009. In fiscal year 2009 the fund received its highest amount ever of $1.7 billion. The OVC submits a biennial report to Congress on the status of the fund. In *OVC Report to the Nation 2009* (December 2009, http://www.ojp.usdoj.gov/ovc/welcovc/reporttonation2009/ReporttoNation09full.pdf), the OVC notes that through fiscal year 1999 the money deposited into the fund each year was completely distributed the following year. In 2000 Congress capped the amount that could be distributed each year. The OVC reports in *OVC Fact Sheet: Crime Victims Fund* (April 2010, http://www.ojp.usdoj.gov/ovc/publications/factshts/cvf2010/intro.html) that the cap for fiscal year 2009 was $635 million.

The primary programs supported by the fund are:

- State crime victim assistance grants

- State crime victim compensation grants

- Victim-witness coordinators who assist victims of federal crimes

- FBI victim specialists who assist victims of federal crimes

- The federal Victim Notification System, which notifies victims of federal crimes about key events, such as offender release dates

- The Children's Justice Act grant for state and tribal programs that handle crimes against children

According to the OVC, in *OVC Report to the Nation 2009*, in fiscal years 2007 and 2008 VOCA distributed $863 million for 294,857 compensation claims.

National Crime Victims' Rights Week

The OVC encourages local communities to observe a National Crime Victims' Rights Week. The event is held annually in April and includes rallies, candlelight vigils, and other activities that are designed to honor or memorialize crime victims and highlight their rights in the criminal justice system.

Offender Restitution Programs

Restitution programs require those who have harmed an individual to repay the victim. In the past, the criminal justice system focused primarily on punishing the criminal and leaving the victims to rely on civil court cases for damage repayment. By the 21st century most states permitted criminal courts to allow restitution payments as a condition of probation and/or parole. In addition, courts had the statutory authority to order restitution, and several states had passed constitutional amendments that specifically enumerated a victim's right to restitution.

Most restitution laws provide for restitution to the direct victim(s) of a crime, including the surviving family members of homicide victims. Restitution is usually only provided to victims of crimes for which a defendant was convicted. Many states allow victims to claim medical expenses and property damage or loss, and several permit families of homicide victims to claim costs for loss of support. In assessing damages, the courts must consider the offender's ability to pay.

Civil Suits

A victim can sue in civil court for damages even if the offender has not been found guilty of a criminal offense. Victims often pursue this course of action because it is easier to win civil cases than criminal cases. In a criminal case, a jury or judge can find an alleged offender guilty only if the proof is "beyond a reasonable doubt." In a civil case, the burden of proof requires merely a "preponderance of the evidence" against the accused. Proof is still needed that a crime was committed, that there were damages, and that the accused is liable to pay for those damages. In addition, any restitution amounts that remain unpaid at the end of an offender's parole or probation period may be converted into civil judgments. However, even when victims secure a civil judgment, they often have trouble collecting their damage payments. Such has been the case with O. J. Simpson (1947–), a former professional football player, who was acquitted in 1995 of killing his former wife and her friend. In 1997 the victims' families won a multimillion-dollar civil judgment against Simpson. However, quirks of state laws have shielded his pension and primary residence from seizure to pay the debts.

CHAPTER 4
DRUG CRIMES

As noted in Chapter 2, the Federal Bureau of Investigation's (FBI) Uniform Crime Reports (UCR) Program indicates that reported rates of violent crimes and property crimes have decreased dramatically over the past two decades. The UCR Program does not track the number of drug crimes that are reported by the police, but it does track the number of arrests for drug crimes. State and local arrests for drug crimes skyrocketed from 580,900 in 1980 to 1.7 million in 2009, an increase of 193.1%. (See Figure 4.1.) According to the FBI, in *Crime in the United States, 2009* (September 2010, http://www2.fbi.gov/ucr/cius2009/index.html), the arrests for drug abuse violations in 2009 were one of the highest numbers for any single crime category.

SELF-REPORTED ILLICIT DRUG USE

The Substance Abuse and Mental Health Services Administration (SAMHSA), which is part of the U.S. Department of Health and Human Services, conducts an annual survey on the use of illegal drugs by the U.S. population. In *Results from the 2009 National Survey on Drug Use and Health: Volume I. Summary of National Findings* (September 2010, http://www.oas.samhsa.gov/NSDUH/2k9NSDUH/2k9ResultsP.pdf), SAMHSA notes that it surveys approximately 67,500 people each year in the civilian noninstitutionalized population (people who are not in the U.S. military, school, jail, or mental health facilities) of the United States.

SAMHSA finds that in 2009, 21.8 million Americans aged 12 years and older had used illicit drugs within the previous month. (See Figure 4.2.) The vast majority (16.7 million) of these illicit drug users had used marijuana during the past month. Much smaller numbers had used psychotherapeutics (7 million), cocaine (1.6 million), hallucinogens (1.3 million), inhalants (600,000), and heroin (200,000). Psychotherapeutics are defined by SAMHSA as prescription drugs, such as pain relievers, tranquilizers, stimulants, and sedatives, that are used for nonmedical purposes.

Figure 4.3 shows past-month use of various illicit drugs by people aged 12 years and older between 2002 and 2009. In 2009, 8.7% of the U.S. population aged 12 years and older admitted using illicit drugs during the previous month. The most widely consumed illicit drug was marijuana (6.6%), followed by psychotherapeutics (2.8%), cocaine (0.7%), and hallucinogens (0.5%). Figure 4.4 provides a breakdown of past-month nonmedical use of psychotherapeutics between 2002 and 2009. Pain relievers were consistently the most used of the psychotherapeutic drugs.

As shown in Figure 4.5, SAMHSA finds that self-reported illicit drug use in 2008 and 2009 was most common among teens and young adults aged 16 to 29 years.

THE WAR ON DRUGS

The nation has waged a so-called War on Drugs for decades, yet the number of current drug users is staggering: in 2009 there were 21.8 million admitted users of illegal drugs and 1.7 million drug arrests. (See Figure 4.2 and Figure 4.1.) In addition, experts estimate that millions of other crimes are connected to illicit drug use. In *Drugs and Crime* (2011, http://bjs.ojp.usdoj.gov/index.cfm?ty=tp&tid=35), the Bureau of Justice Statistics (BJS), a division of the U.S. Department of Justice, defines three types of drug-crime relationships:

- Drug-defined offenses—these are violations of the drug abuse laws. Examples include drug possession, marijuana cultivation, methamphetamine production, and sales of cocaine, heroin, marijuana, and other illicit drugs.

- Drug-related offenses—these are offenses related to the pharmacologic effects of drugs, drug users' needs for money, and distribution-related violence. Examples

FIGURE 4.1

Drug crime arrests, 1980–2009

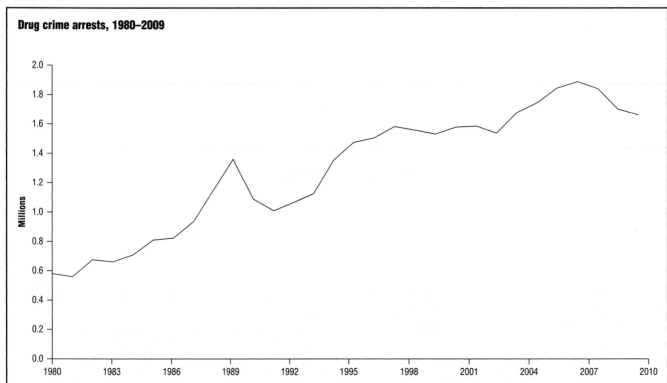

SOURCE: Adapted from Tina Dorsey and Doris J. James, "Total Estimated Drug Law Violation Arrests in the United States, 1980–2007," in *Drugs and Crime Facts*, U.S. Department of Justice, Office of Justice Programs, Bureau of Justice Statistics, August 17, 2009, http://bjs.ojp.usdoj.gov/content/dcf/tables/arrtot.cfm (accessed October 25, 2010); "Table 29. Estimated Number of Arrests, United States, 2009," in *Crime in the United States, 2009*, U.S. Department of Justice, Federal Bureau of Investigation, September 2010, http://www2.fbi.gov/ucr/cius2009/data/documents/09tbl29.xls (accessed October 5, 2010); and "Table 29. Estimated Number of Arrests, United States, 2008," in *Crime in the United States, 2008*, U.S. Department of Justice, Federal Bureau of Investigation, September 2009, http://www2.fbi.gov/ucr/cius2008/data/documents/08tbl29.xls (accessed October 25, 2010)

include drug-induced violent behavior, stealing to get money to buy drugs, and violence between rival drug dealers.

- Drug-using lifestyle offenses—these offenses result from habitual drug use and the associated criminal lifestyle rather than from participation in the "legitimate economy." Examples include drug abusers with extensive contacts in the criminal community who learn new criminal skills from other offenders and frequently seize opportunities to commit crimes.

Drug Crime through the 1950s

Throughout its history the United States has struggled with how best to tackle the problem of drug abuse and the crimes linked to it. During the 1700s a number of potions containing opium and promising cures for a variety of ailments were available as so-called patent medicines, and physicians routinely prescribed opium medications to their patients. In 1805 the discovery of morphine by the German pharmacist Friedrich Sertürner (1793–1841) introduced another powerful drug to the medicines of the day. By the end of the 19th century cocaine, codeine, and dozens of similar drugs were in common use. However, doctors were increasingly concerned about the side effects and

addictiveness of these drugs and began issuing stern warnings about them to the public.

At the federal level, Congress passed the Pure Food and Drug Act of 1906, the Opium Exclusion Act of 1909, and the Harrison Narcotic Act of 1914 in attempts to quell the widespread availability of highly addictive drugs. The Progressive movement and religious revival that swept the country during the late 1800s and early 1900s made drug abuse socially unacceptable. By the 1920s drug use had been driven underground into the criminal world along with alcohol, which was banned by the 18th Amendment in 1919. During the 1930s several laws were passed against marijuana, including the Marihuana Tax Act of 1937, which restricted the legal use of marijuana-based products via high taxes and heavy fines. By the 1950s drug abuse was considered a problem only among distinct and socially outcast populations. These included the African-American inhabitants of inner-city ghettos and certain bohemian elements that rejected the social norms of the time.

Drug Crime during the 1960s

The 1960s ushered in a completely new drug culture to the United States: recreational drug use among middle- and upper-class white youths in suburban and rural areas.

FIGURE 4.2

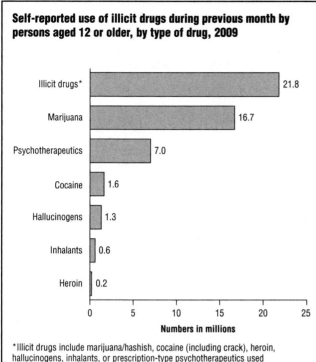

Self-reported use of illicit drugs during previous month by persons aged 12 or older, by type of drug, 2009

*Illicit drugs include marijuana/hashish, cocaine (including crack), heroin, hallucinogens, inhalants, or prescription-type psychotherapeutics used nonmedically.

SOURCE: "Figure 2.1. Past Month Illicit Drug Use among Persons Aged 12 or Older: 2009," in *Results from the 2009 National Survey on Drug Use and Health: Volume I. Summary of National Findings*, U.S. Department of Health and Human Services, Substance Abuse and Mental Health Services Administration, Office of Applied Studies, September 2010, http://www.oas.samhsa.gov/NSDUH/2k9NSDUH/2k9ResultsP.pdf (accessed October 25, 2010)

Marijuana and a relatively new hallucinogenic drug called D-lysergic acid diethylamide (LSD) surged in popularity. Other drugs of choice during this era were amphetamines (also called speed or uppers). Amphetamines stimulate the central nervous system. The drugs were widely dispensed by U.S. military authorities during World War II (1939–1945) to keep soldiers alert during battle. After the war amphetamines remained popular among students and workers who wanted to stay awake for long periods. They also used them to lose weight because amphetamines suppress the appetite. According to Celinda Franco of the Congressional Research Service (CRS), in *Methamphetamine: Background, Prevalence, and Federal Drug Control Policies* (January 24, 2007, http://assets.opencrs.com/rpts/RL33857_20070124.pdf), amphetamines could be easily purchased over the counter (i.e., without a prescription) until 1951. By the end of the 1960s new laws had been passed to combat the growing problems with LSD and amphetamine abuse.

A National Emergency Is Declared

In 1969 President Richard M. Nixon (1913–1994) asked Congress to pass extensive legislation giving the federal government more control over the problem of drug abuse. The result was the Comprehensive Drug Abuse Prevention and Control Act of 1970. The act gave the U.S. attorney general greater jurisdiction over drug crimes and provided for the rehabilitation of drug addicts. It also placed new restrictions on the pharmaceutical industry and the medical professionals to better control and monitor the supply and dispensing of prescription drugs. On June 17, 1971, Nixon addressed Congress about the nation's drug problem with this warning: "We must now candidly recognize that the deliberate procedures embodied in present efforts to control drug abuse are not sufficient in themselves. The problem has assumed the dimensions of a national emergency" (http://www.presidency.ucsb.edu/ws/index.php?pid=3048). In a statement to the public made that same day, Nixon said, "America's public enemy number one in the United States is drug abuse. In order to fight and defeat this enemy, it is necessary to wage a new, all-out offensive" (http://www.presidency.ucsb.edu/ws/index.php?pid=3047). Over time, Nixon's statement became known as the declaration of the War on Drugs. In 1973 he created the U.S. Drug Enforcement Administration (DEA) to coordinate drug control efforts for the federal government.

Drug Crime during the 1970s and 1980s

Despite the declaration of the War on Drugs, illicit drug use continued to thrive. During the 1970s the sedative methaqualone, commonly known by the brand-name Quaalude, became a popular street drug. It was heartily embraced by the American medical establishment as a safe and nonaddictive alternative to barbiturates and easily found its way from medicine cabinets to the streets.

Another drug that gained prominence during this period was 3,4 methylenedioxymethamphetamine (MDMA, also known as ecstasy). In "MDMA (Ecstasy)" (December 2010, http://www.nida.nih.gov/InfoFacts/ecstasy.html), the National Institute on Drug Abuse notes that ecstasy is a synthetic psychoactive drug. It initially became popular among middle-class white teens and young adults at youth-friendly nightclubs and dance parties called raves. Ecstasy is one of several so-called club drugs that are associated with these types of users.

During the 1970s and 1980s cocaine use soared in the United States with the rise of large well-funded drug cartels in South America, particularly in Colombia. The cartels used their extensive criminal networks to import the drug into the United States and sell it for premium prices. Cocaine became the drug of choice for wealthy celebrities and professionals. It developed a reputation as a trendy, glamorous, and nonaddictive drug that was too expensive for street users. Meanwhile, a cheaper form of cocaine called crack cocaine was introduced to the street users. Unlike powdered cocaine, the crack version was a crystal that could be smoked. It was also more potent than the same amount of powdered cocaine and cost much less. A crack cocaine epidemic developed in U.S. cities, particularly in inner cities

FIGURE 4.3

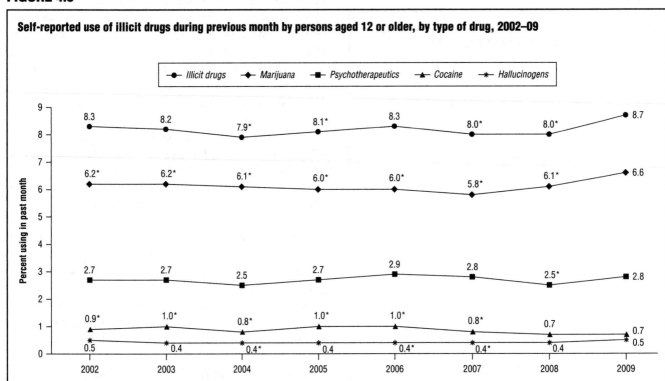

Self-reported use of illicit drugs during previous month by persons aged 12 or older, by type of drug, 2002–09

*Difference between this estimate and the 2009 estimate is statistically significant at the 0.05 level.

SOURCE: "Figure 2.2. Past Month Use of Selected Illicit Drugs among Persons Aged 12 or Older: 2002–2009," in *Results from the 2009 National Survey on Drug Use and Health: Volume I. Summary of National Findings*, U.S. Department of Health and Human Services, Substance Abuse and Mental Health Services Administration, Office of Applied Studies, September 2010, http://www.oas.samhsa.gov/NSDUH/2k9NSDUH/2k9ResultsP.pdf (accessed October 25, 2010)

with large populations of low-income African-Americans. Gang wars and other crack-related crimes skyrocketed.

Drug Crime during the 1990s and the First Decade of the 21st Century

By the early 1990s the crack epidemic was over and the United States enjoyed a brief downturn in the number of drug arrests. (See Figure 4.1.) This decline coincided with a national drop in overall crime that was described in Chapter 2. However, the overall crime rate continued a downward trend through the end of the decade, even as drug crime began to increase again. Drug arrests reached nearly 1.4 million in 1989, but decreased to 1.1 million in 1992. They then began a sustained rise that lasted through 2006. Drug arrests dropped somewhat between 2007 and 2009. It remains to be seen whether this decrease is a temporary blip or the beginning of a downturn in drug crime.

The most striking feature of drug crime during the 1990s and the first decade of the 21st century, as compared with previous decades, has been the dramatic comeback of marijuana as the drug of choice among users. Since the early 1990s there has been a large increase in the number of marijuana arrests. (See Figure 4.6.) This occurred after a nine-year decline from 1982 to 1991, when marijuana arrests were down to 290,000. Over the following decade

they climbed to 735,000 arrests and continued to increase through 2007. Marijuana arrests decreased slightly between 2008 and 2009, but were still high by historical standards.

As shown in Figure 4.2, marijuana was the most-used drug in 2009. Nearly 17 million people aged 12 years and older admitted they had used marijuana during the previous month.

ILLICIT DRUG SCHEDULES

Titles II and III of the Comprehensive Drug Abuse Prevention and Control Act of 1970 are called the Controlled Substances Act (CSA). The CSA places all illicit drugs into one of five schedules or categories based on the characteristics of the drugs and their potential for abuse. According to the DEA, in *Drugs of Abuse* (June 2004, http://www.usdoj.gov/dea/pubs/abuse/doa-p.pdf), the five schedules are:

- Schedule I—the drugs have a high potential for abuse, have no accepted use in medical treatment in the United States, and lack acceptable safety for use even under medical supervision.

- Schedule II—the drugs have a high potential for abuse that could cause severe physical or psychological

FIGURE 4.4

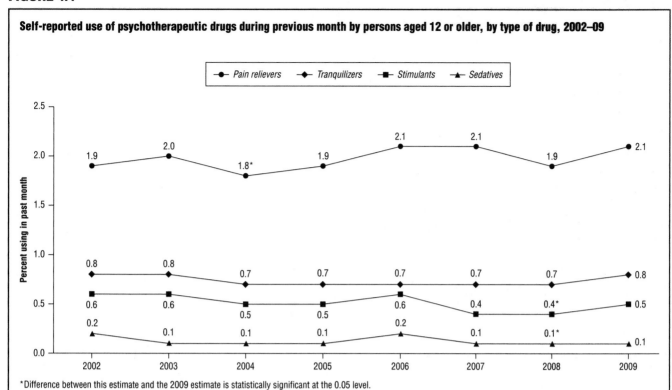

Self-reported use of psychotherapeutic drugs during previous month by persons aged 12 or older, by type of drug, 2002–09

*Difference between this estimate and the 2009 estimate is statistically significant at the 0.05 level.

SOURCE: "Figure 2.3. Past Month Nonmedical Use of Types of Psychotherapeutic Drugs among Persons Aged 12 or Older: 2002–2009," in *Results from the 2009 National Survey on Drug Use and Health: Volume I. Summary of National Findings*, U.S. Department of Health and Human Services, Substance Abuse and Mental Health Services Administration, Office of Applied Studies, September 2010, http://www.oas.samhsa.gov/NSDUH/2k9NSDUH/2k9ResultsP.pdf (accessed October 25, 2010)

dependence. They have accepted uses in medical treatment in the United States (perhaps with many restrictions).

- Schedule III—the drugs have a lower abuse potential than Schedule I or II drugs, and such abuse "may lead to moderate or low physical dependence or high psychological dependence." They have accepted uses in medical treatment in the United States.

- Schedule IV—the drugs have a lower abuse potential than Schedule III drugs, and such abuse could cause limited physical or psychological dependence. They have accepted uses in medical treatment in the United States.

- Schedule V—the drugs have a lower abuse potential than Schedule IV drugs, and such abuse could cause limited physical or psychological dependence. They have accepted uses in medical treatment in the United States.

Table 4.1 lists the common illicit drugs and their CSA schedule numbers, medical uses (if any), and levels of physical and psychological dependence. Heroin, morphine, cocaine, and the cannabis drugs (e.g., marijuana) are derived primarily from organic sources. Heroin, morphine, and cocaine originate from opium poppies. Cannabis is a species

of flowering plants. Some illicit drugs are considered synthetic drugs because their origins are not primarily organic. Examples include amphetamines, methamphetamines, MDMA drugs (e.g., ecstasy), and LSD.

DRUG LAW VIOLATIONS

Drug offenses include the possession, sale, or manufacture of illicit drugs. Many drug offenses are felonies and are punishable by at least one year in prison. Some drug offenses—particularly the possession of small amounts of marijuana—are misdemeanors. People convicted of misdemeanor drug crimes may receive a fine and/or a sentence of less than one year in a local jail. Some jurisdictions treat the possession of very small amounts of marijuana (e.g., less than 1 ounce [28 g]) as an infraction, rather than as a misdemeanor. Infractions are minor offenses, such as traffic violations, that are punishable only with fines, not with incarceration.

Drug laws are complex and can differ between jurisdictions. In general, the seriousness of an offense and the harshness of its penalty are based on the type and amount of drug involved and whether the offender possesses the drug for his or her own use or is a seller, manufacturer, or distributor. First-time offenders may receive less harsh charges and sentences than repeat offenders. Other

FIGURE 4.5

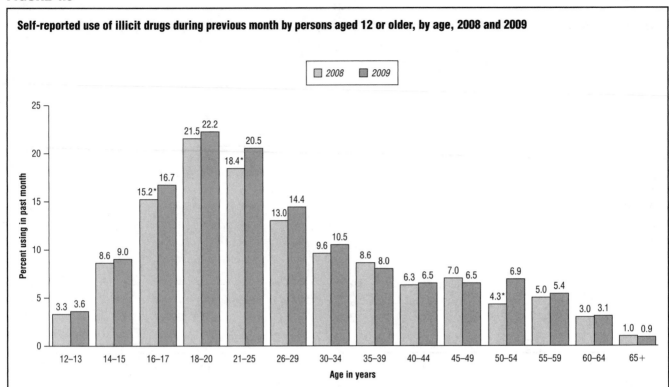

Self-reported use of illicit drugs during previous month by persons aged 12 or older, by age, 2008 and 2009

□ 2008   ■ 2009

*Difference between this estimate and the 2009 estimate is statistically significant at the 0.05 level.

SOURCE: "Figure 2.4. Past Month Illicit Drug Use among Persons Aged 12 or Older, by Age: 2008 and 2009," in *Results from the 2009 National Survey on Drug Use and Health: Volume I. Summary of National Findings*, U.S. Department of Health and Human Services, Substance Abuse and Mental Health Services Administration, Office of Applied Studies, September 2010, http://www.oas.samhsa.gov/NSDUH/2k9NSDUH/2k9ResultsP.pdf (accessed October 25, 2010)

factors also play a role. For example, New York City treats possession of very small amounts of marijuana as an infraction, unless the drug is "in public view," upon which the offense is a misdemeanor.

Drug Arrests by Drug and Violation Type

Table 4.2 breaks down drug arrests in 2009 by drug law violation (sale/manufacturing or possession) and by drug type (heroin or cocaine and their derivatives, marijuana, synthetic or manufactured drugs, and other dangerous non-narcotic drugs). The majority (82%) of the drug arrests in 2009 were for possession, whereas only 18% were for sale/manufacturing. (See Figure 4.7.)

Arrests for heroin and cocaine peaked at 730,000 in 1989 before beginning a sustained decline until 2002. (See Figure 4.6.) In 2009 law enforcement agencies made over 415,000 arrests for heroin and cocaine offenses, which accounted for 25% of all drug arrests that year. (See Figure 4.8.) Marijuana arrests declined during the 1980s and then climbed significantly through the 1990s and into the first decade of the 21st century. In 2009 there were nearly 860,000 marijuana arrests—the highest number of arrests for any drug type. As shown in Figure 4.8, marijuana arrests accounted for more than half (52%) of

all drug arrests in 2009. In 1982 synthetic or manufactured drug arrests totaled less than 30,000; by 2009 they exceeded 89,000, accounting for 18% of total drug arrests. Arrests for other drugs increased from around 80,000 in 1982 to over 301,000 in 2009, accounting for 5% of total drug arrests.

The Crack Epidemic

Arrests for heroin and cocaine skyrocketed during the 1980s. (See Figure 4.6.) Cocaine, in particular, was popular during the 1980s in two forms: powdered cocaine that was snorted or liquefied and injected into the veins and rock crystal cocaine (or crack) that was smoked in pipes. Both are considered highly addictive. Nonmedical use of cocaine has been illegal since the passage of the Harrison Narcotics Act of 1914. In 1970 cocaine was classified as a CSA Schedule II drug.

During the early 1980s crack cocaine was introduced as a much cheaper alternative to the powdered form of the drug. It also provided a much quicker high than powdered cocaine. Crack soon became the drug of choice among low-income users, particularly in inner cities with large minority populations. The country experienced a so-called crack epidemic. Americans were appalled by media reports about

FIGURE 4.6

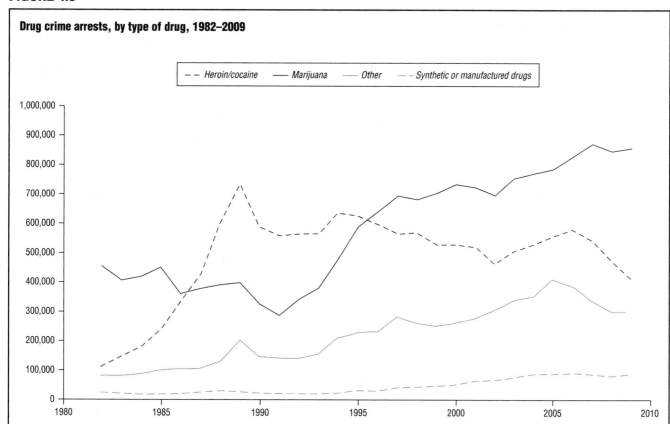

Drug crime arrests, by type of drug, 1982–2009

Legend: – – Heroin/cocaine — Marijuana — Other – – Synthetic or manufactured drugs

SOURCE: Adapted from "Arrest Table. Arrests for Drug Abuse Violations: Percent Distribution by Region, 2008," in *Crime in the United States, 2008*, U.S. Department of Justice, Federal Bureau of Investigation, September 2009, http://www2.fbi.gov/ucr/cius2008/documents/08arresttbl.xls (accessed October 25, 2010); Tina Dorsey and Doris J. James, "Total Estimated Drug Law Violation Arrests in the United States, 1980–2007," in *Drugs and Crime Facts*, U.S. Department of Justice, Office of Justice Programs, Bureau of Justice Statistics, August 17, 2009, http://bjs.ojp.usdoj.gov/content/dcf/tables/arrtot.cfm (accessed October 25, 2010); "Arrest Table. Arrests for Drug Abuse Violations, Percent Distribution by Region, 2009," in *Crime in the United States, 2009*, U.S. Department of Justice, Federal Bureau of Investigation, September 2010, http://www2.fbi.gov/ucr/cius2009/arrests/index.html (accessed September 29, 2010); and Tina Dorsey and Doris James, "Number of Arrests, by Drug Type, 1982–2007," in *Drugs and Crime Facts*, U.S. Department of Justice, Office of Justice Programs, Bureau of Justice Statistics, August 17, 2009, http://bjs.ojp.usdoj.gov/content/dcf/tables/drugtype.cfm (accessed October 25, 2010)

crack-induced street crime and crack-addicted babies born to mothers abusing the drug. The social effects of the crack epidemic are described by the DEA, in *A Tradition of Excellence* (January 2009, http://www.usdoj.gov/dea/pubs/history/1985-1990.pdf): "The crack trade had created a violent sub-world, and crack-related murders in many large cities were skyrocketing. For example, a 1988 study by the Bureau of Justice Statistics found that in New York City, crack use was tied to 32% of all homicides and 60% of drug-related homicides. On a daily basis, the evening news reported the violence of drive-by shootings and crack users trying to obtain money for their next hit."

THE CRACKDOWN ON CRACK. In 1986 Congress passed the Anti-drug Abuse Act, a comprehensive law that imposed mandatory minimum prison sentences for people convicted of federal drug crimes. The new law made an important distinction between crack cocaine and powdered cocaine. A person convicted of possessing only 0.2 ounces (5 g) of crack cocaine faced the same mandatory prison sentence as a person convicted of possessing 17.6 ounces (500 g) of powdered cocaine. In other words, there was a 100 to 1 sentencing disparity between the two forms of the drug. At the time, politicians defended the disparity as a reasonable response to the harm that crack cocaine was doing to American society. However, the law soon became controversial because relatively low-level crack users and suppliers (many of whom were low-income African-Americans) received harsher sentences than users and suppliers of much larger amounts of powdered cocaine. Because most of the latter offenders were white, activists decried the law as racist.

After nearly two decades of controversy, the issue was addressed by the U.S. Supreme Court in *Kimbrough v. United States* (552 U.S. 85 [2007]). The case involved Derrick Kimbrough, an African-American defendant who had pleaded guilty in federal court to offenses involving both powdered and crack cocaine. The original court sentenced Kimbrough in accordance with the federal

TABLE 4.1

Characteristics of commonly abused drugs

Drugs	CSA, Schedules	Trade or other names	Medical uses	Dependence — Physical	Dependence — Psychological
Narcotics					
Heroin	Substance I	Diamorphine, Horse, Smack, Black tar, Chiva, Negra (black tar)	None in U.S., analgesic, antitussive	High	High
Morphine	Substance II	MS-Contin, Roxanol, Oramorph SR, MSIR	Analgesic	High	High
Hydrocodone	Substance II, Product III, V	Hydrocodone w/Acetaminophen, Vicodin, Vicoprofen, Tussionex, Lortab	Analgesic, antitussive	High	High
Hydromorphone	Substance II	Dilaudid	Analgesic	High	High
Oxycodone	Substance II	Roxicet, Oxycodone w/Acetaminophen, OxyContin, Endocet, Percocet, Percodan	Analgesic	High	High
Codeine	Substance II, Products III, V	Acetaminophen, Guaifenesin or Promethazine w/ Codeine, Fiorinal, Fioricet or Tylenol w/Codeine	Analgesic, antitussive	Moderate	Moderate
Other narcotics	Substance II, III, IV	Fentanyl, Demerol, Methadone, Darvon, Stadol, Talwin, Paregoric, Buprenex	Analgesic, antidiarrheal, antitussive	High-Low	High-Low
Depressants					
gamma Hydroxybutyric Acid	Substance I, Product III	GHB, Liquid Ecstasy, Liquid X, Sodium Oxybate, Xyrem®	None in U.S., anesthetic	Moderate	Moderate
Benzodiazepines	Substance IV	Valium, Xanax, Halcion, Ativan, Restoril, Rohypnol (Roofies, R-2), Klonopin	Antianxiety, sedative, Anticonvulsant, Hypnotic, Muscle Relaxant	Moderate	Moderate
Other depressants	Substance I, II, III, IV	Ambien, Sonata, Meprobamate, Chloral Hydrate, Barbiturates, Methaqualone (Quaalude)	Antianxiety, Sedative, Hypnotic	Moderate	Moderate
Stimulants					
Cocaine	Substance II	Coke, Flake, Snow, Crack, Coca, Blanca, Perico, Nieve, Soda	Local anesthetic	Possible	High
Amphetamine/ Methamphetamine	Substance II	Crank, Ice, Cristal, Krystal Meth, Speed, Adderall, Dexedrine, Desoxyn	Attention deficit/hyperactivity disorder, narcolepsy, weight control	Possible	High
Methylphenidate	Substance II	Ritalin (Illy's), Concerta, Focalin, Metadate	Attention deficit/hyperactivity disorder	Possible	High
Other stimulants	Substance III, IV	Adipex P, Ionamin, Prelu-2, Didrex, Provigil	Vasoconstriction	Possible	Moderate
Hallucinogens					
MDMA and Analogs	Substance I	(Ecstasy, XTC, Adam), MDA (Love Drug), MDEA (Eve), MBDB	None	None	Moderate
LSD	Substance I	Acid, Microdot, Sunshine, Boomers	None	None	Unknown
Phencyclidine and Analogs	Substance I, II, III	PCP, Angel Dust, Hog, Loveboat, Ketamine (Special K), PCE, PCPy, TCP	Anesthetic (Ketamine)	Possible	High
Other hallucinogens	Substance I	Psilocybe mushrooms, Mescaline, Peyote Cactus Ayahausca, DMT, Dextromethorphan* (DXM)	None	None	None
Cannabis					
Marijuana	Substance I	Pot, Grass, Sinsemilla, Blunts, Mota, Yerba, Grifa	None	Unknown	Moderate
Tetrahydrocannabinol	Substance I, Product III	THC, Marinol	Antinauseant, Appetite stimulant	Yes	Moderate
Hashish and Hashish Oil	Substance I	Hash, Hash oil	None	Unknown	Moderate
Anabolic Steroids					
Testosterone	Substance III	Depo Testosterone, Sustanon, Sten, Cypt	Hypogonadism	Unknown	Unknown
Other Anabolic Steroids	Substance III	Parabolan, Winstrol, Equipose, Anadrol, Dianabol, Primabolin-Depo, D-Ball	Anemia, breast cancer	Unknown	Yes
Inhalants					
Amyl and Butyl Nitrite		Pearls, Poppers, Rush, Locker Room	Angina (Amyl)	Unknown	Unknown
Nitrous Oxide		Laughing gas, balloons, Whippets	Anesthetic	Unknown	Low
Other inhalants		Adhesives, spray paint, hair spray, dry cleaning fluid, spot remover, lighter fluid	None	Unknown	High
Alcohol		Beer, wine, liquor	None	High	High

SOURCE: Adapted from "Drugs of Abuse/Uses and Effects," in *Drugs of Abuse: 2005 Edition*, U.S. Department of Justice, Drug Enforcement Administration, June 2004 http://www.usdoj.gov/dea/pubs/abuse/doa-p.pdf (accessed November 24, 2010)

guidelines for powdered cocaine, rather than with the harsher crack cocaine sentence structure. The Supreme Court ruled in December 2007 that federal judges can use discretion in such cases and impose shorter sentences for crack cocaine offenses than called for by federal guidelines to reduce the powder-crack disparity. That same month the U.S. Sentencing Commission (USSC) ruled that crack cocaine sentences imposed by federal courts in the past could be shortened accordingly following petition by the convicted defendants. The USSC also recommended that Congress eliminate the 100 to 1 disparity in crack sentencing compared with sentencing for powdered cocaine offenses.

TABLE 4.2

Drug crime arrests, by type of violation and drug, 2009

Drug abuse violations		United States total
Total*		100.0
Sale/manufacturing:	Total	18.4
	Heroin or cocaine and their derivatives	7.1
	Marijuana	6.0
	Synthetic or manufactured drugs	1.7
	Other dangerous nonnarcotic drugs	3.5
Possession:	Total	81.6
	Heroin or cocaine and their derivatives	17.7
	Marijuana	45.6
	Synthetic or manufactured drugs	3.7
	Other dangerous nonnarcotic drugs	14.6

*Because of rounding, the percentages may not add to 100.0.

SOURCE: Adapted from "Arrest Table. Arrests for Drug Abuse Violations: Percent Distribution by Region, 2009," in *Crime in the United States, 2009*, U.S. Department of Justice, Federal Bureau of Investigation, September 2010, http://www2.fbi.gov/ucr/cius2009/arrests/index.html (accessed September 29, 2010)

FIGURE 4.7

Breakdown of drug crime arrests, by type of violation, 2009

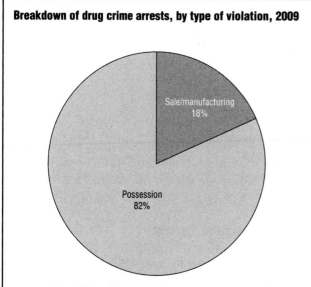

SOURCE: Adapted from "Arrest Table. Arrests for Drug Abuse Violations: Percent Distribution by Region, 2009," in *Crime in the United States, 2009*, U.S. Department of Justice, Federal Bureau of Investigation, September 2010, http://www2.fbi.gov/ucr/cius2009/arrests/index.html (accessed September 29, 2010)

FIGURE 4.8

Breakdown of drug crime arrests, by type of drug, 2009

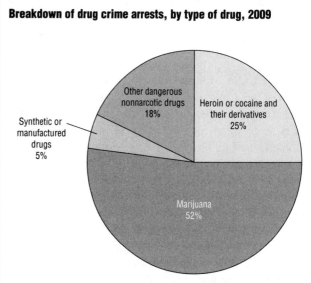

SOURCE: Adapted from "Arrest Table. Arrests for Drug Abuse Violations: Percent Distribution by Region, 2009," in *Crime in the United States, 2009*, U.S. Department of Justice, Federal Bureau of Investigation, September 2010, http://www2.fbi.gov/ucr/cius2009/arrests/index.html (accessed September 29, 2010)

THE CRACK EPIDEMIC ENDS. Heroin and cocaine arrests plummeted suddenly in 1990, after peaking at 730,000 arrests in 1989. (See Figure 4.6.) By 2002 arrests were down to around 460,000. Criminologists and sociologists present a number of possible causes for the sudden end to the crack epidemic. Some tie it to the overall downward trend in crime that occurred during the 1990s. As noted in Chapter 2, the reasons for the crime decline are not known for certain, but could include tougher sentencing laws, higher incarceration rates, better policing, and a robust economy.

Some analysts believe the epidemic's end was precipitated, in part, by changing consumer tastes. During the 1990s crack lost favor as the drug of choice among inner-city youths as they increasingly turned to marijuana. Denise Herd of the University of California, Berkeley, suggests in "Changes in Drug Use Prevalence in Rap Music Songs, 1979–1997" (*Addiction Research and Theory*, vol. 16, no. 2, April 2008) that rap music may have played a role in this social trend. Herd finds that popular rap songs decried the "destructiveness" of crack during the 1980s, but glorified marijuana during the 1990s by tying the drug to "creativity, wealth and status."

Marijuana

As the crack epidemic was ending during the early 1990s, another drug began gaining prominence in arrest records: marijuana. Marijuana arrests fell throughout the 1980s, dropping to 290,000 arrests in 1991. (See Figure 4.6.) Over the following decade arrests nearly tripled, reaching 730,000 in 2000. By 2009 there were approximately 860,000

In August 2010 President Barack Obama (1961–) signed the Fair Sentencing Act. The act eliminated the five-year mandatory minimum prison sentence for first-time crack cocaine possession and increased to 1 ounce (28 g) the amount of crack cocaine that is required for the imposition of mandatory minimum prison terms for drug trafficking. In other words, the 100 to 1 sentencing disparity between crack cocaine and powdered cocaine was reduced to an 18 to 1 sentencing disparity.

marijuana arrests, which made up 52% of all drug arrests. (See Figure 4.8.) As shown in Table 4.2, marijuana possession accounted for 45.6% of all drug abuse arrests in 2009, whereas marijuana sale/manufacturing accounted for just 6% of the total drug arrests.

MARIJUANA MISDEMEANORS AND INFRACTIONS. In *Beyond Our Control?: Confronting the Limits of Our Legal System in the Age of Cyberspace* (2003), Stuart Biegel reports that marijuana arrests in the United States doubled from 7,000 to 15,000 between 1964 and 1966. By 1969 the national total for marijuana arrests had increased nearly 700% to 118,903. Court systems became overrun with cases involving marijuana possession, which at that time could elicit a prison sentence as long as five years for possession of only a single marijuana cigarette (or joint). In response, many jurisdictions began lowering the penalties for possession of small amounts of marijuana. In some areas this offense was essentially decriminalized, meaning that it became an infraction, rather than a misdemeanor. Decriminalization began in Oregon in 1973 and then spread to other states: Alaska, California, Colorado, and Ohio in 1975; Mississippi, New York, and North Carolina in 1977; and Nebraska in 1978. However, the decriminalization trend faded during the 1980s as marijuana use declined and other drugs came into prominence. Also, the movement to decriminalize was not embraced at the federal level.

As a result, some jurisdictions categorize the possession of small amounts of marijuana as either a misdemeanor or an infraction, depending on the circumstances of the offense. This distinction has been a source of great controversy for some social activists. For example, Harry G. Levine and Deborah Peterson Small suggest in *Marijuana Arrest Crusade: Black Bias and Police Policy in New York City, 1997–2007* (April 2008, http://graphics8.nytimes.com/packages/pdf/nyregion/20080429_MARIJUANA.pdf) that marijuana possession arrests in New York City are racially skewed in that African-American and Hispanic offenders are far more likely than white offenders to be charged with misdemeanor possession as opposed to being issued an infraction. Levine and Small note that misdemeanor marijuana possession arrests in New York City skyrocketed between 1997 and 2006, totaling approximately 353,000 arrests during this period. By contrast, only 30,000 arrests were made for misdemeanor marijuana possession in each of the nine-year periods of 1977 to 1986 and 1987 to 1996. In New York City simple possession of less than 0.9 of an ounce (24.8 g) of marijuana is an infraction rather than a misdemeanor. However, possession of even small amounts of marijuana is a misdemeanor if the drug is "in public view." Levine and Small claim that New York City police officers target African-American and Hispanic youths for "stop and frisk" encounters that are intended to bully the offenders into showing their marijuana so they can be charged with a misdemeanor, rather than with an infraction.

LEGALIZED MEDICAL MARIJUANA USE. During the late 1990s some states began legalizing the use of small amounts of marijuana for medical reasons, such as to relieve pain or nausea. According to the nonprofit educational organization ProCon.org (http://medicalmarijuana.procon.org/viewresource.asp?resourceID=000881), as of January 2011, 15 states and the District of Columbia had legalized medical marijuana usage (the year that each state's law was passed is given in parentheses):

- Alaska (1998)
- Arizona (2010)
- California (1996)
- Colorado (2000)
- District of Columbia (2010)
- Hawaii (2000)
- Maine (1999)
- Michigan (2008)
- Montana (2004)
- Nevada (2000)
- New Jersey (2010)
- New Mexico (2007)
- Oregon (1998)
- Rhode Island (2006)
- Vermont (2004)
- Washington (1998)

However, it should be noted that as of February 2011, marijuana usage of any type was still a crime under federal law.

A Methamphetamine Epidemic?

Methamphetamine (or meth) is a stimulant in the amphetamine group. During the 1990s and the first decade of the 21st century methamphetamine abuse became a major problem in some parts of the United States. The rise of this previously obscure drug is described by Franco in *Methamphetamine: Background, Prevalence, and Federal Drug Control Policies.*

Methamphetamine can be synthesized from a naturally occurring chemical called ephedrine. This so-called precursor chemical is commonly synthesized, as are two other methamphetamine precursors: phenylpropanolamine and pseudoephedrine. Both of the latter are widely used in cold and sinus medications, many of which can be purchased over the counter.

THE EVOLUTION OF ILLICIT METHAMPHETAMINE LABORATORIES. Franco notes that methamphetamine is classified as a Schedule II drug under the CSA. The drug had been used medically in the United States for several decades. During the 1950s methamphetamine was widely prescribed for a variety of ailments; however, growing concern about the abuse of methamphetamine (and amphetamines, in general) led to severe government restrictions on dispensing the drug. In response, underworld methamphetamine laboratories began springing up during the 1960s. These illicit laboratories were primarily located in the western United States and mostly operated by outlaw motorcycle gangs. They produced a crude form of methamphetamine that was known as crank on the streets. Crank was less potent than pharmaceutical-grade methamphetamine, but it still became popular with certain users. During the 1980s more sophisticated amateur chemists developed a new method for synthesizing a much more potent form of crank using ephedrine-based reactions. This led to a variety of forms that could be ingested, snorted, injected, or smoked. A popular type of smokable methamphetamine is a crystalline powder known as ice.

During the 1990s illicit amateur methamphetamine laboratories became a cause of great concern. Many of the laboratories were operated in homes, putting the residents—particularly children—at great danger of fires and explosions due to the volatile nature of the chemicals involved.

As the so-called methamphetamine epidemic attracted national attention, legislators rushed to pass laws making it more difficult for amateur chemists to obtain the ephedrine-type precursors that are used to synthesize methamphetamine. The Comprehensive Methamphetamine Control Act of 1996 added the precursor chemicals to Schedule II of the CSA. That act and a subsequent law—the Methamphetamine Trafficking Penalty Enhancement Act of 1998—increased the penalties for manufacturing and selling methamphetamine. After 2000 legislators tackled the easy availability of precursor chemicals in over-the-counter cold and sinus medications. By 2006 many states and the federal government had laws in place restricting purchases by individual consumers of these medications from retail and mail-order stores. The clampdown is believed to have reduced the number of amateur methamphetamine laboratories in the United States. The DEA notes in "Maps of Methamphetamine Lab Incidents" (September 2010, http://www.usdoj.gov/dea/concern/map_lab_seizures.html) that the number of these laboratories known to law enforcement officials decreased from 18,581 in 2004 to only 6,233 in 2007, but then rebounded to more than 10,000 in 2009. Figure 4.9 shows the locations of the 10,064 laboratories (and related facilities) that were reported in 2009.

Franco notes that by 2007 the clampdown on ephedrine-containing medications had made it much more difficult for the so-called mom-and-pop methamphetamine laboratories to operate. As a result, large-scale methamphetamine production has shifted to more sophisticated super laboratories often under the control of Mexican drug-trafficking organizations. According to Franco, DEA officials estimated in 2007 that more than 80% of illicit methamphetamine in the United States was supplied by these Mexican drug cartels. They reportedly purchase tons of precursor chemicals from companies around the world and synthesize a potent form of methamphetamine in large laboratories in Mexico and in the western United States.

METHAMPHETAMINE HOT SPOTS. Even though methamphetamine abuse is often described by the media as a national epidemic, analysts assert that it is actually a regional problem in that certain so-called hot spots exist around the country. Franco notes that methamphetamine abuse is largely associated with states in the Midwest and in some parts of the West and south central United States. In 2009 clandestine methamphetamine laboratory incidents occurred mainly in Missouri (1,784 incidents), Indiana (1,267 incidents), Mississippi (714 incidents), Kentucky (707 incidents), Michigan (648 incidents), Alabama (614 incidents), and Tennessee (589 incidents). (See Figure 4.9.)

DRUG USE REPORTED BY PRISON INMATES AND ARRESTEES

In *Drug Use and Dependence, State and Federal Prisoners, 2004* (October 2006, http://bjs.ojp.usdoj.gov/content/pub/pdf/dudsfp04.pdf), Christopher J. Mumola and Jennifer C. Karberg of the BJS note that in 2004, 56% of all state prisoners reported using drugs in the month before committing their offense(s). This percentage changed little from 1997, when 57% of state prisoners reported previous drug use. A slightly lower percentage of federal prison inmates, 50%, reported drug use in the month before their offense in 2004, compared with 45% in 1997.

Nearly one-third (32.1%) of state prison inmates in 2004 said they had committed their current offense while under the influence of drugs. The most common drug used by state prisoners was marijuana; 77.6% of state prisoners in 2004 reported they had used marijuana at some point in their life. The percentage of prisoners who said they used cocaine or crack cocaine in the month before their offense declined from 25% in 1997 to 21.4% in 2004. During this period the use of heroin and other opiates in the month preceding the offense dropped slightly from 9.2% in 1997 to 8.2% in 2004, whereas the use of hallucinogens rose from 4% to 5.9%.

According to Mumola and Karberg, 26.4% of federal prison inmates reported using drugs at the time of their offense in 2004, an increase from 22.4% in 1997. Between 1997 and 2004 marijuana use increased from 30.4% to 36.2%. However, the percentage of federal prisoners who reported using cocaine or crack cocaine in the month before their offense fell from 20% in 1997 to 18% in 2004, and use at the time of the offense dropped from 9.3% in 1997 to 7.4% in 2004.

FIGURE 4.9

Number of methamphetamine clandestine laboratory incidents, 2009

[Includes labs, dumpsites, chem/glass/equipment]

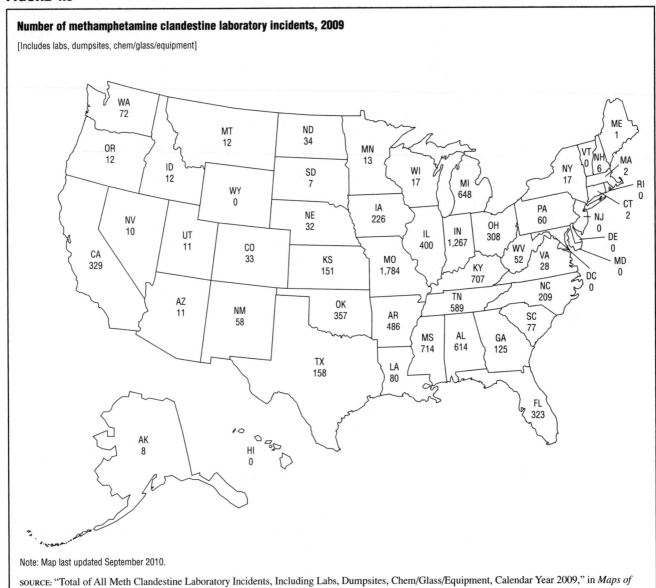

Note: Map last updated September 2010.

SOURCE: "Total of All Meth Clandestine Laboratory Incidents, Including Labs, Dumpsites, Chem/Glass/Equipment, Calendar Year 2009," in *Maps of Methamphetamine Lab Incidents*, U.S. Department of Justice, U.S. Drug Enforcement Administration, September 2010, http://www.justice.gov/dea/concern/map_lab_seizures.html (accessed October 26, 2010)

Since 2007 the Office of National Drug Control Policy (ONDCP) within the Executive Office of the President has operated the Arrestee Drug Abuse Monitoring (ADAM) program. The ONDCP's ADAM II program replaces an earlier ADAM I program that was operated by the National Institute of Justice. In *ADAM II 2009 Annual Report* (June 2010, http://www.whitehousedrugpolicy.gov/publications/pdf/adam2009.pdf), the ONDCP notes that the ADAM II program monitors drug use trends among newly arrested males at 10 jail systems around the country:

- Atlanta, Georgia (Fulton County)
- Charlotte, North Carolina (Mecklenburg County)
- Chicago, Illinois (Cook County)
- Denver, Colorado (Denver County)
- Indianapolis, Indiana (Marion County)
- Minneapolis, Minnesota (Hennepin County)
- New York, New York (Borough of Manhattan)
- Portland, Oregon (Multnomah County)
- Sacramento, California (Sacramento County)
- Washington, D.C.

Participation by arrestees is voluntary; however, the ONDCP reports that 86% of all arrestees interviewed in 2009 agreed to participate by providing urine samples for drug testing. The ADAM II program is not limited to people arrested for drug crimes. In fact, the ONDCP notes that arrestees eligible to participate in the program have been arrested for a variety of crimes, "ranging from

FIGURE 4.10

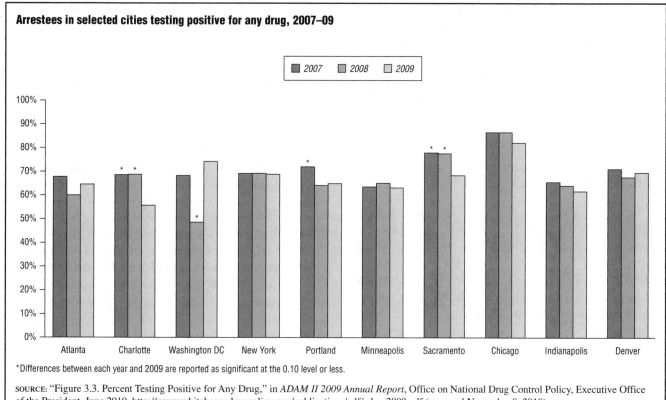

Arrestees in selected cities testing positive for any drug, 2007–09

*Differences between each year and 2009 are reported as significant at the 0.10 level or less.

SOURCE: "Figure 3.3. Percent Testing Positive for Any Drug," in *ADAM II 2009 Annual Report*, Office on National Drug Control Policy, Executive Office of the President, June 2010, http://www.whitehousedrugpolicy.gov/publications/pdf/adam2009.pdf (accessed November 8, 2010)

a traffic violation to burglary to homicide." As shown in Figure 4.10, the vast majority of arrestees subjected to drug testing at each location in 2009 tested positive for at least one drug. The drugs tested included amphetamine, barbiturates, benzodiazepines, cocaine, marijuana, methadone, methamphetamine, opiates, oxycodone, phencyclidine, and propoxyphene.

Marijuana was the most commonly used drug with 36.2% to 49.4% of arrestees at each location testing positive for it. It was followed by cocaine, at 10.5% to 36.9%; opiates, at 1.7% to 17.8%; and methamphetamine, at 0% to 30.7%. Usage of the latter three drugs varied significantly from location to location. Overall, the ONDCP reports that ADAM II results consistently show that marijuana has been the most commonly used illegal substance among booked arrestees since the original program began in 2000.

IS THE UNITED STATES WINNING ITS WAR ON DRUGS?

In 1971 President Nixon launched the nation's War on Drugs. After nearly four decades of battle, analysts disagree on whether the United States is winning or losing the war. However, researchers point to data indicating that juvenile drug use and arrest rates are not increasing as rapidly as they once did.

SAMHSA examines youth drug use trends in *Results from the 2009 National Survey on Drug Use and Health*.

It also reports on its surveys and Monitoring the Future (MTF) studies, which are sponsored by the National Institute on Drug Abuse. The MTF surveys students in the eighth, 10th, and 12th grades during the spring of each year. SAMHSA notes that its surveys and MTF studies indicate declining use of marijuana and cocaine among the surveyed youths.

In *Key Facts at a Glance* (February 2, 2011, http://bjs .ojp.usdoj.gov/content/glance/tables/drugtab.cfm), the BJS indicates that juvenile drug arrests totaled 93,300 in 1970. The number rose and fell over the following decades, but peaked at 213,200 arrests in 1997 before beginning to decline. According to the FBI, in *Crime in the United States, 2009*, UCR data from 12,371 law enforcement agencies indicate that 134,610 people under the age of 18 years were arrested for drug abuse violations in 2009.

The number of adults arrested for drug offenses has also shown a recent decline. The BJS reports in *Key Facts at a Glance* that drug arrests of people aged 18 years and older totaled 322,300 in 1970. By 1989 the number reached 1,247,800 arrests. Following a slight decline during the early 1990s adult drug arrests began rising again, peaking at 1,693,100 in 2006. The FBI reports in *Crime in the United States, 2009* that 1,170,581 people over the age of 18 years were arrested for drug crimes in 2009 based on UCR data from 12,371 law enforcement agencies.

Like all commodities, illicit drugs operate under the economic principles of supply and demand. Federal, state, and local law enforcement officials attack the supply side by arresting and prosecuting sellers and manufacturers of illicit drugs. Because many illicit drugs are imported from foreign countries, the federal government plays an active role in trying to control and stop these international suppliers. This has proved to be extremely difficult. Liana Sun Wyler of the CRS states in *International Drug Control Policy* (August 24, 2009, http://www.fas.org/sgp/crs/row/RL34543.pdf) that "illegal drug use generates a lucrative illegal drug trade that affects countries worldwide. Estimates of the global proceeds from illegal drugs vary significantly, ranging from $100 billion to more than $1 trillion per year. A substantial portion of profits generated by illegal drug trade—as much as 70%—are laundered and invested through foreign banks and institutions. This transnational illegal drug industry also provides international drug trafficking organizations with resources to evade and compete with law enforcement agencies; penetrate legitimate economic structures; and, in some instances, challenge the authority of national governments."

Opium production in war-torn Afghanistan is of particular concern to authorities. The United Nations Office on Drugs and Crime indicates in *Afghanistan: Opium Winter Rapid Assessment Survey* (February 2008, http://www.unodc.org/documents/crop-monitoring/Afghan-winter-survey-Feb08-short.pdf) that Afghanistan produced more than 90% of the world's illegal opium in 2007. In *Afghanistan Drug Control: Strategy Evolving and Progress Reported, but Interim Performance Targets and Evaluation of Justice Reform Efforts Needed* (March 2010, http://www.gao.gov/new.items/d10291.pdf), the U.S. Government Accountability Office estimates that the drug trade in Afghanistan generates approximately $3 billion annually. Authorities believe that some of this money is used to fund terrorist operations in Afghanistan against a coalition of military forces from the United States and other countries that are trying to restore peace there.

The War on Drugs is an expensive war. According to Raphael Perl of the CRS, in *Drug Control: International Policy and Approaches* (February 2, 2006, http://fpc.state.gov/documents/organization/61518.pdf), between 1981 and 2001 the United States spent $8.6 billion on international narcotics control, primarily in South America. Nevertheless, estimated cocaine production in that region nearly quadrupled during that same period and the average price per gram of cocaine in the United States decreased by half. Table 4.3 shows the federal government budget for drug control by agency for fiscal years 2009, 2010, and 2011. The federal government spent $15.3 billion in fiscal year 2009 on drug control, enacted $15 billion for fiscal year 2010, and was expected to spend $15.5 billion in fiscal year 2011.

TABLE 4.3

Drug control funding, by national agency, fiscal years 2009–11

[Budget authority in millions]

	Fiscal years		
	2009 **Final**	**2010** **Enacted**	**2011** **Request**
Department of Defense	1,405.1	1,598.8	1,588.5
Department of Education	429.8	175.8	283.1
Department of Health and Human Services			
Centers for Medicare & Medicaid Services	215.0	430.0	400.0
Substance Abuse and Mental Health Services Administration	2,494.1	2,557.4	2,688.2
National Institutes of Health—National Institute on Drug Abuse	1,293.6	1,059.4	1,094.1
Indian Health Service	91.5	96.0	103.1
Total HHS	**4,094.2**	**4,142.8**	**4,285.4**
Department of Homeland Security			
Customs and Border Protection	2,101.0	2,108.6	2,086.1
Immigration and Customs Enforcement	437.1	477.7	499.8
Coast Guard	1,096.9	1,162.3	1,208.1
Office of Counternarcotics Enforcement	3.7	3.6	3.9
Total DHS	**3,638.7**	**3,752.2**	**3,797.9**
Department of the Interior			
Bureau of Indian Affairs	6.3	10.0	10.0
Department of Justice			
Bureau of Prisons	79.2	87.6	93.5
Drug Enforcement Administration	2,203.5	2,271.5	2,421.9
Organized Crime Drug Enforcement Task Force Program	515.0	528.6	579.3
Office of Justice Programs	397.5	288.4	307.6
National Drug Intelligence Center	44.0	44.0	44.6
Total Justice	**3,239.2**	**3,220.1**	**3,446.9**
Office of National Drug Control Policy			
Counterdrug Technology Assessment Center	3.0	5.0	0.0
High Intensity Drug Trafficking Areas	234.0	239.0	210.0
Other Federal Drug Control Programs	174.7	154.4	165.3
Salaries and Expenses	27.2	29.6	26.2
Total ONDCP	**438.9**	**428.0**	**401.4**
Department of State			
Bureau of International Narcotics and Law Enforcement Affairs	1,150.4	870.7	892.0
United States Agency for International Development	418.6	365.1	365.1
Total State	**1,569.0**	**1,235.9**	**1,257.1**
Department of Transportation			
National Highway Traffic Safety Administration	2.7	2.7	2.7
Department of the Treasury			
Internal Revenue Service	60.6	59.2	60.3
Department of Veterans Affairs			
Veterans Health Administration	392.8	405.0	418.0
Small Business Administration	1.0	1.0	1.0
	15,278.4	**15,031.5**	**15,552.5**

Note: Detail may not add to total because of rounding.

SOURCE: "Table 2. Federal Drug Control Spending by Agency, FY 2009–FY 2011," in *National Drug Control Strategy 2010*, Office on National Drug Control Policy, Executive Office of the President, May 11, 2010, http://www.whitehousedrugpolicy.gov/publications/policy/ndcs10/ndcs2010.pdf (accessed October 25, 2010)

CHAPTER 5
WHITE-COLLAR CRIME

DEFINING WHITE-COLLAR CRIME

The term *white-collar crime* was first used by the American criminologist Edwin Hardin Sutherland (1883–1950) in 1939 to define a violation of the criminal law committed by "a person of respectability and high social status in the course of his occupation" (Cornell University Law School, "White Collar Crime," August 19, 2010, http://topics.law.cornell.edu/wex/White-collar_crime). Over time, the definition has become much broader and can include a variety of crimes committed by perpetrators that use deceptive means for financial gain. The Federal Bureau of Investigation (FBI) investigates violations of federal laws. In *Financial Crimes Report to the Public, Fiscal Year 2009 (October 1, 2008–September 30, 2009)* (2009, http://www2.fbi.gov/publications/financial/fcs_report2009/financial_crime_2009.htm), the FBI notes that white-collar crimes are "characterized by deceit, concealment, or violation of trust and are not dependent upon the application or threat of physical force or violence."

Thus, the term *white-collar crime* is a generic term for a broad set of criminal offenses that include fraud, embezzlement, bribery, swindles, counterfeiting, identity theft, confidence games, money laundering, environmental crimes, copyright violations, computer hacking, and a number of other offenses.

ARRESTS FOR WHITE-COLLAR CRIMES

The FBI's Uniform Crime Reporting (UCR) Program gathers crime data from law enforcement agencies around the country and publishes selected data in an annual report. Arrest data for 2009 are provided in *Crime in the United States, 2009* (September 2010, http://www2.fbi.gov/ucr/cius2009/index.html). The UCR Program provides 2009 arrest data for only three crimes that are widely considered to be white-collar crimes:

- Embezzlement—17,920 arrests
- Forgery and counterfeiting—85,844 arrests
- Fraud—210,255 arrests

The FBI defines these crimes as:

- Embezzlement—"The unlawful misappropriation or misapplication by an offender to his/her own use or purpose of money, property, or some other thing of value entrusted to his/her care, custody, or control."

- Forgery and counterfeiting—"The altering, copying, or imitating of something, without authority or right, with the intent to deceive or defraud by passing the copy or thing altered or imitated as that which is original or genuine; or the selling, buying, or possession of an altered, copied, or imitated thing with the intent to deceive or defraud. Attempts are included."

- Fraud—"The intentional perversion of the truth for the purpose of inducing another person or other entity in reliance upon it to part with something of value or to surrender a legal right. Fraudulent conversion and obtaining of money or property by false pretenses. Confidence games and bad checks, except forgeries and counterfeiting, are included."

According to the UCR Program, there were nearly 13.7 million arrests in 2009; thus, arrests for these three white-collar crimes made up only a very small portion (less than 3%) of the total arrests.

The FBI provides 10-year arrest trends for all crimes that are tracked through the UCR Program. The data indicate that arrests for fraud between 2000 and 2009 decreased by 32.5% among male offenders and by 38.7% among female offenders. Arrests for embezzlement decreased by 7.5% among male offenders and by 3.8% among female offenders. Arrests for forgery and counterfeiting decreased by 23.6% among male offenders and by 28.8% among female offenders.

SURVEY RESULTS ON WHITE-COLLAR CRIME VICTIMIZATIONS

The National White Collar Crime Center (NW3C) is a congressionally funded nonprofit corporation whose members are involved in the investigation and enforcement of laws dealing with white-collar crime. In 2010 the NW3C conducted a national survey of 2,503 adults in which the participants were asked about their experiences and those of their households with white-collar crime during the previous 12 months. The results are presented by Rodney Huff, Christian Desilets, and John Kane in *The 2010 National Public Survey on White Collar Crime* (December 2010, http://crimesurvey.nw3c.org/docs/nw3c 2010survey.pdf).

Twenty-four percent of households and 17% of individuals surveyed reported they had been a victim of white-collar crime during the previous year. The most common white-collar crimes experienced by households included credit card fraud (39.6% of reported incidents), being misled about the price of a product or service (28.1%), paying for unnecessary repairs (22.3%), monetary losses due to Internet fraud (15.8%), and identity theft (12.2%). Of the households that experienced a white-collar crime, 54.7% reported the crime to at least one organization (such as a credit card company, business, or personal attorney) and 18.8% reported the crime to the police. The most commonly reported crimes to law enforcement by individuals were false stockbroker information (56.3%), identity theft (46.6%), and mortgage fraud (42.9%).

IDENTITY THEFT STATISTICS FROM THE BUREAU OF JUSTICE STATISTICS

As the 21st century progresses, more and more transactions of every type are handled remotely using cellular phones, computers, and the Internet. Identity thieves steal personal information from victims, such as their Social Security, driver's license, credit card, or other identification numbers, and then set up new bank or credit card accounts or otherwise misrepresent themselves as their victims to obtain money, goods, or services fraudulently.

As noted in Chapter 3, the Bureau of Justice Statistics (BJS) performs a detailed examination of U.S. crime victims through its National Crime Victimization Survey (NCVS). This annual survey measures the levels of victimization resulting from specific criminal acts. The data collected are extrapolated to the entire U.S. population to provide estimates of criminal victimization at the national level.

In 2004 the BJS first added questions about identity theft to the NCVS survey. The results for the 2007 survey are reported by Lynn Langton and Katrina Baum of the BJS in *Identity Theft Reported by Households, 2007— Statistical Tables* (June 2010, http://bjs.ojp.usdoj.gov/con tent/pub/pdf/itrh07st.pdf).

According to Langton and Baum, the NCVS defines identity theft as any one of the following criminal acts:

- Unauthorized use or attempted unauthorized use of a victim's credit cards

- Unauthorized use or attempted unauthorized use of a victim's accounts, for example, bank, checking or debit, or cellular phone accounts

- Misuse of a victim's personal information for the purpose of opening new accounts, obtaining loans, or committing other crimes

Langton and Baum note that 7.9 million U.S. households reported experiencing identity theft in 2007, representing 6.6% of all U.S. households. The latter value is up from 5.5% in 2005. About 49% of the victimized households in 2007 experienced unauthorized use of credit cards, 24% had unauthorized use of other existing accounts (such as a bank account), and 13% reported misuse of their personal information. The remaining 14% of victimized households experienced multiple types of identity theft.

Demographic data reveal that whites suffered the most identity theft victimizations in 2007. White victims numbered more than 6.5 million, accounting for 82% of all victims. High-income households (i.e., those with annual incomes of $75,000 or more) were more likely to be victimized than lower-income households.

Overall, the average loss per victimized household from all types of identity theft was $1,830. Households that experienced misuse of personal information lost approximately three times the average amount.

IDENTITY THEFT AND CONSUMER FRAUD REPORTED BY THE FEDERAL TRADE COMMISSION

The Federal Trade Commission (FTC) operates a complaint database known as the Consumer Sentinel Network (CSN) that compiles consumer complaints about identity theft, consumer fraud, and related offenses. The data are made available to law enforcement agencies, such as the FBI, to assist in their investigations of white-collar crimes. The FTC publishes an annual report that summarizes CSN data collected within the previous year. According to the FTC, in *Consumer Sentinel Network Data Book for January–December 2009* (February 2010, http://www.ftc.gov/sentinel/reports/senti nel-annual-reports/sentinel-cy2009.pdf), the CSN compiles complaints that are filed with the FTC and other agencies and organizations, including the following:

- Better Business Bureaus

- Internet Crime Complaint Center

- Canada's PhoneBusters

- U.S. Postal Inspection Service

FIGURE 5.1

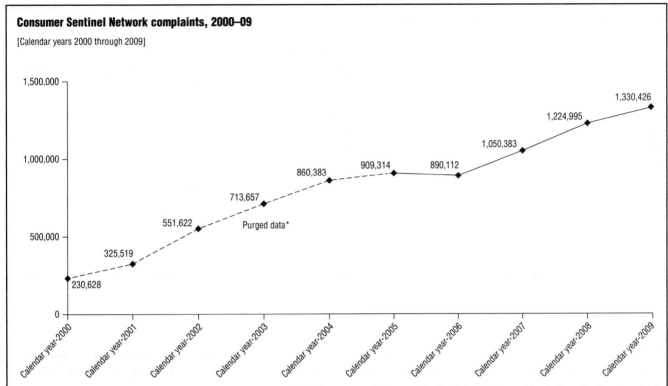

Consumer Sentinel Network complaints, 2000–09

[Calendar years 2000 through 2009]

*Complaint counts from calendar year 2000 to calendar year 2004 represent historic figures as per the Consumer Sentinel Network's five-year data retention policy. These complaint figures exclude National Do Not Call Registry complaints.

SOURCE: "Consumer Sentinel Network Complaint Count, Calendar Years 2000 through 2009," in *Consumer Sentinel Network Data Book for January–December 2009*, U.S. Federal Trade Commission, February 2010, http://www.ftc.gov/sentinel/reports/sentinel-annual-reports/sentinel-cy2009.pdf (accessed October 26, 2010)

- Identity Theft Assistance Center
- National Fraud Information Center

As of 2009, the CSN had over 5.4 million complaints in its database. Figure 5.1 shows the number of complaints that were registered each year between 2000 and 2009. Note that complaints are purged (eliminated) from the database after five years. In 2009 the CSN received more than 1.3 million complaints, the highest number ever recorded.

Table 5.1 provides a breakdown by complaint type (fraud, identity theft, or other) between 2000 and 2009. In every year that is listed, fraud complaints outnumbered identity theft and other complaints. In 2009 the CSN recorded 721,418 fraud complaints, which represented 54.2% of the total complaints that year. Identity theft complaints accounted for 20.9% (278,078) of the total and other complaints made up 24.9% (330,930) of the total.

Fraud Victims

CSN data indicate that fraud victims lost a total of $1.7 billion in 2009. As shown in Figure 5.2, Internet-based e-mail was the most commonly cited method by which fraudsters contacted victimized consumers in 2009. Nearly half (48%) of the contacts that were associated with CSN-reported fraud occurred via this method. Another 12% of

contacts occurred through other Internet means (e.g., web-sites), and 22% occurred more traditionally through the mail system (12%) or by telephone (10%).

Identity Theft Victims

Table 5.2 lists the top-20 CSN complaint categories for 2009. Identity theft (21%) was the most prevalent complaint. It was followed by complaints about third-party and creditor debt collections (9%), Internet services (6%), shop-at-home and catalog sales (6%), and foreign money offers and counterfeit check scams (5%).

According to the FTC, fraudulent use of a credit card was reported by 17% of identity theft complainants during 2009. This entails thieves using stolen identities to open new credit card accounts or tapping into victims' existing credit card accounts. Another significant type of identity theft was government documents/benefits fraud, which accounted for 16% of the total. Thieves used stolen identities to file fraudulent tax returns or to apply for or obtain government benefits or documents, such as driver's licenses or Social Security cards. In 15% of the total identity fraud complaints, stolen identities were used by thieves to open new telephone, wireless, or utilities accounts or to fraudulently make charges to victims' existing accounts. Another 13% of identity theft complaints involved

TABLE 5.1

Consumer Sentinel Network complaints, by type of complaint, 2000–09

| Calendar year | Consumer Sentinel Network complaint count | | | |
	Fraud	Identity theft	Other	Total complaints
2000	111,255	31,140	88,233	230,628
2001	137,306	86,250	101,963	325,519
2002	242,783	161,977	146,862	551,622
2003	331,366	215,240	167,051	713,657
2004	410,298	246,909	203,176	860,383
2005	437,585	255,687	216,042	909,314
2006	428,398	246,214	215,500	890,112
2007	577,902	259,314	213,167	1,050,383
2008	644,356	314,484	266,155	1,224,995
2009	721,418	278,078	330,930	1,330,426

Note: Complaint counts from calendar year 2000 to calendar year 2004 represents historic figures as per the Consumer Sentinel Network's five-year data retention policy. These complaint figures exclude National Do Not Call Registry complaints.

SOURCE: "Consumer Sentinel Network Complaint Type Count, Calendar Years 2000 through 2009," in *Consumer Sentinel Network Data Book for January–December 2009*, U.S. Federal Trade Commission, February 2010, http://www.ftc.gov/sentinel/reports/sentinel-annual-reports/sentinel-cy2009.pdf (accessed October 26, 2010)

FIGURE 5.2

Consumer Sentinel Network complaints, by company's method of contacting consumer, 2009

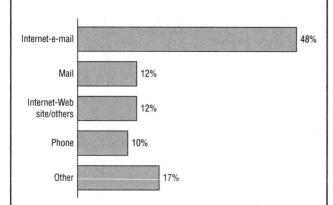

Internet-e-mail 48%
Mail 12%
Internet-Web site/others 12%
Phone 10%
Other 17%

Note: Percentages are based on the total number of Consumer Sentinel Network fraud complaints for each calendar year where consumers reported the company's method of initial contact: Calendar year 2007 = 307,265; calendar year 2008 = 376,698; and calendar year 2009 = 449,563. Sixty-two percent of consumers reported this information during calendar year 2009, 53 percent and 58 percent for calendar year 2007 and calendar year 2008, respectively.

SOURCE: "Consumer Sentinel Network Fraud Complaints by Company's Method of Contacting Consumers, January 1–December 31, 2009," in *Consumer Sentinel Network Data Book for January–December 2009*, U.S. Federal Trade Commission, February 2010, http://www.ftc.gov/sentinel/reports/sentinel-annual-reports/sentinel-cy2009.pdf (accessed October 26, 2010)

TABLE 5.2

Top 20 Consumer Sentinel Network complaint categories, 2009

Rank	Category	No. of complaints	Percentages
1	Identity theft	278,078	21%
2	Third party and creditor debt collection	119,549	9%
3	Internet services	83,067	6%
4	Shop-at-home and catalog sales	74,581	6%
5	Foreign money offers and counterfeit check scams	61,736	5%
6	Internet auction	57,821	4%
7	Credit cards	45,203	3%
8	Prizes, sweepstakes and lotteries	41,763	3%
9	Advance-fee loans and credit protection/repair	41,448	3%
10	Banks and lenders	32,443	2%
11	Credit bureaus, information furnishers and report users	31,629	2%
12	Television and electronic media	26,568	2%
13	Health care	25,414	2%
14	Business opportunities, employment agencies and work-at-home plans	22,896	2%
15	Computer equipment and software	22,621	2%
16	Telecom equipment	22,377	2%
17	Auto related complaints	22,372	2%
18	Travel, vacations and timeshare plans	15,386	1%
19	Debt management and credit counseling	13,401	1%
20	Telephone and mobile services	10,939	1%

Notes: Percentages are based on the total number of Consumer Sentinel Network complaints (1,330,426) received by the Federal Trade Commission between January 1 and December 31, 2009. Thirteen percent (178,878) of the total Consumer Sentinel Network complaints received by the Federal Trade Commission were coded Other (Note in Comments).

SOURCE: Adapted from "Consumer Sentinel Network Complaint Categories, January 1–December 31, 2009," in *Consumer Sentinel Network Data Book for January–December 2009*, U.S. Federal Trade Commission, February 2010, http://www.ftc.gov/sentinel/reports/sentinel-annual-reports/sentinel-cy2009.pdf (accessed October 26, 2010)

---

employment-related fraud, such as obtaining employment by pretending to be someone else.

CSN data indicate that 62% of identity theft victims filed reports about the incidents with the police in 2009. Another 11% said they notified the police about the incidents, but either the reports were not filed or the victims did not indicate if a report was taken. The remaining 28% of self-reported identity theft victims in 2009 said they did not notify the police about the incidents.

DATA BREACHES AND IDENTITY THEFT

Since the 1990s well-organized rings of identity thieves have emerged that engage in large-scale thefts known as data breaches. These are crimes in which the computer records of businesses, government agencies, universities, or other organizations are breached for the purpose of obtaining the personal and/or financial data of large numbers of people. The phenomenon is described by Kimberly Kiefer Peretti of the U.S. Department of Justice (DOJ) in *Data Breaches: What the Underground World of "Carding" Reveals* (May 2008, http://www.cybercrime.gov/DataBreachesArticle.pdf).

Peretti defines *carding* as the large-scale theft of credit and/or debit card account numbers and other financial information. (See Table 5.3.) She notes that carding is an especially worrisome crime because carders have created fast and effective methods for disseminating the stolen information to other criminals. This is achieved through websites known as carding forums, where fraudsters buy and sell stolen personal and financial information. Large-scale data breaches first gained public attention in 2005, when carders stole the financial records of 163,000 consumers from the computer systems of Choicepoint, Inc. The company notified California consumers about the breach in accordance with a 2003 law requiring companies to alert individuals whose data records have been stolen.

Since that time other large data breaches have prompted many states to pass similar legislation.

FINANCIAL CRIMES REPORTED BY THE FBI

The FBI's Financial Crime Section investigates certain offenses relating to fraud, theft, and embezzlement. According to the FBI, in *Financial Crimes Report to the Public, Fiscal Year 2009 (October 1, 2008–September 30, 2009)*, these white-collar crimes include corruption by public officials, corporate fraud, mortgage fraud, securities and commodities fraud, health care fraud, financial institution fraud, insurance fraud, mass marketing fraud, and money laundering. Data on all these offenses, excluding corruption by public officials, are addressed in the FBI report.

Corporate Fraud Reported by the FBI

According to the FBI, most of the corporate fraud cases it investigates involve accounting schemes that businesses use to deceive their investors, analysts, or auditors about the financial soundness of their companies. Corporations may overstate their financial worth to artificially inflate the value of their stock on the stock markets. Executives participating in these schemes often sell their stock for a high profit before the deception is discovered, bringing them significant personal financial gain. Other investors lose large sums of money after the truth comes out and the company's stock plummets in value.

TABLE 5.3

Definitions of various white collar crimes

Account takeover	A type of identity theft involving fraud on existing financial accounts, for example, when a criminal uses a stolen credit card number to make fraudulent purchases on an existing credit line.
Carders	Individuals engaged in criminal carding activities.
Carding	Large scale theft of credit and/or debit card account numbers and other financial information.
Carding forums	Criminal websites dedicated to the sale of stolen personal and financial information to fraudsters worldwide.
Carding online	Using stolen credit card information to make purchases of goods and services online from merchants.
Cashing	Obtaining money, rather than retail goods and services, with the unauthorized use of stolen financial information, for example, withdrawing cash at ATMs.
Data breach	An organization's unauthorized or unintentional exposure, disclosure, or loss of sensitive personal information, such as Social Security numbers or credit card numbers.
Dumps	Information electronically copied from the magnetic stripe on the back of credit and debit cards. This information includes customer name, account number, etc.
Dumpster diving	Rummaging through garbage cans or trash bins to obtain copies of checks, credit card or bank statements, etc., and using this information to assume a person's identity.
Full info (or fulls)	A package of data about a victim, including address, phone number, social security number, credit or debit account numbers and PINs, credit history report, mother's maiden name, and other identifying information.
Gift card vending	Purchasing gift cards from retail merchants at their physical stores using counterfeit credit cards and reselling the gift cards for a percentage of their actual value.
In-store carding	Presenting a counterfeit credit card that had been encoded with stolen account information to a cashier at a physical retail store location.
Malicious code	For hacking purposes, this is a computer program placed unknowingly on a victim's computer that allows for the capture of personal and financial data.
New account creation	A type of identity theft involving fraudulent creation of new accounts, for example, when a criminal uses stolen data to open a bank or credit card account in someone else's name.
Phishing	Using 'spoofed' emails to "lead consumers to counterfeit websites designed to trick them into divulging financial data such as credit card numbers. Phishing can also involve placing malicious code onto an individual's computer without the individual's awareness to steal personal information directly.
Skimming	Criminal use of an electronic storage device to read and record the encoded data on the magnetic stripe on the back of a credit or debit card. Typical examples involve rogue employees at restaurants that swipe a patron's card in the skimming device prior to swiping it through the restaurant's own card reader or attaching the skimming device to an ATM.
Wardriving	Driving around in a vehicle with a laptop and a high-powered antenna to locate, and potentially exploit, wireless computer systems of vulnerable targets. Once inside the system, a criminal can intercept wireless communications and capture credit card numbers and other personal identification information.

SOURCE: Adapted from Kimberly Kiefer Peretti, *Data Breaches: What the Underground World of "Carding" Reveals*, U.S. Department of Justice, Computer Crime and Intellectual Property Section, May 2008, http://www.cybercrime.gov/DataBreachesArticle.pdf (accessed November 24, 2010)

FIGURE 5.3

Pending federal court cases of corporate fraud, fiscal years 2005–09

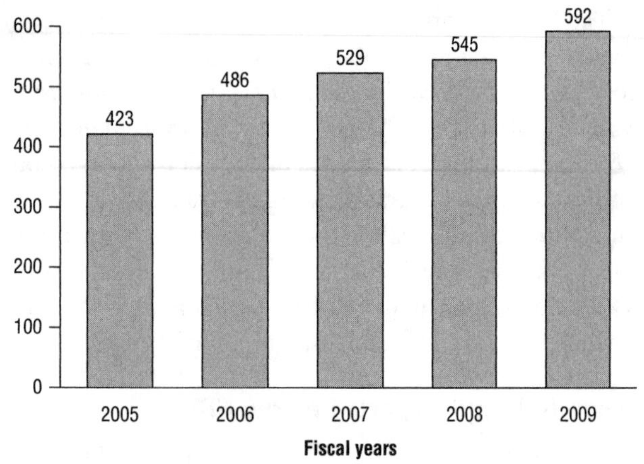

[Bar chart showing pending federal court cases of corporate fraud by fiscal year:
2005: 423
2006: 486
2007: 529
2008: 545
2009: 592
Y-axis ranges from 0 to 600. X-axis labeled "Fiscal years"]

SOURCE: "Corporate Fraud Pending Cases," in *Financial Crimes Report to the Public, Fiscal Year 2009 (October 1, 2008–September 30, 2009)*, U.S. Department of Justice, Federal Bureau of Investigation, undated, http://www2.fbi.gov/publications/financial/fcs_report2009/financial_crime_2009.htm (accessed October 26, 2010)

FIGURE 5.4

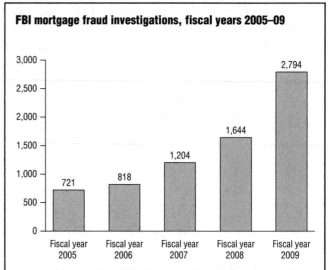

FBI mortgage fraud investigations, fiscal years 2005–09

[Bar chart showing FBI mortgage fraud investigations by fiscal year:
Fiscal year 2005: 721
Fiscal year 2006: 818
Fiscal year 2007: 1,204
Fiscal year 2008: 1,644
Fiscal year 2009: 2,794
Y-axis ranges from 0 to 3,000.]

SOURCE: "Mortgage Fraud," in *Financial Crimes Report to the Public, Fiscal Year 2009 (October 1, 2008–September 30, 2009)*, U.S. Department of Justice, Federal Bureau of Investigation, undated, http://www2.fbi.gov/publications/financial/fcs_report2009/financial_crime_2009.htm (accessed October 26, 2010)

Figure 5.3 shows the number of corporate fraud cases being pursued by the FBI between fiscal years (FYs) 2005 and 2009. The number grew from 423 cases in FY 2005 to 592 cases in FY 2009. The FBI's investigations into corporate fraud resulted in 153 indictments and 156 convictions in FY 2009. A total of $6.1 billion in restitutions (an amount of money that is set by a court to be paid to the victim of a crime for property losses or injuries caused by the crime) and $5.4 million in fines were secured by the federal government from convicted corporate criminals in FY 2009.

Mortgage Fraud Reported by the FBI

The FBI indicates that mortgage fraud typically involves "material misstatement, misrepresentation, or omission relating to the property or potential borrower which is relied on by an underwriter or lender to fund, purchase, or insure a loan." These cases fall into two broad categories: fraud for profit and fraud for housing. Fraud for profit is conducted by industry insiders, for example, loan officers or appraisers. Fraud for housing is perpetrated by individuals who seek housing through false pretenses, for example, by lying about their assets or income on a mortgage loan application.

Figure 5.4 shows the number of mortgage fraud cases pending in federal courts between FYs 2005 and 2009. The number skyrocketed from 721 cases in FY 2005 to 2,794 cases in FY 2009. The FBI achieved 822 indictments and 494 convictions for mortgage fraud through FY 2009. Approximately $2.5 billion in restitutions, $7.5 million in recoveries, and $58.4 million in fines were collected.

One of the notable convictions reported by the FBI is of Viktor Kobzar, a mortgage broker based in Seattle, Washington. He and his coconspirators were accused of buying "luxury" homes and illegally flipping them. Flipping is a crime in which a buyer purchases a property and pays an appraiser to create false documents saying the property is worth much more than it is actually worth. The buyer then sells the property for a huge profit. In January 2010 Kobzar was sentenced to five years in prison for his role in the flipping scheme.

Mortgage fraud is often brought to the FBI's attention through the filing of a Suspicious Activity Report (SAR) by a financial institution or the U.S. Department of Housing and Urban Development. SARs are filed with the U.S. Department of the Treasury and shared with law enforcement agencies. They can be triggered by any financial transaction that arouses the suspicion of a participating business. The number of mortgage-related SARs surged from 21,994 in FY 2005 to 67,190 in FY 2009. (See Figure 5.5.) This huge increase is believed to be related to the significant downturn in the real estate and housing market in 2005 and the subsequent economic recession that lasted from late 2007 to mid-2009.

In December 2008 the FBI created the National Mortgage Fraud Team (NMFT) to investigate "criminal organizations and individuals" engaging in mortgage fraud schemes against financial institutions. The NMFT spearheaded the creation of dozens of regional task forces and working groups around the country composed of federal, state, and local law enforcement representatives to investigate mortgage fraud complaints.

FIGURE 5.5

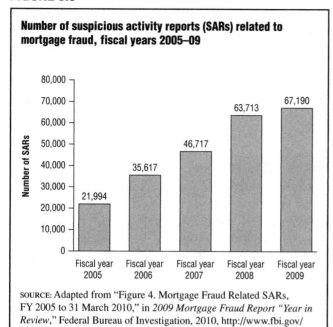

Number of suspicious activity reports (SARs) related to mortgage fraud, fiscal years 2005–09

SOURCE: Adapted from "Figure 4. Mortgage Fraud Related SARs, FY 2005 to 31 March 2010," in *2009 Mortgage Fraud Report "Year in Review*," Federal Bureau of Investigation, 2010, http://www.fbi.gov/stats-services/publications/mortgage-fraud-2009 (accessed November 22, 2010)

FIGURE 5.6

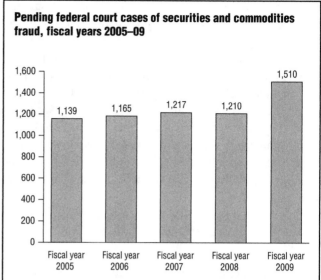

Pending federal court cases of securities and commodities fraud, fiscal years 2005–09

SOURCE: "Securities and Commodities Fraud Pending Cases," in *Financial Crimes Report to the Public, Fiscal Year 2009 (October 1, 2008–September 30, 2009)*, U.S. Department of Justice, Federal Bureau of Investigation, undated, http://www2.fbi.gov/publications/financial/fcs_report2009/financial_crime_2009.htm (accessed October 26, 2010)

Securities and Commodities Fraud Reported by the FBI

Securities are financial instruments, such as stocks, bonds, and mutual funds. Commodities are raw materials, foreign currencies, or other objects of investment. Securities and commodities fraud offenses are complicated crimes in which investment companies or managers use sophisticated schemes to trick investors out of their money. According to the FBI, the most common schemes involve manipulating the price of securities or commodities or selling them under false pretenses.

Figure 5.6 shows the number of securities and commodities fraud cases being investigated by the FBI between FYs 2005 and 2009. The number grew from 1,139 cases in FY 2005 to 1,510 cases in FY 2009. The FBI reports achieving 412 indictments and 306 convictions in FY 2009 for these types of fraud cases. In FY 2009, $8.1 billion in restitutions, $63.4 million in recoveries, and $12.8 million in fines were collected.

One of the most significant cases investigated by the FBI was the enormous Ponzi scheme managed by Bernard Madoff (1938–), an influential Wall Street executive who had served as the chairman of NASDAQ during the 1990s. Named after Charles Ponzi (1883–1949), an Italian immigrant who defrauded investors in Boston, Massachusetts, in the early 20th century, a Ponzi scheme is also known as a pyramid scheme. Its victims are lured with promises of large, quick returns on their investments. Rather than providing legitimate investment services, however, the swindler uses the investment monies of those lower on the pyramid (the new investors) to provide payouts to those higher up in the scheme. Larger and larger numbers of investors are always needed to keep sending money up the levels of the pyramid, a situation that cannot be sustained forever, and the scheme is eventually exposed. At the time of Madoff's arrest, the U.S. Securities and Exchange Commission (SEC) reported in the press release "SEC Charges Bernard L. Madoff for Multi-billion Dollar Ponzi Scheme" (December 11, 2008, http://www.sec.gov/news/press/2008/2008-293.htm) that Madoff estimated the fraud losses to his victims to total "at least $50 billion."

Madoff was the founder and chairman of Bernard L. Madoff Investment Securities LLC, a leading Wall Street firm established in 1960. Ruthie Ackerman indicates in "Market Maker Arrested in Ponzi Scheme He Estimated at $50B" (*Forbes*, December 11, 2008) that at the time of Madoff's arrest the firm claimed $700 million in capital and prided itself, according to its website, on the "unblemished record of value, fair-dealing, and high ethical standards that has always been the firm's hallmark." However, besides the investment firm, Madoff also conducted a side business as an investment adviser, kept multiple sets of books, maintained secrecy about his investments, and provided false reports of his activities to federal regulators and to his clients. In the press release "Statement Regarding Madoff Investigation" (December 16, 2008, http://www.sec.gov/news/press/2008/2008-297.htm), Christopher Cox (1952–), the chairman of the SEC, explains that Madoff's influence included an advisory role to the SEC, a relationship Madoff used to his advantage and one that led SEC staff to dismiss accusations against him that first came to their attention during the late 1990s.

When Madoff's list of clients was made public in early February 2009, it included thousands of institutions and individuals, including investment funds, pension funds, charitable organizations, financiers, Hollywood celebrities, and many private investors who expressed alarm at the sudden, unsought media exposure of their personal finances. In March 2009 Madoff pleaded guilty to 11 felony counts against him in federal court, including securities fraud, investment adviser fraud, mail fraud, wire fraud, money laundering, making false statements, perjury, making false filings with the SEC, and theft from an employee benefit plan. In June 2009 Madoff was sentenced to 150 years in prison.

Health Care Fraud Reported by the FBI

Health care fraud occurs when individuals or businesses cheat public or private health care systems out of money. Many of these crimes are perpetrated by insiders, for example, by doctors or other practitioners who overbill insurance companies or perform unnecessary services. Many other offenses are included in this category, such as selling medical equipment or prescription drugs under false pretenses. The latter can occur through Internet pharmacies or businesses that illegally sell prescription-only drugs, appliances, or counterfeit or stolen pharmaceuticals.

Figure 5.7 shows the number of health care fraud cases pending in federal courts between FYs 2005 and 2009. The number has hovered around 2,400 to 2,500 cases each year. FBI investigations produced 945 indictments and 640 convictions through FY 2009. In addition, the agency secured $1.6 billion in restitutions, $853 million in recoveries, $68 million in fines, and $54 million in seizures in FY 2009.

FIGURE 5.7

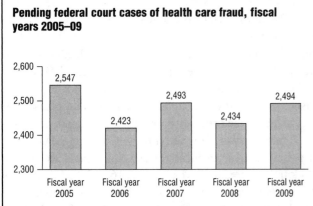

Pending federal court cases of health care fraud, fiscal years 2005–09

SOURCE: "Health Care Fraud," in *Financial Crimes Report to the Public, Fiscal Year 2009 (October 1, 2008–September 30, 2009)*, U.S. Department of Justice, Federal Bureau of Investigation, undated, http://www2.fbi.gov/publications/financial/fcs_report2009/financial_crime_2009.htm (accessed October 26, 2010)

The FBI reports that one of its most significant cases involved a medical doctor who was accused of defrauding Medicare, Medicaid, and other health care benefit programs. Hany M. Iskander operated pain management clinics in Ohio. He allegedly submitted millions of dollars in fraudulent insurance claims for medical services that were either not performed on patients or were medically unnecessary. In February 2010 he was sentenced to 42 months in prison and ordered to pay nearly $7 million in restitution.

Insurance Fraud Reported by the FBI

Insurance fraud involves a number of crimes that may be perpetrated by industry insiders against policyholders or vice versa. Note that fraud involving health care insurance is not included in this category, but is tracked separately. The FBI reports that the most common types of insider insurance fraud involve misuse of policyholder premiums. This can occur when insurance agents or brokers keep premiums for their own financial gain. Fraud by policyholders most often takes the form of willful destruction of property (e.g., arson to collect insurance proceeds) or making other false claims.

The FBI reports that it was investigating 152 insurance fraud cases in FY 2009. The agency achieved 43 indictments, 22 arrests, and 42 convictions that year. In addition, $22.9 million in restitutions, $31.4 million in recoveries, and $618,480 in seizures were obtained in FY 2009.

One case cited by the FBI involved an insurance executive who was accused of collecting workers' compensation premiums and then not submitting those monies to insurance companies. In 2009 John Wayne Goff was sentenced to 12 years in prison for various charges including filing a false report with the Alabama Department of Insurance. The FBI notes that Goff used the proceeds from his scheme to finance his own "exorbitant salary" and to support a "lavish lifestyle."

Mass Marketing Fraud Reported by the FBI

Mass marketing fraud is a general term for fraud that is perpetrated by a form of mass communications, such as the telephone or Internet. Typically, the victim of the scam is asked to pay some fee to secure a prize from a lottery or sweepstakes or to facilitate the transfer of a larger sum of money to the victim's possession. One of the best-known schemes in this category is the so-called Nigerian e-mail fraud wherein victims are asked to pay fees to help transfer a large sum of money out of Nigeria. For their help, the victims are promised a substantial payment from the transferred funds. Victims pay the up-front fee, but never receive the promised payment.

The FBI reports that it was investigating 89 cases of mass marketing fraud at year-end FY 2009. The FBI acknowledges that many of these crimes are perpetrated by criminals in foreign nations, making them difficult to prosecute. The agency believes the best solution for combating mass marketing fraud lies in better consumer education.

One significant case that the FBI investigated involved a criminal enterprise operating in Israel. The perpetrators told elderly people in the United States they had won large cash prizes in an international sweepstakes lottery, but had to pay thousands of dollars in fees to collect the winnings. The victims were reportedly duped out of at least $2 million. The investigation by the FBI in concert with the Tel Aviv Fraud Division of the Israel National Police resulted in the arrests of eight suspects in 2009.

Money Laundering Reported by the FBI

The FBI defines money laundering as "the process by which criminals conceal or disguise the proceeds of their crimes or convert those proceeds into goods and services. It allows criminals to infuse their illegal money into the stream of commerce, thus corrupting financial institutions and the money supply, thereby giving criminals unwarranted economic power." In other words, money laundering is the process of making criminally obtained money look legitimate. The FBI's Financial Crimes Section focuses only on money laundering cases in which the money is derived from other white-collar crimes, for example, securities fraud.

Figure 5.8 shows the number of money laundering cases pending in federal courts between FYs 2005 and 2009. The number gradually declined over this period, from 507 cases in FY 2005 to 350 cases in FY 2009. The agency obtained 43 indictments and 84 convictions and secured $81.9 million in restitutions, $643,000 in recoveries, and $1.5 million in fines associated with these types of cases in FY 2009.

The FBI reports that it has been investigating money laundering conducted by members of La Cosa Nostra, an organized crime group also known as the Mafia. The perpetrators were allegedly operating an Internet gambling operation based in Costa Rica. According to the FBI, the investigation has uncovered evidence of money laundering and other white-collar crimes, including the movement of "vast sums of money around the world while effectively masking the associated transactions."

FAMOUS CORPORATE CRIMES: ENRON

The collapse of Enron Corporation is one of the most glaring examples of corporate crime and falsification of corporate data in recent history. Based in Houston, Texas, Enron was an energy broker that traded in electricity and other energy commodities. During the late 1990s, however, instead of simply brokering energy deals, Enron devised increasingly complex contracts with buyers and sellers that allowed Enron to profit from the difference in the selling price and the buying price of commodities such as electricity. Enron executives created a number of partnerships—in effect, companies that existed only on paper whose sole function was to hide debt and make Enron appear to be much more profitable than it actually was.

In December 2001 Enron filed for bankruptcy protection, listing some $13.1 billion in liabilities and $24.7 billion in assets—$38 billion less than the assets listed only two months earlier. As a result, thousands of Enron employees lost their jobs. In addition, many Enron staff—who had been encouraged by company executives to invest monies from their 401(k) retirement plans in Enron stock—had their retirement savings reduced to almost nothing as a result of the precipitous decline in value of Enron stock.

In the wake of Enron's collapse, several committees in the U.S. Senate and U.S. House of Representatives began to investigate whether Enron defrauded investors by deliberately concealing financial information. Many lawsuits were filed against Enron, its accounting firm Arthur Andersen, and former Enron executives including the former chairman Kenneth L. Lay (1942–2006) and the former chief executive officer Jeffrey Skilling (1953–).

The Enron treasurer Ben Glisan Jr. (1966–) was convicted of conspiracy charges to commit wire and securities fraud. He was sentenced to five years in prison and was released in January 2007. Lay and Skilling went on trial in January 2006. Kristen Hays reports in "Prosecutor: Lay, Skilling Committed Crimes" (Associated Press, May 16, 2006) that the federal prosecutor Kathryn H. Ruemmler (1971–) accused the men of using "accounting tricks, fiction, hocus-pocus, trickery, misleading statements, half-truths, omissions and outright lies" in committing their crimes. On May 25 a jury found Lay guilty of all six counts against him in the corporate trial; he was also convicted of four counts of fraud in a separate trial relating to his personal finances. He faced 20 to 30 years in prison

FIGURE 5.8

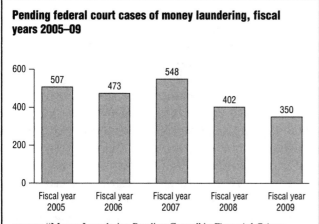

Pending federal court cases of money laundering, fiscal years 2005–09

SOURCE: "Money Laundering Pending Cases," in *Financial Crimes Report to the Public, Fiscal Year 2009 (October 1, 2008–September 30, 2009),* U.S. Department of Justice, Federal Bureau of Investigation, undated, http://www2.fbi.gov/publications/financial/fcs_report2009/financial_crime_2009.htm (accessed October 26, 2010)

but died of a heart attack in July 2006, before the judge set his sentence. The jury found Skilling guilty of 19 of the 28 counts against him, and he was sentenced to 24 years and four months in federal prison. Skilling began serving his sentence at a low-security federal facility in Waseca, Minnesota, and is projected to be released in 2028. Dozens of other people were charged in the Enron scandal. In February 2008 three British bankers prosecuted for their roles were given 37-month prison terms.

In June 2002 a New York jury found the accounting firm Arthur Andersen guilty of obstructing justice in connection with the Enron collapse. The firm was convicted of destroying Enron documents during an ongoing federal investigation of Enron's accounting practices. As a result of the verdict, Arthur Andersen faced a fine of $500,000 and a probation term of up to five years. In 2005 the U.S. Supreme Court overturned this conviction due to flaws in the instructions that had been given to the jury. However, the firm was effectively out of the accounting business with its few remaining U.S. employees responsible for administrating the many legal cases generated by the scandal.

The Enron scandal helped lead to the passage of the Sarbanes-Oxley Act (SOX), which was signed into law in July 2002. The law was designed to rebuild public trust in the U.S. corporate sector by imposing new criminal and civil penalties for security violations and establishing a new certification system for internal audits. SOX also grants independent auditors more access to company data and requires increased disclosure of compensation methods and systems, especially for upper management.

COMPUTER CRIME
Federal Computer Crime Legislation

In 1986 Congress passed the Computer Fraud and Abuse Act (CFAA), which makes it illegal to perpetrate fraud on a computer. This law was followed in 1994 by the Computer Abuse Amendments Act, which makes it a federal crime "through means of a computer used in interstate commerce or communications ... [to] damage, or cause damage to, a computer, computer system, network, information, data, or program ... with reckless disregard" for the consequences of these actions to the computer owner. This law pertains to maliciously destroying or changing computer records or knowingly distributing malware (i.e., malicious software or programs, such as viruses, Trojans, or worms, that are designed to interfere in the working of a computer system and/or allow a perpetrator access to someone else's computer system). Malware can be transmitted by downloading music, games, or other types of software or by clicking on e-mail attachments.

The 2001 Uniting and Strengthening America by Providing Appropriate Tools Required to Intercept and Obstruct Terrorism (USA PATRIOT) Act, which gave increased powers to U.S. law enforcement and intelligence agencies to help prevent terrorist attacks, amended the CFAA. The act was expanded to include the types of electronic records that law enforcement authorities may obtain without a subpoena, including records of Internet session times and durations, as well as temporarily assigned network addresses. The PATRIOT Act was reauthorized in March 2006 in the USA PATRIOT Improvement and Reauthorization Act of 2005.

Internet Fraud

In *IC3 2009 Internet Crime Report* (March 2010, http://www.ic3.gov/media/annualreport/2009_ic3report.pdf), the Internet Crime Complaint Center (IC3) notes that it received 336,655 complaints of Internet crime in 2009. This represents a 22.3% increase from 2008, when the center received 275,284 complaints. The total dollar cost of all cases of Internet fraud referred to law enforcement agencies was $559.7 million, with a median loss (half of the losses where higher and half of the losses were lower) of $575 per complaint. This shows a significant upward trend from $264.6 million in 2008. According to IC3, the top-three complaint categories in 2009 were nondelivered merchandise and/or payment (19.9% of complaints), identity theft (14.1% of complaints), and credit card/debit card fraud (10.4% of complaints).

SPAM. The IC3 defines the term *spam* as unsolicited bulk e-mail. According to IC3, spam is widely used to commit traditional white-collar crimes, including financial institution fraud, credit card fraud, and identity theft. Spam messages are usually considered unsolicited because the recipients have not chosen to receive the messages. Generally, spam involves multiple identical messages sent simultaneously. Spam can also be used to access computers and servers without authorization and transmit viruses or forward spam. Spam senders often sell open proxy information, credit card information, and e-mail lists illegally.

The Controlling the Assault of Non-Solicited Pornography and Marketing (CAN-SPAM) Act of 2003 established requirements for those who send commercial e-mail. CAN-SPAM requires that all spam contain a legitimate return address as well as instructions on how to opt out of receiving additional spam from the sender. Spam must also state in the subject line if the e-mail is pornographic in nature. Violators of these rules are subject to heavy fines.

The law's main provisions include:

- Banning false or misleading header information—the "from," "to," and routing information (including the originating name and e-mail address) must be accurate and identify the person who initiated the e-mail
- Prohibiting deceptive subject lines—the subject line must not mislead the recipient about the e-mail's content or subject matter

- Requiring an opt-out method—senders must provide a return e-mail address or another Internet-based way that allows the recipient to ask the sender not to send any more e-mail messages to him or her

The first person convicted by a jury in a CAN-SPAM case was Jeffrey Brett Goodin (1961–) of California. He was found guilty in January 2007 of operating an Internet-based scheme to obtain personal and credit card information. Goodin sent e-mails to AOL users that appeared to be from AOL's billing department. The messages, which instructed recipients to update their AOL billing information or lose service, referred users to web pages that were actually scam pages set up by Goodin to collect the users' personal and credit card information.

SPYWARE. The Anti-Spyware Coalition (2011, http://www.antispywarecoalition.org/about/FAQ.html), a group that consists of software manufacturers, academics, and consumer advocates, defines spyware as:

> Technologies deployed without appropriate user consent and/or implemented in ways that impair user control over:
>
> - Material changes that affect their user experience, privacy, or system security
> - Use of their system resources, including what programs are installed on their computers, and/or
> - Collection, use and distribution of their personal or other sensitive information

Some states have enacted antispyware legislation. For example, California's Consumer Protection against Computer Spyware Act makes it illegal for anyone to install software on someone else's computer deceptively and use it to modify settings, including the user's home page, default search page, or bookmarks. The act also outlaws collecting, through intentionally deceptive means, personally identifiable information by logging keystrokes, tracking website visits, or extracting personal information from a user's hard drive.

Computer Hacking

Computer hacking takes place when an outsider gains unauthorized access to a secure computer by identifying and exploiting system vulnerabilities. Criminal hackers use their software expertise to crack security codes to access stored information or hijack a computer (i.e., take it over and instruct it to generate spam or perform other malicious actions). The Web Application Security Consortium tracks hacking incidents that have been reported in the media and that result from vulnerabilities in web application security. The consortium (2011, http://projects.webappsec.org/w/page/13246995/Web-Hacking-Incident-Database) reports that the number of web hacking incidents has increased significantly in recent years, from just three in 2000 to 222 in 2010.

One famous hacking case involves Robert Tappan Morris (1965–), the first person ever to be charged under the CFAA. In 1988 Morris allegedly released the first-known computer worm on the Internet. He did not serve prison time, but was put on probation for his crime and had to perform community service and pay a fine. As of February 2011, Morris was a computer science professor at the Massachusetts Institute of Technology.

Two notorious hackers pursued by the FBI during the 1990s were Kevin D. Mitnick (1965–) and Kevin Poulsen (1965–). Both served four- to five-year prison sentences for their computer crimes, and both later became successful businessmen. As of February 2011, Mitnick had his own security consulting firm and Poulsen was a senior editor for *Wired News*.

In 2002 the United Kingdom resident Gary McKinnon was arrested for allegedly hacking into U.S. military computers from his home near London. He claimed he was looking for information about unidentified flying objects, whereas U.S. officials accused him of deliberately deleting important files and crashing computer systems. As of February 2011, McKinnon was fighting extradition to the United States to face trial on the charges.

In "The Great Cyberheist" (*New York Times Magazine*, November 10, 2010), James Verini details the life and crimes of Albert Gonzalez (1981–), who is considered to be the most financially successful hacker in U.S. history. Gonzalez was first arrested in 2003 and became an informant for the federal government to help the U.S. Secret Service capture top members of the Shadowcrew, a semi-organized group of sophisticated cybercriminals. However, Gonzalez secretly continued his own hacking career. He masterminded schemes for breaching corporate computer systems and gained access to millions of credit and debit card account numbers. In 2008 the FBI arrested Gonzalez on multiple charges. He pleaded guilty and in March 2010 was sentenced to 20 years in prison. Verini notes that Gonzalez's crimes allegedly cost the victimized corporations more than $400 million in losses.

INTELLECTUAL PROPERTY

According to the World Intellectual Property Organization (2011, http://www.wipo.int/about-ip/en/), intellectual property consists of "creations of the mind: inventions, literary and artistic works, and symbols, names, images, and designs used in commerce." These include industrial property such as trademarks, chemical formulas, patents, and designs, and copyrighted material such as literary works, films, musical compositions and recordings, graphic and architectural designs, works of art in any medium, and domain names.

In the United States intellectual property is protected by the joint efforts of the U.S. Patent and Trademark

Office, the U.S. Copyright Office, the DOJ, the U.S. Department of Commerce, and two agencies that focus on international aspects of intellectual property: the U.S. Customs and Border Protection, which monitors incoming goods arriving from other nations, and the Office of the U.S. Trade Representative, which negotiates on behalf of U.S. interests and develops and implements trade agreements and policies.

TAX FRAUD

For most Americans, failure to pay the correct amount of taxes to the Internal Revenue Service (IRS) results in an agreement to pay off the taxes in some manner. However, when the IRS believes it has found a pattern of deception designed to avoid paying taxes, criminal charges can be brought against someone. The IRS indicates in "Fiscal Year 2009 Enforcement Results" (December 22, 2010, http://www.irs.gov/pub/irs-drop/fy_2009_enforcement_results.pdf) that in FY 2009 it recommended 2,570 cases for prosecution. The IRS also notes that it had an 87.2% conviction rate for cases that were prosecuted in FY 2009.

FORGERY AND COUNTERFEITING

As technology advances, forgers can use sophisticated computers, scanners, and laser printers to make copies of more and more documents, including counterfeit checks, identification badges, driver's licenses, and money.

Making counterfeit U.S. currency or altering genuine currency to increase its value is punishable by a fine, imprisonment of up to 15 years, or both. Possession of counterfeit U.S. currency is also a crime that is punishable by a fine, imprisonment of up to 15 years, or both. Counterfeiting is not limited to paper money. Manufacturing counterfeit U.S. coins in any denomination above five cents is subject to the same penalties as all other counterfeit activities. Anyone who alters a real coin to increase its value to collectors can be punished by a fine, imprisonment of up to five years, or both.

In response to the growing use of computer-generated counterfeit money, the Department of the Treasury redesigned the $50 and $100 notes during the 1990s and introduced new $5, $10, and $20 notes between 1998 and 2000. These notes contained a watermark that made them harder to copy accurately. According to the Bureau of Engraving and Printing, in "Currency Redesign" (2010, http://www.newmoney.gov/currency/default.htm), another change in currency design was introduced in October 2003: a new $20 note with shades of green, peach, and blue in the background. A blue eagle and metallic green eagle and shield were also added to the note's design. A new $50 note was issued in September 2004, a new $10 note in March 2006, and a new $5 note in March 2008.

In "Know Your Money: Advanced Technologies in Counterfeiting" (2010, http://www.secretservice.gov/money_technologies.shtml), the Secret Service explains that many counterfeiters have abandoned the traditional method of offset printing, which requires specialized skills and machinery. Instead, counterfeiters produce fake currency with basic computer training and typical office equipment. The number of counterfeit notes in circulation is likely to increase because more people have access to the machines and methods that are required to produce them; however, the security features added to the design and manufacture of U.S. currency have also made it easier to detect bogus notes.

PUBLIC CORRUPTION

The abuse of public trust may be found wherever the interest of individuals or businesses overlaps with government interest. It ranges from the health inspector who accepts a bribe from a restaurant owner or the police officer who "shakes down" a drug dealer, to the council member or legislator who accepts money to vote a certain way. These crimes are often difficult to uncover because typically few willing witnesses are available.

According to the DOJ, in *Report to Congress on the Activities and Operations of the Public Integrity Section for 2009* (2010, http://www.justice.gov/criminal/pin/docs/arpt-2009.pdf), the number of people who are convicted for offenses involving the abuse of public office has remained relatively stable since 2002. In 2009, 1,082 federal, state, and local officials and private citizens were indicted and 1,061 were convicted in public corruption cases. Of those convicted, 426 were elected or appointed federal officials, 102 were state officials, 257 were local officials, and the remaining 276 were private citizens not employed by the government.

Jack Abramoff

In one of the most notable cases involving bribery and kickbacks, Jack Abramoff (1958–), a prominent lobbyist in Washington, D.C., pleaded guilty to fraud, tax evasion, and conspiracy to bribe public officials in January 2006. He was originally sentenced to 70 months in prison. However, because of the assistance he provided federal prosecutors, his sentence was reduced to 48 months in September 2008. The court also ordered him to pay more than $23 million in restitution to his victims.

Abramoff received kickbacks from his former business partner, Michael Scanlon (1970–), in a conspiracy to defraud Native American tribes who sought government approval to operate casinos. The tribes hired Abramoff to represent their interests, and he then recommended Scanlon's public relations firm to the tribes. Abramoff received a kickback from Scanlon for the referral. Abramoff and Scanlon supplied financial incentives, trips, and entertainment expenses to public officials whose support was needed for the projects they represented.

Abramoff was also listed as a coconspirator in the charges against Representative Robert W. Ney (1954–; R-OH), who pleaded guilty in October 2006 to honest services fraud, lobbying violations, and making false statements to the House of Representatives. Ney represented the 18th District of Ohio from 1995 to 2006. He admitted that he accepted domestic and international trips, meals, sports and concert tickets, and other incentives from Abramoff and others in exchange for his support on matters before the House of Representatives. Ney also received financial services from a foreign businessman in return for his support in obtaining a travel visa and an exemption from legal restrictions against foreign nationals selling U.S. aircraft abroad. In January 2007 Ney was sentenced to 30 months in prison and two years of supervised release. In addition, he was ordered to serve 100 hours of community service for each year of supervised release and to pay a $6,000 fine.

Public Corruption Cases

Because public officials have sworn to uphold the law and to act in the interest of the communities they represent, their failure to do so is considered particularly reprehensible, and cases of public corruption often receive much media attention. Common public corruption charges include perjury, obstruction of justice, and bribery. "Pay-to-play" is a form of bribery in which a public official demands benefits (often in the form of campaign contributions) in exchange for government appointments or contracts. The following section highlights some of the more notable corruption cases that involve public officials.

KWAME KILPATRICK. Mayor Kwame Kilpatrick (1970–) of Detroit, Michigan, pleaded guilty to two felony counts of obstruction of justice and resigned from office as part of a September 2008 plea agreement. The charges arose from the settlement of a 2007 court case, for which the city of Detroit paid a premium to hide evidence that the mayor and his chief of staff had an affair and lied about it under oath. In the case, two whistle-blowers—a deputy chief of police and one of Kilpatrick's former bodyguards—claimed to have been dismissed in retaliation for their parts in an investigation of the mayor and his security detail on accusations that included throwing wild parties at the mayor's residence, improper use of city vehicles, and inflated overtime claims. During the trial Kilpatrick and Christine Beatty (1970–), his former chief of staff, had testified that they had not had an affair; however, after the whistle-blowers won a $6.5 million judgment, they discovered thousands of text messages sent by the couple to each other that revealed an intimate relationship. Faced with evidence that he and Beatty had perjured themselves, Kilpatrick pushed through a city-funded $8.4 million settlement of the case to keep the text messages from becoming

public. In 2008 Kilpatrick spent 99 days in jail for lying under oath about the affair.

In May 2010 Kilpatrick was sentenced to up to five years in prison for violating the terms of probation that was handed out in his earlier conviction. In December 2010 he was indicted by a federal grand jury and charged with committing racketeering, bribery, extortion, and fraud while in office. The indictment alleges that the former mayor used his political power to steer millions of dollars in government contracts to a company that was owned by one of his friends. As of February 2011, Kilpatrick had not gone to trial for the new charges laid out in the indictment.

TED STEVENS. In October 2008 Senator Ted Stevens (1923–2010; R-AK)—the longest-serving Republican in Senate history—was convicted on bribery charges that were related to gifts allegedly given to him by an oil company executive. Less than a week after his conviction, Stevens was narrowly defeated in his reelection bid by Mark Begich (1962–), the Democratic challenger. In April 2009 the DOJ (http://www.usdoj.gov/opa/pr/2009/April/09-ag-288.html) moved to have Stevens's conviction dismissed on procedural grounds. The U.S. attorney general Eric Holder Jr. (1951–) said of the Stevens's case, "After careful review, I have concluded that certain information should have been provided to the defense for use at trial. In light of this conclusion, and in consideration of the totality of the circumstances of this particular case, I have determined that it is in the interest of justice to dismiss the indictment and not proceed with a new trial." In August 2010 Stevens died in a plane crash in Alaska.

CITY OFFICIALS IN BELL, CALIFORNIA. In September 2010 eight current and former city officials in Bell, California, were arrested and charged with numerous counts of corruption. The officials allegedly paid themselves high salaries, misappropriated city funds, and participated in illegal loan schemes. As of February 2011, the accused perpetrators had not gone to trial.

ALABAMA STATE LEGISLATORS. In October 2010 federal authorities charged four members of the Alabama legislature with conspiring with lobbyists and other associates to "buy and sell votes" to influence proposed state legislation dealing with casino gambling. As of February 2011, the cases had not gone to trial.

PUERTO RICO POLICE DEPARTMENT. In October 2010 over 130 of Puerto Rican police officers were arrested by federal agents and accused of providing security services to suspected drug dealers, accepting payments for those services, and in some cases engaging in drug dealing themselves. In "133 Charged in Puerto Rico Graft Inquiry" (*New York Times*, October 6, 2010), Charlie Savage notes that this incident was described by federal officials as the largest investigation of police corruption in FBI history. As of February 2011, none of the cases had been tried in court.

ROD R. BLAGOJEVICH. The Illinois governor Rod R. Blagojevich (1956–) was impeached and removed from office in January 2009 following his arrest the previous month on federal charges of solicitation of bribery, mail fraud, and abuse of power. The accusations against Blagojevich included charges that he attempted to sell to the highest bidder the Senate seat that had been vacated by Barack Obama (1961–) at the time of his election to the presidency; that Blagojevich demanded editorial favor with the *Chicago Tribune* in exchange for state funds for a large financial transaction being negotiated by the newspaper's parent company; and that he solicited bribes in the form of campaign contributions from various sources in exchange for favorable treatment in state business. In April 2009 the federal charges against Blagojevich were expanded in a 19-count indictment that included wire fraud, attempted extortion, and racketeering conspiracy, among other charges. According to the DOJ, in the press release "Former Illinois Gov. Rod R. Blagojevich, His Brother, Two Former Top Aides and Two Businessmen Indicted on Federal Corruption Charges Alleging Pervasive Fraud" (April 2, 2009, http://www.usdoj.gov/usao/iln/pr/chicago/2009/pr0402_01.pdf), Blagojevich conspired with his brother, Robert Blagojevich, his chief of staff, John Harris, and others in various influence-peddling and pay-to-play activities that made up "a wide-ranging scheme to deprive the people of Illinois of honest government."

In August 2010 Blagojevich was convicted of only one of the charges against him: making false statements to investigators. A mistrial was declared for the other charges against him. As of February 2011, the federal government planned to retry Blagojevich on those charges sometime in 2011.

CHAPTER 6
CONTROLLING CRIME

Criminologists state that every criminal act involves three elements: motivation, resources, and opportunity. A person who is motivated to commit a crime and has the resources to do so (e.g., a weapon or the physical or mental prowess needed to carry out a crime) seeks criminal opportunities, such as victims or targets. Societies try to control crime by controlling these three primary elements of criminality.

Controlling crime in the United States is a multipronged effort that includes interrelated acts of prevention, deterrence, and punishment. Private citizens may take actions that are designed to prevent and deter crimes on their person and property. Examples include installing alarm systems in their home, taking self-defense classes, and participating in neighborhood watch programs. Taxpayer funds are used by governments to establish crime-controlling entities at the local, state, and federal levels for the overall good of society. There are four major governmental components that work together to control crime:

- Law enforcement agencies
- The legal system
- The judicial system
- The corrections system

LAW ENFORCEMENT AGENCIES

The primary role of law enforcement agencies is to investigate crimes, gather evidence, and arrest suspected perpetrators. Agencies differ by geographic jurisdictions (e.g., federal, state, or local) and by enforcement responsibilities (e.g., the types of laws they enforce or the types of crimes they investigate).

Agencies and Employees

The vast majority of law enforcement in the United States is carried out by local agencies. The Federal Bureau of Investigation (FBI) tracks local law enforcement employment as part of its Uniform Crime Reporting (UCR) Program. In 2009 the UCR Program reported that 14,614 city and county police agencies around the country had just over 1 million full-time employees. (See Table 6.1.) Of these employees, 706,886 were law enforcement officers, such as police officers or sheriff deputies, and the remainder were civilian employees (e.g., receptionists or clerks). More than half of all local law enforcement employees worked for city governments, most for cities with populations of 250,000 or more.

As of February 2011, every state except Hawaii had a state police agency or highway patrol force. These officers patrol state highways and often provide law enforcement assistance to local agencies within their state, particularly those in rural areas or small towns.

The federal government has several law enforcement agencies with specific responsibilities. The largest agencies are:

- FBI
- U.S. Drug Enforcement Administration
- Bureau of Alcohol, Tobacco, Firearms, and Explosives
- U.S. Customs and Border Protection
- U.S. Immigration and Customs Enforcement
- U.S. Secret Service

The latter three agencies operate under the U.S. Department of Homeland Security.

OFFICERS KILLED IN THE LINE OF DUTY. Between 2000 and 2009 felons killed 536 federal, state, and local law enforcement officers. (See Table 6.2.) This excludes officers who were killed in the September 11, 2001, terrorist attacks against the United States. The largest number of officers (121) were feloniously killed during arrest situations. Another 115 of the officers were killed during ambushes and 101 were killed during traffic pursuits or stops.

TABLE 6.1

Number of full-time law enforcement employees (officers and civilians) and number of law enforcement agencies, total and by jurisdiction size, 2009

Population group	Total law enforcement employees	Percent law enforcement employees Male	Percent law enforcement employees Female	Total officers	Percent officers Male	Percent officers Female	Total civilians	Percent civilians Male	Percent civilians Female	Number of agencies	2009 estimated population
Total agencies	1,021,456	73.1	26.9	706,886	88.3	11.7	314,570	39.0	61.0	14,614	289,417,471
Total cities	584,672	75.4	24.6	452,037	88.2	11.8	132,635	31.5	68.5	11,218	195,945,107
Group I (250,000 and over)	206,064	71.6	28.4	157,079	83.2	16.8	48,985	34.2	65.8	75	56,942,042
1,000,000 and over (Group I subset)	111,779	70.0	30.0	83,976	81.8	18.2	27,803	34.4	65.6	10	25,873,144
500,000 to 999,999 (Group I subset)	56,824	74.6	25.4	44,603	84.5	15.5	12,221	38.3	61.7	25	17,183,941
250,000 to 499,999 (Group I subset)	37,461	71.7	28.3	28,500	85.4	14.6	8,961	27.9	72.1	40	13,884,957
Group II (100,000 to 249,999)	67,620	73.0	27.0	51,236	88.1	11.9	16,384	25.9	74.1	188	27,843,405
Group III (50,000 to 99,999)	67,603	76.1	23.9	51,954	90.6	9.4	15,649	27.9	72.1	439	29,972,217
Group IV (25,000 to 49,999)	64,238	77.8	22.2	50,701	91.4	8.6	13,537	26.7	73.3	815	27,953,975
Group V (10,000 to 24,999)	70,228	79.4	20.6	56,342	92.2	7.8	13,886	27.6	72.4	1,839	29,047,897
Group VI (under 10,000)	108,919	79.4	20.6	84,725	91.5	8.5	24,194	37.2	62.8	7,862	24,185,571
Metropolitan counties	303,722	69.2	30.8	177,518	86.5	13.5	126,204	45.0	55.0	1,245	65,937,797
Nonmetropolitan counties	133,062	71.9	28.1	77,331	92.7	7.3	55,731	43.0	57.0	2,151	27,534,567
Suburban areas*	471,235	72.7	27.3	308,436	88.6	11.4	162,799	42.6	57.4	7,561	122,719,200

*Suburban areas include law enforcement agencies in cities with less than 50,000 inhabitants and county law enforcement agencies that are within a Metropolitan Statistical Area. Suburban areas exclude all metropolitan agencies associated with a principal city. The agencies associated with suburban areas also appear in other groups within this table.

SOURCE: "Table 74. Full-Time Law Enforcement Employees, by Population Group, Percent Male and Female, 2009," in *Crime in the United States, 2009*, U.S. Department of Justice, Federal Bureau of Investigation, September 2010, http://www2.fbi.gov/ucr/cius2009/data/documents/09tbl74.xls (accessed November 4, 2010)

TABLE 6.2

Number of law enforcement officers feloniously killed, 2000–09

[Circumstance at scene of incident, 2000–2009]

Circumstance		Total	2000	2001*	2002	2003	2004	2005	2006	2007	2008	2009
Number of victim officers	Total	536	51	70	56	52	57	55	48	58	41	48
Disturbance call	Total	77	8	13	9	10	10	7	8	5	1	6
	Disturbance (bar fight, person with firearm, etc.)	35	4	5	4	5	1	2	6	3	1	4
	Domestic disturbance (family quarrel, etc.)	42	4	8	5	5	9	5	2	2	0	2
Arrest situation	Total	121	12	24	10	8	13	8	12	17	9	8
	Burglary in progress/pursuing burglary suspect	14	3	3	0	1	2	1	0	1	2	1
	Robbery in progress/pursuing robbery suspect	38	1	4	4	1	7	4	6	7	1	3
	Drug-related matter	19	3	8	3	1	0	0	2	1	1	0
	Attempting other arrest	50	5	9	3	5	4	3	4	8	5	4
Civil disorder (mass disobedience, riot, etc.)	Total	0	0	0	0	0	0	0	0	0	0	0
Handling, transporting, custody of prisoner	Total	13	2	2	0	2	1	1	1	1	1	2
Investigating suspicious person/circumstance	Total	59	6	8	6	4	7	7	6	4	7	4
Ambush situation	Total	115	10	9	17	9	15	8	10	16	6	15
	Entrapment/premeditation	42	2	3	4	6	6	4	1	9	1	6
	Unprovoked attack	73	8	6	13	3	9	4	9	7	5	9
Investigative activity (surveillance, search, interview, etc.)	Total	9	0	0	0	2	0	4	0	1	2	0
Handling person with mental illness	Total	12	0	3	4	0	2	2	1	0	0	0
Traffic pursuit/stop	Total	101	13	8	10	14	6	15	8	11	8	8
	Felony vehicle stop	36	4	5	6	4	0	5	0	5	5	2
	Traffic violation stop	65	9	3	4	10	6	10	8	6	3	6
Tactical situation (barricaded offender, hostage taking, high-risk entry, etc.)	Total	29	0	3	0	3	3	3	2	3	7	5

*The deaths of the 72 law enforcement officers that resulted from the events of September 11, 2001, are not included in this table.

SOURCE: "Table 19. Law Enforcement Officers Feloniously Killed, Circumstances at Scene of Incident, 2000–2009," in *Law Enforcement Officers Killed and Assaulted, 2009*, U.S. Department of Justice, Federal Bureau of Investigation, October 2010, http://www2.fbi.gov/ucr/killed/2009/data/table_19.html (accessed October 26, 2010)

Key Law Enforcement Agency Components

Even though law enforcement agencies differ in their geographic and criminal jurisdictions, there are some components that are considered key to modern crime control, particularly at the local level. These components are neighborhood patrols, detectives, and forensic science.

Local law enforcement agencies may assign uniformed officers to regularly patrol specific neighborhoods for the purpose of developing relationships with the residents and business owners in the area. These officers are known informally as "beat cops," because each officer patrols a particular "beat" within the community. The use of beat cops is an example of community policing, whereby law enforcement agencies seek to forge a cooperative bond with people in the community to better fight crime.

Community policing was commonly practiced in the United States in the early part of the 20th century. However, beginning in the 1950s and 1960s police departments shifted beat cops from their foot patrols to patrol cars so that larger areas could be covered. Eventually, law enforcement agencies became almost completely reactive—that is, they reacted after a crime was committed with officers dispatched in response to 911 calls. During the high-crime decades of the 1970s and 1980s, some criminologists began advocating a return to community policing. Joseph F. Ryan describes this evolution in "Community Policing and the Impact of the COPS Federal Grants: A Potential Tool in the Local War on Terrorism" (Albert R. Roberts, ed., *Critical Issues in Crime and Justice*, 2003). Ryan notes that community policing was a key component of the Violent Crime Control and Law Enforcement Act of 1994, which allocated billions of federal dollars for the hiring of more police officers and the development of community policing programs.

Community policing is an example of proactive policing. Proactive means taking action before a situation or event becomes a problem. Proactive policies are designed to prevent crimes from occurring in the first place. Activities that are designed to deter criminals include visible police patrols, such as beat cops regularly walking or driving around neighborhoods. Some jurisdictions install video cameras in public places, such as parks or street corners, to deter criminal activity. Local law enforcement agencies also work with private citizens and business owners to encourage the reporting of suspicious-acting people or situations that present opportunities to criminals.

Many law enforcement agencies also employ detectives. These are plainclothes officers who are specially trained to investigate particular crimes (such as homicides). Detectives interview witnesses and suspects, gather facts, examine records, and collect evidence. They may also participate in the apprehension of perpetrators.

Forensic science is the application of scientific knowledge and methods to solve crime. Forensic investigators (or criminalists) are employed by some law enforcement agencies. These specialists commonly investigate crime scenes where they collect and analyze physical evidence. They may perform deoxyribonucleic acid (DNA) or firearms analyses or conduct laboratory tests on blood, semen, hair, tissue, fibers, and other evidentiary materials that are associated with criminal acts.

Arrests

One of the most important aspects of crime control that law enforcement agencies practice is the apprehension and arrest of suspected perpetrators. According to the FBI, in 2009 law enforcement agencies made nearly 13.7 million arrests for all criminal infractions, excluding traffic violations. (See Table 6.3.)

The FBI notes that there were 581,765 arrests for violent crimes (murder and nonnegligent manslaughter, forcible rape, robbery, and aggravated assault) and 1.7 million arrests for property crimes (burglary, larceny-theft,

TABLE 6.3

Estimated number of arrests, 2009

Total[a]	**13,687,241**
Murder and nonnegligent manslaughter	12,418
Forcible rape	21,407
Robbery	126,725
Aggravated assault	421,215
Burglary	299,351
Larceny-theft	1,334,933
Motor vehicle theft	81,797
Arson	12,204
Violent crime[b]	581,765
Property crime[b]	1,728,285
Other assaults	1,319,458
Forgery and counterfeiting	85,844
Fraud	210,255
Embezzlement	17,920
Stolen property; buying, receiving, possessing	105,303
Vandalism	270,439
Weapons; carrying, possessing, etc.	166,334
Prostitution and commercialized vice	71,355
Sex offenses (except forcible rape and prostitution)	77,326
Drug abuse violations	1,663,582
Gambling	10,360
Offenses against the family and children	114,564
Driving under the influence	1,440,409
Liquor laws	570,333
Drunkenness	594,300
Disorderly conduct	655,322
Vagrancy	33,388
All other offenses	3,764,672
Suspicion	1,975
Curfew and loitering law violations	112,593
Runaways	93,434

[a]Does not include suspicion.
[b]Violent crimes are offenses of murder and nonnegligent manslaughter, forcible rape, robbery, and aggravated assault. Property crimes are offenses of burglary, larceny-theft, motor vehicle theft, and arson.

SOURCE: "Table 29. Estimated Number of Arrests, United States, 2009," in *Crime in the United States, 2009*, U.S. Department of Justice, Federal Bureau of Investigation, September 2010, http://www2.fbi.gov/ucr/cius2009/data/documents/09tbl29.xls (accessed October 5, 2010)

motor vehicle theft, and arson) in 2009. (See Table 6.3.) Of the arrests for specific offenses on which the FBI collects statistics, the five crimes with the most arrests were:

- Drug abuse violations—1.7 million arrests

- Driving under the influence—1.4 million arrests

- Larceny-theft—1.3 million arrests

- Assaults, other than aggravated assaults—1.3 million arrests

- Disorderly conduct—655,322 arrests

AGE OF ARRESTEES. Age data were reported to the FBI in 2009 for 10.7 million arrestees. (See Table 6.4.) Of this number, nearly 4.7 million (43.6%) people arrested nationwide were under the age of 25 years. Among those arrestees for whom age is known, people under 25 years old accounted for more than three-quarters (76.7%) of those arrested for liquor law infractions and nearly two-thirds of those arrested for robbery (65.2%), arson (64.3%), vandalism (64.1%), or burglary (60.3%). People in this age group made up much lower percentages of those arrested for offenses against the family and children (22.3%), fraud (25.7%), driving under the influence (27%), and drunkenness (27.1%). Arrestees for these crimes were more often people older than 25 years of age.

Overall, people under 25 years old made up 44.7% of those arrested for violent crimes and 55.8% of those arrested for property crimes. (See Table 6.4.)

GENDER OF ARRESTEES. A gender breakdown for all 13.7 million arrests shown in Table 6.3 is not provided by the FBI. However, the FBI estimates that in 2009 male arrestees outnumbered female arrestees by a margin of almost three to one. (See Table 6.5.) Out of a total of 8.3 million arrests in 2009 for which gender information was reported, almost 6.2 million of those arrested were male and nearly 2.1 million were female.

TABLE 6.4

Arrests of persons of all ages and those under 25 years of age, 2009

[12,371 agencies; 2009 estimated population 239,839,971]

Offense charged	Total all ages	Number of persons arrested Under 25	Percent of total all ages Under 25
Total	**10,741,157**	**4,683,319**	**43.6**
Murder and nonnegligent manslaughter	9,775	4,779	48.9
Forcible rape	16,442	6,995	42.5
Robbery	100,702	65,648	65.2
Aggravated assault	331,372	127,514	38.5
Burglary	235,226	141,939	60.3
Larceny-theft	1,060,754	580,101	54.7
Motor vehicle theft	64,169	36,154	56.3
Arson	9,509	6,116	64.3
Violent crime*	458,291	204,936	44.7
Property crime*	1,369,658	764,310	55.8
Other assaults	1,036,754	424,561	41.0
Forgery and counterfeiting	67,357	20,968	31.1
Fraud	162,243	41,743	25.7
Embezzlement	14,097	5,520	39.2
Stolen property; buying, receiving, possessing	82,944	42,557	51.3
Vandalism	212,981	136,616	64.1
Weapons; carrying, possessing, etc.	130,941	72,605	55.4
Prostitution and commercialized vice	56,640	15,920	28.1
Sex offenses (except forcible rape and prostitution)	60,422	24,398	40.4
Drug abuse violations	1,305,191	610,372	46.8
Gambling	8,067	4,331	53.7
Offenses against the family and children	87,889	19,622	22.3
Driving under the influence	1,112,384	300,776	27.0
Liquor laws	447,496	343,030	76.7
Drunkenness	471,727	127,741	27.1
Disorderly conduct	518,374	276,872	53.4
Vagrancy	26,380	8,306	31.5
All other offenses (except traffic)	2,946,277	1,073,879	36.4
Suspicion	1,517	729	48.1
Curfew and loitering law violations	89,733	89,733	100.0
Runaways	73,794	73,794	100.0

*Violent crimes are offenses of murder and nonnegligent manslaughter, forcible rape, robbery, and aggravated assault. Property crimes are offenses of burglary, larceny-theft, motor vehicle theft, and arson.

SOURCE: Adapted from "Table 41. Arrests: Persons under 15, 18, 21, and 25 Years of Age, 2009," in *Crime in the United States, 2009*, U.S. Department of Justice, Federal Bureau of Investigation, September 2010, http://www2.fbi.gov/ucr/cius2009/data/documents/09tbl41.xls (accessed October 11, 2010)

TABLE 6.5

Ten-year arrest trends, by gender, 2000–09

[8,649 agencies; 2009 estimated population 186,864,905; 2000 estimated population 172,176,040]

	Male			Female		
	Total			Total		
Offense charged	2000	2009	Percent change	2000	2009	Percent change
Total[a]	6,491,372	6,174,287	−4.9	1,874,217	2,087,303	+11.4
Murder and nonnegligent manslaughter	6,755	6,437	−4.7	844	756	−10.4
Forcible rape	16,139	12,469	−22.7	169	148	−12.4
Robbery	58,443	67,906	+16.2	6,663	9,384	+40.8
Aggravated assault	240,528	209,078	−13.1	60,787	58,236	−4.2
Burglary	151,244	159,017	+5.1	23,497	29,764	+26.7
Larceny-theft	454,947	451,750	−0.7	258,379	354,854	+37.3
Motor vehicle theft	67,551	38,987	−42.3	12,558	8,486	−32.4
Arson	8,820	6,432	−27.1	1,556	1,300	−16.5
Violent crime[b]	321,865	295,890	−8.1	68,463	68,524	+0.1
Property crime[b]	682,562	656,186	−3.9	295,990	394,404	+33.2
Other assaults	590,790	592,155	+0.2	179,874	211,334	+17.5
Forgery and counterfeiting	40,765	31,152	−23.6	26,468	18,840	−28.8
Fraud	116,447	78,550	−32.5	100,219	61,385	−38.7
Embezzlement	6,207	5,743	−7.5	6,249	6,013	−3.8
Stolen property; buying, receiving, possessing	62,320	52,247	−16.2	13,151	14,057	+6.9
Vandalism	143,680	133,421	−7.1	26,230	29,090	+10.9
Weapons; carrying, possessing, etc.	86,024	90,182	+4.8	7,614	8,040	+5.6
Prostitution and commercialized vice	18,886	11,639	−38.4	25,779	25,757	−0.1
Sex offenses (except forcible rape and prostitution)	50,319	42,609	−15.3	3,831	4,019	+4.9
Drug abuse violations	771,170	806,669	+4.6	167,968	189,039	+12.5
Gambling	3,984	2,877	−27.8	584	482	−17.5
Offenses against the family and children	67,421	53,001	−21.4	18,828	17,574	−6.7
Driving under the influence	734,872	651,424	−11.4	144,794	190,445	+31.5
Liquor laws	311,989	244,047	−21.8	94,783	96,795	+2.1
Drunkenness	363,705	331,804	−8.8	56,312	66,608	+18.3
Disorderly conduct	280,158	257,713	−8.0	89,049	96,319	+8.2
Vagrancy	13,151	13,189	+0.3	3,721	3,628	−2.5
All other offenses (except traffic)	1,720,089	1,746,701	+1.5	460,661	530,612	+15.2
Suspicion	2,757	958	−65.3	696	335	−51.9
Curfew and loitering law violations	67,275	50,288	−25.3	30,078	21,915	−27.1
Runaways	37,693	26,800	−28.9	53,571	32,423	−39.5

[a]Does not include suspicion.
[b]Violent crimes are offenses of murder and nonnegligent manslaughter, forcible rape, robbery, and aggravated assault. Property crimes are offenses of burglary, larceny-theft, motor vehicle theft, and arson.

SOURCE: Adapted from "Table 33. Ten-Year Arrest Trends, by Sex, 2000–2009," in *Crime in the United States, 2009*, U.S. Department of Justice, Federal Bureau of Investigation, September 2010, http://www2.fbi.gov/ucr/cius2009/data/documents/09tbl33.xls (accessed October 5, 2010)

Between 2000 and 2009 the number of males arrested for all offenses declined by 4.9%, whereas female arrests for all offenses increased by 11.4%. (See Table 6.5.) Male arrests during this period increased the most for robbery (up 16.2%), burglary (up 5.1%), weapons violations (up 4.8%), and drug abuse violations (up 4.6%). Male arrests declined substantially for suspicion (down 65.3%), motor vehicle theft (down 42.3%), prostitution and commercialized vice (down 38.4%), and fraud (down 32.5%).

By contrast, female arrests between 2000 and 2009 increased for nearly all crimes, particularly robbery (up 40.8%), larceny-theft (up 37.3%), driving under the influence (up 31.5%), and burglary (up 26.7%). (See Table 6.5.) Female arrests declined for suspicion (down 51.9%), runaways (down 39.5%), fraud (down 38.7%), and motor vehicle theft (down 32.4%).

Overall, male arrests were down 8.1% for violent crimes and down 3.9% for property crimes between 2000 and 2009. Female arrests increased by 0.1% for violent crimes and increased by 33.2% for property crimes during this same period.

RACE AND ETHNICITY OF ARRESTEES. Of the 10.7 million arrests reported to the UCR Program that included race information in 2009, 69.1% of the arrestees were white and 28.3% were African-American. (See Table 6.6.) The remaining arrestees were Native American or Alaskan Native (1.4%) and Asian or Pacific Islander (1.2%). Whites accounted for large percentages of those arrested for driving under the influence (86.3%), liquor law violations (84%), and drunkenness (82.5%). African-American arrestees accounted for over two-thirds (68.6%) of all arrests for illegal gambling and more than half of all arrests for

TABLE 6.6

Arrests, by race, 2009

[12,371 agencies; 2009 estimated population 239,839,971]

Offense charged	Total arrests					Percent distribution[a]				
	Total	White	Black	American Indian or Alaskan Native	Asian or Pacific Islander	Total	White	Black	American Indian or Alaskan Native	Asian or Pacific Islander
Total	**10,690,561**	**7,389,208**	**3,027,153**	**150,544**	**123,656**	**100.0**	**69.1**	**28.3**	**1.4**	**1.2**
Murder and nonnegligent manslaughter	9,739	4,741	4,801	100	97	100.0	48.7	49.3	1.0	1.0
Forcible rape	16,362	10,644	5,319	169	230	100.0	65.1	32.5	1.0	1.4
Robbery	100,496	43,039	55,742	726	989	100.0	42.8	55.5	0.7	1.0
Aggravated assault	330,368	209,922	111,904	4,613	3,929	100.0	63.5	33.9	1.4	1.2
Burglary	234,551	155,994	74,419	2,021	2,117	100.0	66.5	31.7	0.9	0.9
Larceny-theft	1,056,473	719,983	306,625	14,646	15,219	100.0	68.1	29.0	1.4	1.4
Motor vehicle theft	63,919	39,077	23,184	817	841	100.0	61.1	36.3	1.3	1.3
Arson	9,466	7,085	2,154	115	112	100.0	74.8	22.8	1.2	1.2
Violent crime[b]	456,965	268,346	177,766	5,608	5,245	100.0	58.7	38.9	1.2	1.1
Property crime[b]	1,364,409	922,139	406,382	17,599	18,289	100.0	67.6	29.8	1.3	1.3
Other assaults	1,032,502	672,865	332,435	15,127	12,075	100.0	65.2	32.2	1.5	1.2
Forgery and counterfeiting	67,054	44,730	21,251	345	728	100.0	66.7	31.7	0.5	1.1
Fraud	161,233	108,032	50,367	1,315	1,519	100.0	67.0	31.2	0.8	0.9
Embezzlement	13,960	9,208	4,429	75	248	100.0	66.0	31.7	0.5	1.8
Stolen property; buying, receiving, possessing	82,714	51,953	29,357	662	742	100.0	62.8	35.5	0.8	0.9
Vandalism	212,173	157,723	48,746	3,352	2,352	100.0	74.3	23.0	1.6	1.1
Weapons; carrying, possessing, etc.	130,503	74,942	53,441	951	1,169	100.0	57.4	41.0	0.7	0.9
Prostitution and commercialized vice	56,560	31,699	23,021	427	1,413	100.0	56.0	40.7	0.8	2.5
Sex offenses (except forcible rape and prostitution)	60,175	44,240	14,347	715	873	100.0	73.5	23.8	1.2	1.5
Drug abuse violations	1,301,629	845,974	437,623	8,588	9,444	100.0	65.0	33.6	0.7	0.7
Gambling	8,046	2,290	5,518	27	211	100.0	28.5	68.6	0.3	2.6
Offenses against the family and children	87,232	58,068	26,850	1,690	624	100.0	66.6	30.8	1.9	0.7
Driving under the influence	1,105,401	954,444	121,594	14,903	14,460	100.0	86.3	11.0	1.3	1.3
Liquor laws	444,087	373,189	50,431	14,876	5,591	100.0	84.0	11.4	3.3	1.3
Drunkenness	469,958	387,542	71,020	8,552	2,844	100.0	82.5	15.1	1.8	0.6
Disorderly conduct	515,689	326,563	176,169	8,783	4,174	100.0	63.3	34.2	1.7	0.8
Vagrancy	26,347	14,581	11,031	543	192	100.0	55.3	41.9	2.1	0.7
All other offenses (except traffic)	2,929,217	1,937,221	911,670	43,880	36,446	100.0	66.1	31.1	1.5	1.2
Suspicion	1,513	677	828	1	7	100.0	44.7	54.7	0.1	0.5
Curfew and loitering law violations	89,578	54,439	33,207	872	1,060	100.0	60.8	37.1	1.0	1.2
Runaways	73,616	48,343	19,670	1,653	3,950	100.0	65.7	26.7	2.2	5.4

[a]Because of rounding, the percentages may not add to 100.0.

[b]Violent crimes are offenses of murder and nonnegligent manslaughter, forcible rape, robbery, and aggravated assault. Property crimes are offenses of burglary, larceny-theft, motor vehicle theft, and arson.

SOURCE: "Table 43A. Arrests, by Race, 2009," in *Crime in the United States, 2009*, U.S. Department of Justice, Federal Bureau of Investigation, September 2010, http://www2.fbi.gov/ucr/cius2009/data/documents/09tbl43a.xls (accessed October 27, 2010)

FIGURE 6.1

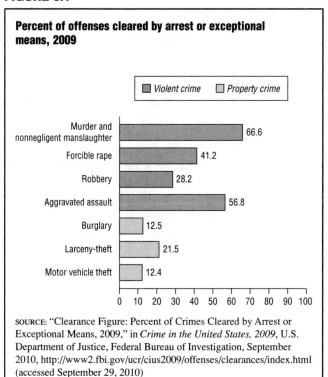

Percent of offenses cleared by arrest or exceptional means, 2009

Legend: ■ Violent crime □ Property crime

Offense	Percent
Murder and nonnegligent manslaughter	66.6
Forcible rape	41.2
Robbery	28.2
Aggravated assault	56.8
Burglary	12.5
Larceny-theft	21.5
Motor vehicle theft	12.4

SOURCE: "Clearance Figure: Percent of Crimes Cleared by Arrest or Exceptional Means, 2009," in *Crime in the United States, 2009*, U.S. Department of Justice, Federal Bureau of Investigation, September 2010, http://www2.fbi.gov/ucr/cius2009/offenses/clearances/index.html (accessed September 29, 2010)

robbery (55.5%) and suspicion (54.7%). As shown in Table 6.6, whites made up 58.7% of arrests for violent crimes, whereas African-Americans accounted for 38.9%. Likewise, whites made up a larger percentage of those arrested for property crimes (67.6%) than did African-Americans (29.8%).

OFFENSES CLEARED BY ARREST OR EXCEPTIONAL MEANS. Figure 6.1 shows the percentage of known offenses that were cleared by arrest or exceptional means in 2009. Offenses cleared by exceptional means are those for which there can be no arrest, such as in a murder-suicide, when the perpetrator is known to be deceased.

Because murder is considered the most serious crime, it receives the most police attention and, therefore, has the highest arrest rate of all felonies. In 2009, 66.6% of murders and nonnegligent manslaughters were cleared by arrest or exceptional means. (See Figure 6.1.) The only other offense for which more than half of the crimes were cleared in 2009 was aggravated assault (56.8%). Clearance rates were much lower for the other crimes listed in Figure 6.1, particularly motor vehicle theft (12.4% clearance rate) and burglary (12.5% clearance rate).

Figure 6.2 uses data from the FBI's UCR Program to compare the number of violent crimes that were

FIGURE 6.2

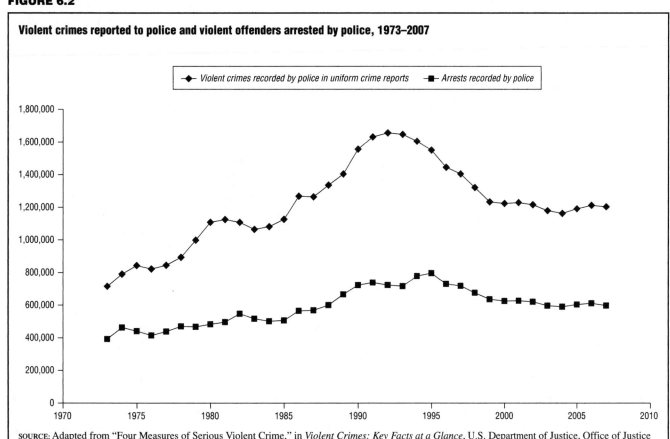

Violent crimes reported to police and violent offenders arrested by police, 1973–2007

Legend: ◆ Violent crimes recorded by police in uniform crime reports   ■ Arrests recorded by police

SOURCE: Adapted from "Four Measures of Serious Violent Crime," in *Violent Crimes: Key Facts at a Glance*, U.S. Department of Justice, Office of Justice Programs, Bureau of Justice Statistics, September 18, 2006, http://bjs.ojp.usdoj.gov/content/glance/tables/4meastab.cfm (accessed November 10, 2010)

recorded by the police each year between 1973 and 2007 to the number of arrests for violent crimes. In all years the number of recorded crimes far exceeded the number of arrests. This was particularly true from the late 1980s to the mid-1990s, a time of historically high crime rates.

Making an arrest does not mean the alleged offender is guilty or will be convicted of the crime. Law enforcement agencies do not determine the guilt or innocence of suspected perpetrators. That task is left up to the judicial system.

THE LEGAL SYSTEM

Even though *mala in se* (morally wrong or inherently wrong) behaviors are universally condemned as wrong, punishments for these crimes can vary significantly between societies. Many of the legal decisions concerning *mala in se* crimes have evolved over time through what is known as common law. Common law refers to the legal precedents that are established by court decisions over time, as opposed to laws that are passed by legislative bodies. The U.S. legal system relies heavily on common-law decisions dating back to the legal system that was used in England before the establishment of the United States.

People enter the U.S. criminal justice system through a variety of means. They may be issued a citation for a traffic violation witnessed by a law enforcement officer. They may be arrested for a more serious crime by a law enforcement officer who has probable cause to believe they committed a crime. They may be arrested due to issuance of a warrant for their arrest by a court. An arrest warrant is a legal document signed by a judge or a magistrate who believes there is compelling evidence that the person named in the warrant has committed a particular crime.

A person charged with a crime falls under the legal and judicial system of the government body with appropriate jurisdiction, for example, the city, county, state, or federal government. These systems may differ in structure and mode of operation, but under U.S. law they all must provide certain legal rights to arrested people.

The Rights of the Arrested

People placed under arrest (with or without a warrant) must be told their Miranda rights before being questioned about their alleged crime by law enforcement officials. Miranda rights stem from the 1966 U.S. Supreme Court decision *Miranda v. Arizona* (384 U.S. 436). The court ruled that arrested individuals must be told about their constitutional rights to an attorney and against self-incrimination before they are subjected to any questioning about their alleged crime. Even though the so-called Miranda warning takes several forms, it must cover the following basic concepts:

- The arrestee has the right to remain silent during police questioning.

- Anything the arrestee says to the police can be used against him or her at trial.

- The arrestee has the right to an attorney.

- If the arrestee cannot afford an attorney, one will be appointed for him or her at the government's expense.

In addition, arrested individuals have the right to know the charges against them and to see any arrest warrants that are used to make the arrest. According to the American Bar Association, in "Steps in a Trial: Arrest Procedures" (2011, http://www.americanbar.org/groups/public_education/resources/law_related_education_network/how_courts_work/arrestprocedure.html), a person arrested without a warrant can only be held by the police for a limited time period (typically 48 hours) before making his or her first court appearance, or arraignment, before a judge or magistrate. The granting of bail is not specifically a right, but most arrestees are given a bail hearing during which a court sets the monetary amount for bail. The U.S. Constitution prohibits excessive bail. It also guarantees the defendant the right to a speedy trial and prohibits the imposition of cruel and unusual punishment.

The Role of Prosecutors

Government jurisdictions have their own unique legal systems. Each system is typically headed by a public official. At the state level this official may be called the state attorney. At the lower levels of government, such as counties or cities, officials may be called district attorneys, county or city attorneys, or simply prosecutors. A prosecutor represents the legal authority of his or her geographical area and supervises the legal prosecution of suspected criminals. These cases are often referred to prosecutors' offices by law enforcement agencies. Some states also use grand juries to file criminal charges against suspected criminals. Grand juries consist of local citizens who are summoned by a court to serve for a specified period of time. They do not determine the guilt or innocence of the accused, but they do determine if there is enough evidence to bind over the accused to stand trial. If so, the grand jury issues a formal charge called an indictment.

Some district attorneys are elected into office, whereas others are appointed by higher public officials. A prosecutor acts on behalf of the people within a jurisdiction to ensure that its criminal laws are enforced and that criminals are prosecuted. Prosecution for criminal activity sometimes proceeds to court, where the guilt or innocence of the defendant is determined during a trial. The judicial system tries perpetrators in a court of law and, if they are found guilty, sentences them to a period of incarceration or some other form of punishment, restitution (an amount of money that is set by a court to be paid to the victim of a crime for property losses or injuries caused by the crime), and/or treatment.

Not all criminal cases proceed to trial. In fact, many are settled through alternative means, such as plea bargains.

PLEA BARGAINS. In a plea bargain the prosecutor (acting on behalf of the people of the jurisdiction) and the defendant's attorney reach an agreement about how a case should be settled before it goes to trial. A typical example involves an offer from the prosecutor for the defendant to plead guilty to a lesser charge than the one originally filed against him or her. Another common plea bargain occurs when the defendant agrees to plead guilty to a charge in exchange for a recommendation by the prosecutor for a lighter sentence than would be expected to result from a guilty verdict if the case went to trial. Prosecutors are motivated to negotiate plea bargains because criminal trials can be long and costly and their outcomes are not certain. Defendants may choose to plea bargain to avoid the publicity and legal expense of a trial and the likely harsher sentence that will result from a guilty verdict. The American Bar Association indicates in "Steps in a Trial: Plea Bargaining" (2011, http://www.americanbar.org/groups/public_education/resources/law_related_education_network/how_courts_work/pleabargaining.html) that plea bargains resolve most of the criminal cases in most jurisdictions in the United States.

The Bureau of Justice Statistics (BJS) within the U.S. Department of Justice (DOJ) tracks national conviction and sentencing rates for state courts. As of February 2011, the most recent data available were for 2004. In *State Court Sentencing of Convicted Felons, 2004—Statistical Tables* (July 1, 2007, http://bjs.ojp.usdoj.gov/index.cfm?ty=pbdetail&iid=1533), Matthew R. Durose of the BJS reports that 95% of all felons convicted in state courts in 2004 pleaded guilty, presumably as a result of plea bargains. Only 5% of state felony cases went to trial in 2004. Of these, 3% were tried by the bench (i.e., by a judge) and 2% were tried by juries. The percentage of felons convicted in 2004 by a guilty plea exceeded 90% for all felonies except murder (69% convicted by a guilty plea) and rape (83% convicted by a guilty plea).

THE JUDICIARY SYSTEM

The judiciary system includes all criminal courts and the judges and juries that operate within them. There are two main levels of the judiciary system in the United States: federal courts and state/local courts. In "District Courts" (2011, http://www.uscourts.gov/districtcourts.html), U.S. Courts notes that the federal judiciary system includes 94 U.S. judicial districts that are organized into 12 regional circuits. (See Figure 6.3; note that the 12th circuit is the District of Columbia.) The district courts serve as trial courts in the federal system. Each circuit has a U.S. court

of appeals. The U.S. Supreme Court is the highest court in the United States. It hears a limited number of cases each year that primarily address issues related to federal law or the U.S. Constitution.

Every state has its own court system. These systems differ by state, but in general they include local or municipal courts, county-level courts, district courts, state appeals courts, and state supreme courts. Figure 6.4 shows the court structure for Texas. Note that municipal and county courts have jurisdiction over misdemeanors, whereas district courts have jurisdiction over felony criminal cases.

Sentences

One of the roles of the judiciary system is to impose sentences on convicted criminals. Most convicted felons are sentenced to incarceration. Nonincarceration sentences include probation (a period of intense supervision) and other alternatives, such as a fine or community service.

Durose indicates in *State Court Sentencing of Convicted Felons, 2004—Statistical Tables* that there were over 1.1 million felony convictions in state and federal courts in 2004. Only 5.8% of the convictions were in federal court. The vast majority (94.2%) were in state courts. At the state and federal levels, 70% and 85%, respectively, of convicted felons were sentenced to prison or jail. The mean (average) maximum incarceration length for felons sentenced to incarceration was 37 months at the state level and 61 months at the federal level. The average maximum incarceration lengths were much higher for the most serious violent crimes, such as murder and nonnegligent manslaughter, rape, and robbery.

Durose also reports the percentage of felons sentenced in 2004 by state courts to prison, jail, probation, or other nonincarceration options. Note that only the most severe penalty is counted for felons who received a combination of sentences. Overall, 70% of state-convicted felons (40% in prisons and 30% in jails) were sentenced to incarceration. Another 28% of state-convicted felons were sentenced to probation. Only 2% received another type of sentence, such as a fine or community service. The incarceration rate was much higher for felons convicted of the most violent offenses, such as murder and nonnegligent manslaughter. Of these felons, 92% (89% in prisons and 3% in jails) received a sentence of incarceration, whereas only 7% received probation and 1% were given another nonincarceration sentence.

Truth-in-Sentencing

During the 1970s and early 1980s the United States experienced a historically high crime rate. Politicians responded to public pressure with policies that aimed to "get tough on crime," including new sentencing

FIGURE 6.3

Map of the geographical boundaries of the U.S. Courts of Appeal and U.S. District Courts

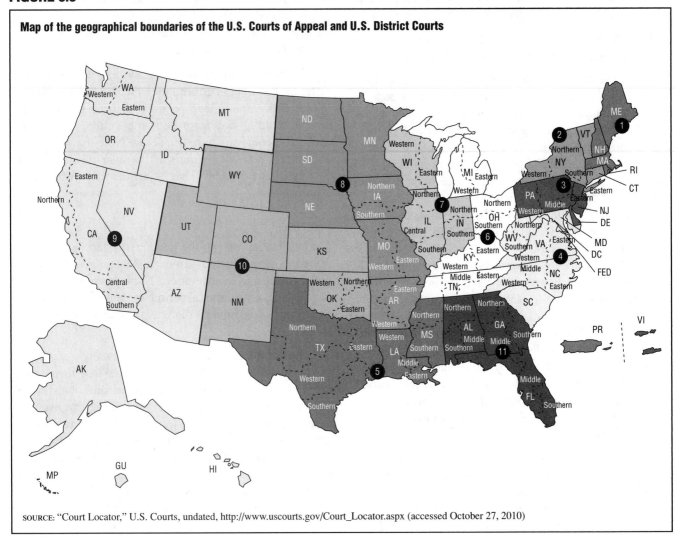

SOURCE: "Court Locator," U.S. Courts, undated, http://www.uscourts.gov/Court_Locator.aspx (accessed October 27, 2010)

guidelines that imposed mandatory minimum sentences and other reforms that established stiffer penalties for certain offenses. Sentence reforms enacted by states came to be known as "truth-in-sentencing" statutes.

Truth-in-sentencing is intended to tell the public that a sentence announced by the court will actually be served—rather than the offender serving only some small fraction of the sentence, being released on parole, or having the sentence commuted to probation and serving no time at all. Under truth-in-sentencing statutes, offenders are required to spend substantial portions of their sentence in prison.

With truth-in-sentencing came the distinction between determinate and indeterminate sentencing. Determinate sentencing takes decision-making power away from parole boards, fixes the term to be served, and provides or denies the means to shorten the sentence by good behavior or other "earned" time. Indeterminate sentencing gives parole boards the authority to release offenders at their option after a process of review. Part of the truth-in-sentencing statutes is mandatory minimum sentences for specific offenses and circumstances. Guidelines define the range

of sentences the judge may apply, which are governed by the offense and the prior history of the offender (e.g., first-time or repeat-offender, severity of the offense, and so on).

Setting uniform sentences for offenses and requiring that fixed proportions of them be served by those convicted put pressure on prison and jail capacities. In response, Congress passed the Violent Crime Control and Law Enforcement Act of 1994. The act gave the federal government the authority to offer grants to states to expand their prison capacity if they imposed truth-in-sentencing requirements on violent offenders. To qualify for the grants, the states had to pass laws requiring that serious violent offenders serve at least 85% of their imposed sentences in prison.

JUDGES' SENTENCING POWER. Some states that adopted truth-in-sentencing laws during the 1970s and 1980s included provisions allowing judges great leeway in deciding sentencing factors. This was also true for some state hate crime laws that were first passed during the 1980s. However, legal analysts complained that these provisions violated the Sixth and 14th Amendments to

FIGURE 6.4

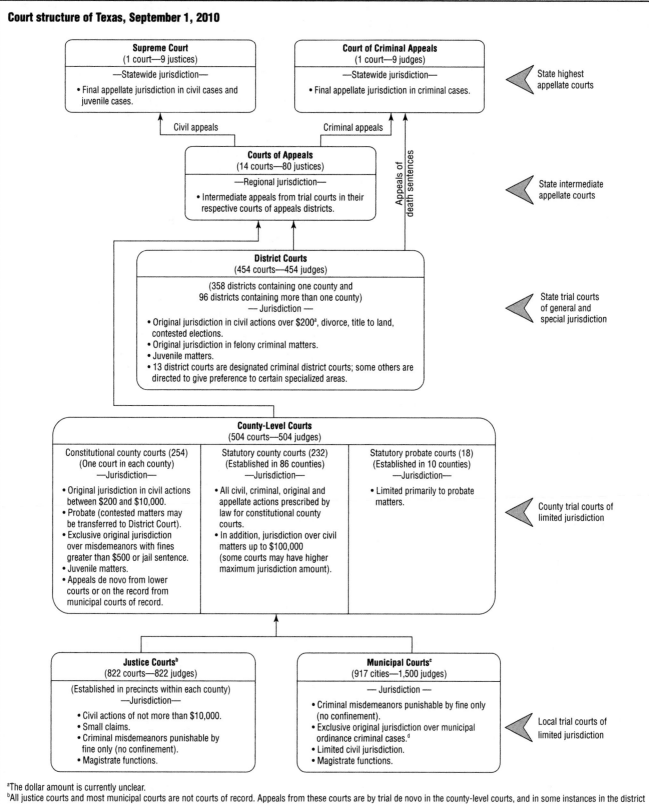

Court structure of Texas, September 1, 2010

Supreme Court
(1 court—9 justices)

—Statewide jurisdiction—

• Final appellate jurisdiction in civil cases and juvenile cases.

Court of Criminal Appeals
(1 court—9 judges)

—Statewide jurisdiction—

• Final appellate jurisdiction in criminal cases.

State highest appellate courts

Civil appeals — Criminal appeals — Appeals of death sentences

Courts of Appeals
(14 courts—80 justices)

—Regional jurisdiction—

• Intermediate appeals from trial courts in their respective courts of appeals districts.

State intermediate appellate courts

District Courts
(454 courts—454 judges)

(358 districts containing one county and 96 districts containing more than one county)
— Jurisdiction —

• Original jurisdiction in civil actions over $200[a], divorce, title to land, contested elections.
• Original jurisdiction in felony criminal matters.
• Juvenile matters.
• 13 district courts are designated criminal district courts; some others are directed to give preference to certain specialized areas.

State trial courts of general and special jurisdiction

County-Level Courts
(504 courts—504 judges)

Constitutional county courts (254) (One court in each county) —Jurisdiction—	Statutory county courts (232) (Established in 86 counties) —Jurisdiction—	Statutory probate courts (18) (Established in 10 counties) —Jurisdiction—
• Original jurisdiction in civil actions between $200 and $10,000. • Probate (contested matters may be transferred to District Court). • Exclusive original jurisdiction over misdemeanors with fines greater than $500 or jail sentence. • Juvenile matters. • Appeals de novo from lower courts or on the record from municipal courts of record.	• All civil, criminal, original and appellate actions prescribed by law for constitutional county courts. • In addition, jurisdiction over civil matters up to $100,000 (some courts may have higher maximum jurisdiction amount).	• Limited primarily to probate matters.

County trial courts of limited jurisdiction

Justice Courts[b]
(822 courts—822 judges)

(Established in precincts within each county)
—Jurisdiction—

• Civil actions of not more than $10,000.
• Small claims.
• Criminal misdemeanors punishable by fine only (no confinement).
• Magistrate functions.

Municipal Courts[c]
(917 cities—1,500 judges)

— Jurisdiction —

• Criminal misdemeanors punishable by fine only (no confinement).
• Exclusive original jurisdiction over municipal ordinance criminal cases.[d]
• Limited civil jurisdiction.
• Magistrate functions.

Local trial courts of limited jurisdiction

[a]The dollar amount is currently unclear.
[b]All justice courts and most municipal courts are not courts of record. Appeals from these courts are by trial de novo in the county-level courts, and in some instances in the district courts.
[c]Some municipal courts are courts of record—appeals from those courts are taken on the record to the county-level courts.
[d]An offense that arises under a municipal ordinance is punishable by a fine not to exceed: (1) $2,000 for ordinances that govern fire safety, zoning, and public health or (2) $500 for all others.

SOURCE: "Court Structure of Texas, September 1, 2010," in *Texas Courts Online*, Texas Office of Court Administration, September 1, 2010, http://www.courts.state.tx.us/oca/pdf/Court_Structure_Chart.pdf (accessed October 27, 2010)

the U.S. Constitution. The Sixth Amendment states in part "in all criminal prosecutions, the accused shall enjoy the right to a speedy and public trial, by an impartial jury." The 14th Amendment states in part "nor shall any state deprive any person of life, liberty, or property, without due process of law." Both provisions have historically been interpreted as a limit on the power of judges (as opposed to juries) in the criminal justice system.

In 2000 the U.S. Supreme Court found in *Apprendi v. New Jersey* (530 U.S. 466) that a state judge had violated the due process clause of the 14th Amendment by deciding on his own that a defendant who had pleaded guilty to a firearms charge had actually committed a hate crime and should receive an enhanced sentence allowed under New Jersey's hate crime law. In 2004 the court ruled in *Blakely v. Washington* (542 U.S. 296) that a state judge cannot impose a longer sentence when the basis for the enhanced sentence was not admitted by the defendant or found by the jury. In 2007 the Supreme Court similarly ruled in *Cunningham v. California* (U.S. 05-6551) that a state judge had violated a defendant's right to trial by jury by making findings on his own (i.e., findings not considered by the jury) that justified a longer sentence for a crime than the sentence called for under state law. In simple terms, these rulings mean that only facts proved to a jury (or admitted to by a defendant pleading guilty) can justify imposition by a state judge of a sentence longer than that called for under state law.

Federal Sentencing Guidelines

The Sentencing Reform Act of 1984 was the federal approach to truth-in-sentencing, or determinate sentencing. The act was designed to eliminate the unregulated power of federal judges to impose sentences of indeterminate length. Because of this unregulated power, some people were convicted of the same crime but sentenced by different judges to receive entirely different terms of incarceration. The U.S. Sentencing Commission (USSC) developed federal guidelines to give a range of sentencing options to federal judges while guaranteeing minimum and maximum sentencing lengths.

The USSC continues to update the guidelines as laws administered by the federal courts are changed or new laws are passed. The USSC also issues supplemental volumes. As of February 2011, the most recent edition of the guidelines was *2010 Federal Sentencing Guidelines Manual and Supplement* (November 1, 2010, http://www.ussc.gov/Guidelines/2010_guidelines/ToC_PDF.cfm).

At the core of the guidelines are offenses as defined by federal statutes. The USSC assigns an offense level to each offense, known as the base offense level, which ranges from 1 to 43. The lowest actual offense for which the USSC has a level is trespass. Trespass is level 4. First-degree murder has a base offense level of 43. Based on the circumstances that are associated with an offense, additional levels can be added or taken away until a particular offense has been assigned to the appropriate level. Judges and prosecutors use these levels to find the relevant sentence in the federal sentencing table, which determines the number of months of imprisonment.

An illustration is provided for kidnapping, abduction, and unlawful restraint in Table 6.7. The table displays the USSC's guideline for this offense. The offense has a base offense level of 32, but additional levels can be added. For example, if the victim was not released before seven days had passed, the level is increased by one, to 33. If the victim sustained permanent or life-threatening bodily injury, the level is increased by four, to 36. If the victim was sexually exploited, the level is increased by six levels, to 38.

According to the USSC's 2010 sentencing table, level 28, for example, points to six columns of sentence ranges indicating a minimum and a maximum sentence in each column. (See Table 6.8.) The first column, where the sentence range is 78 to 97 months, applies to offenders with no prior convictions or one prior conviction. The sixth column, where the sentence is 140 to 175 months, provides sentencing guidelines for offenders with 13 or more prior convictions. A single level thus provides six different levels of

TABLE 6.7

Federal sentencing guidelines on kidnapping, abduction, and unlawful restraint, 2010

(a) Base offense level: 32

(b) Specific offense characteristics

    (1) If a ransom demand or a demand upon government was made, increase by 6 levels.

    (2) (A) If the victim sustained permanent or life-threatening bodily injury, increase by 4 levels; (B) if the victim sustained serious bodily injury, increase by 2 levels; or (C) if the degree of injury is between that specified in subdivisions (A) and (B), increase by 3 levels.

    (3) If a dangerous weapon was used, increase by 2 levels.

    (4) (A) If the victim was not released before thirty days had elapsed, increase by 2 levels.

    (B) If the victim was not released before seven days had elapsed, increase by 1 level.

    (5) If the victim was sexually exploited, increase by 6 levels.

    (6) If the victim is a minor and, in exchange for money or other consideration, was placed in the care or custody of another person who had no legal right to such care or custody of the victim, increase by 3 levels.

    (7) If the victim was kidnapped, abducted, or unlawfully restrained during the commission of, or in connection with, another offense or escape therefrom; or if another offense was committed during the kidnapping, abduction, or unlawful restraint, increase to—

      (A) the offense level from the chapter two offense guideline applicable to that other offense if such offense guideline includes an adjustment for kidnapping, abduction, or unlawful restraint, or otherwise takes such conduct into account; or

      (B) 4 plus the offense level from the offense guideline applicable to that other offense, but in no event greater than level 43, in any other case, if the resulting offense level is greater than that determined above.

SOURCE: "§2A4.1. Kidnapping, Abduction, Unlawful Restraint," in *2008 Federal Sentencing Guidelines Manual*, U.S. Sentencing Commission, November 2008, http://www.ussc.gov/Guidelines/2008_guidelines/Manual/GL2008.pdf (accessed December 2, 2008)

TABLE 6.8

Federal sentencing table, 2010

[In months of imprisonment]

		Criminal history category (criminal history points)					
	Offense level	I (0 or 1)	II (2 or 3)	III (4, 5, 6)	IV (7, 8, 9)	V (10, 11, 12)	VI (13 or more)
Zone A	1	0–6	0–6	0–6	0–6	0–6	0–6
	2	0–6	0–6	0–6	0–6	0–6	1–7
	3	0–6	0–6	0–6	0–6	2–8	3–9
	4	0–6	0–6	0–6	2–8	4–10	6–12
	5	0–6	0–6	1–7	4–10	6–12	9–15
	6	0–6	1–7	2–8	6–12	9–15	12–18
	7	0–6	2–8	4–10	8–14	12–18	15–21
	8	0–6	4–10	6–12	10–16	15–21	18–24
Zone B	9	4–10	6–12	8–14	12–18	18–24	21–27
	10	6–12	8–14	10–16	15–21	21–27	24–30
Zone C	11	8–14	10–16	12–18	18–24	24–30	27–33
	12	10–16	12–18	15–21	21–27	27–33	30–37
Zone D	13	12–18	15–21	18–24	24–30	30–37	33–41
	14	15–21	18–24	21–27	27–33	33–41	37–46
	15	18–24	21–27	24–30	30–37	37–46	41–51
	16	21–27	24–30	27–33	33–41	41–51	46–57
	17	24–30	27–33	30–37	37–46	46–57	51–63
	18	27–33	30–37	33–41	41–51	51–63	57–71
	19	30–37	33–41	37–46	46–57	57–71	63–78
	20	33–41	37–46	41–51	51–63	63–78	70–87
	21	37–46	41–51	46–57	57–71	70–87	77–96
	22	41–51	46–57	51–63	63–78	77–96	84–105
	23	46–57	51–63	57–71	70–87	84–105	92–115
	24	51–63	57–71	63–78	77–96	92–115	100–125
	25	57–71	63–78	70–87	84–105	100–125	110–137
	26	63–78	70–87	78–97	92–115	110–137	120–150
	27	70–87	78–97	87–108	100–125	120–150	130–162
	28	78–97	87–108	97–121	110–137	130–162	140–175
	29	87–108	97–121	108–135	121–151	140–175	151–188
	30	97–121	108–135	121–151	135–168	151–188	168–210
	31	108–135	121–151	135–168	151–188	168–210	188–235
	32	121–151	135–168	151–188	168–210	188–235	210–262
	33	135–168	151–188	168–210	188–235	210–262	235–293
	34	151–188	168–210	188–235	210–262	235–293	262–327
	35	168–210	188–235	210–262	235–293	262–327	292–365
	36	188–235	210–262	235–293	262–327	292–365	324–405
	37	210–262	235–293	262–327	292–365	324–405	360–life
	38	235–293	262–327	292–365	324–405	360–life	360–life
	39	262–327	292–365	324–405	360–life	360–life	360–life
	40	292–365	324–405	360–life	360–life	360–life	360–life
	41	324–405	360–life	360–life	360–life	360–life	360–life
	42	360–life	360–life	360–life	360–life	360–life	360–life
	43	Life	Life	Life	Life	Life	Life

SOURCE: "Sentencing Table," in *2008 Federal Sentencing Guidelines Manual*, U.S. Sentencing Commission, November 2008, http://www.ussc.gov/Guidelines/2008_guidelines/Manual/GL2008.pdf (accessed November 24, 2010)

confinement, and, within each level, a minimum and a maximum number of months of imprisonment. This leaves judges with some discretion to determine sentencing.

Level 28 falls into the sentencing table's Zone D. (See Table 6.8.) Individuals in this zone are not permitted to receive any probation and must serve at least the minimum sentence shown in the applicable column.

Property crimes are handled in the USSC guidelines in a similar manner. The base level is increased with the value of the property that is involved.

DEPARTURES FROM THE GUIDELINES. As noted earlier, U.S. Supreme Court decisions in *Apprendi v. New Jersey*, *Blakely v. Washington*, and *Cunningham v. California* struck down state laws that allowed state judges to make

findings on their own (i.e., not jury findings) that imposed longer sentences than those called for under state law.

In 2005 the Supreme Court made a related ruling in *United States v. Booker* (543 U.S. 220). In this case the subject had been charged with possession with intent to distribute 1.8 ounces (50 grams) of crack cocaine, a crime for which the federal sentencing guidelines set a 262-month sentence. However, the judge later determined that Booker had possessed 3.2 ounces (92 grams) of crack cocaine and had also obstructed justice. Because of these additional offenses, the judge sentenced Booker to 360 months in prison. In language similar to the *Blakely* ruling, the court ruled that federal judges cannot determine facts that are used to increase a defendant's punishment beyond what is authorized by a jury verdict or the defendant's own admissions. In its ruling, the court struck down the mandatory application of sentencing guidelines and instructed courts to apply reasonableness in determining sentences. Guidelines should be considered, but judges are not required to follow them. The legal impact of these two decisions continues to be worked out in the courts.

According to the USSC, in an analysis of cases that were decided in fiscal year 2009, 56.8% of offenders were sentenced within the guideline range. (See Table 6.9.) Another 2% of offenders received departures above the guideline range, and 41.2% received departures below the guideline range. Of the latter, 25.3% received government-sponsored below-range sentences and 15.9% received non-government-sponsored below-range sentences.

REVISED SENTENCING GUIDELINES LEADING TO LESSER SENTENCES. As noted earlier, the USSC has occasionally amended the federal sentencing guidelines. Section

TABLE 6.9

National comparison of federal sentences imposed relative to federal sentencing guideline ranges, fiscal year 2009

	Number	%
Total cases	**79,153**	**100.0**
Cases sentenced within guideline range	44,991	56.8
Cases sentenced above guideline range	1,496	2.0
Departure above guideline range	533	0.7
Upward departure from guideline range[a]	382	0.5
Upward departure with *Booker*/18 U.S.C. §3553[b]	151	0.2
Otherwise above guideline range	963	1.3
Above guideline range with *Booker*/18 U.S.C. §3553[c]	842	1.1
All remaining cases above guideline range[d]	121	0.2
Government sponsored below range[e]	20,011	25.3
§5K1.1 Substantial Assistance Departure	9,855	12.5
§5K3.1 Early Disposition Program Departure	7,242	9.1
Other government sponsored below range	2,914	3.7
Non-government sponsored below range	12,655	15.9
Departure below guideline range	2,403	3.0
Downward departure from guideline range[a]	1,542	1.9
Downward departure with *Booker*/18 U.S.C. §3553[b]	861	1.1
Otherwise below guideline range	10,252	12.9
Below guideline range with *Booker*/18 U.S.C. §3553[c]	9,358	11.8
All remaining cases below guideline range[d]	894	1.1

Note: This table reflects the 81,372 cases sentenced in fiscal year 2009. Of these, 2,219 cases were excluded because information was missing from the submitted documents that prevented the comparison of the sentence and the guideline range.

[a]All cases with departures in which the court did not indicate as a reason either *United States v. Booker*, 18 U.S.C. §3553, or a factor or reason specifically prohibited in the provisions, policy statements, or commentary of the *Guidelines Manual*.

[b]All cases sentenced outside of the guideline range in which the court indicated both a departure (see footnote a) and a reference to either *United States v. Booker*, 18 U.S.C. §3553, or related factors as a reason for sentencing outside of the guideline system.

[c]All cases sentenced outside of the guideline range in which no departure was indicated and in which the court cited *United States v. Booker*, 18 U.S.C. §3553, or related factors as one of the reasons for sentencing outside of the guideline system.

[d]All cases sentenced outside of the guideline range that could not be classified into any of the three previous outside of the range categories. This category includes cases in which no reason was provided for a sentence outside of the range.

[e]Cases in which a reason for the sentence indicated that the prosecution initiated, proposed, or stipulated to a sentence outside of the guideline range, either pursuant to a plea agreement or as part of a non-plea negotiation with the defendant.

SOURCE: "Table N. National Comparison of Sentence Imposed and Position Relative to the Guideline Range, Fiscal Year 2009," in *U.S. Sentencing Commission's Sourcebook of Federal Sentencing Statistics*, U.S. Sentencing Commission, 2009, http://www.ussc.gov/Data_and_Statistics/Annual_Reports_and_Sourcebooks/2009/TableN.pdf (accessed November 8, 2010)

1B1.10 of the *2010 Federal Sentencing Guidelines Manual and Supplement* provides for the reduction of an inmate's prison term when a "guideline range applicable to that defendant" is subsequently lowered. This reduction is not applied in every case. For example, the USSC does not allow the reduced term to be less than the term the inmate has already served. In addition, the reduction is not automatic; the defendant's lawyer must file a motion with the court seeking the reduction. As described in Chapter 4, this situation arose in late 2010, when the USSC issued *Supplement to the 2010 Guidelines Manual* (November 1, 2010, http://www.ussc.gov/Guidelines/2010_guidelines/Manual_PDF/2010_Guidelines_Manual_Supplement.pdf) in response to the Fair Sentencing Act, which was signed by President Barack Obama (1961–) in August 2010. This supplement lowered the sentencing range for people convicted of crack cocaine offenses.

"Three Strikes, You're Out"

Nine years after passing the first truth-in-sentencing law, Washington State passed the first of the so-called three-strikes laws in December 1993. The measure took effect in the wake of a voter initiative, which passed by a three-to-one margin. Three-strikes laws are the functional equivalent of sentencing guidelines in that they mandate a fixed sentence length for repeat offenders for specified crimes or a mix of crimes—but their formulation in public debate, using the baseball analogy, is much easier to understand than the complexities of thick books of codes and sentencing tables.

Three-strikes laws were originally intended to ensure that the offender receives a mandatory long sentence upon conviction for the third offense, for example, life imprisonment without parole (as in Washington State) or 25 years without parole (as in California). These sentences guaranteed that the criminal would be removed from society for a long period of time or, in some instances, for life. Even though three-strikes laws are best known for their imposition of long sentences on a third offense, they also feature longer-than-average sentences for second offenses.

The Washington law identifies specific offenses that are "strikable." California, which passed its own (and more famous) three-strikes law just months after Washington passed its measure, specifies the categories of offenses that must precede the third felony conviction.

OPPOSITION AND CHALLENGES TO THREE-STRIKES LAWS. Opponents of three-strikes laws charge that the laws unfairly target African-Americans, who are disproportionately represented among felony convicts. They argue that three-strikes laws remove proportion and reasonableness from sentencing by making all third strikes punishable by the same prison sentence, whether it is for stealing a small item or killing someone. Opponents also note that incarcerating more people for longer periods requires more prisons and increases corrections costs for maintaining prisoners. Reducing the possibility of parole results in an increasing number of elderly prisoners, who are statistically much less likely to commit crimes than younger prisoners and who have increasing health care needs. Lastly, some critics suggest that the finality of three-strikes laws may make active criminals more desperate and, thus, more violent. According to this view, if criminals know they will be sentenced to life in prison, then they have nothing to lose and might be more likely to kill witnesses or to resist arrest through violent means.

In 2002 the U.S. Supreme Court agreed to consider whether California's three-strikes law, which was considered to be one of the toughest in the country, violates the Eighth Amendment's ban against cruel and unusual punishment. More than half of California prisoners sentenced under the three-strikes law were convicted of nonviolent third-strike felonies, including drug possession and petty theft, and are serving mandatory sentences of 25 years to life without the possibility of parole. In *Lockyer v. Andrade* (538 U.S. 63 [2003]), the court considered the case of Leandro Andrade, an inmate serving two consecutive 25-year sentences in California for stealing videotapes valued at $150 from two different video stores. Because each theft counted as an offense and Andrade had two prior convictions, the new crimes counted as his third and fourth strikes for purposes of sentencing. In a 5–4 decision, the court upheld the sentence imposed on Andrade and thereby upheld the right of states to impose long sentences on repeat felony offenders, regardless of the relative seriousness of the third-strike felony.

In 2003 the Supreme Court again ruled on the constitutionality of the California three-strikes law. The case involved the defendant Gary Albert Ewing, who had been sentenced to 25 years to life for a third offense, the theft of three golf clubs, with each valued at $399. His previous offenses included (among others) a burglary and a robbery while threatening his victim with a knife. *Ewing v. California* (538 U.S. 11 [2003]) was a good test of the California statute because neither of Ewing's first two offenses were seriously violent and the third, the triggering offense, was what is known under California law as a "wobbler," namely an offense that can be tried, at the prosecutor's option, as either a felony or a misdemeanor.

The petition in *Ewing* argued that the punishment was cruel, unusual, and disproportionate to the offense that was committed. In effect, Ewing had the profile of a habitual but petty criminal whose theft of golf clubs should have been tried as a misdemeanor. In this case the court dismissed the proportionality argument and, instead, affirmed the state's right to set policy for the protection of the public. Quoting from another case, the court said, "The Eighth Amendment does not require strict proportionality between crime and sentence [but] forbids only extreme sentences that are 'grossly disproportionate' to the crime." California had the right to incapacitate repeat offenders by incarcerating them. According to the court, the U.S. Constitution did not mandate that the states apply any one penological theory.

IMPACT AND EFFECTIVENESS OF THREE-STRIKES LAWS. In *An Examination of the Impact of 3-Strike Laws, 10 Years after Their Enactment* (September 21, 2004, http://www.soros.org/initiatives/usprograms/focus/justice/articles_publications/publications/threestrikes_20040923/three_strikes.pdf), Vincent Schiraldi, Jason Colburn, and Eric Lotke note that between 1993 and 2002, 23 states had passed three-strikes laws.

According to Schiraldi, Colburn, and Lotke, the three-strikes laws had little impact on state prison populations after they were enacted, except for California, Florida, and Georgia. Of the 21 three-strikes states on which data on the number of people incarcerated were available, 14 had incarcerated fewer than 100 people under three strikes. Only three states had more than 400 people imprisoned under three strikes: California (42,322 inmates), Georgia (7,631), and Florida (1,628). The researchers also report that between 1993 and 2002 states with three-strikes laws experienced a decline in serious crime rates only slightly greater (26.8%) than states without three-strikes laws (22.3%).

Further scientific analyses of three-strikes laws have been conducted by Brian Brown and Greg Jolivette of the Legislative Analyst's Office in *A Primer: Three Strikes—The Impact after More Than a Decade* (October 2005, http://www.lao.ca.gov/2005/3_strikes/3_strikes_102005.htm), by Eric Helland and Alexander Tabarrok in *Does Three Strikes Deter? A Non-parametric Estimation* (December 22, 2006, http://mason.gmu.edu/~atabarro/ThreeStrikes.pdf), and by Radha Iyengar in *I'd Rather Be Hanged for a Sheep Than a Lamb: The Unintended Consequences of "Three-Strikes" Laws* (February 2008, http://www.nber.org/papers/w13784).

Brown and Jolivette report that at year-end 2004 there were nearly 43,000 inmates in California prisons who had been sentenced under the three-strikes law. They made up just over one-fourth (26%) of the state's total prison population. Most of the so-called strikers (more than 35,000) were serving time for their second strike. Approximately 7,500 of the strikers were third strikers. From 1994 to 2001 the percent of second and third strikers grew quickly, from less than 5% to approximately 25% of California's total prison population. Through 2004 the percentage remained about 25%. Thirty-seven percent of the strikers were convicted of serious crimes, such as assault, robbery, and burglary. Nearly one-fourth (23%) of the strikers were serving time for drug charges. More than half (56%) of the strikers had been most recently convicted of a nonviolent nonserious crime. However, Brown and Jolivette find that the criminal histories of the strikers were "more serious," on average, than the criminal histories of nonstrikers.

Brown and Jolivette list the racial makeup of California's second and third strikers as 37% African-American, 33% Hispanic, and 26% white. This breakdown is described as "similar" to the overall prison population in the state. African-Americans make up 45% of the third-striker population, but only 30% of the overall prison population. The researchers examine the effects of California's three-strikes law on public safety. The state's crime rate had already begun to decline at the time the law was implemented in 1994 and continued to decline over the following decade. However, a variety of factors is believed to have played a role in the decline. Brown and Jolivette conclude that it is "difficult to conclusively evaluate the law's impact on crime and safety."

Helland and Tabarrok examine the arrest and conviction records of a large subset of criminals who were released from California prisons in 1994. They determine that the state's three-strikes law reduced felony arrest rates by 17% to 20% among second strikers and kept them from committing further serious crimes.

Iyengar finds a similar result in her study. She estimates that California's three-strikes law "reduced participation in criminal activity" by 20% for first strikers (i.e., criminals facing second-strike sentences on their next offense) and by 28% for second strikers. However, Iyengar concludes that second strikers who did choose to commit further crimes were more likely to commit more violent crimes than they otherwise would have committed because the consequences were the same regardless of the violent nature of the third strike. For example, second strikers were more willing to commit robbery than burglary and more willing to commit a rape or assault during the commission of a burglary. In addition, Iyengar claims the state's three-strikes law encouraged some strikers to commit their next serious crime outside of the state. According to Iyengar, "Three strikes appears to have imposed 50,000 crimes on other states due to the migration of criminals out of California."

AMENDING THREE-STRIKES LAWS. The three-strikes laws were a product of the early 1990s, a time of historically high crime rates and a booming national economy. By the end of the first decade of the 21st century, however, decreasing crime rates and increasing budget pressures led many states to water down their three-strikes laws. The National Conference of State Legislators (NCSL) is a bipartisan organization that provides research and technical assistance on legislative issues to state policy makers. In "Three Strikes Laws: Past and Present" (October 2010, http://www.ncsl.org/portals/1/Documents/cj/BulletinOct-2010.pdf), the NCSL notes that 24 states enacted three-strikes laws between 1993

and 1995. However, since that time the majority of these states have amended their laws to make them less rigid. The biggest change has been the elimination of mandatory sentences in favor of "judicial discretion." In other words, judges do not have to automatically apply specific sentences, although they may be bound by sentencing guidelines. According to the NCSL, nearly a third of the states with three-strikes laws have either eliminated or limited the imposition of a life sentence without the possibility for parole as the penalty for third strikers.

The NCSL reports that some states (Arkansas, Georgia, New Mexico, North Dakota, Tennessee, Utah, Vermont, and Virginia) have not amended their original three-strikes laws. California has changed its law to allow for more flexibility in sentencing, but the sentence choices can be even harsher than those originally prescribed. For example, California's law originally included a mandatory life sentence that required third strikers to serve at least 25 years. The NCSL notes that in 2010 California law required third strikers to serve the longest prison term of the following three choices: 25 years, a term of three times the sentence prescribed for the offense for nonthird strikers, or the latter plus any allowed sentence enhancements.

Alternative Sentencing

Forms of sentencing other than incarceration, probation, or a combination of the two (split sentences) are widely used in virtually every state. State departments of correction, the District of Columbia, and the Federal Bureau of Prisons offer a range of alternative sentencing options for criminal offenders. Even though programs can vary among regions, these options include work-release and weekender programs, shock incarceration (sometimes called boot camp), community service programs, day fines, day reporting centers, intensive probation supervision, house arrest and electronic monitoring, residential community corrections, and diversionary treatment programs. Other types of alternative sentencing options, such as mediation and restitution, are sometimes available.

WORK RELEASE AND WEEKENDER PROGRAMS. Work-release programs permit selected prisoners nearing the end of their sentence to work in the community and return to prison facilities or community residential facilities during nonworking hours. Such programs are designed to prepare inmates to return to the community in a relatively controlled environment while they are learning how to work productively. Work release also allows inmates to earn an income, reimburse the state for part of their confinement costs, build up savings for their eventual full release, and acquire more positive living habits. Those on weekender programs spend certain days in prison, usually weekends, but are free the remainder of the time. Both of these types of sentences are known as intermittent incarceration.

Violent offenders and those convicted of drug offenses are usually excluded from these programs by the courts.

SHOCK INCARCERATION. Shock incarceration is another name for reformatories or boot camps that use military discipline for juveniles and adults. The DOJ explains in *Correctional Boot Camps: Lessons from a Decade of Research* (June 2003, http://www.ncjrs.gov/pdffiles1/nij/197018.pdf) that boot camps became popular in the United States during the 1980s and early 1990s. By 1995 more than 120 of them were in operation. Most boot camp sentences were short, for example, three to four months.

Typically, boot camp programs include physical training and regular drill-type exercise, housekeeping and maintenance of the facility, and hard labor. Virtually all these programs are based on the assumption that a military regimen is beneficial. Despite great public expectations, by 2009 many boot camps had closed for failing to meet their primary objectives: reduce recidivism (relapse into criminal activity) and reduce prison populations. According to the DOJ, research indicates that boot camps are effective only at achieving short-term changes in inmate attitudes and behavior.

COMMUNITY SERVICE PROGRAMS. Community service is most often a supplement to other penalties and mainly given to white-collar criminals, juvenile delinquents, and those who commit nonserious crimes. Offenders are usually required to work for government or private nonprofit agencies cleaning parks, collecting roadside trash, setting up chairs for community events, painting community projects, and helping out at nursing homes.

DAY FINES. Under the day-fines type of alternative sentence, the offender pays a monetary sum rather than spending time in jail or prison. Day-fines are fines that are assessed for a specific number of days in which the fine amount is based on the seriousness of the crime, the criminal record of the offender, and the offender's income. The fines are paid into the jurisdiction's treasury.

DAY REPORTING CENTERS. Day reporting centers (DRCs) allow offenders to reside in the community. DRCs are often populated by people with drug and alcohol problems and require offenders to appear on a frequent and regular basis to participate in services or activities that are provided by the center or other community agencies. Random drug screening and breathalyzer tests may be administered. The centers may provide employment and educational training and conduct classes on topics such as anger management, substance abuse, life skills, and cognitive skills. Failure to adhere to program requirements or to report at stated intervals can lead to commitment to prison or jail. DRC participation can also be terminated if the offender is charged with a new crime.

INTENSIVE PROBATION SUPERVISION. Intensive probation supervision (IPS) is another method of closely supervising offenders while they reside in the community. Routine probation is not designed or structured to handle high-risk probationers. Therefore, IPS was developed as an alternative that is stricter than routine probation.

The caseloads of officers assigned to IPS offenders are kept low. In most IPS programs the offender must contact a supervising officer frequently, pay restitution to victims, participate in community service, have and keep a job, and, if appropriate, undergo random and unannounced drug testing. Offenders are often required to pay a probation fee.

HOUSE ARREST AND ELECTRONIC MONITORING. Some nonviolent offenders are sentenced to house arrest (or home confinement), which means that they are legally required to remain confined in their own home. They are allowed to leave only for medical purposes or to go to work, although some curfew programs permit offenders to work during the day and have a specified number of hours of free time before returning home. The idea began as a way to keep drunk drivers off the street, but it quickly expanded to include other nonviolent offenders.

The most severe type of house arrest is home incarceration, where the offender's home actually becomes a prison that he or she cannot leave except for very special reasons, such as medical emergencies. Home-detention programs require the offender to be at home when he or she is not working. Some offenders are required to perform a certain number of hours of community service and, if they are employed, to repay the cost of probation and/or restitution.

An electronic monitoring program (EMP) that is used in tandem with house arrest involves attaching a small radio transmitter to the offender in a nonremovable bracelet or anklet. Some systems send a signal to a small monitoring box, which is programmed to call a department of corrections computer if the signal is broken; other systems randomly call probationers and the computer verifies each prisoner's identity through voice recognition software. In some cases a special device in the electronic monitor sends a confirmation to the computer. Some systems have global positioning system technologies to help corrections officers ensure that offenders are not violating any territorial restrictions.

EMPs are often used to monitor the whereabouts of those who are under house arrest and permitted to work. Electronic monitoring is sometimes used to ensure that child molesters stay a specified distance from schools. EMPs cost much less than building new prison cells or housing more inmates. However, close supervision by officers is crucial to the success of EMPs. Officers must ensure that the participants are indeed working when they leave the house and that they are not using illegal drugs. Electronic monitoring equipment must also be checked periodically to make certain that the offenders have not attempted to disable the equipment.

RESIDENTIAL COMMUNITY CORRECTIONS. Residential community corrections facilities are known informally as halfway houses because they are designed to help prisoners reintegrate into community life. Some offenders are sentenced to halfway houses directly in lieu of incarceration if their offenses and general profile indicate they will benefit from the structure and counseling available in such facilities. Many states frequently use halfway houses to relieve prison overcrowding.

Residential centers house offenders in a structured environment. Offenders work full time, maintain the residence center, perform community service, and sometimes attend educational or counseling programs. They may leave the centers only for work or approved programs such as substance-abuse treatment. One type of residential program, called the restitution center, allows offenders to work to pay restitution and child support. The centers regularly test the residents for drugs.

DIVERSIONARY TREATMENT PROGRAMS. Probation combined with mandatory treatment programs is used as an alternative sentence for nonviolent offenders convicted of drug offenses, alcohol abuse, or nonviolent sex offenses. Sentenced individuals are free on probation but typically are required to attend group therapy and supervised professional treatment sessions.

MEDIATION AND RESTITUTION. In mediation the victims and the offenders meet under the auspices of a community representative and work out a "reconciliation," usually involving some type of restitution and requiring the offenders to take responsibility for their actions. This technique is used mainly for minor crimes and often involves private organizations; therefore, the judiciary does not always accept its resolution. Most often, restitution is not considered the complete punishment but part of a broader punishment, such as probation or working off the restitution dollar amount while in prison.

Death Penalty

The ultimate penalty that can be imposed by the U.S. judiciary system is the death penalty, also known as capital punishment. The Eighth Amendment of the U.S. Constitution guarantees that "cruel and unusual punishments [not be] inflicted." In recent decades debates have raged about the morality and deterrent effect of the death penalty and whether or not capital punishment is cruel and unusual punishment under the Constitution. According to Tracy L. Snell of the BJS, in *Capital Punishment, 2009—Statistical Tables* (December 2010, http://bjs.ojp.usdoj.gov/content/

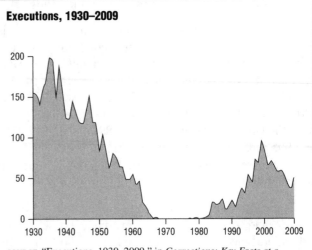

FIGURE 6.5

Executions, 1930–2009

SOURCE: "Executions, 1930–2009," in *Corrections: Key Facts at a Glance*, U.S. Department of Justice, Office of Justice Programs, Bureau of Justice Statistics, 2010, http://bjs.ojp.usdoj.gov/content/glance/exe .cfm (accessed September 30, 2010)

pub/pdf/cp09st.pdf), 3,173 state and federal prisoners were under a sentence of death at year-end 2009. Figure 6.5 shows the number of executions that were carried out annually between 1930 and 2009. In 2009 there were 52 executions.

KEY U.S. SUPREME COURT CASES. Three Supreme Court cases, all decided during the 1970s, have produced the current interpretation of the Eighth Amendment relative to the death penalty. In *Furman v. Georgia* (408 U.S. 238 [1972]), the court held that the death penalty in three cases under review was cruel and unusual because under the then-prevailing statutes juries had "untrammeled discretion ... to pronounce life or death in capital cases." Due process required procedural fairness, including consideration of the severity and circumstances of the crime. In the three cases decided in *Furman*, three individuals were condemned to die, two for rape and one for murder. All three of the offenders were African-American.

In response to *Furman*, states modified their statutes. North Carolina imposed a mandatory death sentence for first-degree murder. This law was tested by the Supreme Court in *Woodson v. North Carolina* (428 U.S. 280 [1976]). The court held that even though the death penalty was not a cruel and unusual punishment in every circumstance, a mandatory death sentence did not satisfy the requirements laid down in *Furman*. The court stated, "North Carolina's mandatory death penalty statute for first-degree murder departs markedly from contemporary standards respecting the imposition of the punishment of death and thus cannot be applied consistently with the Eighth and Fourteenth Amendments' requirement that the State's power to punish 'be exercised within the limits of civilized standards.'" The court overturned the North Carolina law.

Woodson was decided on July 2, 1976. On that same day the court rendered its judgment in *Gregg v. Georgia* (428 U.S. 153), the case of a man who was sentenced to death for murder and robbery under new legislation that passed in Georgia following *Furman*. In this case the court upheld the death penalty, saying, in part:

> The Georgia statutory system under which petitioner was sentenced to death is constitutional. The new procedures on their face satisfy the concerns of *Furman*, since before the death penalty can be imposed there must be specific jury findings as to the circumstances of the crime or the character of the defendant, and the State Supreme Court thereafter reviews the comparability of each death sentence with the sentences imposed on similarly situated defendants to ensure that the sentence of death in a particular case is not disproportionate. Petitioner's contentions that the changes in Georgia's sentencing procedures have not removed the elements of arbitrariness and capriciousness condemned by *Furman* are without merit.

Death Penalty for Juveniles

In *Roper v. Simmons* (543 U.S. 551 [2005]), the Supreme Court ruled that the death penalty for minors is cruel and unusual punishment. In a 5–4 ruling, the court found it unconstitutional to sentence someone to death for a crime he or she committed when he or she was younger than the age of 18 years. As a result of the ruling, dozens of prisoners were removed from death row.

As part of its argument for outlawing the death penalty for minors, the court cited scientific opinion that teenagers are too immature to be held accountable in the same way as adults for the crimes they commit. Justice Anthony M. Kennedy (1936–), who spoke for the majority, explained that "from a moral standpoint it would be misguided to equate the failings of a minor with those of an adult, for a greater possibility exists that a minor's character deficiencies will be reformed."

As will be explained in Chapter 10, in May 2010 the Supreme Court ruled in *Graham v. Florida* (560 U.S. ___) that a sentence of life imprisonment with no chance for parole is unconstitutional when applied to minors who are convicted of committing crimes in which no one is killed. As of February 2011, this sentence remained legal

FIGURE 6.6

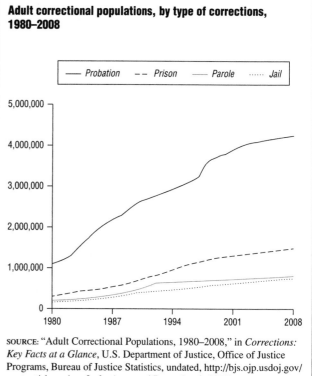

Adult correctional populations, by type of corrections, 1980–2008

SOURCE: "Adult Correctional Populations, 1980–2008," in *Corrections: Key Facts at a Glance*, U.S. Department of Justice, Office of Justice Programs, Bureau of Justice Statistics, undated, http://bjs.ojp.usdoj.gov/content/glance/corr2.cfm (accessed December 2, 2010)

for minors who are convicted of crimes in which someone is killed.

THE CORRECTIONS SYSTEM

The corrections system operates prisons, jails, and other places of confinement; oversees parole; and administers probation. Figure 6.6 shows the adult correctional population in the United States between 1980 and 2008. According to Lauren E. Glaze and Thomas P. Bonczar of the BJS, in *Probation and Parole in the United States, 2007 Statistical Tables* (December 2008, http://bjs.ojp.usdoj.gov/content/pub/pdf/ppus07st.pdf), 3.2% of the U.S. adult population was incarcerated or on probation or parole at year-end 2007. Detailed information about correctional facilities, inmates, and people on probation or parole is provided in Chapters 7, 8, and 9, respectively.

CHAPTER 7
CORRECTIONAL FACILITIES: PRISONS AND JAILS

Public views of crime and punishment have changed over the centuries. In general, most societies have moved away from the extraction of personal or family justice (vengeful acts such as blood feuds or the practice of taking "an eye for an eye") toward formal systems that are based on written codes and orderly processes. Prisons and jails have changed from being holding places where prisoners awaited deportation, maiming, whipping, or execution to places of extended—even lifelong—incarceration. Confinement itself has become the punishment.

THE HISTORY OF CORRECTIONS IN THE UNITED STATES

During the colonial period in U.S. history physical punishment was more common than incarceration. Stocks, pillories, branding, flogging, and maiming (such as cutting off an ear or slitting the nostrils) were typical punishments meted out to offenders. The death penalty was also used frequently. The Puritans of Massachusetts believed that humans were naturally depraved, which made it easier for some of the colonies and the first states to enforce harsh punishments. In addition, because Puritans maintained the view that individuals had no control over their fate (predestination), few early Americans supported the idea that criminals could be rehabilitated.

The Quakers, led by William Penn (1644–1718), made colonial Pennsylvania an exception to the harsh practices that were often found in the other colonies. The early criminal code of colonial Pennsylvania abolished executions for all crimes except homicide, replaced physical punishments with imprisonment and hard labor, and did not charge the prisoners for their food and housing.

The Reform Movement

The idea of individual freedom and the concept that people could change society for the better by using reason permeated American society during the 1800s. Reformers worked to abolish slavery, secure women's rights, and prohibit liquor, as well as to change the corrections system. Rehabilitation of prisoners became the goal of criminal justice, and inmates were given work to keep them busy and to defray the cost of their confinement. Prison administrators began constructing factories within prison walls or hiring inmates out as laborers in chain gangs. In rural areas inmates worked on prison-owned farms. In the South prisoners were often leased out to local farmers. Prison superintendents justified the hard labor by arguing that it taught the offenders the value of work and self-discipline. With the rise of labor unions in the North, the 1930s saw an end to the large-scale prison industry. Unions complained about competing with the inmates' free labor, especially amid the rising unemployment of the Great Depression (1929–1939). As a result, states began limiting what inmates could produce.

As crime increased from the 1970s through the early 1990s, criminal justice practices such as indeterminate sentencing, probation, parole, and treatment programs came under attack. Support decreased for rehabilitative programs and increased for keeping offenders incarcerated; many people subscribed to the idea that keeping criminals off the streets was the surest way to keep them from committing more crimes. In response, the federal government and a growing number of states introduced mandatory sentencing and life terms for habitual criminals. They also limited the use of probation, parole, and time off for good behavior. As a result, the incarceration rate skyrocketed through the early 1990s. Crime rates began falling during the late 1990s and this trend continued through the first decade of the 21st century. The decrease in crime rates led to a much slower growth in the incarcerated population.

TYPES OF PRISONER COUNTS

The Bureau of Justice Statistics (BJS) within the U.S. Department of Justice (DOJ) compiles detailed data on federal, state, and local correctional facilities and inmates.

It is important to note that some BJS reports distinguish between two different types of prisoner counts: a custody count and a count of the number of inmates under jurisdiction. A custody count is the number of inmates physically located within a particular facility, correctional system, or state. The number of inmates under jurisdiction is the number of inmates under the legal authority of a particular jurisdiction, for example, the state of California. These inmates may or may not be physically located in facilities in the same jurisdiction. In addition, inmates under the legal authority of one type of jurisdiction, such as a state, may be physically located in a facility of another jurisdiction, such as a county jail.

PRISONS AND JAILS COMPARED

Corrections institutions are organized into tiers by level of government, and at each level (federal, state, and local) specific types of institutions provide corrections functions based on the relative severity of the offenses committed. The most restrictive form of corrections is incarceration in a prison. Both the federal and the state governments operate their own prison systems; within the federal government, the military maintains its own prisons. Prison inmates serve time for serious offenses that carry a sentence of at least one year of incarceration.

Most people sentenced to jail serve less than a year for misdemeanors and offenses against the public order. The vast majority of jails are operated at the local level by cities and counties. The federal government operates some jails as well, and within the federal government the U.S. Immigration and Customs Enforcement has its own detention facilities. Prisons and jails are operated under a single state authority in Alaska, Connecticut, Delaware, Hawaii, Rhode Island, and Vermont.

PUBLIC VERSUS PRIVATE CORRECTIONAL FACILITIES

During the 1980s the rapidly rising prison and jail populations led a few jurisdictions to privatize some of their correctional facilities. The basic assumption behind this idea is that the private sector is inherently more efficient, flexible, and cost effective than the government sector because it is less constrained by bureaucracy. It is also argued that private facilities save the public the initial costs of prison construction because those costs are assumed by private contractors. This saves the government from taking on long-term debt to build housing for more prisoners. In this view, a privatized or even a partially privatized corrections system would cost taxpayers less money. Corrections functions, however, are ultimately vested in governmental hands, and private prisons must operate under established rules and regulations.

According to Heather C. West of the BJS, in *Prison Inmates at Midyear 2009—Statistical Tables* (June 2010,

http://bjs.ojp.usdoj.gov/content/pub/pdf/pim09st.pdf), 7.9% of the prisoners under state or federal jurisdiction were held in private correctional facilities as of midyear 2009. That percentage was up from 6.3% in 2000.

FEDERAL CORRECTIONS

The Federal Bureau of Prisons (BOP; http://www.bop .gov) was established in 1930 as an agency of the DOJ to oversee the corrections system for federal inmates and to administer federal prisons. The BOP notes in "Weekly Population Report" (http://www.bop.gov/locations/weekly _report.jsp) that as of February 3, 2011, it oversaw 209,521 federal inmates. Most of the inmates (171,296 or 81.8% of the total) were in BOP facilities. An additional 23,988 inmates (11.4% of the total) were in privately managed facilities, and 14,237 inmates (6.8% of the total) were held in other contract facilities, such as jails or community corrections centers, or were under home confinement.

The BOP directly operated 183 facilities around the country at that time. The five states with the largest number of BOP facilities were Texas (22), California (16), Pennsylvania (14), Florida (12), and Kentucky (10). The 10 BOP facilities housing the largest number of inmates were:

- Fort Dix Federal Correctional Institute, New Jersey— 4,397 inmates
- Brooklyn Metropolitan Detention Center, New York—2,661 inmates
- Forrest City Federal Correctional Institute, Arkansas—2,030 inmates
- Beaumont Low-Security Federal Correctional Institute, Texas—2,011 inmates
- Atlanta U.S. Penitentiary, Georgia—1,985 inmates
- Coleman Low-Security Federal Correctional Institute, Florida—1,923 inmates
- Seagoville Federal Correctional Institute, Texas— 1,918 inmates
- Leavenworth U.S. Penitentiary, Kansas—1,877 inmates
- Elkton Federal Correctional Institute, Ohio—1,859 inmates
- Yazoo City Federal Correctional Institute, Mississippi— 1,833 inmates

Security Levels of Federal Prisons

The BOP maintains institutions at five different security levels, and each prisoner is assigned to a particular level based on that individual's offenses and behavioral history:

- Minimum security—at the lowest security level are federal prison camps. These facilities have dormitory housing, a relatively low staff-to-inmate ratio, and limited or no perimeter fencing. They are located on or near larger institutions or military bases, where the inmates participate in work programs.

- Low-security federal correctional institutions (FCIs)—FCIs have fenced perimeters and a dormitory that consists of cubicle housing. Inmates are typically involved in work programs.

- Medium-security FCIs—these facilities feature reinforced perimeter fencing, usually a double fence with an electronic detection system. In addition, inmates are housed in cells and have access to work and treatment programs.

- High-security U.S. penitentiaries (USPs)—the most secure environment in the federal prison system includes highly secured perimeters with walls and reinforced fences. Inmates are held in multiple- or single-occupant cells, are closely watched, and do not have freedom to move around within the facility without supervision.

- Administrative facilities—these facilities hold offenders awaiting trial or treat inmates with serious medical needs. Special facilities may also be used to house the most dangerous, violent, or escape-prone inmates. These include metropolitan correctional centers, metropolitan detention centers, federal detention centers, federal medical centers, the Federal Transfer Center in Oklahoma City, Oklahoma, and the Administrative-Maximum USP in Florence, Colorado.

CENSUS OF STATE AND FEDERAL CORRECTIONAL FACILITIES

Since 1974 the DOJ has performed a census of state and federal correctional facilities every five to seven years. As of February 2011, the most recent results were published by James J. Stephan of the BJS in *Census of State and Federal Correctional Facilities, 2005* (October 2008, http://bjs.ojp.usdoj.gov/content/pub/pdf/csfcf05.pdf). In 2005 there were 1,821 facilities—1,719 state facilities and 102 federal facilities. The vast majority of the facilities were publicly operated (1,406 facilities) rather than privately operated (415 facilities). Between 2000 and 2005 the total number of state prisons increased by 8.5%, whereas the total number of federal prisons increased by 21.4%. The number of inmates housed in state and federal prisons increased by 9.6% during this same period.

In 2005 state prisons housed nearly 1.3 million inmates, whereas federal prisons held less than 146,000 inmates. The number of state inmates increased by 7.5% between 2000 and 2005. A much larger increase (31.4%)

occurred in federal prisons. The number of combined state and federal inmates per 100,000 U.S. residents increased from 464 in 2000 to 480 in 2005.

In 2005 the largest number of prisons (946) housed fewer than 500 inmates each. Likewise, the largest number of prisons (969) were minimum-security facilities. The number of prisons holding 2,500 inmates or more rose from 65 in 2000 to 76 in 2005, an increase of 16.9%, which was the largest increase for any size range. The number of minimum-security prisons increased by 19% during this same period, from 814 in 2000 to 969 in 2005.

Correctional Facility Employees

State and federal correctional facilities employed more than 445,000 people as of December 30, 2005. Nearly two-thirds (67%) of the employees were male. Correctional officers, who work in direct contact with inmates, numbered 295,261 (66% of the total). Clerical and maintenance workers include secretaries, clerks, janitors, cooks, and groundskeepers. They accounted for 12% of state and federal prison employees. Professional and technical staff members are doctors, nurses, dentists, counselors, and other medical and social workers. They made up 10% of total employees. Academic and technical educators made up 3% of the workforce, and prison administrators (such as wardens) accounted for 2% of the workforce. Another 7% of state and federal prison workers were not specifically classified in the 2005 census.

State Prisons and Inmates

As of 2005, the 10 states with the largest numbers of state prisons were:

- Texas—132
- Florida—109
- California—100
- North Carolina—88
- Georgia—87
- New York—77
- Michigan—62
- Ohio—59
- Virginia—59
- Colorado—58

In 2005 the states housing the most state inmates were California (169,988), Texas (163,556), Florida (86,705), New York (63,855), and Georgia (51,822).

Work, Educational, and Counseling Programs for Inmates

As of December 30, 2005, a large majority of state and federal prisons offered inmate work, educational, and counseling programs. Most facilities (88%) offered inmate work programs, typically in facility support services. Similarly, 85% of state and federal prisons offered educational programs to the inmates, mostly for secondary education and general education diploma testing. Even more facilities (92%) offered counseling programs, mainly in life skills and community adjustment.

PRISON INMATES AT YEAR-END 2009

State correctional facilities, including prisons, are commonly overseen by state corrections or public safety agencies. Table 7.1 lists the responsible agency for each state and the District of Columbia.

Every year the DOJ collects data on the nation's state and federal inmate population. Surveys are conducted at midyear and at the end of the year. Survey results from year-end 2009 were reported by West in *Prisoners at Yearend 2009—Advance Counts* (June 2010, http://bjs.ojp .usdoj.gov/content/pub/pdf/py09ac.pdf). Just over 1.6 million inmates were under state or federal jurisdiction at year-end 2009. (See Table 7.2.) The vast majority (87.1% or 1.4 million) of the inmates were in state prisons and 12.9% (208,118) were in federal prisons.

Table 7.2 lists the number of inmates under state or federal jurisdiction by state at year-end 2009. The states

TABLE 7.1

State correctional departments, 2010

Alabama	Alabama Department of Corrections	http://www.doc.state.al.us/
Alaska	Alaska Department of Corrections	http://www.correct.state.ak.us/corrections/index.jsf
Arizona	Arizona Department of Corrections	http://www.adc.state.az.us/
Arkansas	Arkansas Department of Correction	http://www.adc.arkansas.gov/
California	California Department of Corrections and Rehabilitation	http://www.cdcr.ca.gov/
Colorado	Colorado Department of Corrections	http://www.doc.state.co.us/
Connecticut	Connecticut Department of Correction	http://www.ct.gov/doc/site/default.asp
Delaware	Delaware Department of Correction	http://www.doc.delaware.gov/
District of Columbia	District of Columbia Department of Corrections	http://doc.dc.gov/doc/site/default.asp
Florida	Florida Department of Corrections	http://www.dc.state.fl.us/
Georgia	Georgia Department of Corrections	http://www.dcor.state.ga.us/
Hawaii	Hawaii Department of Public Safety, Corrections Division	http://hawaii.gov/psd/corrections
Idaho	Idaho Department of Correction	http://www.corr.state.id.us/
Illinois	Illinois Department of Corrections	http://www.idoc.state.il.us/
Indiana	Indiana Department of Correction	http://www.in.gov/idoc/
Iowa	Iowa Department of Corrections	http://www.doc.state.ia.us/
Kansas	Kansas Department of Corrections	http://www.dc.state.ks.us/
Kentucky	Kentucky Department of Corrections	http://www.corrections.ky.gov/
Louisiana	Louisiana Department of Public Safety and Corrections	http://www.corrections.state.la.us/
Maine	Maine Department of Corrections	http://www.maine.gov/corrections/
Maryland	Maryland Department of Public Safety and Correctional Services	http://www.dpscs.state.md.us/
Massachusetts	Massachusetts Department of Correction	http://www.mass.gov/?pageID=eopsagencylanding& L=3&L0=Home&L1=Public+Safety+Agencies&L2= Massachusetts+Department+of+Correction&sid=Eeops
Michigan	Michigan Department of Corrections	http://www.michigan.gov/corrections
Minnesota	Minnesota Department of Corrections	http://www.doc.state.mn.us/
Mississippi	Mississippi Department of Corrections	http://www.mdoc.state.ms.us/
Missouri	Missouri Department of Corrections	http://doc.mo.gov/
Montana	Montana Department of Corrections	http://www.cor.mt.gov/default.mcpx
Nebraska	Nebraska Department of Corrections	http://www.corrections.nebraska.gov/
Nevada	Nevada Department of Corrections	http://www.doc.nv.gov/
New Hampshire	New Hampshire Department of Corrections	http://www.nh.gov/nhdoc/
New Jersey	New Jersey Department of Corrections	http://www.state.nj.us/corrections/
New Mexico	New Mexico Corrections Department	http://www.corrections.state.nm.us/
New York	New York State Department of Correctional Services	http://www.docs.state.ny.us/
North Carolina	North Carolina Department of Correction	http://www.doc.state.nc.us/
North Dakota	North Dakota Department of Corrections and Rehabilitation	http://www.nd.gov/docr/
Ohio	Ohio Department of Rehabilitation and Correction	http://www.drc.ohio.gov/
Oklahoma	Oklahoma Department of Corrections	http://www.doc.state.ok.us/
Oregon	Oregon Department of Correction	http://www.oregon.gov/DOC/index.shtml
Pennsylvania	Pennsylvania Department of Corrections	http://www.cor.state.pa.us/portal/server.pt/community/ department_of_corrections/4604
Rhode Island	Rhode Island Department of Corrections	http://www.doc.ri.gov/index.php
South Carolina	South Carolina Department of Corrections	http://www.doc.sc.gov/
South Dakota	South Dakota Department of Corrections	http://doc.sd.gov/
Tennessee	Tennessee Department of Correction	http://www.state.tn.us/correction/
Texas	Texas Department of Criminal Justice	http://tdcj.state.tx.us/
Utah	Utah Department of Corrections	http://corrections.utah.gov/
Vermont	Vermont Department of Corrections	http://www.doc.state.vt.us/
Virginia	Virginia Department of Corrections	http://www.vadoc.state.va.us/
Washington	Washington State Department of Corrections	http://www.doc.wa.gov/
West Virginia	West Virginia Division of Corrections	http://www.wvdoc.com/wvdoc/
Wisconsin	Wisconsin Department of Corrections	http://www.wi-doc.com/
Wyoming	Wyoming Department of Corrections	http://doc.state.wy.us/

SOURCE: Created by Kim Masters Evans for Gale, 2010

TABLE 7.2

State and federal inmates at yearend, by jurisdiction, 2009

Region and jurisdiction	Number of prisoners 12/31/2009
U.S. total[a]	1,613,656
Federal	208,118
State	1,405,538
Northeast	**177,361**
Connecticut[a]	19,716
Maine	2,206
Massachusetts	11,316
New Hampshire	2,731
New Jersey	25,382
New York	58,687
Pennsylvania	51,429
Rhode Island[a]	3,674
Vermont[a]	2,220
Midwest	**261,603**
Illinois	45,161
Indiana	28,808
Iowa[b]	8,813
Kansas	8,641
Michigan	45,478
Minnesota	9,986
Missouri	30,563
Nebraska	4,474
North Dakota	1,486
Ohio	51,606
South Dakota	3,434
Wisconsin	23,153
South	**649,451**
Alabama	31,790
Arkansas	15,208
Delaware[a]	6,794
District of Columbia	~
Florida	103,915
Georgia[b]	53,371
Kentucky	21,638
Louisiana	39,780
Maryland	22,255
Mississippi	21,482
North Carolina	39,860
Oklahoma	26,397
South Carolina	24,288
Tennessee	26,965
Texas	171,249
Virginia	38,092
West Virginia	6,367

TABLE 7.2

State and federal inmates at yearend, by jurisdiction, 2009 [CONTINUED]

Region and jurisdiction	Number of prisoners 12/31/2009
West	**317,123**
Alaska[a]	5,285
Arizona[b]	40,627
California	171,275
Colorado	22,795
Hawaii[a]	5,891
Idaho	7,400
Montana	3,605
Nevada	12,482
New Mexico	6,519
Oregon	14,403
Utah	6,533
Washington	18,233
Wyoming	2,075

~Not applicable. As of December 31, 2001, sentenced felons from the District of Columbia were the responsibility of the Federal Bureau of Prisons.
[a]Prisons and jails form one integrated system. Data include total jail and prison populations.
[b]Prison population based on custody counts.
[c]Data for 2008 and 2009 are not comparable.

SOURCE: Adapted from Heather C. West, "Appendix Table 1. Prisoners under the Jurisdiction of State or Federal Correctional Authorities, by Jurisdiction, December 31, 2000 and 2008, with Advanced Counts for 2009," in *Prisoners at Yearend 2009—Advance Counts*, U.S. Department of Justice, Office of Justice Programs, Bureau of Justice Statistics, June 2010, http://bjs.ojp.usdoj.gov/content/pub/pdf/py09ac.pdf (accessed November 8, 2010)

Figure 7.1 shows the annual percent change in the number of inmates under state and federal jurisdiction between 2000 and 2009, based on an advanced count at year-end 2009. The annual percent increased by 2% or more during most years from 2000 to 2006. After 2006 the annual percent continued to increase, but its pace slowed to approximately 1.8% in 2007, to 0.7% in 2008, and to 0.2% in 2009.

JAILS

Besides confining offenders for short terms (usually a sentence of less than one year), jails administer community justice programs that offer alternatives to incarceration. Jails also hold suspects awaiting arraignment, trial, or sentencing, and detainees such as juveniles and mental patients who are being transferred to other facilities.

Jail Inmates at Midyear 2009

Data from the DOJ survey of the nation's jail population conducted June 30, 2010, were reported by Todd D. Minton in *Jail Inmates at Midyear 2009—Statistical Tables* (June 2010, http://bjs.ojp.usdoj.gov/content/pub/pdf/jim09st.pdf). At midyear 2009, 767,620 inmates were being held in local jails. (See Figure 7.2.) As shown in Table 7.3, the number of local jail inmates was 621,149 in 2000. The jail inmate population grew at an average annual rate of around 2% to 5% between 2000 and 2006.

with the highest number of inmates under their jurisdiction were:

• California—171,275

• Texas—171,249

• Florida—103,915

• New York—58,687

• Florida—53,371

• Ohio—51,606

• Pennsylvania—51,429

• Michigan—45,478

• Illinois—45,161

• North Carolina—39,860

FIGURE 7.1

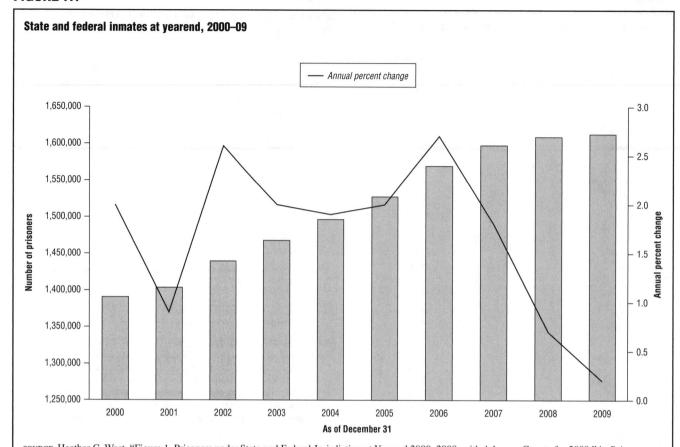

State and federal inmates at yearend, 2000–09

SOURCE: Heather C. West, "Figure 1. Prisoners under State and Federal Jurisdiction at Yearend 2000–2008, with Advance Counts for 2009," in *Prisoners at Yearend 2009—Advance Counts*, U.S. Department of Justice, Office of Justice Programs, Bureau of Justice Statistics, June 2010, http://bjs.ojp.usdoj.gov/content/pub/pdf/py09ac.pdf (accessed November 8, 2010)

Between 2007 and 2008 the annual change slowed to 1.9% and 0.7%, respectively. In 2009 the jail inmate population decreased 2.3%.

Local Jail Sizes

Table 7.4 breaks down the nation's local jail inmates by size of facility as of midyear 2009. Only 2.9% of the inmates were incarcerated in jail facilities that held fewer than 50 inmates each. The largest percentage (50.7%) of inmates were in facilities that held 1,000 or more inmates each.

Table 7.5 lists the 20 largest local jail jurisdictions (based on the number of inmates held) at midyear 2009. Seven of the nation's largest jail jurisdictions were in California. Los Angeles County, California, was the largest with 19,869 inmates. The county's average daily population in 2009 was 19,437. With a rated capacity of 22,477 inmates, the county had 88% of its jail capacity occupied at midyear 2009.

Other states with local jail jurisdictions among the 20 largest at midyear 2009 included Arizona, Florida, Illinois, Maryland, New York, Pennsylvania, Tennessee, and Texas. (See Table 7.5.)

Table 7.6 lists the number of people that were held in local jails or under local correctional supervision at midyear 2000, 2006, 2007, 2008, and 2009. Of the 837,833 people under confinement status at midyear 2009, the vast majority (767,620 or 91.6% of the total) were incarcerated full time. The remaining 8.4% (70,213) were in various types of supervised programs outside of jail facilities. At midyear 2009, 17,738 people were involved in community service programs under the supervision of local jurisdictions. More than 11,000 people were in weekender programs. These programs allow sentenced individuals (typically those convicted of nonserious and nonviolent misdemeanors) to serve jail time on the weekends only.

OVERALL INCARCERATION NUMBERS AND RATES

In *Key Facts at a Glance* (February 8, 2011, http://bjs.ojp.usdoj.gov/content/glance/corr2.cfm), the BJS indicates that the total number of prison and jail inmates in the United States has risen steadily for more than two decades. Between 1980 and 1990 the prison and jail population more than doubled, from just over 500,000 inmates to more than 1.1 million inmates, and then continued to grow. By 2002 the prison and jail inmate population exceeded 2 million.

FIGURE 7.2

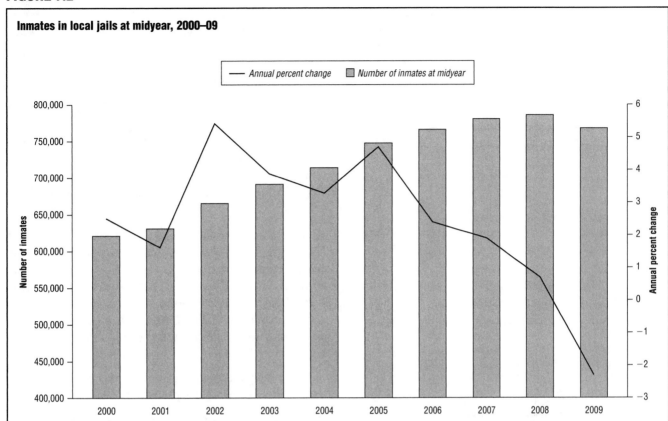

Inmates in local jails at midyear, 2000–09

SOURCE: Todd D. Minton, "Figure 1. Inmates Confined in Local Jails at Midyear and Annual Percent Change in the Jail Population, 2000–2009," in *Jail Inmates at Midyear 2009—Statistical Tables*, U.S. Department of Justice, Office of Justice Programs, Bureau of Justice Statistics, June 2010, http://bjs.ojp .usdoj.gov/content/pub/pdf/jim09st.pdf (accessed November 8, 2010)

TABLE 7.3

Inmates in local jails at midyear and jail incarceration rates, 2000–09

Year	Inmates confined at midyear		Average daily population[a]		Jail incarceration rate[b]
	Number	Percent change	Number	Percent change	
2000	621,149	2.5%	618,319	1.7%	226
2001	631,240	1.6	625,966	1.2	222
2002	665,475	5.4	652,082	4.2	231
2003	691,301	3.9	680,760	4.4	238
2004	713,990	3.3	706,242	3.7	243
2005	747,529	4.7	733,442	3.9	252
2006	765,819	2.4	755,320	3.0	256
2007	780,174	1.9	773,138	2.4	259
2008	785,556	0.7	776,573	0.4	258
2009	767,620	−2.3	767,992	−1.1	250
Average annual change,					
2000–2008	3.0%		2.9%		
2008–2009	−2.3		−1.1		

[a]Average daily population is the sum of all inmates in jail each day for a year, divided by the number of days in the year.
[b]Number of inmates confined at midyear per 100,000 U.S. residents.

SOURCE: Todd D. Minton, "Table 1. Inmates Confined in Local Jails at Midyear, Average Daily Population, and Incarceration Rates, 2000–2009," in *Jail Inmates at Midyear 2009—Statistical Tables*, U.S. Department of Justice, Office of Justice Programs, Bureau of Justice Statistics, June 2010, http://bjs.ojp.usdoj.gov/ content/pub/pdf/jim09st.pdf (accessed November 8, 2010)

Table 7.7 provides a breakdown of the number of inmates in federal, state, and local facilities between 2000 and 2009. The federal and state prison populations are based on annual year-end surveys, whereas the local jail populations are based on annual midyear surveys. Overall, the inmate population increased by 2.2% between 2000 and 2008. The rate of increase was highest for federal prisoners at 4.4%, compared with 3% for jail inmates and 1.5% for state inmates. In other words, the federal inmate population grew at a faster annual rate between 2000 and 2008 than did the state or local jail inmate populations.

The incarceration rate is the number of people sent by the courts to prisons and jails per 100,000 people in the general population. The incarceration rate for people in state and federal prisons and local jails was 684 at year-end 2000. (See Table 7.7.) By midyear 2009 the incarceration rate was 748 inmates per 100,000 U.S. residents.

Crime rates, as calculated by the Federal Bureau of Investigation (FBI), have decreased since the 1990s while the incarceration rate has increased. It should be noted, however, that FBI crime rate statistics do not include drug offenses or related money laundering offenses and illegal weapons violations, which have been growing at high rates. Some additional reasons for the rising incarceration rate include:

- More people are serving time in prison; that is, fewer convicts are receiving probation or parole.

- Mandatory sentencing rules require that some criminals be held for longer periods.

TABLE 7.4

Inmates in local jails at midyear, by size of jurisdiction, 2009

Jurisdiction size*	Number of inmates 2009	Percent of all inmates 2009
Total	767,620	100.0%
Fewer than 50 inmates	22,046	2.9%
50 to 99	37,838	4.9
100 to 249	86,279	11.2
250 to 499	108,462	14.1
500 to 999	123,442	16.1
1,000 or more	389,554	50.7

Note: Detail may not add to total because of rounding.
*Based on the average daily population. Average daily population is the sum of all inmates in jail each day for a year, divided by the number of days in the year.

SOURCE: Adapted from Todd D. Minton, "Table 3. Inmates Confined in Local Jails at Midyear, by Size of Jurisdiction, 2008 and 2009," in *Jail Inmates at Midyear 2009—Statistical Tables*, U.S. Department of Justice, Office of Justice Programs, Bureau of Justice Statistics, June 2010, http://bjs.ojp.usdoj.gov/content/pub/pdf/jim09st.pdf (accessed November 8, 2010)

TABLE 7.5

Twenty largest local jail jurisdictions, 2009

	Number of inmates[a]	Average daily population[b]	Rated capacity[c]	Percent of capacity occupied[d]
Total	226,073	225,068	245,270	92%
Los Angeles County, CA	19,869	19,437	22,477	88
New York City, NY	13,130	13,365	19,636	67
Harris County, TX	11,360	11,361	9,391	121
Cook County, IL	9,737	9,383	10,607	92
Philadelphia City, PA	9,436	9,359	8,685	109
Maricopa County, AZ	8,745	9,215	9,395	93
Orange County, CA	5,990	6,255	7,019	85
Miami-Dade County, FL	5,992	6,051	5,845	103
Dallas County, TX	6,222	6,039	8,097	77
Shelby County, TN	5,961	5,943	6,669	89
San Bernardino County, CA	5,923	5,591	5,914	100
San Diego County, CA	5,215	5,263	4,664	112
Broward County, FL	4,915	4,981	5,504	89
Sacramento County, CA	4,796	4,700	5,075	95
Santa Clara County, CA	4,244	4,498	3,825	111
Alameda County, CA	4,405	4,444	4,673	94
Orange County, FL	3,721	4,206	4,721	79
Bexar County, TX	4,377	4,093	4,528	97
Baltimore City, MD	3,957	3,997	3,683	107
Jacksonville City, FL	3,950	3,728	3,137	126

Note: Jurisdictions are ordered by their average daily population in 2009.
[a]Number of inmates held in jail facilities on the last weekday in June.
[b]Based on the average daily population for the year ending June 30. Average daily population is the sum of all inmates in jail each day for a year, divided by the number of days in the year.
[c]Number of beds or inmates assigned by a rating official to facilities within each jurisdiction.
[d]Number of inmates at midyear divided by the rated capacity and multiplied by 100.

SOURCE: Adapted from Todd D. Minton,"Table 9. The 50 Largest Local Jail Jurisdictions: Number of Inmates Held, Average Daily Population, and Rated Capacity, Midyear 2007–2009," in *Jail Inmates at Midyear 2009—Statistical Tables*, U.S. Department of Justice, Office of Justice Programs, Bureau of Justice Statistics, June 2010, http://bjs.ojp.usdoj.gov/content/pub/pdf/jim09st.pdf (accessed November 8, 2010)

- Some courts are requiring stiffer sentences.
- There is a rising incidence of rearrest of those who have been paroled.

TABLE 7.6

Inmates in local jails at midyear, by confinement status and type of program, 2000 and 2009

Confinement status and type of program	Number of persons under jail supervision	
	2000	2009
Total	**687,033**	**837,833**
Held in jail	621,149	767,620
Supervised outside of a jail facility[a]	65,884	70,213
Weekender programs	14,523	11,212
Electronic monitoring	10,782	11,834
Home detention[b]	332	738
Day reporting	3,969	6,492
Community service	13,592	17,738
Other pretrial supervision	6,279	12,439
Other work programs[c]	8,011	5,912
Treatment programs[d]	5,714	2,082
Other	2,682	1,766

[a]Excludes persons supervised by a probation or parole agency.
[b]Includes only persons without electronic monitoring.
[c]Includes persons in work release programs, work gangs, and other alternative work programs.
[d]Includes persons under drug, alcohol, mental health, and other medical treatment.

SOURCE: Adapted from Todd D. Minton, "Table 10. Persons under Jail Supervision, by Confinement Status and Type of Program, Midyear 2000 and 2006–2009," in *Jail Inmates at Midyear 2009—Statistical Tables*, U.S. Department of Justice, Office of Justice Programs, Bureau of Justice Statistics, June 2010, http://bjs.ojp.usdoj.gov/content/pub/pdf/jim09st.pdf (accessed November 8, 2010)

OVERCROWDING IN PRISONS AND JAILS

The booming inmate populations in state and federal prisons and local jails have led, in some facilities, to overcrowding. When overcrowding occurs, two inmates are often assigned to a cell that is designed for one person, or temporary housing units are set up to take prison overflow. Overcrowding makes it more likely that disagreements will arise between inmates, leading to violence and injuries. In addition, diseases are more likely to spread among the inmate population.

State and Federal Prison Capacity

In *Census of State and Federal Correctional Facilities, 2005*, Stephan lists the percent of rated capacity (the maximum number of beds or inmates that may be housed in a correctional facility) that was occupied by inmates in state and federal prisons as of December 30, 2005. Overall, U.S. prisons were at 111% of capacity on that date. Publicly operated prisons were at 112% of capacity, whereas privately operated prisons were at 95% of capacity. Federal prisons were much more troubled by overcrowding than state prisons. Federal prisons reported being at 137% of capacity, whereas state prisons were at 108% of capacity. On a regional basis, state prisons in the western United States reported the most overcrowding (120% of capacity), followed by the Midwest (110% of capacity), the South (104% of capacity), and the Northeast (102% of capacity).

TABLE 7.7

Inmates in state and federal prisons and local jails, selected dates, 2000–09

	Number of inmates					Average annual change, 2000–2008	Percent change, 12/31/2008– 06/30/2009
	12/31/2000	12/31/2007	6/30/2008	12/31/2008	6/30/2009		
Total inmates in custody	**1,937,482**	**2,298,041**	**2,308,561**	**2,308,390**	**2,297,400**	**2.2%**	**−0.5 %**
Federal prisoners[a]							
Total	**140,064**	**197,285**	**198,402**	**198,414**	**203,233**	**4.4%**	**2.4%**
Prisons	133,921	189,154	190,273	189,770	194,435	4.5	2.5
Federal facilities	124,540	165,975	165,690	165,252	170,354	3.6	3.1
Privately operated facilities	9,381	23,179	24,583	24,518	24,081	12.8	−1.8
Community corrections centers[b]	6,143	8,131	8,129	8,644	8,798	4.4	1.8
State prisoners	1,176,269	1,320,582	1,324,603	1,324,420	1,326,547	1.5%	0.2%
Local jails[c]	621,149	780,174	785,556	785,556	767,620	3.0%	−2.3%
Incarceration rate[d]	684	756	762	756	748	1.3%	−1.0%

Note: Total includes all inmates held in state or federal prison facilities or in local jails. It does not include inmates held in U.S. territories, military facilities, U.S. Immigration and Customs Enforcement facilities, jails in Indian country, and juvenile facilities.
[a]After 2001, responsibility for sentenced prisoners from the District of Columbia was transferred to the Federal Bureau of Prisons.
[b]Non-secure, privately operated community corrections centers.
[c]Counts for inmates held in local jails are for the last working day of June in each year.
[d]The total number in custody per 100,000 U.S. residents. Resident population estimates were as of January 1 of the following year for December 31 estimates and July 1 of the same year for June 30 estimates.

SOURCE: Heather C. West, "Table 15. Inmates Held in Custody in State or Federal Prisons or in Local Jails, December 31, 2000–2008 and June 30, 2008 and 2009," in *Prison Inmates at Midyear 2009—Statistical Tables*, U.S. Department of Justice, Office of Justice Programs, Bureau of Justice Statistics, June 2010, http://bjs.ojp.usdoj.gov/content/pub/pdf/pim09st.pdf (accessed November 8, 2010)

TABLE 7.8

Rated capacity of local jails and percent of capacity occupied, 2000–09

| Year | Rated capacity[b] | Year-to-year change in capacity[a] | | Percent of capacity occupied[c] |
		Number	Percent	
2000	677,787	25,466	3.9%	92.0%
2001	699,309	21,522	3.2	90.0
2002	713,899	14,590	2.1	93.0
2003	736,471	22,572	3.2	94.0
2004	755,603	19,132	2.6	94.0
2005	786,954	33,398	4.1	95.0
2006	794,984	8,638	1.0	96.3
2007	810,543	15,863	2.0	96.3
2008	828,413	17,870	2.2	94.8
2009	849,544	21,131	2.6	90.4
Average annual increase,				
2000–2008	2.5%	22,381		
2008–2009	2.6	21,131		

Note: Capacity data for 2000–2004 and 2006–2009 were survey estimates subject to sampling error.
[a]Increase or reduction in the number of beds during the 12 months ending midyear of each year. Number and percent change for 2000 are calculated using the rated capacity of 652,321 for 1999.
[b]Rated capacity is the number of beds or inmates assigned by a rating official to facilities within each jurisdiction.
[c]Number of confined inmates on the last weekday in June divided by the rated capacity and multiplied by 100.

SOURCE: Todd D. Minton, "Table 2. Rated Capacity of Local Jails and Percent of Capacity Occupied, 2000–2009," in *Jail Inmates at Midyear 2009—Statistical Tables*, U.S. Department of Justice, Office of Justice Programs, Bureau of Justice Statistics, June 2010, http://bjs.ojp.usdoj.gov/content/pub/pdf/jim09st.pdf (accessed November 8, 2010)

TABLE 7.9

Percent of jail capacity occupied at midyear, by size of jurisdiction, 2000 and 2009

| Jurisdiction size[b] | Percent of capacity occupied[a] | |
	2000	2009
Total	91.6%	90.4%
Fewer than 50 inmates	66.4%	62.2%
50 to 99	80.4	78.6
100 to 249	94.1	84.3
250 to 499	95.7	93.5
500 to 999	94.3	91.3
1,000 or more	94.1	94.5

[a]Number of inmates at midyear divided by the rated capacity multiplied by 100.
[b]Based on the average daily population.

SOURCE: Adapted from Todd D. Minton, "Table 5. Percent of Jail Capacity Occupied at Midyear, by Size of Jurisdiction, 2000, 2008, and 2009," in *Jail Inmates at Midyear 2009—Statistical Tables*, U.S. Department of Justice, Office of Justice Programs, Bureau of Justice Statistics, June 2010, http://bjs.ojp.usdoj.gov/content/pub/pdf/jim09st.pdf (accessed November 8, 2010)

As of December 30, 2005, the 10 most overcrowded state prison systems were:

- California—141% of capacity
- Illinois—136% of capacity
- Washington—131% of capacity
- Florida—128% of capacity
- Ohio—122% of capacity
- Iowa—116% of capacity
- Hawaii—110% of capacity
- New Hampshire—109% of capacity
- Wisconsin—109% of capacity
- Pennsylvania—108% of capacity

Jail Capacity

Overall, the nation's jails do not suffer as much overcrowding as the state and federal prisons. Table 7.8 shows the rated capacity of local jails and the percent of capacity occupied between 2000 and 2009. Note that data were compiled based on midyear surveys. Local jails had a rated capacity of 677,787 beds in 2000. This is the number of beds that were available. In 2008 the local jail capacity had reached 828,413 beds. The average annual increase in local jail capacity was 2.5% between 2000 and 2008. In 2009 the local jail capacity rose slightly to 849,544 beds, which was an increase of 2.6% from the year before. In 2000 local jails were at approximately 92% of rated capacity. In 2009 they were at 90.4% of rated capacity.

The percents of capacity occupied of local jails differ greatly by jurisdiction size. As shown in Table 7.9, jails with fewer than 50 inmates were at 62.2% of capacity in 2009, whereas those holding 1,000 or more inmates were at 94.5% of capacity. Smaller jails also had a much higher weekly turnover rate (the sum of weekly admissions and releases divided by the average daily population and multiplied by 100) than did larger jails. In 2009 the weekly turnover rate for jails holding fewer than 50 inmates was 137.8%. (See Table 7.10.) By contrast, the weekly turnover rate for jails holding 1,000 or more inmates was 52.5%.

TABLE 7.10

Inmates in local jails at midyear, average daily population and weekly turnover rate, by size of jurisdiction, 2009

Jurisdiction size[c]	Average daily population[a]		Weekly turnover rate[b]	
	2008	2009	2008	2009
Total	776,573	767,992	66.5%	63.7%
Fewer than 50 inmates	21,860	22,012	112.7%	137.8%
50 to 99	40,414	37,992	100.6	90.8
100 to 249	88,378	85,650	84.1	84.2
250 to 499	104,290	108,025	80.8	68.5
500 to 999	115,212	123,243	57.6	59.2
1,000 or more	406,419	391,070	55.7	52.5

[a]Average daily population is the sum of all inmates in jail each day for a year, divided by the number of days in the year.
[b]Turnover rate was calculated by adding weekly admissions and releases, dividing by the average daily population and multiplying by 100.
[c]Based on the average daily population.

SOURCE: Adapted from Todd D. Minton, "Table 4. Average Daily Jail Population, Admissions, and Turnover Rate, by Size of Jurisdiction, Week Ending June 30, 2008 and 2009," in *Jail Inmates at Midyear 2009—Statistical Tables*, U.S. Department of Justice, Office of Justice Programs, Bureau of Justice Statistics, June 2010, http://bjs.ojp.usdoj.gov/content/pub/pdf/jim09st.pdf (accessed November 8, 2010)

COSTS OF CORRECTIONS

As shown in Figure 1.2 in Chapter 1, the total amount spent on corrections facilities and functions at the federal, state, and local levels rose from $9 billion in 1982 to $74.2 billion in 2007.

Prisoner Work Programs

State and local governments prevent prisoners from working at some jobs because they would be in competition with private enterprise or workers. In 1936 Congress barred convicts from working on federal contracts worth more than $10,000. In 1940 Congress made it illegal to transport convict-made goods through interstate commerce. These rules were changed in 1979, when Congress established the Prison Industry Enhancement Certification Program (PIECP). The PIECP allows state correctional industries that meet certain requirements to sell inmate-produced goods to the federal government and in interstate commerce. The National Correctional Industries Association (NCIA), the professional organization for prison industry employees, provides training and technical assistance to the PIECP.

The NCIA indicates in "Prison Industry Enhancement Certification Program: Cumulative Data, 1979 through 2nd Quarter (April 1 through June 30) 2010" (September 14, 2010, http://www.nationalcia.org/wp-content/uploads/2008/05/qtr0210cumulative.pdf) that the program paid gross wages of $537.6 million from 1979 to the second quarter of 2010. From this total the following deductions were made: room and board ($158.1 million), taxes ($69.5 million), victims programs ($52.6 million), and family support ($34.4 million). In addition, $28.6 million went to mandatory savings accounts. Overall, the program paid over $223 million in net wages.

Many prison administrators generally favor work programs. Some believe work keeps prisoners productive and occupied, thus leading to a safer prison environment. Another benefit is that work programs prepare prisoners for reentry into the noninstitutionalized world by helping them develop job skills and solid work habits that will be needed for postincarceration employment. Some prisons report that inmates who work in industry are less likely to cause problems in prison or be rearrested after release than convicts who do not participate in work programs.

In addition, many inmates report they like the opportunity to work. They assert that it provides relief from boredom and gives them some extra money. Inmates find that the money they earn helps them to meet financial obligations for their families even while they are in prison.

Work Programs for Federal Inmates

According to the BOP, in "Work Programs" (2010, http://www.bop.gov/inmate_programs/work_prgms.jsp), federal prison inmates are required to work if they are medically able to do so. Their work assignments typically contribute to the facility operations and maintenance in areas such as food service, plumbing, painting, or landscaping. Inmates earn $0.12 to $0.40 per hour for these in-house work assignments. The BOP also reports that 16% of federal prison inmates work in Federal Prison Industries factories. This program provides slightly higher wages to inmates, from $0.23 to $1.15 per hour. Work includes manufacturing jobs in areas such as furniture, electronics, textiles, and graphic arts. With a high school diploma or its equivalent inmates can be promoted to a managerial role.

UNICOR. UNICOR (http://www.unicor.gov/) is the trade name for Federal Prison Industries, Inc. (FPI), the government corporation that employs inmates in federal prisons. UNICOR should not be confused with state prison industry programs that are administered by the states. Under UNICOR, which was established in 1934, federal inmates get job training by producing goods and services for federal agencies. In 2009 items that were produced by inmates included clothing and textiles (military items and apparel, protective clothing for law enforcement, mattresses, and medical textiles), electronics (circuit boards, electrical cables, and outdoor lighting systems/flood lights), industrial products (prescription and nonprescription safety eyewear, traffic and safety signage, license plates, air filters, and perimeter fencing), and office furniture (systems furniture, seating, and filing and storage products). Inmates also provided fleet management and vehicular components (fleet vehicle and vehicular component remanufacturing, fleet vehicle uplifting, and fleet management services), recycling (computers and electronic equipment), and other services (data services, printing and binding, and contact center/help desk support).

UNICOR products and services must be purchased by federal agencies and are not for sale in interstate commerce or to nonfederal entities. UNICOR is not permitted to compete with private industry. If UNICOR cannot make the needed product or provide the required service, federal agencies may buy the product or service from the private sector through a waiver that is issued by UNICOR.

According to the FPI, in *Annual Report 2009* (2010, http://www.unicor.gov/information/publications/pdfs/corporate/catar2009_C.pdf), UNICOR employed 18,972 inmates in 98 factories at 71 prison locations at the end of September 2009. Of all eligible inmates in BOP facilities, 16% worked for UNICOR that year. The agency's goal is to employ 25% of all work-eligible prisoners who have no existing job skills.

UNICOR is a self-supporting government corporation that may borrow funds from the U.S. Department of the Treasury and use the proceeds to purchase equipment, pay wages to inmates and staff, and invest in expansion of facilities. However, no funds are appropriated for UNICOR operations. During fiscal year 2009 its net sales were $885.3 million.

CHAPTER 8
CHARACTERISTICS AND RIGHTS OF INMATES

CHARACTERISTICS OF INMATES
Federal, State, and Local Inmates

Heather C. West of the Bureau of Justice Statistics (BJS) reports in *Prison Inmates at Midyear 2009—Statistical Tables* (June 2010, http://bjs.ojp.usdoj.gov/content/pub/pdf/pim09st.pdf) that as of June 30, 2009, there were 2.3 million federal, state, and local inmates in custody. Of these inmates, 1.3 million (57.7%) were in state prisons. Inmates in local jails numbered 767,620 (33.4% of the total). The remaining 203,233 (8.8%) were in federal prisons. The overall incarceration rate (the number of prisoners in custody per 100,000 U.S. residents) was 748. This number was up from 684 at year-end 2000, an increase of 9.4%.

The inmates in custody were overwhelmingly male (2.1 million or 91.2% of the total). West provides breakdowns by race and Hispanic origin of the male and female inmates. Note that these totals do not include inmates who reported being of two or more races. Also excluded are inmates who identified themselves as Native American, Alaskan Native, Asian-American, Native Hawaiian, or other Pacific Islander. The racial and Hispanic breakdown of the male inmates in custody as of midyear 2009 was as follows:

- Non-Hispanic white—693,800 (33.1% of the total male inmate population)
- Non-Hispanic African-American—841,000 (40.1%)
- Hispanic—442,000 (21.1%)

Overall, the incarceration rate for males was 1,398 inmates in custody per 100,000 U.S. residents. The incarceration rate for non-Hispanic African-American males (4,749) was nearly seven times that for non-Hispanic white males (708). By contrast, the incarceration rate for Hispanic males was 1,822, which was two and a half times that for non-Hispanic white males.

West notes that 201,200 female inmates were in federal, state, or local custody as of midyear 2009. Their racial and Hispanic breakdown was as follows:

- Non-Hispanic white—92,100 (45.8% of the total female inmate population)
- Non-Hispanic African-American—64,800 (32.2%)
- Hispanic—32,300 (16.1%)

Overall, the incarceration rate for females was 131 inmates in custody per 100,000 U.S. residents. The incarceration rate for non-Hispanic African-American females (333) was more than three and a half times that for non-Hispanic white females (91). By contrast, the incarceration rate for Hispanic females was 142, which was one and a half times that for non-Hispanic white females.

Nearly all (99.3%) of the inmates in custody at midyear 2009 were aged 18 years and older. The breakdown by age bracket of the adult inmates was as follows:

- 18 to 19 years old—3.2%
- 20 to 24 years old—15%
- 25 to 29 years old—17%
- 30 to 34 years old—15.7%
- 35 to 39 years old—15.1%
- 40 to 44 years old—13.5%
- 45 to 49 years old—9.7%
- 50 to 54 years old—5.3%
- 55 to 59 years old—2.7%
- 60 to 64 years old—1.2%
- 65 years and older—1%

The inmates tended to be younger adults; more than half (50.9%) were between the ages of 18 and 34 years.

FIGURE 8.1

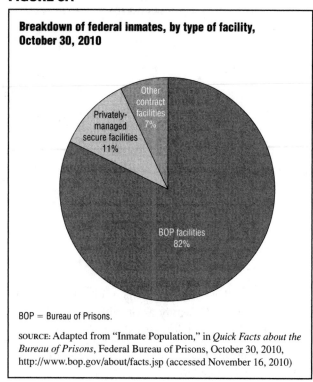

Breakdown of federal inmates, by type of facility, October 30, 2010

BOP = Bureau of Prisons.

SOURCE: Adapted from "Inmate Population," in *Quick Facts about the Bureau of Prisons*, Federal Bureau of Prisons, October 30, 2010, http://www.bop.gov/about/facts.jsp (accessed November 16, 2010)

FIGURE 8.2

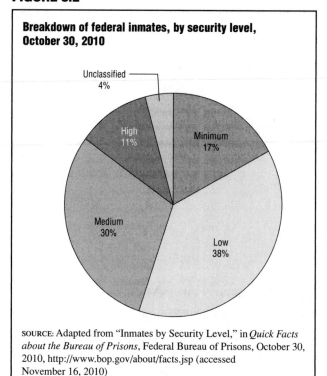

Breakdown of federal inmates, by security level, October 30, 2010

SOURCE: Adapted from "Inmates by Security Level," in *Quick Facts about the Bureau of Prisons*, Federal Bureau of Prisons, October 30, 2010, http://www.bop.gov/about/facts.jsp (accessed November 16, 2010)

Federal Inmates Only

The Federal Bureau of Prisons (BOP) is an agency of the U.S. Department of Justice (DOJ). The BOP oversees the corrections system for federal inmates and administers federal prisons. In "Quick Facts about the Bureau of Prisons" (October 30, 2010, http://www.bop.gov/about/facts.jsp), the BOP provides a snapshot in time of the federal inmate population. As of October 30, 2010, the BOP had jurisdiction over 210,148 federal inmates. As shown in Figure 8.1, 82% of the inmates were being held in BOP facilities. Smaller percentages were confined in privately managed facilities (11%) and other contract facilities (7%).

Figure 8.2 shows a breakdown by security level under which the inmates were being held. More than a third (38%) were in low security, 30% were in medium security, 17% were in minimum security, 11% were in high security, and 4% were unclassified. Table 8.1 provides demographic data about the inmates. The vast majority (196,426 or 93.5%) of the prisoners were male, and only 13,722 (6.5%) were female. Concerning the ethnic and racial composition of the inmates, 57.7% were white, 38.9% were African-American, 1.8% were Native American, and 1.7% were Asian-American. Nearly one-third (32.8%) of BOP prisoners were Hispanic.

Almost three-fourths (73.9%) of federal inmates were U.S. citizens. (See Table 8.1.) Mexican citizens, the next largest group of inmates, made up 17.5% of the total. Much smaller proportions of federal inmates were citizens of

TABLE 8.1

Federal inmates, by gender, race, ethnicity, age, and citizenship, October 30, 2010

Inmates by gender		
Male	196,426	(93.5%)
Female	13,722	(6.5%)
Inmates by race		
White	121,155	(57.7%)
Black	81,653	(38.9%)
Native American	3,766	(1.8%)
Asian	3,574	(1.7%)
Ethnicity		
Hispanic	68,905	(32.8%)
Inmate age		
Average inmate age	39	
Citizenship		
United States	155,394	(73.9%)
Mexico	36,729	(17.5%)
Colombia	2,635	(1.3%)
Cuba	1,779	(0.8%)
Dominican Republic	2,607	(1.2%)
Other/unknown	11,004	(5.3%)

SOURCE: Adapted from "Inmate Breakdown," in *Quick Facts about the Bureau of Prisons*, Federal Bureau of Prisons, October 30, 2010, http://www.bop.gov/about/facts.jsp (accessed November 16, 2010)

Colombia (1.3%), the Dominican Republic (1.2%), and Cuba (0.8%). The remaining 5.3% of inmates were of other or unknown citizenship. The average inmate age was 39 years.

Table 8.2 provides a breakdown of federal inmate offenses as of October 30, 2010. More than half (51.4%)

TABLE 8.2

Federal inmates, by type of offense, October 30, 2010

Drug offenses	100,439	51.4%
Weapons, explosives, arson	29,894	15.3%
Immigration	21,399	11.0%
Robbery	8,594	4.4%
Burglary, larceny, property offenses	6,882	3.5%
Extortion, fraud, bribery	9,966	5.1%
Homicide, aggravated assault, and kidnapping offenses	5,388	2.8%
Miscellaneous	1,865	1.0%
Sex offenses	8,840	4.5%
Banking and insurance, counterfeit, embezzlement	866	0.4%
Courts or corrections	650	0.3%
Continuing criminal enterprise	524	0.3%
National security	93	0.0%

Note: Data calculated for those with offense-specific information available.

SOURCE: "Types of Offenses," in *Quick Facts about the Bureau of Prisons*, Federal Bureau of Prisons, October 30, 2010, http://www.bop.gov/about/facts .jsp (accessed November 16, 2010)

TABLE 8.3

Federal inmates, by sentence imposed, October 30, 2010

Less than 1 year	3,061	(1.6%)
1–3 years	23,171	(11.9%)
3–5 years	28,035	(14.3%)
5–10 years	58,179	(29.8%)
10–15 years	40,272	(20.6%)
15–20 years	17,601	(9.0%)
More than 20 years	19,041	(9.7%)
Life	6,090	(3.1%)
Death	57	

Note: Data is only calculated for cases where sentencing information is available.

SOURCE: "Sentence Imposed," in *Quick Facts about the Bureau of Prisons*, Federal Bureau of Prisons,October 30, 2010, http://www.bop.gov/about/ facts.jsp (accessed November 16, 2010)

FIGURE 8.3

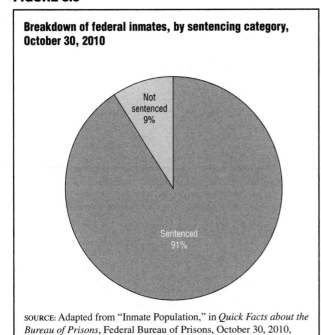

Breakdown of federal inmates, by sentencing category, October 30, 2010

SOURCE: Adapted from "Inmate Population," in *Quick Facts about the Bureau of Prisons*, Federal Bureau of Prisons, October 30, 2010, http://www.bop.gov/about/facts.jsp (accessed November 16, 2010)

---

of the prisoners were incarcerated for drug crimes—the largest single category. Another 15.3% of inmates were in prison for charges involving weapons, explosives, and/or arson, and 11% of inmates had been sentenced for immigration offenses. Together, these three crime categories accounted for 77.7% of the offenses of federal inmates. Each of the other crime categories listed in Table 8.2 accounted for less than 5% of the total offenses.

As shown in Figure 8.3, the vast majority (91%) of the federal inmate population as of October 30, 2010, had been sentenced for their crimes. Only 9% of the inmates had not yet been sentenced at that time. Table 8.3 lists the sentences

that were imposed on federal inmates as of October 30, 2010. The largest single contingent of prisoners (29.8%) was serving a sentence of five to 10 years. Nearly 21% of the inmates had received a sentence of 10 to 15 years, and 14.3% were serving three- to five-year sentences. Smaller contingents were serving sentences of 1 to 3 years (11.9%), more than 20 years (9.7%), 15 to 20 years (9%), and less than 1 year (1.6%). Just over 3% of federal inmates had received life sentences, and 57 inmates had been given death sentences.

State Inmates Only

As noted earlier, West reports in *Prison Inmates at Midyear 2009—Statistical Tables* that as of June 30, 2009, there were 1.3 million inmates in custody in state prisons. Overall, 1.4 million prisoners were under state jurisdiction as of June 30, 2009. As noted in Chapter 7, the BJS tracks two different inmate counts: inmates in custody and inmates under jurisdiction. The count of inmates in state custody is a count of the prisoners physically located in state prisons. The count of inmates under state jurisdiction includes the latter plus other inmates who are under state jurisdiction, but are physically located in nonstate prisons, such as county jails. The vast majority of prisoners (1.3 million or 92.8%) were male. The female inmate population was 101,233, which accounted for 7.2% of the total.

West does not provide detailed demographic data about state prisoners as of midyear 2009. However, such data are reported for year-end 2006 by William J. Sabol, Heather C. West, and Matthew Cooper of the BJS in *Prisoners in 2008* (December 2009, http://bjs.ojp.usdoj .gov/content/pub/pdf/p08.pdf).

Sabol, West, and Cooper note that 1.3 million state inmates were serving sentences of at least one year as of year-end 2006. They included over 1.2 million males (93% of the total) and 92,200 females (6.9% of the total). Concerning the race and Hispanic origin of the inmates,

TABLE 8.4

TABLE 8.5

Inmates in local jails at midyear, by gender, status, and racial and ethnic origin, 2000 and 2009

Characteristic	2000	2009
Total	621,149	767,620
Sex		
Male	550,162	673,891
Female	70,987	93,729
Adults	**613,534**	**760,400**
Male	543,120	667,201
Female	70,414	93,199
Juveniles[a]	**7,615**	**7,220**
Held as adults[b]	6,126	5,847
Held as juveniles	1,489	1,373
Race/Hispanic origin[c]		
White[d]	260,500	326,500
Black/African American[d]	256,300	300,600
Hispanic/Latino	94,100	124,000
Other[d, e]	10,200	14,800
Two or more races[d]	—	1,800

Note: Detail may not sum to total due to rounding.
—Not collected.
[a] Juveniles are persons under the age of 18 at midyear.
[b] Includes juveniles who were tried or awaiting trial as adults.
[c] Estimates based on reported data adjusted for nonresponse.
[d] Excludes persons of Hispanic or Latino origin.
[e] Includes American Indians, Alaska Natives, Asians, Native Hawaiians, and other Pacific Islanders.

SOURCE: Adapted from Todd D. Minton, "Table 6. Number of Inmates in Local Jails, by Characteristics, Midyear 2000 and 2005–2009," in *Jail Inmates at Midyear 2009—Statistical Tables*, U.S. Department of Justice, Office of Justice Programs, Bureau of Justice Statistics, June 2010, http://bjs.ojp.usdoj.gov/content/pub/pdf/jim09st.pdf (accessed November 8, 2010)

Percentage of inmates in local jails at midyear, by gender, status, and racial and ethnic origin, 2000 and 2009

Characteristic	2000	2009
Sex		
Male	88.6%	87.8%
Female	11.4	12.2
Adults	98.8%	99.1%
Male	87.4	86.9
Female	11.3	12.1
Juveniles[a]	1.2%	0.9%
Held as adults[b]	1.0	0.8
Held as juveniles	0.2	0.2
Race/Hispanic origin[c]		
White[d]	41.9%	42.5%
Black/African American[d]	41.3	39.2
Hispanic/Latino	15.2	16.2
Other[d, e]	1.6	1.9
Two or more races[d]	. . .	0.2
Conviction status[b]		
Convicted	44.0%	37.8%
Male	39.0	33.0
Female	5.0	4.8
Unconvicted	56.0	62.2
Male	50.0	54.8
Female	6.0	7.4

Note: Detail may not sum to total due to rounding.
. . .Not collected.
[a] Persons under age 18 at midyear.
[b] Includes juveniles who were tried or awaiting trial as adults.
[c] Estimates based on reported data and adjusted for nonresponse.
[d] Excludes persons of Hispanic or Latino origin.
[e] Includes American Indians, Alaska Natives, Asians, Native Hawaiians, and other Pacific Islanders.

SOURCE: Adapted from Todd D. Minton, "Table 7. Percent of Inmates in Local Jails, by Characteristics, Midyear 2000 and 2005–2009," in *Jail Inmates at Midyear 2009—Statistical Tables*, U.S. Department of Justice, Office of Justice Programs, Bureau of Justice Statistics, June 2010, http://bjs.ojp.usdoj.gov/content/pub/pdf/jim09st.pdf (accessed November 8, 2010)

474,200 (35.6%) were non-Hispanic white, 508,700 (38.2%) were non-Hispanic African-American, and 248,900 (18.7%) were Hispanic.

Approximately 667,900 (50.2%) of the sentenced inmates under state jurisdiction at year-end 2006 were incarcerated for violent crimes, including murder, manslaughter, rape and other sexual assaults, robbery, assault, and other violent offenses. Another 277,900 (20.9%) inmates were serving time for property crimes, such as burglary, larceny, motor vehicle theft, fraud, and other property crimes. Twenty percent (265,800) of the prisoners were incarcerated for drug crimes. A smaller percentage (8% or 112,300) had been sentenced to state prison for public-order offenses involving weapons, drunk driving, court offenses, commercialized vice, morals and decency offenses, liquor law violations, and other public-order offenses. The remaining 7,200 (0.5%) inmates were incarcerated for other crimes or their crimes were not specified.

Local Jail Inmates Only

As noted earlier, at midyear 2009 there were 767,620 inmates in local jails. Table 8.4 and Table 8.5 provide demographic details about local jail inmates as of midyears 2000 and 2009. At midyear 2009, 673,891 (87.8%) of jail

inmates were male and 93,729 (12.2%) were female. The racial breakdown was non-Hispanic white (326,500 inmates or 42.5% of the total), non-Hispanic African-American (300,600 inmates or 39.2%), non-Hispanic inmates of other races (14,800 inmates or 1.9%), and non-Hispanic inmates of two or more races (1,800 inmates or 0.2%). Hispanic inmates (124,000) made up 16.2% of the jail population at midyear 2009.

At midyear 2009 nearly all inmates in local jails were adults. Approximately 7,200 of the inmates were juveniles, making up 0.9% of the total inmate population. (See Table 8.4 and Table 8.5.)

Convicted inmates include those awaiting sentencing, serving a sentence, or returned to jail for a violation of probation or parole. Jails also hold people who have not been convicted of a crime but who are awaiting arraignment and those who are being detained pending transfer to a juvenile or mental health facility. More local jail inmates were classified as unconvicted (62.2%) than convicted (37.8%) at midyear 2009. (See Table 8.5.)

PRISONERS WITH MINOR CHILDREN

Lauren E. Glaze and Laura M. Maruschak of the BJS estimate in *Parents in Prison and Their Minor Children* (August 2008, http://bjs.ojp.usdoj.gov/content/pub/pdf/pptmc.pdf) that 809,800 state and federal prisoners were parents of minor children (i.e., children under the age of 18 years) as of midyear 2007. These parents accounted for 52% of state inmates and 63% of federal inmates. Together, the parents had more than 1.7 million minor children, or 2.3% of the total U.S. population of minor children. The breakdown by race and Hispanic origin for the minor children of inmates was non-Hispanic African-American children (6.7%), Hispanic children (2.4%), and non-Hispanic white children (0.9%). In other words, non-Hispanic African-American children were seven and a half times more likely than non-Hispanic white children and over two and half times more likely than Hispanic children to have an incarcerated parent.

As of midyear 2007, the vast majority of the parents (744,200) were fathers, whereas 65,600 were mothers. Inmate fathers reported having nearly 1.6 million minor children, whereas inmate mothers reported having 147,400 minor children. According to Glaze and Maruschak, the number of minor children with a mother in prison grew by 131% between 1991 and 2006, whereas those with a father in prison grew by 77%.

WOMEN PRISONERS

Female prisoners make up a small part of the overall prison population, but their treatment is an issue for many human rights groups. The American Civil Liberties Union (ACLU) is particularly critical of the practice of shackling pregnant inmates. Shackling can consist of handcuffs and/or chains around the ankles or midsection. It is a common practice at many prisons for inmates to be shackled under certain circumstances, for example, during transport to and from court or other locations and while being treated in hospitals. Critics suggest that shackled women are in danger of seriously harming their unborn babies if they should fall. Human rights advocates also abhor the practice of shackling women inmates to their hospital beds while the women are in labor.

In "Washington Restricts Shackling of Pregnant Inmates" (April 2, 2010, http://www.aclu-wa.org/news/washington-restricts-shackling-pregnant-inmates), the ACLU notes that in 2010 the state of Washington joined seven other states (Arkansas, California, Illinois, New Mexico, New York, Texas, and Vermont) in passing some type of antishackling legislation. The Washington law bans restraints during labor and postpartum recovery, except during "emergency circumstances," and limits shackling during the third trimester of pregnancy. In October 2010 Governor Arnold Schwarzenegger (1947–) vetoed a bill passed by the California legislature that would have expanded that state's ban on shackling during labor to all stages of pregnancy.

MEDICAL PROBLEMS IN INMATES

The latest data on the medical problems of state and federal prisoners are addressed by Maruschak in *Medical Problems of Prisoners* (April 22, 2008, http://bjs.ojp.usdoj.gov/content/pub/pdf/mpp.pdf). Maruschak presents findings from the 2004 Survey of Inmates in State and Federal Correctional Facilities. According to Maruschak, 44% of state inmates and 39% of federal inmates reported a current medical problem other than a cold or virus. The most common medical problems reported by inmates were arthritis (15.3% of state inmates and 12.4% of federal inmates), hypertension (13.8% of state inmates and 13.2% of federal inmates), and asthma (9.1% of state inmates and 7.2% of federal inmates). Female inmates and inmates older than 45 years of age were much more likely to report having a current medical problem than male inmates and those younger than 45 years of age, respectively.

HIV/AIDS

Maruschak reports in *HIV in Prisons, 2007—08* (December 2009, http://bjs.ojp.usdoj.gov/content/pub/pdf/hivp08.pdf) that the number of inmates with the human immunodeficiency virus (HIV) or confirmed cases of acquired immunodeficiency syndrome (AIDS) in state and federal prisons as of year-end 2008 was 21,987. The percentage of inmates with HIV/AIDS was 1.9% for female inmates and 1.5% for male inmates. The three states with the largest contingents of state prisoners known to be infected with HIV/AIDS were Florida (3,626 inmates), New York (3,500 inmates), and Texas (2,450 inmates). Together, these three states accounted for nearly half of all HIV/AIDS cases among state inmates.

Concerning prison inmates who were diagnosed with AIDS, the rate was 0.41% in 2007, compared with a rate of 0.17% for the general U.S. population.

Mental Health Problems of Inmates

A movement began during the 1970s to deinstitutionalize the mentally ill and reintegrate them into society. This widespread trend resulted in the closing of many large mental hospitals and treatment centers. With fewer options open to them, the mentally ill came into contact with law enforcement authorities more often. Holly Hills, Christine Siegfried, and Alan Ickowitz state in *Effective Prison Mental Health Services: Guidelines to Expand and Improve Treatment* (May 2004, http://www.nicic.org/pubs/2004/018604.pdf) that "since the early 1990s, an increasing number of adults with mental illness have become involved with the criminal justice system. State and federal prisons, in particular, have undergone a dramatic transformation, housing a growing number of inmates with serious mental disorders. Complicating this situation is the high proportion of mentally ill inmates who have co-occurring substance use disorders."

In *Mental Health Problems of Prison and Jail Inmates* (September 2006, http://bjs.ojp.usdoj.gov/content/pub/pdf/mhppji.pdf), Doris J. James and Lauren E. Glaze of the BJS report that more than half of all prison and jail inmates had a mental health problem at midyear 2005. Specifically, 705,600 inmates in state prisons (56% of all state prison inmates), 78,800 inmates in federal prisons (45% of all federal prison inmates), and 479,900 inmates in local jails (64% of all local jail inmates) reported symptoms of a mental health problem. For example, 35.1% of federal prisoners, 43.2% of state prisoners, and 54.5% of jail inmates reported symptoms of mania; 16% of federal prisons, 23.5% of state prisoners, and 29.7% of jail inmates reported symptoms of major depression; and 10.2% of federal prisoners, 15.4% of state prisoners, and 23.9% of jail inmates reported symptoms of a psychotic disorder.

DIFFERENCES BY GENDER. James and Glaze indicate that female inmates have much higher rates of mental health problems than male inmates. At midyear 2005, 73% of female state prison inmates had a mental health problem, compared with 55% of male inmates. Similarly, 61% of female federal inmates reported a mental health problem, compared with 44% of male inmates, and 75% of female jail inmates had a mental health problem, compared with 63% of male inmates.

HISTORY OF HOMELESSNESS AND FOSTER CARE. According to James and Glaze, state prison and local jail inmates who reported a mental health problem were more likely than other inmates to have been homeless in the year before they entered prison or jail. Specifically, 13.2% of state prisoners and 17.2% of jail inmates had both a mental health problem and a recent experience of homelessness, compared with 6.3% of state prisoners and 8.8% of jail inmates who did not have a mental health problem but said they had been homeless in the year before they were incarcerated. Approximately 18.5% of state prisoners who had a mental health problem had lived in a foster home, agency, or institution while growing up, compared with 9.5% of state prisoners who did not report a mental health problem. Similarly, 14.5% of jail inmates who had a mental health problem had lived in a foster home, agency, or institution, compared with 6% of jail inmates who did not have a mental health problem.

SEXUAL VIOLENCE IN PRISONS AND JAILS

In response to concerns about sexual misconduct in prisons, President George W. Bush (1946–) signed into law the Prison Rape Elimination Act (PREA) in September 2003. As part of this legislation, the BJS is charged with developing a national data collection on the incidence and prevalence of sexual assault within correctional facilities. As of February 2011, the most recent report on sexual violence involving adult inmates was by Allen J. Beck et al. in *Sexual Victimization in Prisons and Jails Reported by Inmates, 2008–09* (August 2010, http://bjs.ojp.usdoj.gov/content/pub/pdf/svpjri0809.pdf).

Beck et al. note that the data are based on the second National Inmate Survey, which was conducted between October 2008 and December 2009 in 167 state and federal prisons, 286 jails, and 10 special confinement facilities that were operated by the U.S. Immigration and Customs Enforcement, the U.S. military, and correctional authorities on Native American tribal lands. More than 76,000 inmates participated in the survey. The inmates were questioned about acts of nonconsensual sex between inmates and between inmates and facility staff. The results were extrapolated to provide estimates of sexual misconduct in the nation's entire inmate population.

According to Beck et al., 4.4% of prison inmates and 3.1% of jail inmates reported one or more incidents of sexual victimization by another inmate or a facility staff member during the previous 12 months or since their admission to the facility if they had been there less than 12 months. These percentages, when extrapolated to the national inmate population, suggest that approximately 88,500 adult inmates in prisons and jails were sexually victimized over the same period while incarcerated. Unwanted sexual misconduct by facility staff was reported by 2.8% of prison inmates and 2% of jail inmates. In most cases the inmates were male and the staff members were female. In addition, 1.8% of prison inmates and 1.1% of jail inmates admitted willingly participating in sexual activities with staff. Sexual victimization by another inmate was reported by 2.1% of prison inmates and 1.5% of jail inmates. The rates for this type of victimization were higher for female inmates (4.7% in prisons and 3.1% in jails) than for male inmates (1.9% in prisons and 1.3% in jails).

INMATE DEATHS

The BJS initiated the Deaths in Custody Reporting Program in response to the Deaths in Custody Reporting Act of 2000. The program requires state prisons and local jails to report annually the cause of death and certain demographic data for all inmates who die in their custody. The data are summarized in Table 8.6 and Table 8.7 for state prisoners between 2001 and 2007. In total, 3,388 state inmates died while incarcerated in 2007. The vast majority (2,860 inmates or 84.4%) died of illnesses other than AIDS. Other primary causes of death were suicide (214 inmates or 6.3%) and AIDS (120 inmates or 3.5%).

Table 8.8 lists the mortality rate per 100,000 state prisoners by cause of death between 2001 and 2007. In 2007 the mortality rate due to all causes was 257. This was the second-highest rate recorded for all causes of deaths between 2001 and 2007. The mortality rate due to illness in 2007 was 217, the highest reported rate during this period.

TABLE 8.6

Deaths of inmates in state prisons, by cause of death, 2001–07

	Number of state prisoner deaths							
	2001–2007	**2001**	**2002**	**2003**	**2004**	**2005**	**2006**	**2007**
All causes	21,936	2,878	2,946	3,167	3,138	3,177	3,242	3,388
Illness	18,193	2,303	2,379	2,633	2,645	2,668	2,705	2,860
AIDS	1,274	270	245	210	145	153	131	120
Suicide	1,386	169	168	200	200	215	220	214
Homicide	356	39	48	50	51	56	55	57
Drug/alcohol intoxication	254	36	37	23	23	37	57	41
Accident	208	23	31	26	37	30	33	28
Other/don't know	265	38	38	25	37	18	41	68

Note: Executions are not included.

SOURCE: Margaret E. Noonan, "Table 1. Number of State Prisoner Deaths, by Cause of Death, 2001–2007," in *Deaths in Custody: State Prison Deaths, 2001–2007—Statistical Tables*, U.S. Department of Justice, Office of Justice Programs, Bureau of Justice Statistics, 2010, http://bjs.ojp.usdoj.gov/content/dcrp/prisonindex.pdf (accessed November 9, 2010)

TABLE 8.7

Percent of deaths of inmates in state prisons, by cause of death, 2001–07

	Percent of state prisoner deaths							
	2001–2007	**2001**	**2002**	**2003**	**2004**	**2005**	**2006**	**2007**
All causes	100%	100%	100%	100%	100%	100%	100%	100%
Illness	82.9	80.8	84.3	83.4	84.3	84.0	83.4	84.4
AIDS	5.8	8.3	4.6	4.0	4.6	4.8	4.0	3.5
Suicide	6.3	5.7	6.4	6.8	6.4	6.8	6.8	6.3
Homicide	1.6	1.6	1.6	1.7	1.6	1.8	1.7	1.7
Drug/alcohol intoxication	1.2	1.3	0.7	1.8	0.7	1.2	1.8	1.2
Accident	0.9	1.1	1.2	1.0	1.2	0.9	1.0	0.8
Other/don't know	1.2	1.3	1.2	1.3	1.2	0.6	1.3	2.0

Note: Executions are not included.

SOURCE: Margaret E. Noonan, "Table 2. Percent of State Prisoner Deaths, by Cause of Death, 2001–2007," in *Deaths in Custody: State Prison Deaths, 2001–2007—Statistical Tables*, U.S. Department of Justice, Office of Justice Programs, Bureau of Justice Statistics, 2010, http://bjs.ojp.usdoj.gov/content/dcrp/prisonindex.pdf (accessed November 9, 2010)

TABLE 8.8

Mortality rate per 100,000 state prisoners, by cause of death, 2001–07

	Average annual mortality rate per 100,000 state prisoners, 2001–2007	Mortality rate, per 100,000 state prisoners						
		2001	**2002**	**2003**	**2004**	**2005**	**2006**	**2007**
All causes	251	242	246	258	253	254	250	257
Illness	208	194	198	215	213	213	209	217
AIDS	15	23	20	17	12	12	10	9
Suicide	16	14	14	16	16	17	17	16
Homicide	4	3	4	4	4	4	4	4
Drug/alcohol intoxication	3	3	3	2	2	3	4	3
Accident	2	2	3	2	3	2	3	2
Other/don't know	3	3	3	2	3	1	3	5

Notes: Mortality rates are based on the June 30 state prison custody population count, collected in the National Prisoner Statistics (NPS) program. Executions are not included.

SOURCE: Margaret E. Noonan, "Table 3. Mortality Rate per 100,000 State Prisoners, by Cause of Death, 2001–2007," in *Deaths in Custody: State Prison Deaths, 2001–2007—Statistical Tables*, U.S. Department of Justice, Office of Justice Programs, Bureau of Justice Statistics, May 2010, http://bjs.ojp.usdoj.gov/content/dcrp/prisonindex.pdf (accessed November 9, 2010)

TABLE 8.9

State inmate mortality characteristics, by cause of death, 2001–07

				Percent of state prisoner deaths, by cause of death, 2001–2007			
	Illness	AIDS	Suicide	Homicide	Drug/alcohol intoxication	Accident	Other/ don't know
Total	100%	100%	100%	100%	100%	100%	100%
Gender							
Male	96.0%	95.2%	95.2%	98.9%	96.5%	96.6%	94.1%
Female	4.0	4.8	4.8	1.1	3.5	3.4	5.9
Race/Hispanic origin							
White	51.2%	19.9%	57.9%	46.3%	57.6%	54.8%	43.7%
Black	37.2	67.9	22.0	32.8	20.2	30.3	45.4
Hispanic	10.3	11.5	16.6	18.4	17.7	11.5	8.0
Other*	1.3	0.8	3.6	2.5	4.5	3.4	2.9
Age							
Under 18	0.0%	0.0%	0.4%	0.3%	0.0%	0.5%	0.0%
18–24	1.0	0.9	15.6	12.6	5.5	9.1	4.6
25–34	4.7	14.2	33.5	27.8	28.0	23.1	13.1
35–44	16.4	45.7	29.8	31.7	37.0	26.0	24.5
45–54	33.0	31.7	15.6	18.3	22.4	24.0	26.2
55 or older	44.9	7.5	5.1	9.3	7.1	17.3	31.6

Note: Executions are not included.
*Includes American Indians, Alaska Natives, Asians, Native Hawaiians, other Pacific Islanders, and persons of two or more races.

SOURCE: Margaret E. Noonan, "Table 10. Percent of State Prisoner Deaths, by Cause of Death and Selected Characteristics, 2001–2007," in *Deaths in Custody: State Prison Deaths, 2001–2007—Statistical Tables*, U.S. Department of Justice, Office of Justice Programs, Bureau of Justice Statistics, May 2010, http://bjs.ojp.usdoj.gov/content/dcrp/prisonindex.pdf (accessed November 9, 2010)

The 2007 mortality rate for AIDS was 9, having dropped from a high of 23 in 2001.

Table 8.9 provides detailed demographic data on the state prisoners who died between 2001 and 2007. The vast majority of the deaths (94.1%) occurred among male inmates. Roughly half of the inmates who died from illness, suicide, homicide, drug/alcohol intoxication, or accidents were white. Nearly two-thirds (67.9%) of deaths due to AIDS occurred among African-American inmates.

As shown in Table 8.9, 44.9% of the state inmates who died of illness between 2001 and 2007 were 55 years and older. Other causes of death were more common among younger inmates, particularly AIDS (45.7% of those who died were aged 35 to 44 years). The victims of suicide, homicide, drug/alcohol intoxication, and accidents were most commonly between 25 and 44 years of age.

Margaret Noonan of the BJS reports in *Mortality in Local Jails, 2000–2007* (July 2010, http://bjs.ojp.usdoj.gov/content/pub/pdf/mlj07.pdf) that 8,110 jail inmates died while incarcerated between 2000 and 2007. As shown in Table 8.10, more than half (53%) died due to illness, primarily heart disease. Another 29% died due to suicide. The annual average mortality rate between 2000 and 2007 was 145 deaths per 100,000 jail inmates. Figure 8.4 shows that the mortality rate trended downward during this period as the average jail population increased each year.

As shown in Figure 8.5, the mortality rate due to suicide declined from around 50 deaths per 100,000 jail

TABLE 8.10

Deaths and mortality rate per 100,000 jail inmates, by cause of death, 2000–07

All causes	Jail inmate deaths		Average annual mortality rate per 100,000 jail inmates
	Number	Percent	
Total	8,110	100%	145
Suicide	2,363	29%	42
Illness	4,288	53%	77
Heart disease	1,789	22	32
AIDS	410	5	7
Cancer	273	3	5
Liver disease	234	3	4
All other illnesses*	1,582	20	28
Drug/alcohol intoxication	567	7%	10
Accident	229	3%	4
Homicide	172	2%	3
Other/unknown	491	6%	8

Note: Mortality rates are based on average daily population as reported to the Deaths in Custody Reporting Program.
*Includes other specified (such as influenza, septicemia, diabetes, and hepatitis) and unspecified or unknown illnesses.

SOURCE: Margaret Noonan, "Table 1. Number of Deaths and Mortality Rate per 100,000 Jail Inmates, by Cause, 2000–2007," in *Mortality in Local Jails, 2000–2007*, U.S. Department of Justice, Office of Justice Programs, Bureau of Justice Statistics, July 2010, http://bjs.ojp.usdoj.gov/content/pub/pdf/mlj07.pdf (accessed November 8, 2010)

inmates in 2000 to less than 40 deaths per 100,000 jail inmates in 2007. The mortality rate due to AIDS also decreased from around 10 deaths per 100,000 jail inmates in 2000 to approximately 5 deaths per 100,000 jail inmates in 2007. The mortality rate due to heart disease hovered

FIGURE 8.4

Mortality rate per 100,000 jail inmates, 2000–07

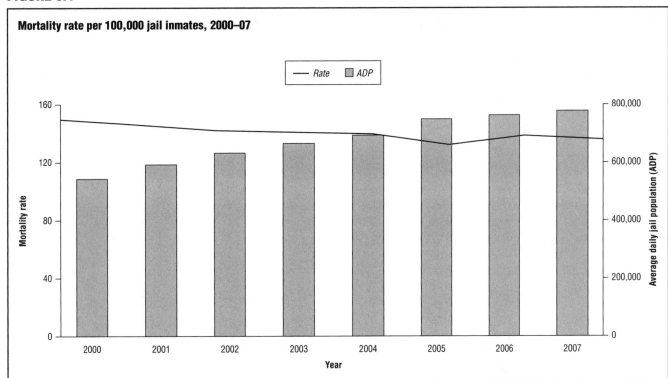

SOURCE: Margaret Noonan, "Figure 1. Mortality Rate per 100,000 Jail Inmates and the Average Daily Population, 2000–2007," in *Mortality in Local Jails, 2000–2007*, U.S. Department of Justice, Office of Justice Programs, Bureau of Justice Statistics, July 2010, http://bjs.ojp.usdoj.gov/content/pub/pdf/mlj07 .pdf (accessed November 8, 2010)

FIGURE 8.5

Top four causes of death in local jails, 2000–07

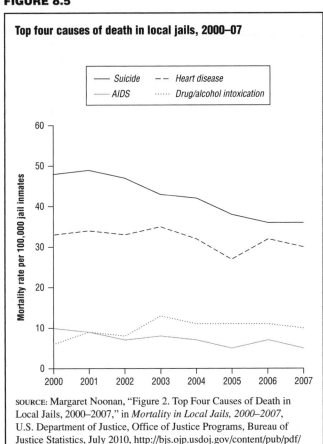

SOURCE: Margaret Noonan, "Figure 2. Top Four Causes of Death in Local Jails, 2000–2007," in *Mortality in Local Jails, 2000–2007*, U.S. Department of Justice, Office of Justice Programs, Bureau of Justice Statistics, July 2010, http://bjs.ojp.usdoj.gov/content/pub/pdf/ mlj07.pdfzz (accessed November 8, 2010)

around 30 deaths per 100,000 jail inmates between 2000 and 2007. The mortality rate due to drug/alcohol intoxication increased slightly from around 7 deaths per 100,000 jail inmates in 2000 to around 10 deaths per 100,000 jail inmates in 2007.

Table 8.11 breaks down mortality rates by inmate demographic data. The rate due to all causes was higher for male jail inmates (146 deaths per 100,000 jail inmates) than for female jail inmates (136 deaths per 100,000 jail inmates). Male inmates had somewhat higher mortality rates than did female inmates for heart disease and suicide. Female mortality rates were higher for other types of illnesses (such as influenza, septicemia, diabetes, and hepatitis) and drug/alcohol intoxication. The mortality rates due to all causes showed significant racial differences. The rate for non-Hispanic white inmates (172 deaths per 100,000 jail inmates) was significantly higher than the rate for non-Hispanic African-American inmates (123 deaths per 100,000 jail inmates) or Hispanic inmates (111 deaths per 100,000 jail inmates). Older inmates suffered much higher mortality rates than did younger inmates.

The mortality rate due to all causes was around 50 deaths per 100,000 jail inmates for prisoners aged 24 years and younger. (See Table 8.11.) The rate increased dramatically with age, rising to 383 deaths per 100,000 jail inmates for prisoners aged 45 to 54 years and to 892 deaths per 100,000 jail inmates for prisoners aged 55

TABLE 8.11

Deaths and mortality rate per 100,000 jail inmates, by cause of death and selected inmate characteristics, 2000–07

Characteristic	All causes	All illnesses	Heart disease	AIDS	Cancer	All other illnesses[a]	Suicide	Drug/alcohol intoxication	Accidental	Homicide
Total	145	77	32	7	5	32	42	10	4	3
Sex										
Male	146	76	33	7	5	31	44	9	4	3
Female	136	78	25	7	3	44	28	17	3	1
Race/Hispanic origin										
White, non-Hispanic	172	73	34	3	5	32	68	14	6	3
Black, non-Hispanic	123	87	35	13	6	33	16	6	3	3
Hispanic	111	57	18	6	3	30	33	8	3	4
Age										
Under 18	49	6	2	1	0	3	37	2	1	1
18–24	52	9	3	1	0	5	31	5	2	3
25–34	88	28	10	5	1	12	40	10	3	2
35–44	163	85	33	12	3	36	49	12	5	3
45–54	383	268	113	22	17	117	57	20	9	6
55 or older	892	730	357	20	85	267	72	14	12	9
Legal Status										
Convicted	83	55	25	5	4	22	18	4	3	2
Unconvicted[b]	176	101	41	10	6	44	66	16	5	4

Note: Mortality rates are based on the average daily population (ADP). In 2000 and 2001, ADP was estimated by taking the average of January 1 and December 31 one-day inmate population counts. Inmate populations for age and offense are estimates based on the 2002 Survey of Inmates in Local Jails. Inmate populations for sex, race/Hispanic origin and legal status are estimates based on the 2000 through 2007 Annual Survey of Jails. Detail may not sum to total due to rounding. All causes of death are included in the calculations of the total mortality rate.

[a]Includes other specified (such as influenza, septicemia, diabetes, and hepatitis) and unspecified or unknown illnesses.
[b]Includes inmates who were returned to jail on a probation or parole violation.

SOURCE: Margaret Noonan, "Table 10. Mortality Rate per 100,000 Jail Inmates, by Selected Inmate Characteristics and Leading Cause of Death, 2000–2007," in *Mortality in Local Jails, 2000–2007*, U.S. Department of Justice, Office of Justice Programs, Bureau of Justice Statistics, July 2010, http://bjs.ojp.usdoj.gov/content/pub/pdf/mlj07.pdf (accessed November 8, 2010)

years and older. Mortality rates due to most causes of death increased with prisoner age.

PRISONERS' RIGHTS UNDER THE LAW

In 1871 a Virginia court, in *Ruffin v. Commonwealth* (62 Va. 790), commented that a prisoner "has, as a consequence of his crime, not only forfeited his liberty, but all his personal rights except those which the law in its humanity accords to him. He is for the time being the slave of the state." Eight decades later, in *Stroud v. Swope* (187 F. 2d. 850 [1951]), the U.S. Court of Appeals for the Ninth Circuit asserted that "it is well settled that it is not the function of the courts to superintend the treatment and discipline of prisoners in penitentiaries, but only to deliver from imprisonment those who are illegally confined." The American Correctional Association explains in *Legal Responsibility and Authority of Correctional Officers: A Handbook on Courts, Judicial Decisions, and Constitutional Requirements* (1987) that correctional administrators believed that prisoners lost all their constitutional rights after conviction. Prisoners had privileges, not rights, and privileges could be taken away arbitrarily.

A significant change in this legal view came during the 1960s. In *Cooper v. Pate* (378 U.S. 546 [1964]), the U.S. Supreme Court held that the Civil Rights Act of 1871 granted protection to prisoners. The U.S. Code states in section 1983, title 42 (which is part of the Civil Rights Act), that "every person who, under color of any statute, ordinance, regulation, custom, or usage, of any State or Territory or the District of Columbia, subjects, or causes to be subjected, any citizen of the United States or other person within the jurisdiction thereof to the deprivation of any rights, privileges, or immunities secured by the Constitution and laws, shall be liable to the party injured in an action at law, suit in equity, or other proper proceeding for redress."

With the *Cooper* decision, the court announced that prisoners had rights that were guaranteed by the U.S. Constitution and could ask the judicial system for help in challenging the conditions of their imprisonment.

HABEAS CORPUS REVIEW

In *Cooper v. Pate*, the Supreme Court relied on civil rights. Another source of prisoners' rights arose from the court's reliance on habeas corpus. This Latin phrase means "have the body" with the rest of the phrase "brought before me" implied. A writ of habeas corpus is therefore the command issued by one court to another court (or to a lesser authority) to produce a person and to explain why that person is being detained. Habeas corpus dates back to an act of the British Parliament passed in 1679. Congress enacted the Judiciary Act of 1789 and gave federal prisoners the right to habeas corpus review. The Habeas Corpus

Act of 1867 later protected the rights of newly freed slaves and extended habeas corpus protection to state prisoners. The effective meaning of habeas corpus for prisoners is that it enables them to petition federal courts to review any aspect of their cases.

FIRST AMENDMENT CASES

The First Amendment of the U.S. Constitution guarantees that "Congress shall make no law respecting an establishment of religion, or prohibiting the free exercise thereof; or abridging the freedom of speech, or of the press; or the right of the people peaceably to assemble, and to petition the government for a redress of grievances."

Censorship

In *Procunier v. Martinez* (416 U.S. 396 [1974]), the Supreme Court ruled that prison officials cannot censor inmate correspondence unless they "show that a regulation authorizing mail censorship furthers one or more of the substantial governmental interests of security, order, and rehabilitation. Second, the limitation of First Amendment freedoms must be no greater than is necessary or essential to the protection of the particular governmental interest involved."

Prison officials may refuse to send letters that detail escape plans or encoded messages but may not censor inmate correspondence simply to "eliminate unflattering or unwelcome opinions or factually inaccurate statements." Because prisoners retain rights "when a prison regulation or practice offends a fundamental constitutional guarantee, federal courts will discharge their duty to protect constitutional rights."

However, the court recognized that it was "ill equipped to deal with the increasingly urgent problems of prison administration and reform." Running a prison takes expertise and planning, all of which, the court explained, is part of the responsibility of the legislative and executive branches. According to the court, the task of the judiciary branch is to establish a standard of review for prisoners' constitutional claims that is responsive to both the need to protect inmates' rights and the policy of judicial restraint.

In *Pell v. Procunier* (417 U.S. 817 [1974]), the court ruled that federal prison officials could prohibit inmates from having face-to-face media interviews. The court reasoned that judgments regarding prison security "are peculiarly within the province and professional expertise of corrections officials, and, in the absence of substantial evidence in the record to indicate that the officials have exaggerated their response to these considerations, courts should ordinarily defer to their expert judgment in such matters."

The U.S. Court of Appeals for the First Circuit ruled in *Nolan v. Fitzpatrick* (451 F. 2d 545 [1985]) that inmates had the right to correspond with newspapers. The prisoners were limited only in that they could not write about escape plans or include contraband material in their letters.

The Missouri Division of Corrections permitted correspondence between immediate family members who were inmates at different institutions and between inmates writing about legal matters. It also allowed other inmate correspondence only if each prisoner's "classification/treatment team" thought it was in the best interests of the parties. Another Missouri regulation permitted an inmate to marry only with the superintendent's permission, which can be given only when there were "compelling reasons" to do so, such as a pregnancy. In *Turner v. Safley* (482 U.S. 78 [1987]), the Supreme Court found the first regulation constitutional and the second one unconstitutional.

The court held that the "constitutional right of prisoners to marry is impermissibly burdened by the Missouri marriage regulation." The court had ruled earlier in *Zablocki v. Redhail* (434 U.S. 374 [1978]) that prisoners had a constitutionally protected right to marry, subject to restrictions because of incarceration such as time and place and prior approval of a warden. However, the Missouri regulation practically banned all marriages.

The findings in *Turner v. Safley* have become a guide for prison regulations in the United States. In its decision, the court observed that:

> When a prison regulation impinges on inmates' constitutional rights, the regulation is valid if it is reasonably related to legitimate penological interests.... First, there must be a "valid, rational connection" between the prison regulation and the legitimate governmental interest put forward to justify it.... Moreover, the governmental objective must be a legitimate and neutral one.... A second factor relevant in determining the reasonableness of a prison restriction ... is whether there are alternative means of exercising the right that remain open to prison inmates.... A third consideration is the impact accommodation of the asserted constitutional right will have on guards and other inmates, and on the allocation of prison resources generally.

Religious Beliefs

Even though inmates retain their First Amendment right to practice their religion, the courts have upheld restrictions on religious freedom when corrections departments need to maintain security, when economic considerations are involved, and when the regulation is reasonable.

The Religious Land Use and Institutionalized Persons Act was signed into law in September 2000 by President Bill Clinton (1946–). Section 3 of the law indicates that prison officials are required to accommodate inmates' religious needs in certain cases, even if this means exempting the inmates from general prison rules. The state of Ohio challenged the act's constitutionality by arguing that it violates the First Amendment's prohibition on the establishment of religion. Because the law does not require prison officials to accommodate inmates' secular needs or desires in similar ways, Ohio claimed the statute impermissibly advances religion. The state also argued that the law creates incentives for prisoners to feign religious belief to gain privileges. The Supreme Court upheld the constitutionality of the act in *Cutter v. Wilkinson* (544 U.S. 709 [2005]), reversing a ruling by the U.S. Court of Appeals for the Sixth Circuit, which had agreed with Ohio's argument.

FOURTH AMENDMENT CASES

The Fourth Amendment guarantees the "right of the people to be secure … against unreasonable searches and seizures … and no warrants shall issue, but upon probable cause." The courts have not been as active in protecting prisoners under the Fourth Amendment as under the First and Eighth Amendments. In *Bell v. Wolfish* (441 U.S. 520 [1979]), the Supreme Court asserted that:

> simply because prison inmates retain certain constitutional rights does not mean that these rights are not subject to restrictions and limitations…. Maintaining institutional security and preserving internal order and discipline are essential goals that may require limitation or retraction of the retained constitutional rights of both convicted prisoners and pretrial detainees. Since problems that arise in the day-to-day operation of a corrections facility are not susceptible of easy solutions, prison administrators should be accorded wide-ranging deference in the adoption and execution of policies and practices that in their judgment are needed to preserve internal order and discipline and to maintain institutional security.

Based on this reasoning, the court ruled that body searches did not violate the Fourth Amendment: "Balancing the significant and legitimate security interests of the institution against the inmates' privacy interests, such searches can be conducted on less than probable cause and are not unreasonable."

In another Fourth Amendment case, *Hudson v. Palmer* (468 U.S. 517 [1984]), the court upheld the right of prison officials to search a prisoner's cell and seize property. The court explained that "the recognition of privacy rights for prisoners in their individual cells simply cannot be reconciled with the concept of incarceration and the needs and objectives of penal institutions…. [However, the fact that a prisoner does not have a reasonable expectation of privacy] does not mean that he is without a remedy for calculated harassment unrelated to prison needs. Nor does it mean that prison attendants can ride roughshod over inmates' property rights with impunity. The Eighth Amendment always stands as a protection against 'cruel and unusual punishments.'"

EIGHTH AMENDMENT CASES

The Eighth Amendment states that "excessive bail shall not be required, nor excessive fines imposed, nor cruel and unusual punishments inflicted." The prohibition against "cruel and unusual punishments" has been used to challenge numerous aspects of the criminal justice system, including the death penalty, three-strikes laws, crowded prisons, lack of health or safety in prisons, and excessive violence by the guards.

Prison Conditions and Medical Care

In *Rhodes v. Chapman* (452 U.S. 337 [1981]), the Supreme Court ruled that housing prisoners in double cells was not cruel and unusual punishment. The justices maintained that "conditions of confinement, as constituting the punishment at issue, must not involve the wanton and unnecessary infliction of pain, nor may they be grossly disproportionate to the severity of the crime warranting imprisonment. But conditions that cannot be said to be cruel and unusual under contemporary standards are not unconstitutional. To the extent such conditions are restrictive and even harsh, they are part of the penalty that criminals pay for their offenses against society."

The court concluded that the Constitution "does not mandate comfortable prisons" and that only those deprivations denying the "minimal civilized measure of life's necessities" violate the Eighth Amendment.

However, Judge Richard A. Enslen (1931–) of the U.S. District Court ruled in *Hadix v. Caruso* (461 F.Supp.2d 574 [2006]) that officials at the Southern Michigan Correctional Facility had to stop using nonmedical restraints on prisoners because the "practice constitutes torture and violates the Eighth Amendment." In November 2006 Judge Enslen issued the opinion in the case of Timothy Souders, a mentally ill detainee who died after spending four days nude and shackled in an isolated cell. Judge Enslen ordered the prison to "immediately cease and desist from the practice of using any form of punitive mechanical restraints [and] shall timely develop practices, protocols and policies to enforce this limitation."

Guards Using Force

The Supreme Court ruled in *Whitley v. Albers* (475 U.S. 312 [1986]) that guards, during prison disturbances or riots, must balance the need "to maintain or restore discipline" through force against the risk of injury to inmates. These situations require prison officials to act quickly and decisively and allow guards and administrators leeway in their actions. In *Whitley*, a prisoner was shot in the knee during an attempt to rescue a hostage. The court found that the injury suffered by the prisoner was not cruel and unusual punishment under the circumstances.

In 1983 Keith Hudson, an inmate at the state penitentiary in Angola, Louisiana, argued with Jack McMillian, a guard. McMillian placed the inmate in handcuffs and shackles to take him to the administrative lockdown area. On the way, according to Hudson, McMillian punched him in the mouth, eyes, chest, and stomach; another guard held him while the supervisor on duty watched. Hudson sued, accusing the guards of cruel and unusual punishment.

A magistrate found that the guards used "force when there was no need to do so" and that the supervisor allowed their conduct, thus violating the Eighth Amendment. However, the U.S. Court of Appeals for the Fifth Circuit reversed the decision, ruling in *Hudson v. McMillian* (929 F. 2d 1014 [1990]) that "inmates alleging use of excessive force in violation of the Eighth Amendment must prove: (1) significant injury; (2) resulting 'directly and only from the use of force that was clearly excessive to the need'; (3) the excessiveness of which was objectively unreasonable; and (4) that the action constituted an unnecessary and wanton infliction of pain."

The court agreed that the use of force was unreasonable and was a clearly excessive and unnecessary infliction of pain. However, the court found against Hudson because his injuries were "minor" and "required no medical attention."

DUE PROCESS COMPLAINTS

The Fifth Amendment provides that no person should "be deprived of life, liberty, or property" by the federal government "without due process of law." The Fourteenth Amendment reaffirms this right and explicitly applies it to the states. Due process complaints brought by prisoners under the Fifth and Fourteenth Amendments are generally centered on questions of procedural fairness. Most of the time disciplinary action in prison is taken on the word of the guard or the administrator, and the inmate has little opportunity to challenge the charges.

The Supreme Court, however, has affirmed that procedural fairness should be used in some institutional decisions. In *Wolff v. McDonnell* (418 U.S. 539 [1974]), the court declared that a Nebraska law providing for sentences to be shortened for good behavior created a "liberty interest." Thus, if an inmate met the requirements, prison officials could not deprive him of the shortened sentence without due process, according to the Fourteenth Amendment.

At the Metropolitan Correctional Center, a federally operated short-term custodial facility in New York City that was designed mainly for pretrial detainees, inmates challenged the constitutionality of the facility's conditions. As this was a pretrial detention center, the challenge was brought under the due process clause of the Fifth Amendment. The district court and the court of appeals found for the inmates, but the Supreme Court disagreed in *Bell v. Wolfish*.

EARLY RELEASE

Beginning in 1983 the Florida legislature enacted a series of laws authorizing the awarding of early release credits to prison inmates when the state prison population exceeded predetermined levels. In 1986 Kenneth Lynce received a 22-year prison sentence on a charge of attempted murder. He was released in 1992, based on the determination that he had accumulated five different types of early release credits totaling 5,668 days, including 1,860 days of provisional credits awarded as a result of prison overcrowding.

Shortly thereafter, the state attorney general issued an opinion interpreting a 1992 statute as having retroactively canceled all provisional credits awarded to inmates convicted of murder and attempted murder. Lynce was rearrested and returned to custody. He filed a habeas corpus petition alleging that the retroactive cancellation of provisional credits violated the ex post facto (from a thing done afterward) clause of the Constitution.

The Supreme Court agreed with Lynce. In *Lynce v. Mathis* (519 U.S. 443 [1997]), the court ruled that "to fall within the ex post facto prohibition, a law must be retrospective and 'disadvantage the offender affected by it.'" The 1992 statute was clearly retrospective and disadvantaged Lynce by increasing his punishment.

LIMITING FRIVOLOUS PRISONER LAWSUITS

In 1995 the Supreme Court made it harder for prisoners to bring constitutional suits to challenge due process rights. In *Sandin v. Conner* (515 U.S. 472), the majority asserted that it was frustrated with the number of due process cases, some of which, it believed, clogged the judiciary with unwarranted complaints, such as claiming a "liberty interest" in not being transferred to a cell with an electrical outlet for a television set.

Sandin concerned an inmate in Hawaii who was not allowed to call witnesses at a disciplinary hearing for misconduct that had placed him in solitary confinement for 30 days. The Court of Appeals for the Ninth Circuit had held in 1993 that the inmate, Demont Conner, had a liberty interest that allowed him a range of procedural protections in remaining free from solitary confinement. The Supreme Court overruled the court of appeals, stating that the inmate had no liberty interest. Due process protections play a role only if the state's action has infringed on some separate, substantive right that the inmate possesses. For example, in *Wolff v. McDonnell* the petitioner's loss of good-time credit was a substantive right that he possessed. The punishment Conner had received "was within the range of confinement to be normally expected for one serving an indeterminate term of 30 years to life" for a number of crimes, including murder.

The court noted that "states may under certain circumstances create liberty interests which are protected by the Due Process Clause," but these should be limited to actions that impose "atypical and significant hardship on the inmate in relation to the ordinary incidents of prison life." According to the court, being put in solitary confinement in a prison where most inmates are limited to their cells most of the day anyway is not a liberty-interest issue. Because there was no liberty interest involved, how the hearing was handled was irrelevant.

Based on this ruling, the court held that a federal court should consider a complaint to be a potential violation of a prisoner's due process rights only when prison staff impose "atypical and significant hardship on the inmate." Mismanaged disciplinary hearings or temporary placement in solitary confinement are just "ordinary incidents of prison life" and should not be considered violations of the Constitution.

Chief Justice William H. Rehnquist (1924–2005) asserted that past Supreme Court decisions have "led to the involvement of federal courts in the day-to-day management of prisons, often squandering judicial resources with little offsetting benefit to anyone." Judges should allow prison administrators the flexibility to fine-tune the ordinary incidents of prison life.

In 1996 Congress passed the Prison Litigation Reform Act (PLRA) in an effort to limit so-called frivolous lawsuits by prisoners. The PLRA requires inmates to exhaust all possible internal prison grievance processes before filing civil rights lawsuits in federal courts. The law states that "no action shall be brought with respect to prison conditions under section 1983 of this title, or any other Federal law, by a prisoner confined in any jail, prison, or other correctional facility until such administrative remedies as are available are exhausted." After a few lower courts handed down controversial rulings on specific procedures that inmates must follow to exhaust administrative grievances, a case was brought before the U.S. Supreme Court. In the consolidated case of *Jones v. Bock* (No. 05-7058 [2007]) and *Williams v. Overton* (No. 05-7142 [2007]), the court overturned strict legal requirements that had been imposed by the U.S. Court of Appeals for the Sixth Circuit on Michigan inmates with grievances against their prison. Lorenzo Jones claimed that prison officials forced him to do "arduous" work even though he had been seriously injured in a car accident. Williams suffered a debilitating medical condition and claimed that his medical needs were not being properly met in prison. Instead of examining the merits of these claims, the Supreme Court chose to focus on specific legal issues associated with lawsuits that the prisoners had filed under the PLRA.

The court clarified that prisoners alleging federal civil rights violations under the PLRA do not have to prove they have exhausted all administrative remedies before filing lawsuits. The burden is on the defense to prove that administrative remedies were not exhausted. In addition, lower courts cannot dismiss lawsuits including multiple claims, even if some of the claims have not been exhausted. Finally, prisoners filing such lawsuits need not have named specific defendants in the administrative grievances to retain their rights to sue those defendants in court.

Complaints about the PLRA

The PLRA is roundly criticized by human rights groups, such as the ACLU and the Southern Center for Human Rights. The ACLU and dozens of other organizations formed the Stop Abuse and Violence Everywhere Coalition (2011, http://www.savecoalition.org/aboutus.html) to establish "proposed reforms to the law that do not interfere with its stated purpose: to reduce frivolous litigation by prisoners." The coalition complains that prisons have implemented complicated grievance systems with strict deadline requirements in order to thwart inmate efforts to file suits under the law. The coalition is also critical of the provision of the PLRA that requires that inmates cannot bring federal civil action unless "physical injury" has occurred. Human rights advocates note that prisoners who have been raped or suffered degrading treatment at the hands of prison staff are barred from filing suits because of this provision. Several PLRA reform bills have been introduced in Congress, most recently the Prison Abuse Remedies Act of 2009. However, as of February 2011 none of the bills had progressed to a vote.

INNOCENCE PROTECTION ACT

Deoxyribonucleic acid (DNA) testing has emerged as a powerful tool that is capable of establishing the innocence of a person in cases where organic matter from the perpetrator of a crime (e.g., blood, skin, or semen) has been obtained by law enforcement officials. This organic matter can be tested against DNA samples that have been taken from an accused or convicted person. If the two samples do not match, then they came from different people and the person being tested is innocent.

The Innocence Protection Act became law in 2004 as part of the Justice for All Act. The act enables people who are "convicted and imprisoned for federal offenses" and who claim to be innocent to have DNA testing on the biological evidence that was originally collected during the investigations of the crimes for which they were convicted. It mandates that the government has to preserve collected biological evidence so that it can be tested after the defendant is convicted. Finally, it provides funds to allow certain agencies to test evidence to identify perpetrators of unsolved crimes.

The Innocence Project is a private organization affiliated with the Benjamin N. Cardozo School of Law at Yeshiva University. The Innocence Project (2011, http://www.innocenceproject.org/) describes itself as "a national litigation and public policy organization dedicated to exonerating wrongfully convicted individuals through DNA testing and reforming the criminal justice system to prevent future injustice." In the fact sheet "Facts on Post-conviction DNA Exonerations" (http://www.innocenceproject.org/Content/351.php) the organization claims that as of 2010, 266 people in the United

States had been exonerated by postconviction DNA testing, including 17 on death row. Furthermore, in the fact sheet "Access to Post-conviction DNA Testing" (2010, http://www.innocenceproject.org/Content/304.php), the Innocence Project states that "although 48 states have post-conviction DNA testing access statutes, many of these testing laws are limited in scope and substance." (As of 2010, Massachusetts and Oklahoma were the only states that did not have any DNA access statutes incorporated into their state laws.) The Innocence Project claims that some state laws are deficient in that they do not include safeguards needed to properly preserve DNA evidence, do not include an appeals process for inmates denied postconviction DNA testing, and do not require "full, fair, and prompt" proceedings after inmates file DNA testing petitions.

CHAPTER 9
PROBATION AND PAROLE

Most of the correctional population of the United States—those under the supervision of correctional authorities—are walking about freely. They are people on probation or parole. A probationer is someone who has been convicted of a crime and sentenced—but the person's sentence has been suspended on condition that he or she behaves in a manner ordered by the court. Probation sometimes follows a brief period of incarceration; more often it is granted by the court immediately. A parolee is an individual who has served a part of his or her sentence in jail or prison but, because of good behavior or legislative mandate, has been granted freedom before the sentence is fully served. The sentence remains in effect, however, and the parolee continues to be under the jurisdiction of a parole board. If the person fails to live up to the conditions of the release, the parolee may be confined again.

According to Lauren E. Glaze, Thomas P. Bonczar, and Fan Zhang of the Bureau of Justice Statistics (BJS), in *Probation and Parole in the United States, 2009* (December 2010, http://bjs.ojp.usdoj.gov/content/pub/pdf/ppus09.pdf), approximately 5 million people (4.2 million on probation and 819,308 on parole) were under community supervision at year-end 2009. Probationers and parolees are still under official supervision and have to satisfy requirements placed on them as a condition of freedom or of early release from correctional facilities.

Glaze, Bonczar, and Zhang indicate that between 2008 and 2009 the number of people on probation and parole decreased by 0.9%, the first annual decline in this population since the BJS began monitoring it in 1980. As shown in Figure 9.1, the number of adults under community supervision increased from just over 4.5 million in 2000 to nearly 5.1 million in 2008, before falling to 5 million in 2009. Probationers have historically made up the largest portion of people under community supervision. In 2009 probationers accounted for 83.7% of the population under community supervision.

As of year-end 2009, Glaze, Bonczar, and Zhang note that approximately 1 out of every 47 adults in the United States was under community supervision (i.e., on probation or parole). This value was down from 2004, when 1 out of every 45 adults in the United States was on probation or parole.

Table 9.1 provides a breakdown by jurisdiction of the adults under community supervision at year-end 2009. The vast majority (4.9 million or 97.5%) were under state jurisdiction. Note that Glaze, Bonczar, and Zhang include the District of Columbia when they used the term *states* or *state jurisdiction*; thus, this chapter does likewise. Only 125,025 (2.5%) were under federal jurisdiction. On a regional basis, the South had the largest adult population under community supervision (1,966,940), followed by the Midwest (1,138,494), the West (920,558), and the Northeast (867,838).

The 10 states with the largest numbers of adults under community supervision at year-end 2009 were:

- Texas—531,274

- California—418,081

- Georgia—416,717

- Florida—272,061

- Ohio—269,524

- Pennsylvania—267,343

- Michigan—199,505

- Massachusetts—184,042

- Illinois—177,854

- New York—169,607

The 10 states with the highest community supervision rates (the number of adults under community supervision per 100,000 adult residents of that state) at year-end 2009 were:

FIGURE 9.1

Number of adults under community supervision, by type of supervision, 2000–09

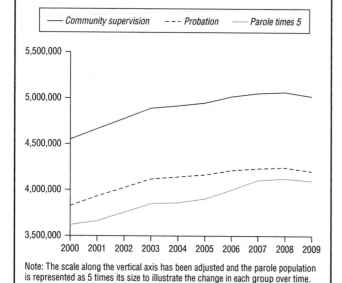

Note: The scale along the vertical axis has been adjusted and the parole population is represented as 5 times its size to illustrate the change in each group over time. The reporting methods for some probation and parole agencies changed over time.

SOURCE: Lauren E. Glaze, Thomas P. Bonczar, and Fan Zhang, "Figure 1. Total Adults Under Community Supervision and on Probation or Parole, 2000–2009," in *Probation and Parole in the United States, 2009*, U.S. Department of Justice, Office of Justice Programs, Bureau of Justice Statistics, December 2010, http://bjs.ojp .usdoj.gov/content/pub/pdf/ppus09.pdf (accessed December 21, 2010)

- Georgia—5,714 adults under community supervision per 100,000 adult residents

- Idaho—5,333 adults under community supervision per 100,000 adult residents

- Massachusetts—3,546 adults under community supervision per 100,000 adult residents

- Rhode Island—3,200 adults under community supervision per 100,000 adult residents

- Minnesota—3,153 adults under community supervision per 100,000 adult residents

- Ohio—3,045 adults under community supervision per 100,000 adult residents

- District of Columbia—3,035 adults under community supervision per 100,000 adult residents

- Texas—2,942 adults under community supervision per 100,000 adult residents

- Indiana—2,900 adults under community supervision per 100,000 adult residents

- Maryland and Pennsylvania—2,708 adults under community supervision per 100,000 adult residents

According to Glaze, Bonczar, and Zhang, the adult community supervision population under state jurisdiction

TABLE 9.1

Adults under community supervision, by jurisdiction, December 31, 2009

Region and jurisdiction	Community supervision population, 12/31/2009[a]	Number under community supervision per 100,000 adult residents, 12/31/2009
U.S. total	5,018,855	2,147
Federal	125,025	53
State	4,893,830	2,094
Alabama	58,384	1,624
Alaska[b]	8,686	1,675
Arizona[c]	86,452	1,764
Arkansas	51,296	2,343
California[b, c]	418,081	1,509
Colorado[b, c, d]	89,769	2,344
Connecticut[c]	59,209	2,175
Delaware	17,350	2,545
District of Columbia	14,889	3,035
Florida[c, d]	272,061	1,871
Georgia[c, e]	416,717	5,714
Hawaii[c]	21,300	2,113
Idaho[c, f]	60,422	5,333
Illinois[c]	177,854	1,820
Indiana[b, c]	140,734	2,900
Iowa[b, c]	26,466	1,148
Kansas[b]	22,246	1,047
Kentucky[c]	66,400	2,004
Louisiana	67,811	2,001
Maine	7,347	701
Maryland	118,283	2,708
Massachusetts[b]	184,042	3,546
Michigan[b, c, d]	199,505	2,616
Minnesota	126,881	3,153
Mississippi	29,702	1,355
Missouri[c, d]	77,338	1,690
Montana[c]	11,092	1,462
Nebraska	19,414	1,436
Nevada	16,486	836
New Hampshire	6,329	610
New Jersey	139,532	2,085
New Mexico[d]	22,206	1,473
New York	169,607	1,117
North Carolina[c]	109,703	1,534
North Dakota	4,530	895
Ohio[b, c, d]	269,524	3,045
Oklahoma[c]	30,037	1,078
Oregon	63,118	2,124
Pennsylvania[d]	267,343	2,708
Rhode Island[b, c]	26,509	3,200
South Carolina	41,300	1,179
South Dakota	9,350	1,516
Tennessee	71,185	1,475
Texas[g]	531,274	2,942

declined by 1% between 2008 and 2009. Overall, 51,652 adults were removed from community supervision in the states. The largest drops were in California (decline of 27,741 adults), Washington (decline of 19,104 adults), and Florida (decline of 11,524 adults). On a percentage basis, the largest decreases were in Washington (down 15.7%), Wyoming (down 14.2%), and California (down 6.2%).

Approximately half the states saw their community supervision population grow between 2008 and 2009. The largest numerical increases were in Idaho (up 7,548 adults), Pennsylvania (up 7,419 adults), and Mississippi (up 4,513 adults). The greatest increases on a percentage basis were in Mississippi (up 17.9%), Idaho (up 14.3%), and the District of Columbia (up 13.1%).

TABLE 9.1

Adults under community supervision, by jurisdiction, December 31, 2009 [CONTINUED]

Region and jurisdiction	Community supervision population, 12/31/2009[a]	Number under community supervision per 100,000 adult residents, 12/31/2009
Utah	14,732	762
Vermont[b, c]	7,920	1,595
Virginia[c]	60,250	992
Washington[b, c, d]	102,932	2,005
West Virginia[c, d]	10,298	716
Wisconsin[c]	64,652	1,482
Wyoming	5,282	1,269
Northeast	867,838	2,015
Midwest	1,138,494	2,233
South	1,966,940	2,290
West	920,558	1,712

[a]Excludes a small number (4,420) of offenders under community supervision who were on both probation and parole.
[b]Population excludes probationers or parolees in one of the following categories: warrant, inactive, or supervised out of state.
[c]Some or all detailed data are estimated.
[d]Data for entries and exits were estimated for nonreporting agencies.
[e]Probation counts include private agency cases and may overstate the number of persons under supervision.
[f]Probation counts include estimates for misdemeanors based on entries.

SOURCE: Adapted from Lauren E. Glaze, Thomas P. Bonczar, and Fan Zhang, "Appendix Table 1. Adults Under Community Supervision, 2009," in *Probation and Parole in the United States, 2009*, U.S. Department of Justice, Office of Justice Programs, Bureau of Justice Statistics, December 2010, http://bjs.ojp.usdoj.gov/content/pub/pdf/ppus09.pdf (accessed December 21, 2010)

Glaze, Bonczar, and Zhang indicate that the adult community supervision population under federal jurisdiction increased by 4.6% between 2008 and 2009. Overall, there were 53 adults under federal community supervision at year-end 2009 for every 100,000 adult residents of the United States. (See Table 9.1.)

PROBATION

Probation Population

In 2000 there were just over 3.8 million probationers. (See Figure 9.1). By 2009 the number had climbed to more than 4.2 million. In each year the number of people entering the system exceeded the number exiting the system. This dynamic changed between 2008 and 2009, when the number of probationers declined by 0.9% because probation exits exceeded entries.

Jurisdiction and Geographical Distribution of Probationers

A breakdown of probationers by jurisdiction (federal and state), by region, and by state is presented in Table 9.2 as of December 31, 2009. At that time the 4.2 million people on probation represented a rate of 1,799 people on probation per 100,000 adult U.S. residents. Nearly all the probationers (nearly 4.2 million or 99.5%) were under

state jurisdiction. Only 22,783 probationers were under federal jurisdiction.

The South had the largest probation population (1.7 million) and the highest regional probation rate (1,997 per 100,000 adult U.S. residents), followed by the Midwest (1 million probationers for a rate of 1,964), the West (747,354 probationers for a rate of 1,390), and the Northeast (717,659 probationers for a rate of 1,666). The 10 states with the highest probation populations at year-end 2009 were:

- Texas—426,331 probationers
- Georgia—392,688 probationers
- California—312,046 probationers

TABLE 9.2

Adults on probation, by jurisdiction, December 31, 2009

Region and jurisdiction	Probation population, 12/31/2009	Number on probation per 100,000 adult residents, 12/31/2009
U.S. total	4,203,967	1,799
Federal	22,783	10
State	4,181,184	1,789
Alabama	49,955	1,389
Alaska[a]	6,747	1,301
Arizona[b]	78,243	1,597
Arkansas	30,130	1,376
California[b]	312,046	1,126
Colorado[a, b, c]	78,114	2,040
Connecticut[b]	56,336	2,070
Delaware	16,831	2,469
District of Columbia	8,955	1,825
Florida[b, c]	267,738	1,841
Georgia[b, d]	392,688	5,385
Hawaii[b]	19,469	1,932
Idaho[b, e]	56,975	5,029
Illinois[b]	144,692	1,480
Indiana[a, b]	130,207	2,683
Iowa[a, b]	23,201	1,007
Kansas	17,236	811
Kentucky[b]	54,205	1,636
Louisiana	42,259	1,247
Maine	7,316	698
Maryland	104,541	2,393
Massachusetts[a]	180,677	3,481
Michigan[a, b, c]	175,131	2,296
Minnesota	121,446	3,018
Mississippi	24,276	1,108
Missouri[b, c]	57,665	1,260
Montana[b]	10,085	1,329
Nebraska	18,591	1,375
Nevada	12,300	624
New Hampshire	4,509	434
New Jersey	124,176	1,856
New Mexico[c]	20,086	1,332
New York	119,657	788
North Carolina[b]	106,581	1,490
North Dakota	4,173	825
Ohio[a, b, c]	254,949	2,880
Oklahoma[b]	27,067	972
Oregon	40,724	1,371
Pennsylvania[c]	192,231	1,947
Rhode Island[b]	25,924	3,129
South Carolina	39,688	1,133
South Dakota	6,602	1,071
Tennessee	59,558	1,234
Texas	426,331	2,361

TABLE 9.2

Adults on probation, by jurisdiction, December 31, 2009 [CONTINUED]

Region and jurisdiction	Probation population, 12/31/2009	Number on probation per 100,000 adult residents, 12/31/2009
Utah	11,528	596
Vermont[a, b]	6,833	1,376
Virginia[b]	55,645	917
Washington[a, b, c]	96,369	1,877
West Virginia[b, c]	8,409	585
Wisconsin[b]	47,421	1,087
Wyoming	4,668	1,121
Northeast	717,659	1,666
Midwest	1,001,314	1,964
South	1,714,857	1,997
West	747,354	1,390

[a]Population excludes probationers in one of the following categories: inactive, warrant, supervised out of jurisdiction, or probationers who had their location tracked by GPS.
[b]Some or all detailed data are estimated.
[c]Data for entries and exits were estimated for nonreporting agencies.
[d]Counts include private agency cases and may overstate the number of persons under supervision.
[e]Counts include estimates for misdemeanors based on entries during the year.

SOURCE: Adapted from Lauren E. Glaze, Thomas P. Bonczar, and Fan Zhang, "Appendix Table 2. Adults on Probation, 2009," in *Probation and Parole in the United States, 2009*, U.S. Department of Justice, Office of Justice Programs, Bureau of Justice Statistics, December 2010, http://bjs.ojp.usdoj.gov/content/pub/pdf/ppus09.pdf (accessed December 21, 2010)

- Florida—267,738 probationers

- Ohio—254,949 probationers

- Pennsylvania—192,231 probationers

- Massachusetts—180,677 probationers

- Michigan—175,131 probationers

- Illinois—144,692 probationers

- Indiana—130,207 probationers

The 10 states with the highest probation rates at year-end 2009 were:

- Georgia—5,385 probationers per 100,000 adult residents

- Idaho—5,029 probationers per 100,000 adult residents

- Massachusetts—3,481 probationers per 100,000 adult residents

- Rhode Island—3,129 probationers per 100,000 adult residents

- Minnesota—3,018 probationers per 100,000 adult residents

- Ohio—2,880 probationers per 100,000 adult residents

- Indiana—2,683 probationers per 100,000 adult residents

- Delaware—2,469 probationers per 100,000 adult residents

- Maryland—2,393 probationers per 100,000 adult residents

- Texas—2,361 probationers per 100,000 adult residents

Glaze, Bonczar, and Zhang report that the population of adult probationers under state jurisdiction decreased by 1% between 2008 and 2009 due to the removal of 40,379 people. The largest declines were in Washington (19,104 removed), California (13,023 removed), and Florida (11,319 removed). On a percentage basis, the largest decreases were in Wyoming (down 14.2%), Washington (down 12.6%), and Nevada (down 7.8%).

Just over half the states experienced increasing probationer populations between 2008 and 2009. The largest numerical increases were in Idaho (up 7,462 adults), Pennsylvania (up 5,258 adults), and Colorado (up 3,991 adults). The greatest increases on a percentage basis were in the District of Columbia (up 16.2%), Idaho (up 15.1%), and Mississippi (up 9%).

The number of adult probationers under federal jurisdiction increased by 1.3% between 2008 and 2009. Overall, there were 10 adults on federal probation at year-end 2009 for every 100,000 adult residents of the United States.

Probation Entries

Glaze, Bonczar, and Zhang note that federal and state governments reported just over 2.1 million entries to their probation systems in 2009. The type of sentence was identified for only 1 million of these new probationers as follows: 649,634 (64.5%) received probation without incarceration, 211,854 (21%) received probation with incarceration, and 145,725 (14.5%) received some other type of sentence, such as probation plus placement in a drug court program.

Probation Exits

According to Glaze, Bonczar, and Zhang, nearly 2.2 million people were reported as exiting probation in 2009. The type of exit was identified for nearly 1.7 million of these exiters. As shown in Table 9.3, nearly two-thirds (65%) of them left the system because they had completed their probation terms successfully—that is, they either completed their full-term sentence or received an early discharge. Sixteen percent left the probation system to be incarcerated because they received a new sentence for committing a new offense, they were incarcerated under their original sentence (i.e., their probation was revoked because they violated the rules of their probation), or they were incarcerated under other or unknown circumstances. Another 3% absconded (disappeared). The remaining exiters left the system for a variety of reasons, including 10% who left for what are called "unsatisfactory" reasons. Unsatisfactory conclusions include those who did not successfully complete all the terms of their supervision, for example, those whose sentences expired before completion and those who failed to fulfill a financial requirement such as restitution.

The breakdown of exit circumstances for 2009 differs little from those reported for 2006, 2007, and 2008. (See Table 9.3.) However, during this period the percent of probationers exiting supervision due to completion grew from 58% in 2006 to 65% in 2009. Likewise, the percentage exiting probation for incarceration declined slightly from 18% in 2006 to 16% in 2009.

Demographics of Probationers

Table 9.4 provides a breakdown of the adult probation population in 2000, 2008, and 2009 for which gender, race, Hispanic or Latino origin, type of probation and supervision, and type and seriousness of offense were identified. Note that this information was not reported by federal and state governments for all probationers, but for a subset of probationers for each category. For example, Glaze, Bonczar, and Zhang indicate that gender information was provided for only 3.1 million of the 4.2 million known probationers as of December 31, 2009.

This subset was 76% male and 24% female. The ratio of males to females was virtually unchanged from 2000, when the population was 78% male and 22% female.

At year-end 2009 race and ethnic origin data were reported for 2.7 million adult probationers. Of these, 55% were non-Hispanic white, 30% were non-Hispanic African-American, and 13% were Hispanic or Latino. (See Table 9.4.) Other races made up 2% of the total. This racial and ethnic breakdown had changed little since 2000.

Supervision status was reported for nearly 2.9 million adult probationers as of December 31, 2009. Over seven out of 10 (72%) of these probationers were under active

TABLE 9.3

Percent and estimated number of probationers who exited community supervision, by type of exit, 2006–09

Type of exit	2006	2007	2008	2009
Total	**100%**	**100%**	**100%**	**100%**
Completion	58%	62%	63%	65%
Incarceration[a]	18	16	17	16
Absconder	4	3	4	3
Discharged to custody, detainer, or warrant	1	1	1	1
Other unsatisfactory[b]	13	11	10	10
Transferred to another probation agency	1	1	1	—
Death	1	1	1	1
Other[c]	5	5	4	4
Estimated number	2,230,200	2,315,800	2,340,800	2,347,500

Note: Detail may not sum to total because of rounding. Distributions are based on probationers for which type of exit was known.
—Less than 0.5%.
[a]Includes probationers who were incarcerated for a new offense, those who had their current probation sentence revoked (e.g. violating a condition of their sentence), and those incarcerated from unspecified reasons.
[b]Includes probationers discharged from supervision who failed to meet all conditions of supervision, including some with only financial conditions remaining, some who had their probation sentence revoked but were not incarcerated because their sentence was immediately reinstated, and other types of unsatisfactory exits; includes some early terminations and expirations of sentence.
[c]Includes probationers discharged through a legislative mandate, because they were deported or transferred to the jurisdiction of Immigration and Customs Enforcement (ICE), transferred to another state through an interstate compact agreement, had their sentence dismissed or overturned by the court through an appeal, had their sentence closed administratively, deferred, or terminated by the court, were awaiting a hearing, were released on bond, some who elected jail time in lieu of probation, and other types of exits.

SOURCE: Lauren E. Glaze, Thomas P. Bonczar, and Fan Zhang, "Table 3. Percent and Estimated Number of Probationers Who Exited Supervision, by Type of Exit, 2006–2009," in *Probation and Parole in the United States, 2009*, U.S. Department of Justice, Office of Justice Programs, Bureau of Justice Statistics, December 2010, http://bjs.ojp.usdoj.gov/content/pub/pdf/ppus09.pdf (accessed December 21, 2010)

TABLE 9.4

Characteristics of adults on probation, 2000, 2008–09

Characteristics	2000	2008	2009
Total	**100%**	**100%**	**100%**
Sex			
Male	78%	76%	76%
Female	22	24	24
Race and Hispanic or Latino origin			
White[a]	54%	56%	55%
Black[a]	31	29	30
Hispanic or Latino	13	13	13
American Indian/Alaska Native[a]	1	1	1
Asian/Native Hawaiian/other Pacific Islander[a]	1	1	1
Two or more races[a]	. . .	1	—
Status of supervision			
Active	76%	71%	72%
Residential/other treatment program	. . .	1	1
Financial conditions remaining	. . .	1	1
Inactive	9	8	6
Absconder	9	8	8
Supervised out of jurisdiction	3	3	3
Warrant status	. . .	6	6
Other	3	2	2
Type of offense			
Felony	52%	49%	51%
Misdemeanor	46	48	47
Other infractions	2	2	2
Most serious offense			
Violent	. . .	19%	19%
Domestic violence	. . .	4	4
Sex offense	. . .	3	3
Other violent offense	. . .	12	13
Property	. . .	25	26
Drug	24	29	26
Public-order	24	17	18
DWI/DUI	18	14	15
Other traffic offense	6	4	4
Other[b]	52	10	10

Note: Each characteristic is based on probationers with a known status. Detail may not sum to total because of rounding.
—Less than 0.5%.
. . .Not available.
[a]Excludes persons of Hispanic or Latino origin.
[b]Includes violent and property offenses in 2000, because those data were not collected separately.

SOURCE: Lauren E. Glaze, Thomas P. Bonczar, and Fan Zhang, "Appendix Table 5. Characteristics of Adults on Probation, 2000, 2008–2009," in *Probation and Parole in the United States, 2009*, U.S. Department of Justice, Office of Justice Programs, Bureau of Justice Statistics, December 2010, http://bjs.ojp.usdoj.gov/content/pub/pdf/ppus09.pdf (accessed December 21, 2010)

supervision. (See Table 9.4.) Much smaller percentages were classified as absconders (8%), inactive (6%), or under warrant status (6%).

Offense categories were reported at year-end 2009 for nearly 3.3 million adult probationers. As shown in Table 9.4, 51% of these probationers had been convicted of a felony and 47% had been convicted of a misdemeanor. Another 2% had been convicted of other infractions, such as traffic offenses or tax crimes. The ratio of felony offenses to misdemeanor offenses in 2009 had changed little since 2000, when 52% of probationers had been convicted of a felony and 46% had been convicted of a misdemeanor.

As of December 31, 2009, specific offense data were available for 2.2 million probationers. The two largest contingents of these probationers had been convicted of drug law violations (26%) and property offenses (26%) as their most serious crime. (See Table 9.4.) Another 19% were on probation for a violent crime and 15% were on probation for driving while intoxicated or driving under the influence.

PAROLE
Trends in Parole

Discretionary parole is administered by parole boards. Their members examine prisoners' criminal histories and prison records and decide whether to release prisoners from incarceration. Since the mid-1990s several states have abolished discretionary parole in favor of mandatory parole. Mandatory parole is legislatively imposed at the state level and, with some exceptions, takes away parole boards' discretion. Mandatory parole provisions ensure that sentences for the same crime require incarceration for the same length of time. The prisoner can shorten his or her sentence only by good behavior—but time off for good behavior is also prohibited in some states. In some jurisdictions parole can only begin after prisoners have served 100% of their minimum sentences. Jeremy Travis and Sarah Lawrence of the Urban Institute report in *Beyond the Prison Gates: The State of Parole in America* (November 2002, http://www.urban.org/UploadedPDF/310583_Beyond_prison_gates.pdf) that the share of discretionary prison releases decreased from 65% in 1976 to 24% by 1999.

The states have different prison release methods. Some states have cut back on parole supervision by releasing more prisoners directly to the community. Other states have aggressively enforced the conditions of parole, leading to the identification of more parole violations. States handle different types of offenses differently. Some allow victims or prosecutors to participate in release decisions, whereas others do not. Some states still rely heavily on parole boards to make release decisions, whereas others no longer use parole boards and have mandatory release

policies for all their prisoners. Furthermore, parolees in some jurisdictions are required to wear electronic bracelets so that officials can monitor their movement.

For example, in 1983 Florida enacted sentencing guidelines that effectively eliminated the option of parole for most crimes that were committed on or after October 1, 1983. According to the Florida Parole Commission (2010, https://fpc.state.fl.us/Parole.htm), the only exceptions to the parole ban are inmates who committed a capital felony murder between October 1, 1983, and May 25, 1994, and all inmates convicted of other capital felonies between October 1, 1983, and October 1, 1995.

Parole Population

The number of adults on parole at year-end 2009 was 819,308. (See Table 9.5.) The vast majority of these parolees (717,066 or 87.5%) were under state jurisdiction. The remaining 102,242 (12.5%) parolees were under federal jurisdiction. The number of adult parolees (state and federal) per 100,000 adult U.S. residents was 351. The 819,308 people on parole at the end of 2009 represented 16.3% of the 5 million people who were under community supervision (i.e., total probationers and parolees).

Geographical Distribution of Parolees

A geographic distribution of adult parolees at year-end 2009 is shown in Table 9.5. On a regional basis, the South had the largest number of people on parole, though not the highest rate (253,363 for a rate of 295 per 100,000 adult residents). The Northeast had the highest rate (349) but not the highest number of people on parole (150,179). The West had 174,241 parolees for a rate of 324, and the Midwest counted 139,283 parolees for a rate of 273.

The 10 states with the highest parolee populations at year-end 2009 were:

- California—106,035
- Texas—104,943
- Pennsylvania—75,112
- New York—49,950
- Illinois—33,162
- Louisiana—25,683
- Michigan—24,374
- Georgia—24,029
- Oregon—22,394
- Arkansas—21,166

The 10 states with the highest parole rates at year-end 2009 were:

- District of Columbia—1,288 parolees per 100,000 adult residents
- Arkansas—967 parolees per 100,000 adult residents

TABLE 9.5

Adults on parole, by jurisdiction, December 31, 2009

Region and jurisdiction	Parole population, 12/31/2009	Number on parole per 100,000 adults residents, 12/31/2009
U.S. total	**819,308**	**351**
Federal	102,242	44
State	717,066	307
Alabama	8,429	234
Alaska	1,939	374
Arizona[a]	8,209	168
Arkansas	21,166	967
California[b]	106,035	383
Colorado	11,655	304
Connecticut	2,873	106
Delaware	519	76
District of Columbia	6,319	1,288
Florida[a]	4,323	30
Georgia	24,029	329
Hawaii	1,831	182
Idaho	3,447	304
Illinois	33,162	339
Indiana[b]	10,527	217
Iowa[b]	3,265	142
Kansas[b]	5,010	236
Kentucky	12,537	378
Louisiana	25,683	758
Maine	31	3
Maryland	13,742	315
Massachusetts	3,365	65
Michigan	24,374	320
Minnesota	5,435	135
Mississippi	5,426	248
Missouri	19,673	430
Montana	1,007	133
Nebraska	823	61
Nevada	4,186	212
New Hampshire	1,820	175
New Jersey	15,356	229
New Mexico	3,157	209
New York	49,950	329
North Carolina[a]	3,544	50
North Dakota	357	71
Ohio	14,575	165
Oklahoma[a]	2,970	107
Oregon	22,394	754
Pennsylvania[c]	75,112	761
Rhode Island[b]	585	71
South Carolina	1,612	46
South Dakota	2,748	446
Tennessee	11,627	241
Texas[a]	104,943	581

- Pennsylvania—761 parolees per 100,000 adult residents

- Louisiana—758 parolees per 100,000 adult residents

- Oregon—754 parolees per 100,000 adult residents

- Texas—581 parolees per 100,000 adult residents

- South Dakota—446 parolees per 100,000 adult residents

- Wisconsin—443 parolees per 100,000 adult residents

- Missouri—430 parolees per 100,000 adult residents

- California—383 parolees per 100,000 adult residents

Glaze, Bonczar, and Zhang indicate that the federal system, most states, and the District of Columbia added to

Region and jurisdiction	Parole population, 12/31/2009	Number on parole per 100,000 adults residents, 12/31/2009
Utah	3,204	166
Vermont[a]	1,087	219
Virginia[a]	4,605	76
Washington	6,563	128
West Virginia	1,889	131
Wisconsin[a]	19,334	443
Wyoming	614	147
Northeast	150,179	349
Midwest	139,283	273
South	253,363	295
West	174,241	324

[a]Some or all data were estimated.
[b]Population excludes parolees in one of the following categories: absconder or supervised out of state.
[c]The December 31, 2009, population includes 25,374 parolees under state parole supervision.

SOURCE: Adapted from Lauren E. Glaze, Thomas P. Bonczar, and Fan Zhang, "Appendix Table 2. Adults on Parole, 2009," in *Probation and Parole in the United States, 2009*, U.S. Department of Justice, Office of Justice Programs, Bureau of Justice Statistics, December 2010, http://bjs.ojp.usdoj.gov/content/pub/pdf/ppus09.pdf (accessed December 21, 2010)

their parolee population in 2009. The largest numerical increases were in Mississippi (net gain of 2,504 parolees), Pennsylvania (net gain of 2,161 parolees), and Texas (net gain of 2,022 parolees). The states with the largest percentage gains were Mississippi (up 85.7%), Rhode Island (up 24.7%), and Connecticut (up 23.4%). The largest net losses of parolees were in California (down 14,718 parolees), Washington (down 5,205 parolees), and Ohio (down 4,544 parolees). On a percentage basis, Washington (down 44.2%), Ohio (down 23.8%), and Wyoming (down 15.5%) had the biggest net losses of parolees.

Parole Entries

Glaze, Bonczar, and Zhang note that federal and state governments reported 545,266 entries to their parole systems in 2009. The type of sentence was identified for 537,956 of these new parolees. Nearly half (46.5%) were mandatory parole entries (i.e., their prison releases were not decided by a parole board). Another 27.3% of the new entries were under discretionary parole as determined by a parole board decision. In addition, 15.1% of the new parolees went into a term of supervised release in the community. Nearly 8% of the new parolees in 2009 were reinstatement entries, meaning that they reentered parole after being incarcerated for a parole violation. The remaining 3.4% of the new parolees were added to parole rolls for other reasons, for example, as part of release to a drug treatment program.

Parole Exits

In 2009 the federal and state governments reported that 552,611 parolees exited their parole systems. Detailed information about exit types is provided by Glaze, Bonczar,

TABLE 9.6

Percent and estimated number of parolees who exited community supervision, by type of exit, 2006–09

Type of exit	2006	2007	2008	2009
Total	100%	100%	100%	100%
Completion	45%	46%	49%	51%
Incarcerated	38	38	36	34
With new sentence	11	10	9	9
With revocation	26	27	25	24
Other/unknown	2	1	1	1
Absconder	11	11	11	9
Other unsatisfactory[a]	2	2	2	2
Transferred to another state	1	1	1	1
Death	1	1	1	1
Other[b]	3	2	1	3
Estimated number	532,200	543,600	574,000	579,100

Note: Detail may not sum to total because of rounding. Distributions are based on parolees for which type of exit was known.

[a]Includes parolees discharged from supervision who failed to meet all conditions of supervision, had their parole sentence rescinded, or had their parole sentence revoked but were not returned to incarceration because their sentence was immediately reinstated, and other types of unsatisfactory exits; includes some early terminations and expirations of sentence.

[b]Includes parolees who were deported or transferred to the jurisdiction of Immigration and Customs Enforcement (ICE), had their sentence terminated by the court through an appeal, were transferred to another state through an interstate compact agreement or discharged to probation supervision, and other types of exits.

SOURCE: Lauren E. Glaze, Thomas P. Bonczar, and Fan Zhang, "Table 6. Percent and Estimated Number of Parolees Who Exited Supervision, by Type of Exit, 2006–2009," in *Probation and Parole in the United States, 2009* U.S. Department of Justice, Office of Justice Programs, Bureau of Justice Statistics, December 2010, http://bjs.ojp.usdoj.gov/content/pub/pdf/ppus09 .pdf (accessed December 21, 2010)

TABLE 9.7

Characteristics of adults on parole, 2000, 2008–09

Characteristics	2000	2008	2009
Total	100%	100%	100%
Sex			
Male	88%	88%	88%
Female	12	12	12
Race and Hispanic or Latino origin			
White[a]	38%	41%	41%
Black[a]	40	38	39
Hispanic or Latino	21	19	18
American Indian/Alaska Native[a]	1	1	1
Asian/Native Hawaiian/other Pacific Islander[a]	—	1	1
Two or more races[a]	...	—	—
Status of supervision			
Active	83%	85%	85%
Inactive	4	4	4
Absconder	7	6	5
Supervised out of state	5	4	4
Financial conditions remaining	...	—	—
Other	1	1	2
Maximum sentence to incarceration			
Less than 1 year	3%	6%	5%
1 year or more	97	94	95
Most serious offense			
Violent	...	26%	27%
Sex offense	...	...	8
Other violent	...	...	19
Property	...	23	23
Drug	...	37	36
Weapon	...	3	3
Other[b]	...	11	10

Note: Each characteristic is based on parolees with a known status. Detail may not sum to total because of rounding.
—Less than 0.5%.
...Not available.
[a]Excludes persons of Hispanic or Latino origin.
[b]Includes public-order offenses.

SOURCE: Lauren E. Glaze, Thomas P. Bonczar, and Fan Zhang, "Appendix Table 15. Characteristics of Adults on Parole, 2000, 2008–2009," in *Probation and Parole in the United States, 2009*, U.S. Department of Justice, Office of Justice Programs, Bureau of Justice Statistics, December 2010, http://bjs.ojp.usdoj.gov/content/pub/pdf/ppus09.pdf (accessed December 21, 2010)

and Zhang for 546,585 of these parolees. As shown in Table 9.6, 51% completed their obligation, meaning that they completed their full-term sentence or received an early discharge. Another 34% were returned to incarceration— 24% whose parole was revoked for a technical violation, 9% who committed a new offense and received a new sentence, and 1% who were incarcerated for other or unknown reasons. An estimated 9% of parolees in 2009 absconded. Another 2% of parolees officially left the parole system, but under "unsatisfactory" conditions. For example, some still had financial obligations that they had not met. The remaining parolees who exited the system in 2009 included those who transferred to another state, died, or left for other or unknown reasons.

As can be seen in Table 9.6, the percentage of adult parolees completing their obligation increased from 45% in 2006 to 51% in 2009. Likewise, the percentage incarcerated declined from 38% in 2006 to 34% in 2009. The percentage of absconders also decreased from 11% in 2006 to 9% in 2009.

Characteristics of Parolees

A breakdown of adult parolees by gender, race, Hispanic or Latino origin, type of supervision, sentence length, and type of offense is provided in Table 9.7 for 2000, 2008,

and 2009. Note that these percentage values apply only to subsets of the entire parolee population.

Glaze, Bonczar, and Zhang note that gender information was available for 817,414 adult parolees reported as of December 31, 2009. The vast majority of the parolees were men (88%), whereas 12% were women. As shown in Table 9.7, the ratio of males to females was unchanged from 2000.

At year-end 2009 race and ethnic origin data were reported for 806,268 adult parolees. This subset contained 41% non-Hispanic whites and 39% non-Hispanic African-Americans. (See Table 9.7.) Eighteen percent of the parolees were Hispanic or Latino. These values had changed only slightly from 2000, when 38% of parolees were non-Hispanic white, 40% were non-Hispanic African-American, and 21% were Hispanic or Latino.

Supervision status was reported for 813,805 adult parolees as of December 31, 2009. Most adult parolees (85%) were under active supervision in 2009, up from 83% in 2000. (See Table 9.7.) In 2009, 5% of the parole population had absconded, which was down slightly from 7% in 2000.

Sentence data were reported at year-end 2009 for 692,379 adult parolees. As shown in Table 9.7, 95% of these parolees had served a sentence of at least one year and 5% had served less than a year.

As of December 31, 2009, specific offense data were available for 720,601 adult parolees. More than a third (36%) of these parolees had been convicted of drug offenses as their most serious crime. (See Table 9.7.) Drug offenses were the largest single crime category. Roughly one-fourth each had served time for violent offenses (27%) or property offenses (23%). Much smaller percentages had been convicted of other crimes (10%) and weapon offenses (3%).

Parolees Returned to Incarceration

As noted earlier, Glaze, Bonczar, and Zhang identified the exit status of 546,585 of the known 552,611 adult parolees who exited the system in 2009; 185,550 (33.9%) of this subset were returned to incarceration. Overall, 131,734 (71%) of these reincarcerated parolees went back to prison because their parole was revoked. The states with the highest number of parolees returned to prison due to parole revocation were California (58,958), Illinois (9,493), and New York (7,967). Another 47,882 parolees were reincarcerated in 2009 because they received new prison sentences. The largest numbers were in California (18,286), Texas (5,844), and Illinois (3,357).

At-risk parolees are those adults who were on parole at the beginning of the year and those who entered parole before the end of the year; by virtue of their release status they are considered at-risk of reincarceration. According to statistics reported by Glaze, Bonczar, and Zhang, the total percentage of at-risk parolees that had been returned to incarceration hovered around 15% between 2000 and 2008. In 2009, 14% of the total at-risk population was returned to incarceration: 9.9% due to parole revocation and 3.6% due to imposition of a new prison sentence.

CHAPTER 10
JUVENILE CRIME

WHO IS A JUVENILE?

Juvenile courts date to the late 19th century, when Cook County, Illinois, established the first juvenile court under the Juvenile Court Act of 1899. The underlying concept was that if parents failed to provide children with proper care and supervision, then the state had the right to intervene benevolently. Other states followed Illinois, and by 1925 juvenile courts were in operation in most states. Juvenile courts favored a rehabilitative philosophy rather than a punitive philosophy and evolved less formal approaches than those in place in adult courts.

In modern law juvenile offenses fall into two main categories: delinquency offenses and status offenses. Delinquency offenses are acts that are illegal regardless of the age of the perpetrator. Status offenses are acts that are illegal only for minors, such as truancy (failure to attend school), running away, or curfew violations. Each state defines by legislation the oldest age at which a youth falls under its juvenile court jurisdiction. As of February 2011, that age was 17 in the vast majority of states. The upper age was set at 16 in nine states (Georgia, Louisiana, Massachusetts, Michigan, Missouri, New Hampshire, South Carolina, Texas, and Wisconsin).

In Illinois the upper age is 17 for misdemeanors and 16 for felonies. New York and North Carolina use an upper age of 15. This means that youths aged 16 and 17 years fall under the jurisdiction of adult courts in these two states. However, New York provides for a "youthful offender" sentence that can be given to certain youths who are tried in adult courts. A "youthful offender" finding results in a shorter sentence than would have been imposed otherwise and no criminal record for the offender.

Many states place certain young offenders in the jurisdiction of the criminal (adult) court rather than the juvenile court based on the youth's age, offense, or previous court history.

CRIMINAL VICTIMIZATIONS BY JUVENILES

As described in Chapter 3, the Bureau of Justice Statistics (BJS) within the U.S. Department of Justice (DOJ) conducts an annual survey called the National Crime Victimization Survey (NCVS) in which a national representative sample of U.S. households is surveyed about criminal victimization. U.S. residents aged 12 years and older are questioned to determine if they have been crime victims during the previous year. If so, information is collected about the circumstances of the crime(s) and the perpetrators involved. Figure 10.1 provides NCVS data for serious violent crimes in which the victims "perceived" that the perpetrators were 12 to 17 years of age. The BJS definition of serious violent crimes includes aggravated assault, rape, and robbery (e.g., stealing that involves the use or threat of force or violence). The data graphed in Figure 10.1 also cover homicides that are believed to have involved one or more juvenile offenders. These homicides were reported to law enforcement agencies. Homicide data are collected and published by the Federal Bureau of Investigation (FBI) as part of its Uniform Crime Reports (UCR) Program, which is described in Chapter 2.

As shown in Figure 10.1, the rate of serious violent crimes attributed to juvenile offenders aged 12 to 17 years peaked during the early 1990s at around 50 crimes per 1,000 U.S. youth aged 12 to 17 years. The rate plummeted over the following decade, dropping to less than 20 crimes per 1,000 youth. In 2008 the rate was 14 crimes per 1,000 youth. Note that homicide data are not included in the 2008 rate.

JUVENILE ARREST STATISTICS

As described in earlier chapters, the FBI oversees the UCR Program and summarizes the data in annual reports. The report *Crime in the United States, 2009* (September 2010, http://www2.fbi.gov/ucr/cius2009/index.html)

FIGURE 10.1

Violent crime rate per 1,000 youths for offenders aged 12–17, 1980–2005 and 2007–08

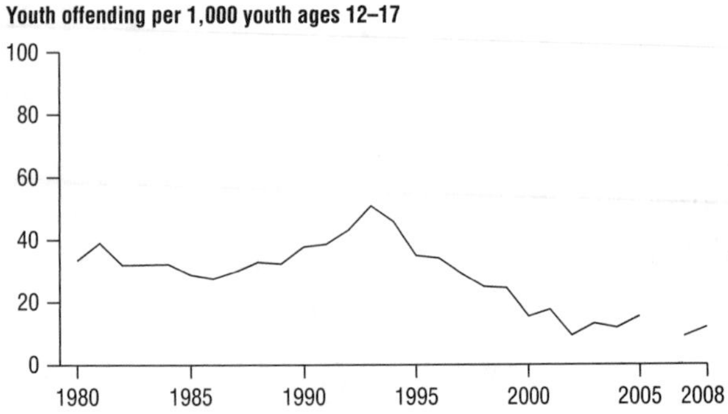

Youth offending per 1,000 youth ages 12–17

Notes: The offending rate is the ratio of the number of crimes (aggravated assault, rape, and robbery, i.e., stealing by force or threat of violence) reported to the National Crime Victimization Survey that involved at least one offender perceived by the victim to be 12–17 years of age, plus the number of homicides reported to the police that involved at least one juvenile offender, to the number of juveniles in the population. Homicide data were not available for 2008 at the time of publication. The number of homicides for 2007 is included in the overall total for 2008. In 2007, homicides represented less than 1 percent of serious violent crime, and the total number of homicides by juveniles has been relatively stable over the last decade. Because of changes made in the victimization survey, data prior to 1992 are adjusted to make them comparable with data collected under the redesigned methodology. Data from 2006 are not included because, due to changes in methodology, 2006 crime perpetration rates are not comparable to other years and cannot be used for yearly trend comparisons.

SOURCE: "Figure 11. Rate of Serious Violent Crimes by Youth Perpetrators Ages 12–17, 1980–2005 and 2007–2008," in *America's Children in Brief: Key National Indicators of Well-Being, 2010*, Federal Interagency Forum on Child and Family Statistics, July 2010, http://www.childstats.gov/pdf/ac2010/ac_10.pdf (accessed November 9, 2010)

includes statistics on crimes reported to law enforcement, arrests, and crimes cleared by arrest or exceptional means through 2009. Crimes cleared by exceptional means are those for which there can be no arrest, such as a murder-suicide, when the perpetrator is known to be deceased. The FBI does provide a partial breakdown of arrest statistics by age, that is, the age of the arrested offender. Because the upper age classification for juveniles differs between states, the FBI does not categorize arrested individuals as adults or juveniles. However, for ease of terminology offenders under the age of 18 years will be referred to as juveniles in this chapter.

Every two years the Office of Juvenile Justice and Delinquency Prevention (OJJDP) under the DOJ conducts a detailed examination of UCR data related to people under the age of 18 years. As of February 2011, the most recent report was *Juvenile Arrests 2008* (December 2009, http://www.ncjrs.gov/pdffiles1/ojjdp/228479.pdf) by Charles Puzzanchera of the OJJDP.

Juvenile Arrests in 2009

Table 10.1 and Table 10.2 show UCR arrest statistics for 2009 for those offenses in which the arrested individuals were under the age of 18 years. The data were reported to the FBI by 12,371 law enforcement agencies around the country. More than 1.5 million people under the age of 18 years were arrested in 2009. They accounted for 14.1% of total arrests that year.

As shown in Table 10.1, the 10 most common specific offenses were:

- Larceny-theft—254,865 arrests
- Assaults other than aggravated assaults—172,984 arrests
- Drug abuse violations—134,610 arrests
- Disorderly conduct—134,301 arrests
- Curfew and loitering law violations—89,733 arrests
- Liquor laws—88,370 arrests
- Running away—73,794 arrests
- Vandalism—71,502 arrests
- Burglary—59,432 arrests
- Aggravated assault—39,467 arrests

Overall, the arrests of people under the age of 18 years in 2009 totaled 68,074 for violent crimes and 334,237 for property crimes. (See Table 10.1.) Juveniles accounted for 14.9% of all violent crime arrests and 24.4% of all property crime arrests. The FBI includes four offenses in its definition of violent crimes: murder and nonnegligent manslaughter, forcible rape, robbery, and aggravated assault. All these offenses involve the use or threat of violence by the perpetrator. Property crimes include burglary, larceny-theft, motor vehicle theft, and arson. The FBI counts only the most serious charge for which a single offender is arrested. Violent crimes are considered more serious than property crimes. Thus, a person arrested for rape and burglary would be counted only once in Table 10.1 (for the rape offense).

JUVENILE ARRESTS BY AGE. As shown in Table 10.2, more than half of the juvenile arrests were of youths aged 17 years (28.9%) or 16 years (25%). Fifteen-year-olds accounted for 19.5% of the juvenile total, and teens aged 13 to 14 years made up 20.6% of the juvenile total. Only 5.4% of all juvenile arrests in 2009 were of children aged 10 to 12 years. Children younger than 10 years accounted for 0.6% of all juvenile arrests.

In general, youths aged 16 or 17 years made up the largest single juvenile contingent arrested for each crime. (See Table 10.2.) However, there were some notable exceptions. More than one-third (35.4%) of juvenile arrests for arson were of 13 to 14 year olds. Another 18.2% of juvenile arrests for arson were of children aged 10 to 12 years. Young teens aged 13 to 14 years also accounted for large percentages of the juveniles arrested for sex offenses, excluding forcible rape and prostitution

TABLE 10.1

Arrests of persons under 18 years of age, by age, 2009

[12,371 agencies]

Offense charged	Ages under 18	Under 10	10–12	13–14	15	16	17
					Number of arrests		
Total	1,515,586	9,737	81,927	312,007	294,866	379,225	437,824
Percent of all offenses charged[a]	14.1	0.1	0.8	2.9	2.7	3.5	4.1
Murder and nonnegligent manslaughter	942	2	11	74	149	290	416
Forcible rape	2,385	10	170	586	460	512	647
Robbery	25,280	31	574	3,996	5,208	7,091	8,380
Aggravated assault	39,467	344	3,035	8,567	7,455	9,451	10,615
Burglary	59,432	487	3,336	12,350	11,809	14,698	16,752
Larceny-theft	254,865	1,295	14,943	53,978	49,213	63,974	71,462
Motor vehicle theft	15,724	27	314	2,753	3,571	4,494	4,565
Arson	4,216	218	769	1,492	697	594	446
Violent crime[b]	68,074	387	3,790	13,223	13,272	17,344	20,058
Violent crime percent distribution[a]	14.9	0.1	0.8	2.9	2.9	3.8	4.4
Property crime[b]	334,237	2,027	19,362	70,573	65,290	83,760	93,225
Property crime percent distribution[a]	24.4	0.1	1.4	5.2	4.8	6.1	6.8
Other assaults	172,984	1,718	16,207	45,480	33,705	38,243	37,631
Forgery and counterfeiting	1,691	8	47	165	234	405	832
Fraud	5,014	35	129	671	775	1,306	2,098
Embezzlement	484	0	7	25	33	118	301
Stolen property; buying, receiving, possessing	14,875	57	550	2,643	3,019	3,918	4,688
Vandalism	71,502	1,210	7,078	19,215	13,394	15,393	15,212
Weapons; carrying, possessing, etc.	26,831	404	2,127	5,768	4,812	6,154	7,566
Prostitution and commercialized vice	1,079	5	15	111	205	277	466
Sex offenses (except forcible rape and prostitution)	10,567	209	1,377	3,481	1,785	1,757	1,958
Drug abuse violations	134,610	149	2,384	18,560	22,916	35,953	54,648
Gambling	1,395	1	6	149	238	404	597
Offenses against the family and children	3,612	38	235	754	727	871	987
Driving under the influence	10,712	52	17	161	455	2,407	7,620
Liquor laws	88,370	101	622	7,324	13,009	24,825	42,489
Drunkenness	11,102	68	98	1,112	1,726	2,660	5,438
Disorderly conduct	134,301	784	11,058	36,160	28,031	30,098	28,170
Vagrancy	2,151	6	50	465	586	554	490
All other offenses (except traffic)	258,293	1,699	9,905	48,501	51,876	66,787	79,525
Suspicion	175	8	15	24	27	47	54
Curfew and loitering law violations	89,733	278	3,357	18,466	20,210	25,523	21,899
Runaways	73,794	493	3,491	18,976	18,541	20,421	11,872

[a]Because of rounding, the percentages may not add to 100.0.
[b]Violent crimes are offenses of murder and nonnegligent manslaughter, forcible rape, robbery, and aggravated assault. Property crimes are offenses of burglary, larceny-theft, motor vehicle theft, and arson.

SOURCE: Adapted from "Table 38. Arrests, by Age, 2009," in *Crime in the United States, 2009*, U.S. Department of Justice, Federal Bureau of Investigation, September 2010, http://www2.fbi.gov/ucr/cius2009/data/documents/09tbl38.xls (accessed October 6, 2010)

(32.9%), vandalism (26.9%), disorderly conduct (26.9%), and assaults other than aggravated assault (26.3%).

JUVENILE ARRESTS BY RACE. Table 10.3 provides a racial breakdown of the 1.5 million juvenile arrestees in 2009. Whites accounted for 993,428 (65.9%) of the total, and African-Americans accounted for 472,929 (31.3%) of the total. Very small contingents consisted of Asians or Pacific Islanders (23,427 or 1.6%) and Native Americans or Alaskan Natives (18,766 or 1.2%). Whites made up the majority of juvenile arrestees for most offenses, particularly driving under the influence (92%), liquor laws (89.4%), drunkenness (88.5%), vandalism (78.4%), and arson (76.7%). African-Americans accounted for large majorities of the juveniles who were arrested for gambling (92.7%) and robbery (67.3%).

Juvenile arrestees for violent crimes in 2009 were 51.6% African-American and 46.4% white. (See Table 10.3.) In contrast, the property crime breakdown was 63.9% white and 33.2% African-American.

JUVENILE ARRESTS BY GENDER. As shown in Table 10.4, nearly 1.1 million (69.6%) of the total 1.5 million juvenile arrestees in 2009 were male. Females made up only 30.4% (460,927) of the total. Male arrests dominated the vast majority of offenses, particularly forcible rape (98.1%), gambling (97.3%), murder and nonnegligent manslaughter (92.7%), weapons violations (89.7%), and sex offenses, excluding forcible rape and prostitution (89.5%). Crimes for which female juveniles accounted for more than 40% of arrests were prostitution and commercialized vice (78.2%), runaways (55.2%), larceny-theft (45.6%), and embezzlement (41.9%).

Males accounted for 81.8% of all juvenile arrests for violent crimes and 62.2% of all juvenile arrests for property crimes in 2009. (See Table 10.4.)

TABLE 10.2

Percent of arrests of persons under 18 years of age, by age, 2009

[12,371 agencies]

Offense charged	Percentage breakdown of arrests by age					
	Under 10	10–12	13–14	15	16	17
Total	**0.6%**	**5.4%**	**20.6%**	**19.5%**	**25.0%**	**28.9%**
Murder and nonnegligent manslaughter	0.2%	1.2%	7.9%	15.8%	30.8%	44.2%
Forcible rape	0.4%	7.1%	24.6%	19.3%	21.5%	27.1%
Robbery	0.1%	2.3%	15.8%	20.6%	28.0%	33.1%
Aggravated assault	0.9%	7.7%	21.7%	18.9%	23.9%	26.9%
Burglary	0.8%	5.6%	20.8%	19.9%	24.7%	28.2%
Larceny-theft	0.5%	5.9%	21.2%	19.3%	25.1%	28.0%
Motor vehicle theft	0.2%	2.0%	17.5%	22.7%	28.6%	29.0%
Arson	5.2%	18.2%	35.4%	16.5%	14.1%	10.6%
Violent crime[b]	0.6%	5.6%	19.4%	19.5%	25.5%	29.5%
Violent crime percent distribution[a]	0.7%	5.4%	19.5%	19.5%	25.5%	29.5%
Property crime[b]	0.6%	5.8%	21.1%	19.5%	25.1%	27.9%
Property crime percent distribution[a]	0.4%	5.7%	21.3%	19.7%	25.0%	27.9%
Other assaults	1.0%	9.4%	26.3%	19.5%	22.1%	21.8%
Forgery and counterfeiting	0.5%	2.8%	9.8%	13.8%	24.0%	49.2%
Fraud	0.7%	2.6%	13.4%	15.5%	26.0%	41.8%
Embezzlement	0.0%	1.4%	5.2%	6.8%	24.4%	62.2%
Stolen property; buying, receiving, possessing	0.4%	3.7%	17.8%	20.3%	26.3%	31.5%
Vandalism	1.7%	9.9%	26.9%	18.7%	21.5%	21.3%
Weapons; carrying, possessing, etc.	1.5%	7.9%	21.5%	17.9%	22.9%	28.2%
Prostitution and commercialized vice	0.5%	1.4%	10.3%	19.0%	25.7%	43.2%
Sex offenses (except forcible rape and prostitution)	2.0%	13.0%	32.9%	16.9%	16.6%	18.5%
Drug abuse violations	0.1%	1.8%	13.8%	17.0%	26.7%	40.6%
Gambling	0.1%	0.4%	10.7%	17.1%	29.0%	42.8%
Offenses against the family and children	1.1%	6.5%	20.9%	20.1%	24.1%	27.3%
Driving under the influence	0.5%	0.2%	1.5%	4.2%	22.5%	71.1%
Liquor laws	0.1%	0.7%	8.3%	14.7%	28.1%	48.1%
Drunkenness	0.6%	0.9%	10.0%	15.5%	24.0%	49.0%
Disorderly conduct	0.6%	8.2%	26.9%	20.9%	22.4%	21.0%
Vagrancy	0.3%	2.3%	21.6%	27.2%	25.8%	22.8%
All other offenses (except traffic)	0.7%	3.8%	18.8%	20.1%	25.9%	30.8%
Suspicion	4.6%	8.6%	13.7%	15.4%	26.9%	30.9%
Curfew and loitering law violations	0.3%	3.7%	20.6%	22.5%	28.4%	24.4%
Runaways	0.7%	4.7%	25.7%	25.1%	27.7%	16.1%

[a]Because of rounding, the percentages may not add to 100.0.

[b]Violent crimes are offenses of murder and nonnegligent manslaughter, forcible rape, robbery, and aggravated assault. Property crimes are offenses of burglary, larceny-theft, motor vehicle theft, and arson.

SOURCE: Adapted from "Table 38. Arrests, by Age, 2009," in *Crime in the United States, 2009*, U.S. Department of Justice, Federal Bureau of Investigation, September 2010, http://www2.fbi.gov/ucr/cius2009/data/documents/09tbl38.xls (accessed October 6, 2010)

Juvenile Arrest Trends between 2000 and 2009

In *Crime in the United States, 2009*, the FBI uses age data from 8,649 law enforcement agencies to compile 10-year arrest trends for people under the age of 18 years. As shown in Table 10.5, overall juvenile arrests declined by 20.2% from 1.5 million in 2000 to 1.2 million in 2009.

Juvenile arrests decreased for nearly all offenses, particularly suspicion (down 79.7%), forgery and counterfeiting (down 69.2%), motor vehicle theft (down 59.6%), offenses against the family and children (down 43.6%), and vagrancy (down 36.4%). Juvenile arrests rose for only two offenses between 2000 and 2009: robbery (up 18%) and prostitution and commercialized vice (up 8.5%). The latter increase is not particularly significant because so few juveniles (less than 800) were arrested for this crime in either year. The increase in robbery arrests is significant, considering that robbery is a violent crime and so many juveniles (19,336 in 2009)

were arrested for it. However, as shown in Table 10.5 the number of juvenile arrests for all violent crimes decreased by 15% between 2000 and 2009. The decline was driven by sharp drops in arrests for forcible rape (down 31.9%) and aggravated assault (down 27.2%). Arrests of juveniles for murder and nonnegligent manslaughter also decreased by 0.6%.

Juvenile arrests for property crimes declined by 20.3% between 2000 and 2009 due to across-the-board decreases in arrests for larceny-theft (down 15.1%), burglary (down 20.9%), arson (down 35.3%), and motor vehicle theft (down 59.6%).

Table 10.6 provides UCR data from 8,649 law enforcement agencies that tracked the gender of arrested juveniles between 2000 and 2009. Arrests of male offenders decreased by 22.9% during this period. Only two crimes—robbery (16.7%) and murder and nonnegligent manslaughter (4%)—saw an increase in arrests.

TABLE 10.3

Percent of arrests of persons under 18 years of age, by race 2009

[12,371 agencies; 2009 estimated population 239,839,971]

	Arrests under 18					Percent distribution[a]				
Offense charged	Total	White	Black	American Indian or Alaskan Native	Asian or Pacific Islander	Total	White	Black	American Indian or Alaskan Native	Asian or Pacific Islander
Total	**1,508,550**	**993,428**	**472,929**	**18,766**	**23,427**	**100.0**	**65.9**	**31.3**	**1.2**	**1.6**
Murder and nonnegligent manslaughter	941	380	546	8	7	100.0	40.4	58.0	0.9	0.7
Forcible rape	2,368	1,501	818	19	30	100.0	63.4	34.5	0.8	1.3
Robbery	25,226	7,854	16,968	112	292	100.0	31.1	67.3	0.4	1.2
Aggravated assault	39,341	21,790	16,694	394	463	100.0	55.4	42.4	1.0	1.2
Burglary	59,237	36,073	22,082	511	571	100.0	60.9	37.3	0.9	1.0
Larceny-theft	253,467	164,701	80,670	3,148	4,948	100.0	65.0	31.8	1.2	2.0
Motor vehicle theft	15,664	8,452	6,765	234	213	100.0	54.0	43.2	1.5	1.4
Arson	4,203	3,222	865	56	60	100.0	76.7	20.6	1.3	1.4
Violent crime[b]	67,876	31,525	35,026	533	792	100.0	46.4	51.6	0.8	1.2
Property crime[b]	332,571	212,448	110,382	3,949	5,792	100.0	63.9	33.2	1.2	1.7
Other assaults	172,000	100,872	67,420	1,849	1,859	100.0	58.6	39.2	1.1	1.1
Forgery and counterfeiting	1,687	1,120	543	9	15	100.0	66.4	32.2	0.5	0.9
Fraud	4,980	3,083	1,793	55	49	100.0	61.9	36.0	1.1	1.0
Embezzlement	481	307	160	1	13	100.0	63.8	33.3	0.2	2.7
Stolen property; buying, receiving, possessing	14,831	8,104	6,461	117	149	100.0	54.6	43.6	0.8	1.0
Vandalism	71,158	55,801	13,683	845	829	100.0	78.4	19.2	1.2	1.2
Weapons: carrying, possessing, etc.	26,666	16,190	9,938	210	328	100.0	60.7	37.3	0.8	1.2
Prostitution and commercialized vice	1,072	426	626	4	16	100.0	39.7	58.4	0.4	1.5
Sex offenses (except forcible rape and prostitution)	10,494	7,468	2,788	89	149	100.0	71.2	26.6	0.8	1.4
Drug abuse violations	134,207	97,232	34,295	1,212	1,468	100.0	72.4	25.6	0.9	1.1
Gambling	1,395	95	1,293	0	7	100.0	6.8	92.7	0.0	0.5
Offenses against the family and children	3,576	2,642	870	48	16	100.0	73.9	24.3	1.3	0.4
Driving under the influence	10,629	9,774	541	191	123	100.0	92.0	5.1	1.8	1.2
Liquor laws	87,811	78,540	5,439	2,704	1,128	100.0	89.4	6.2	3.1	1.3
Drunkenness	11,067	9,799	966	210	92	100.0	88.5	8.7	1.9	0.8
Disorderly conduct	133,674	75,946	55,295	1,362	1,071	100.0	56.8	41.4	1.0	0.8
Vagrancy	2,151	1,539	588	9	15	100.0	71.5	27.3	0.4	0.7
All other offenses (except traffic)	256,855	177,661	71,845	2,844	4,505	100.0	69.2	28.0	1.1	1.8
Suspicion	175	74	100	0	1	100.0	42.3	57.1	0.0	0.6
Curfew and loitering law violations	89,578	54,439	33,207	872	1,060	100.0	60.8	37.1	1.0	1.2
Runaways	73,616	48,343	19,670	1,653	3,950	100.0	65.7	26.7	2.2	5.4

[a]Because of rounding, the percentages may not add to 100.0.

[b]Violent crimes are offenses of murder and nonnegligent manslaughter, forcible rape, robbery, and aggravated assault. Property crimes are offenses of burglary, larceny-theft, motor vehicle theft, and arson.

SOURCE: "Table 43B. Arrests, by Race, 2009," in *Crime in the United States, 2009*, U.S. Department of Justice, Federal Bureau of Investigation, September 2010, http://www2.fbi.gov/ucr/cius2009/data/documents/09tbl43b.xls (accessed November 9, 2010)

TABLE 10.4

Arrests of persons under 18 years of age, by gender, 2009

[12,371 agencies; 2009 estimated population 239,839,971]

Offense charged	Total under 18 Number	Males under 18 Number	Males under 18 Percent	Females under 18 Number	Females under 18 Percent
Total	1,515,586	1,054,659	69.6	460,927	30.4
Murder and nonnegligent manslaughter	942	873	92.7	69	7.3
Forcible rape	2,385	2,340	98.1	45	1.9
Robbery	25,280	22,757	90.0	2,523	10.0
Aggravated assault	39,467	29,720	75.3	9,747	24.7
Burglary	59,432	52,569	88.5	6,863	11.5
Larceny-theft	254,865	138,535	54.4	116,330	45.6
Motor vehicle theft	15,724	13,078	83.2	2,646	16.8
Arson	4,216	3,664	86.9	552	13.1
Violent crime*	68,074	55,690	81.8	12,384	18.2
Property crime*	334,237	207,846	62.2	126,391	37.8
Other assaults	172,984	113,849	65.8	59,135	34.2
Forgery and counterfeiting	1,691	1,187	70.2	504	29.8
Fraud	5,014	3,252	64.9	1,762	35.1
Embezzlement	484	281	58.1	203	41.9
Stolen property; buying, receiving, possessing	14,875	12,064	81.1	2,811	18.9
Vandalism	71,502	61,720	86.3	9,782	13.7
Weapons; carrying, possessing, etc.	26,831	24,064	89.7	2,767	10.3
Prostitution and commercialized vice	1,079	235	21.8	844	78.2
Sex offenses (except forcible rape and prostitution)	10,567	9,458	89.5	1,109	10.5
Drug abuse violations	134,610	113,608	84.4	21,002	15.6
Gambling	1,395	1,357	97.3	38	2.7
Offenses against the family and children	3,612	2,317	64.1	1,295	35.9
Driving under the influence	10,712	8,044	75.1	2,668	24.9
Liquor laws	88,370	54,321	61.5	34,049	38.5
Drunkenness	11,102	8,288	74.7	2,814	25.3
Disorderly conduct	134,301	89,579	66.7	44,722	33.3
Vagrancy	2,151	1,550	72.1	601	27.9
All other offenses (except traffic)	258,293	190,500	73.8	67,793	26.2
Suspicion	175	136	77.7	39	22.3
Curfew and loitering law violations	89,733	62,229	69.3	27,504	30.7
Runaways	73,794	33,084	44.8	40,710	55.2

*Violent crimes are offenses of murder and nonnegligent manslaughter, forcible rape, robbery, and aggravated assault. Property crimes are offenses of burglary, larceny-theft, motor vehicle theft, and arson.

SOURCE: Adapted from "Table 39. Arrests, Males, by Age, 2009," "Table 38. Arrests, by Age, 2009," and "Table 40. Arrests, Females, by Age, 2009," in *Crime in the United States, 2009*, U.S. Department of Justice, Federal Bureau of Investigation, September 2010, http://www2.fbi.gov/ucr/cius2009/arrests/index.html (accessed October 6, 2010).

Arrests for every other crime decreased for male juveniles. As a result, the number of male juveniles who were arrested for violent crimes decreased by 14.5% and for property crimes by 29.2% between 2000 and 2009.

As shown in Table 10.6, the total number of female juveniles arrested decreased by 13.1% between 2000 and 2009. However, arrests increased for several crimes in which relatively large numbers of female juveniles were involved: robbery (up 30.2%), disorderly conduct (up 7.3%), assaults other than aggravated assaults (up 5.7%), and larceny-theft (up 5.2%). Overall, violent crime arrests declined by 16.9% thanks to sharp decreases in arrests for murder and nonnegligent manslaughter (down 33.8%) and aggravated assault (down 24.4%). Arrests of female juveniles for forcible rape increased by 27.3%, but very few offenders (less than 30) were involved in either year. Property crime arrests among female juveniles increased by 0.1% between 2000 and 2009.

Murder: Juvenile Offenders and Victims

Table 2.2 in Chapter 2 provides demographic information about 923 murder offenders under the age of 18 years who were arrested in 2009. The vast majority of these juvenile arrestees (850 or 92.1%) were male. Concerning the racial breakdown, 539 (58.4%) were African-American and 353 (38.2%) were white. Half (465 or 50.4%) of those arrested were aged 13 to 16 years. Ten offenders (1.1%) were 9 to 12 years old and one offender (0.1%) was aged 5 to 8 years.

The FBI also provides demographic data about murder victims in *Crime in the United States, 2009*. Of the 13,636 total victims, 1,348 (9.9%) were under the age of 18 years. Two-thirds (67.7%) of the juvenile victims were male. The racial makeup of the victims was 48.5% (654) white and 47.4% (639) African-American.

Howard N. Snyder and Melissa Sickmund of the National Center for Juvenile Justice (NCJJ) report in

TABLE 10.5

Ten-year arrest trends for persons under 18 years of age, 2000–09

[8,649 agencies; 2009 estimated population 186,864,905; 2000 estimated population 172,176,040]

| | Number of persons arrested | | |
| | Under 18 years of age | | |
Offense charged	2000	2009	Percent change
Total[a]	1,455,216	1,161,830	−20.2
Murder and nonnegligent manslaughter	656	652	−0.6
Forcible rape	2,674	1,820	−31.9
Robbery	16,393	19,336	+18.0
Aggravated assault	41,133	29,932	−27.2
Burglary	58,963	46,637	−20.9
Larceny-theft	231,759	196,863	−15.1
Motor vehicle theft	28,116	11,354	−59.6
Arson	5,584	3,615	−35.3
Violent crime[b]	60,856	51,740	−15.0
Property crime[b]	324,422	258,469	−20.3
Other assaults	142,699	135,125	−5.3
Forgery and counterfeiting	4,144	1,277	−69.2
Fraud	5,874	4,091	−30.4
Embezzlement	1,324	393	−70.3
Stolen property; buying, receiving, possessing	17,991	11,990	−33.4
Vandalism	71,267	55,757	−21.8
Weapons; carrying, possessing, etc.	22,383	20,696	−7.5
Prostitution and commercialized vice	729	791	+8.5
Sex offenses (except forcible rape and prostitution)	10,848	7,799	−28.1
Drug abuse violations	121,666	103,657	−14.8
Gambling	458	312	−31.9
Offenses against the family and children	4,767	2,689	−43.6
Driving under the influence	12,683	8,085	−36.3
Liquor laws	97,338	67,859	−30.3
Drunkenness	14,252	9,837	−31.0
Disorderly conduct	98,834	92,754	−6.2
Vagrancy	1,647	1,047	−36.4
All other offenses (except traffic)	252,417	196,036	−22.3
Suspicion	749	152	−79.7
Curfew and loitering law violations	97,353	72,203	−25.8
Runaways	91,264	59,223	−35.1

[a]Does not include suspicion.

[b]Violent crimes are offenses of murder and nonnegligent manslaughter, forcible rape, robbery, and aggravated assault. Property crimes are offenses of burglary, larceny-theft, motor vehicle theft, and arson.

SOURCE: Adapted from "Table 32. Ten-Year Arrest Trends, Totals, 2000–2009," in *Crime in the United States, 2009*, U.S. Department of Justice, Federal Bureau of Investigation, September 2010, http://www2.fbi.gov/ucr/cius2009/data/documents/09tbl32.xls (accessed October 5, 2010)

Juvenile Offenders and Victims: 2006 National Report (March 2006, http://www.ojjdp.ncjrs.gov/ojstatbb/nr2006/downloads/NR2006.pdf) that murders involving a juvenile offender increased dramatically from the early 1980s to the early 1990s. In 1984 just over 1,000 murders involved a juvenile offender. By 1994 that number had climbed to more than 3,500. Then, murders by juveniles underwent a steep decline. In 2002 it was estimated that approximately 1,300 murders involved a juvenile offender.

Of the known juvenile offenders who committed murder between 1993 and 2002, 74% used a firearm. Snyder and Sickmund report that males (77%) were twice as likely to use a firearm as females (35%). Those aged 17 years were more likely than younger juveniles to use a firearm when committing murder; 77% of 17-year-olds used a gun, compared with 74% of 16-year-olds and 70% of those younger than age 16. African-American youth were more likely to use a gun (80%) than white youth (66%).

SCHOOL CRIME

A comprehensive examination of school crime was conducted for the National Center for Education Statistics and the BJS by Simone Robers et al. in *Indicators of School Crime and Safety: 2010* (November 2010, http://bjs.ojp.usdoj.gov/content/pub/pdf/iscs10.pdf). According to the researchers, approximately 1.2 million students aged 12 to 18 years were the victims of nonfatal crimes at school during the 2008–09 school year. There were 743,100 violent crimes including rape, sexual assault, robbery, aggravated assault, and simple assault. Another 619,000 crimes were thefts.

Among young people aged five to 18 years, Robers et al. note that there were 15 "school-associated" homicides during the 2008–09 school year. In addition, 8% of ninth through 12th graders said they were threatened or attacked and injured by weapon-bearing offenders while on school property. The weapons included firearms, knives, and clubs.

TABLE 10.6

Ten-year arrest trends for persons under 18 years of age, by gender, 2000–09

[8,649 agencies; 2009 estimated population 186,864,905; 2000 estimated population 172,176,040]

Offense charged	Male under 18			Female under 18		
	2000	2009	Percent change	2000	2009	Percent change
Total[a]	1,047,690	807,818	−22.9	407,526	354,012	−13.1
Murder and nonnegligent manslaughter	576	599	+4.0	80	53	−33.8
Forcible rape	2,652	1,792	−32.4	22	28	+27.3
Robbery	14,861	17,342	+16.7	1,532	1,994	+30.2
Aggravated assault	31,550	22,685	−28.1	9,583	7,247	−24.4
Burglary	51,950	40,897	−21.3	7,013	5,740	−18.2
Larceny-theft	146,160	106,852	−26.9	85,599	90,011	+5.2
Motor vehicle theft	23,314	9,412	−59.6	4,802	1,942	−59.6
Arson	4,922	3,138	−36.2	662	477	−27.9
Violent crime[b]	49,639	42,418	−14.5	11,217	9,322	−16.9
Property crime[b]	226,346	160,299	−29.2	98,076	98,170	+0.1
Other assaults	98,731	88,631	−10.2	43,968	46,494	+5.7
Forgery and counterfeiting	2,746	889	−67.6	1,398	388	−72.2
Fraud	3,871	2,637	−31.9	2,003	1,454	−27.4
Embezzlement	686	224	−67.3	638	169	−73.5
Stolen property; buying, receiving, possessing	15,179	9,670	−36.3	2,812	2,320	−17.5
Vandalism	62,404	48,203	−22.8	8,863	7,554	−14.8
Weapons; carrying, possessing, etc.	20,096	18,553	−7.7	2,287	2,143	−6.3
Prostitution and commercialized vice	332	167	−49.7	397	624	+57.2
Sex offenses (except forcible rape and prostitution)	10,103	7,061	−30.1	745	738	−0.9
Drug abuse violations	102,909	86,857	−15.6	18,757	16,800	−10.4
Gambling	431	304	−29.5	27	8	−70.4
Offenses against the family and children	3,029	1,701	−43.8	1,738	988	−43.2
Driving under the influence	10,500	6,033	−42.5	2,183	2,052	−6.0
Liquor laws	66,585	41,879	−37.1	30,753	25,980	−15.5
Drunkenness	11,406	7,381	−35.3	2,846	2,456	−13.7
Disorderly conduct	69,814	61,616	−11.7	29,020	31,138	+7.3
Vagrancy	1,287	824	−36.0	360	223	−38.1
All other offenses (except traffic)	186,628	145,383	−22.1	65,789	50,653	−23.0
Suspicion	575	119	−79.3	174	33	−81.0
Curfew and loitering law violations	67,275	50,288	−25.3	30,078	21,915	−27.1
Runaways	37,693	26,800	−28.9	53,571	32,423	−39.5

[a]Does not include suspicion.

[b]Violent crimes are offenses of murder and nonnegligent manslaughter, forcible rape, robbery, and aggravated assault. Property crimes are offenses of burglary, larceny-theft, motor vehicle theft, and arson.

SOURCE: Adapted from "Table 33. Ten-Year Arrest Trends, by Sex, 2000–2009," in *Crime in the United States, 2009*, U.S. Department of Justice, Federal Bureau of Investigation, September 2010, http://www2.fbi.gov/ucr/cius2009/data/documents/09tbl33.xls (accessed October 5, 2010)

School Shootings

Despite the relative safety of schools, several school shootings by juveniles have received national media attention in the past several years:

- March 21, 2005: 16-year-old Jeff Weise (1988–2005) killed his grandfather and a companion. He then went to Red Lake High School in Red Lake, Minnesota, and killed five students, a security guard, a teacher, and finally himself.

- April 14, 2003: one 15-year-old student was killed and three were wounded at John McDonogh High School in New Orleans, Louisiana, by gunfire from four teenagers who attended a different school.

- March 5, 2001: two students were killed and 13 wounded at Santee High School in Santana, California, when Charles A. Williams (1986–), a 15-year-old student at the school, opened fire from a school bathroom.

- February 29, 2000: a six-year-old student was killed at Theo J. Buell Elementary School near Flint, Michigan, by Dedrick Owens (1993–), a fellow six-year-old student who brought a handgun to school.

- April 20, 1999: 12 students and a teacher were fatally shot at Columbine High School in Littleton, Colorado, by students Eric Harris (1981–1999) and Dylan Klebold (1982–1999), who eventually killed themselves after an hour-long rampage.

YOUTH GANGS

Even though gangs have been a part of American life since the early 18th century, modern street gangs pose a greater threat to public safety and order than ever before. Many gangs originated as social clubs. In the early 20th century most were small groups who engaged in delinquent acts or minor crimes, such as fighting with other gangs. By the late 20th century, however, they were frequently involved in violence, intimidation, and the illegal trafficking of drugs and weapons. An increasing number supported themselves by the sale of crack cocaine, heroin, and other illegal drugs, and had easy access to high-powered guns and rifles.

In the fact sheet "Highlights of the 2008 National Youth Gang Survey" (March 2010, http://www.ncjrs.gov/pdffiles1/ojjdp/229249.pdf), Arlen Egley Jr., James C. Howell, and John P. Moore of the National Gang Center summarize results from a 2008 survey of more than 3,000 police and sheriff's departments around the country. According to the researchers, the results indicate that there were approximately 774,000 gang members and 27,900 gangs in the United States in 2008. The number of gangs is estimated to have increased by 28% since 2002. It should be noted that exact statistics on national gang activity are difficult to compile because local law enforcement agencies may not be aware of gang connections in some cases or may not regularly record offenses as gang related.

Overall, law enforcement agencies in 32.4% of jurisdictions (e.g., cities, suburban areas, towns, and rural counties) reported experiencing gang problems in 2008. Among the jurisdictions with gang problems, over four out of 10 of the agencies reported increases between 2007 and 2008 in gang-related aggravated assaults (44% of agencies), drug sales (41% of agencies), and firearms use (41% of agencies). Almost 20% of the agencies in large cities reported increases in gang-related murders in 2008. Forty-five percent of gang-plagued agencies said their gang problem was "getting worse," whereas less than 10% of gang-plagued agencies described their gang problem as "getting better."

JUVENILE COURT CASES

In "State Juvenile Justice Profiles" (2011, http://70.89.227.250:8080/stateprofiles/), the NCJJ notes that "the United States of America does not have a juvenile justice system. Rather, it has 51 separate systems." In other words, each state and the District of Columbia has its own juvenile justice system.

Even though no nationwide uniform procedure exists for processing juvenile cases, the cases do follow similar paths. An intake department first screens cases. The intake department can be the court itself, a state department of social services, or a prosecutor's office. The intake officer may decide that the case will be dismissed for lack of evidence, handled formally (petitioned), or resolved informally (nonpetitioned). Formal processing can include placement outside the home, probation, a trial in juvenile court, or transfer to an adult court. Informal processing may consist of referral to a social services agency, a fine,

some form of restitution, or informal probation. Both formal and informal processing can result in dismissal of the charges and release of the juvenile.

There are two broad types of cases within juvenile court: petitioned and nonpetitioned. Petitioned cases are those in which a petition is filed requesting a hearing. Nonpetitioned cases do not include such a petition and are handled more informally by the courts.

Juvenile courts may place youths in a detention facility during court processing. Detention may be needed to protect the community from the juvenile, to protect the juvenile, or both. In addition, detention is sometimes necessary to ensure a youth's appearance at scheduled hearings or evaluations.

All states allow certain juveniles to be tried in adult criminal court under some circumstances. These circumstances include the use of firearms or other weapons and a history of criminality. In some states juvenile court judges are allowed to determine whether individual suspects will be prosecuted in juvenile or adult criminal court; some states allow prosecutors to determine whether to file cases in juvenile or adult criminal court; and some states have laws that determine which court holds jurisdiction over cases, depending on the age of the suspect and the crime committed. The NCJJ's "State Juvenile Justice Profiles" is a searchable database that provides information about juvenile justice laws in every state and the District of Columbia.

Even though juvenile justice is governed by state laws, the federal government plays a role by setting standards for juvenile courts and providing funding to state agencies dealing with juvenile crime. In 1968 Congress passed the Juvenile Delinquency Prevention and Control Act; in 1972 it was amended and renamed the Juvenile Delinquency Prevention Act. According to the Cornell University Law School, in "Juvenile Justice" (2011, http://topics.law.cornell.edu/wex/juvenile_justice), "the stated purpose of the act is to assist states and local communities in providing community based preventative services to youths in danger of becoming delinquent, to help train individuals in occupations providing such services, and to provide technical assistance in the field." It also sets standards and rules for state juvenile court "procedures and punishments."

The Juvenile Justice and Delinquency Prevention Act was passed in 1974 and has been amended several times. It provides grant funding to states that comply with its requirements. As explained by Snyder and Sickmund, in *Juvenile Offenders and Victims: 1999 National Report* (September 1999, http://www.ncjrs.gov/html/ojjdp/nationalreport99/toc.html), the act establishes four primary or "core" requirements for the grants:

- Status offenders (e.g., offenders who commit acts such as running away from home, failing to attend school, or violating curfew) should not be placed in secure detention or correctional facilities.

- Detained or confined juveniles cannot have "sight or sound" contact with incarcerated adults.

- Juveniles cannot be detained or confined in adult jails or lockups except under certain circumstances.

- States must determine if they are confining minority juveniles disproportionately to nonminority juveniles and, if so, demonstrate efforts to reduce the disproportionality.

CHANGING APPROACHES TO JUVENILE DELINQUENCY

Before the 1950s the U.S. juvenile justice system was heavily focused on rehabilitation. This approach began to change as the public judged rehabilitation techniques to be ineffective. A growing number of juveniles were being institutionalized until they reached adulthood because the medical treatment they received did not seem to modify their behavior. Under the impetus of a number of U.S. Supreme Court decisions, juvenile courts became more formal to protect juveniles' rights when they were transferred to adult courts or if they were to be confined. During the 1970s the national policy became community-based management of juvenile delinquents.

Public perception changed again during the 1980s. Juvenile crime was growing, and the systems in place were perceived as being too lenient in dealing with delinquents. This spurred a nationwide movement toward tougher treatment of juveniles. In *Juvenile Offenders and Victims: 1999 National Report*, Snyder and Sickmund note that between 1992 and 1997 nearly all the states passed laws making their juvenile justice system more punitive (punishment oriented).

Laurence Steinberg argues in "Introducing the Issue" (*Future of Children*, vol. 18, no. 2, fall 2008) that during the 1990s Americans experienced a "moral panic" about juvenile crime that fueled "get tough" on crime policies that treated many juvenile offenders as adults. However, Steinberg suggests that by the end of the first decade of the 21st century get-tough policies were softening "as politicians and the public come to regret the high economic costs and ineffectiveness of the punitive reforms and the harshness of the sanctions."

Other surveys support the idea that get-tough attitudes appear to be changing. For example, the press release "New NCCD Poll Shows Public Strongly Favors Youth Rehabilitation and Treatment" (February 7, 2007, http://www.nccd-crc.org/nccd/pubs/zogbyPR0207.pdf) notes that a survey conducted by the National Council on Crime and Delinquency found that the American public supports rehabilitation and treatment for young people, not prosecution in adult criminal courts or incarceration in adult jails or prisons. Nine out of 10 people surveyed believed this approach might help prevent crime in the future, and seven out of 10 believed imprisoning juveniles in adult facilities would increase the likelihood that they would commit future crimes. Most people believed that youth should not be automatically transferred to adult court, but that such transfers should be handled on an individual basis.

JUVENILE CRIMES: COURT STATISTICS

As noted earlier, juvenile offenses are either status offenses or delinquency offenses. Status offenses only apply to minors, not to adults. They include acts such as running away from home, truancy (failure to attend school), or violating curfew. Delinquency offenses include murder, rape and other sexual offenses, robbery, burglary, larceny-theft, and other criminal acts for which adults can also be charged.

As shown in Figure 10.2, the number of delinquency cases handled in U.S. juvenile courts increased from around 400,000 cases in 1960 to more than 1.8 million cases per year during the late 1990s. By 2007 the number had declined to nearly 1.7 million cases.

Figure 10.3 shows the outcome of these cases in 2007. Just over half (56%) were petitioned and 44% were not petitioned. In nearly two-thirds (63%) of the petitioned cases the juvenile was adjudicated delinquent (found responsible by a judge for the alleged act). This is procedurally similar to a conviction in criminal court. Another 36% of the petitioned cases resulted in a finding of nonadjudication. Approximately 1% of the petitioned cases were waived to adult criminal court. Most (67%) of the nonadjudicated cases were dismissed. In the remainder the juveniles either received probation (18%) or some other sanction (15%). Probation was given in more than half (56%) of the adjudicated cases. One-fourth of the juveniles who were adjudicated delinquent went into residential placement and 19% received some other sanction. Overall, approximately one-third (561,600) of the nearly 1.7 million juvenile cases handled in 2007 resulted in probation.

Crystal Knoll and Melissa Sickmund of the NCJJ report in "Delinquency Cases in Juvenile Court, 2007" (June 2010, http://ncjrs.gov/pdffiles1/ojjdp/230168.pdf) that male juveniles accounted for 1.2 million of the 1.7 million delinquency cases in 2007, accounting for 73% of the total delinquency caseload. In contrast, female juveniles were involved in 27% of the total delinquency caseload. This value was up from 19% in 1985. The racial and ethnic breakdown of juvenile delinquency cases in 2007 was as follows: whites (64%), African-Americans (33%), Asian-Americans (1%), and Native Americans (1%). At that time

FIGURE 10.2

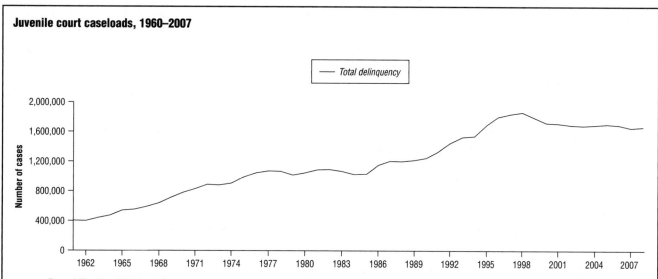

Juvenile court caseloads, 1960–2007

— Total delinquency

SOURCE: Crystal Knoll and Melissa Sickmund, "This decline in juvenile court caseloads since the mid-1990s is the most substantial decline since 1960," in *Delinquency Cases in Juvenile Court, 2007*, U.S. Department of Justice, Office of Justice Programs, Office of Juvenile Justice and Delinquency Prevention, June 2010, http://ncjrs.gov/pdffiles1/ojjdp/230168.pdf (accessed November 9, 2010)

FIGURE 10.3

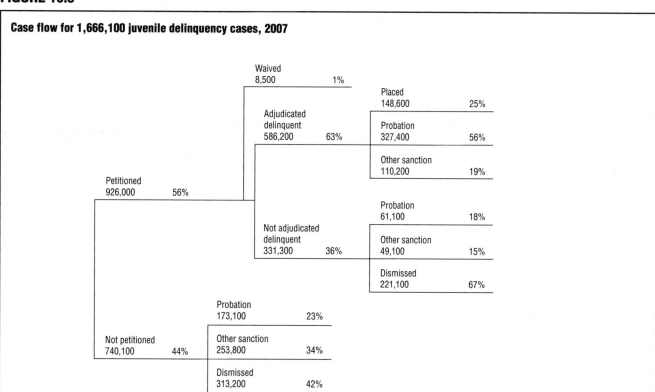

Case flow for 1,666,100 juvenile delinquency cases, 2007

Waived
8,500   1%

Placed
148,600   25%

Adjudicated
delinquent
586,200   63%

Probation
327,400   56%

Other sanction
110,200   19%

Petitioned
926,000   56%

Probation
61,100   18%

Not adjudicated
delinquent
331,300   36%

Other sanction
49,100   15%

Dismissed
221,100   67%

Probation
173,100   23%

Not petitioned
740,100   44%

Other sanction
253,800   34%

Dismissed
313,200   42%

Notes: Cases are categorized by their most severe or restrictive sanction. Detail may not add to totals because of rounding. Flow diagrams for 1985 through 2007 are available.

SOURCE: Crystal Knoll and Melissa Sickmund, "Case Flow for 1,666,100 Delinquency Cases in 2007," in *Delinquency Cases in Juvenile Court, 2007*, U.S. Department of Justice, Office of Justice Programs, Office of Juvenile Justice and Delinquency Prevention, June 2010, http://ncjrs.gov/pdffiles1/ojjdp/230168.pdf (accessed November 9, 2010)

whites accounted for 78% of the overall U.S juvenile population and African-Americans accounted for 16%. Thus, African-American youths were highly overrepresented within the juvenile delinquent population. Knoll and Sickmund provide the following racial breakdown of juvenile delinquency cases in 2007 by offense category:

- Person offenses—56% white and 41% African-American

- Property offenses—66% white and 30% African-American

- Drug offenses—72% white and 25% African-American

- Public-order offenses—63% white and 34% African-American

Table 10.7 provides detailed data about the 409,200 delinquency cases that were handled by juvenile courts in 2007 involving person offenses, such as murder, assault, robbery, rape, and other crimes that included force or the threat of force against people. Overall, the number of person offense cases handled by juvenile courts increased by 122% between 1985 and 2007. The largest increase (174%) was in simple assault cases. Table 10.7 also lists calculated case rates—that is, the number of cases per 1,000 youth aged 10 years through the upper age of the juvenile court jurisdiction. Overall, the case rate for all person offenses handled by juvenile courts increased by 88%, from 7 in 1985 to 13.1 in 2007. Again, the largest increase occurred for simple assaults.

Figure 10.4 shows the number of cases between 1985 and 2007 in which juveniles were placed on probation, put in residential placement, given other sanctions, or waived to criminal court. The probation caseload peaked during the late 1990s at nearly 700,000 cases per year. By 2007 it had declined to less than 600,000 cases. The number of cases resulting in residential placement also peaked during the late 1990s before declining slightly through 2007. Cases resulting in other sanctions showed a sustained upward trend between 1985 and 2007. The number of cases waived to criminal court was nearly flat due to the relatively low number of waived cases each year. However, as shown in Figure 10.5 the number of waived cases increased from around 7,000 in 1985 to around 13,000 during the mid-1990s. The number of delinquency cases waived to criminal court then dropped sharply through 2001 before leveling off. In 2007 just over 8,000 juvenile delinquency cases were waived to criminal court.

STATUS OFFENSE CASES

Status offenses are acts that are against the law only because the people who commit them are juveniles. In many communities social service agencies rather than juvenile courts are responsible for accused status offenders. Because of the differences in screening procedures, national estimates of informally handled status offense cases are not calculated. Therefore, the statistics presented in this chapter report only on status offense cases that are formally handled (petitioned) through the juvenile justice system.

According to Charles Puzzanchera, Benjamin Adams, and Melissa Sickmund of the NCJJ, in *Juvenile Court Statistics 2006–2007* (March 2010, http://www.ncjjservehttp.org/ncjjwebsite/pdf/jcsreports/jcs2007.pdf), the OJJDP uses only five major status offense categories: running away, truancy, liquor law violations, curfew violations, and ungovernability (also known as incorrigibility or being beyond parental control). Puzzanchera, Adams, and Sickmund report that 150,700 status offense cases were petitioned to juvenile courts in 2007. This number was up by 31% from 1995. The following is a breakdown by offenses for 2007:

- Truancy—38% of cases

- Liquor law violations—22% of cases

- Ungovernability—13% of cases

- Running away—12% of cases

- Curfew violations—9% of cases

- Miscellaneous—6% of cases

Age, Sex, and Race

For liquor law violations and curfew violations, Puzzanchera, Adams, and Sickmund indicate that the case rates (the number of cases per 1,000 juveniles in age group) in 2007 increased with violator age across the age group of 10 to 17. That is, the largest rates were reported for 17-year-olds. Different trends are seen in the age breakdowns for runaways, truancy, and ungovernability. For these offenses the highest case rates were for 15- and 16-year-olds.

TABLE 10.7

Person offense cases handled by juvenile courts, 1985–2007

Most severe disposition	1985	2007	Percent change 1985–2007
Cases			
Total person offenses[a]	184,100	409,200	122%
Violent Crime Index	64,500	86,300	34
Criminal homicide	1,200	1,400	18
Forcible rape	3,300	4,300	31
Robbery	25,600	31,000	21
Aggravated assault	34,400	49,600	44
Simple assault	100,500	274,900	174
Case rate[b]			
Total person offenses[a]	7.0	13.1	88%
Violent Crime Index	2.4	2.8	13
Criminal homicide	0.0	0.0	0
Forcible rape	0.1	0.1	10
Robbery	1.0	1.0	2
Aggravated assault	1.3	1.6	22
Simple assault	3.8	8.8	131

[a]Total includes other person offense categories not listed.
[b]Cases per 1,000 youth age 10 through the upper age of juvenile court jurisdiction.
Note: Percent change is calculated using unrounded numbers.

SOURCE: Sarah Hockenberry, "Person Offense Cases Handled by Juvenile Courts, 1985–2007," in *Person Offense Cases in Juvenile Court, 2007*, U.S. Department of Justice, Office of Justice Programs, Office of Juvenile Justice and Delinquency Prevention, June 2010, http://www.ncjrs.gov/pdffiles1/ojjdp/230169.pdf (accessed November 9, 2010)

FIGURE 10.4

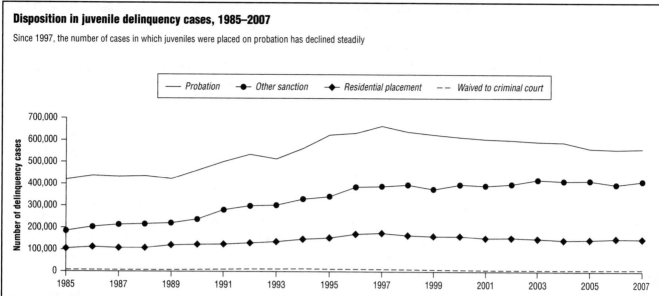

Disposition in juvenile delinquency cases, 1985–2007

Since 1997, the number of cases in which juveniles were placed on probation has declined steadily

Legend: —— Probation ● Other sanction ◆ Residential placement – – Waived to criminal court

Number of delinquency cases (y-axis): 0 to 700,000

Years (x-axis): 1985 1987 1989 1991 1993 1995 1997 1999 2001 2003 2005 2007

Notes: Probation was ordered in 50% of the more than 1.1 million cases that received a juvenile court sanction in 2007 (those that were not dismissed or otherwise released). Probation cases accounted for 34% of the increase between 1985 and 2007 in delinquency cases that received a juvenile court sanction.

SOURCE: Sarah Livsey, "Since 1997, the number of cases in which juveniles were placed on probation has declined steadily," in *Juvenile Delinquency Probation Caseload, 2007*, U.S. Department of Justice, Office of Justice Programs, Office of Juvenile Justice and Delinquency Prevention, June 2010, http://www.ncjrs.gov/pdffiles1/ojjdp/230170.pdf (accessed November 9, 2010)

FIGURE 10.5

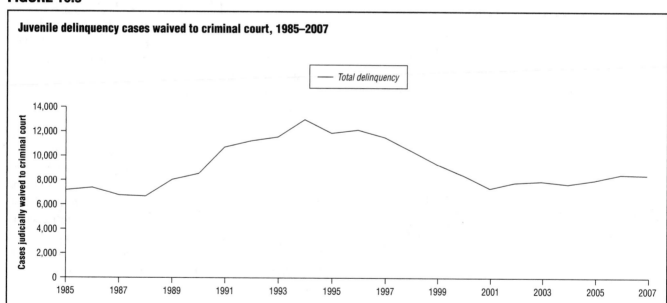

Juvenile delinquency cases waived to criminal court, 1985–2007

Legend: —— Total delinquency

Cases judicially waived to criminal court (y-axis): 0 to 14,000

Years (x-axis): 1985 1987 1989 1991 1993 1995 1997 1999 2001 2003 2005 2007

SOURCE: Benjamin Adams and Sean Addie, "The number of cases judicially waived to criminal court peaked in 1994 and then fell back to the levels of the mid-1980s," in *Delinquency Cases Waived to Criminal Court, 2007*, U.S. Department of Justice, Office of Justice Programs, Office of Juvenile Justice and Delinquency Prevention, June 2010, http://www.ncjrs.gov/pdffiles1/ojjdp/230167.pdf (accessed November 9, 2010)

In 2007 males accounted for 57% of status offense cases, whereas females accounted for 43%. More than one-third (36%) of the cases involving males were for truancy, 24% were for liquor law violations, 13% were for ungovernability, 11% were for curfew violations, 9% were for running away, and 8% were for miscellaneous offenses. Of the status cases involving females, 40% were for truancy, 19% were for liquor law violations, 16% were for running away, 13% were for ungovernability, 7% were for curfew violations, and 5% were for miscellaneous offenses.

Between 1995 and 2007 the number of status cases increased by 29% for males and by 33% for females. The larger increase for female offenders is attributed primarily to increases in violations of liquor and curfew laws. The caseload for liquor law violations increased by 49% for females during this period, compared with a 12% increase for males. Likewise, the caseload for curfew violations increased by 39% for female offenders, but increased by only 15% for male offenders.

Between 1995 and 2007 case rates (the number of cases per 1,000 juveniles aged 10 years and older) increased by 22% for whites, 61% for African-Americans, 56% for Native Americans, and 84% for Asian-Americans. In 2007 the offense profile for each racial group varied somewhat, with truancy making up the largest case rate for whites (38%), followed by liquor law violations (26%) and ungovernability (12%). The largest percentage of African-American status offense cases were brought for truancy (39%) and running away and ungovernability (21% each).

Detention and Case Processing

The handling of status crimes has changed considerably since the mid-1980s. The Juvenile Justice and Delinquency Prevention Act of 1974 offered substantial federal funds to states that tried to reduce the detention of status offenders. The primary responsibility for status offenders was often transferred from the juvenile courts to child welfare agencies. As a result, the character of the juvenile courts' activities changed.

Before this change many juvenile detention centers held a substantial number of young people whose only offense was that their parents could no longer control them. By not routinely institutionalizing these adolescents, the courts demonstrated that children deserved the same rights as adults. A logical extension of this has been that juveniles accused of violent crimes are also now being treated legally as if they are adults.

Those involved in petitioned status offense cases are rarely held in detention. Puzzanchera, Adams, and Sickmund indicate that only 9% of status offenders were detained in 2007. This percentage is virtually unchanged from 7% in 1995.

HOLDING PARENTS RESPONSIBLE

For many decades, civil liability laws held parents at least partly responsible for damages caused by their children. Also, child welfare laws included actions against those who contributed to the delinquency of a minor. Most researchers recognize that parental involvement is key to juvenile rehabilitation; however, that involvement can be problematic because many parents are seen as contributing to their children's problems rather than helping to resolve them. In addition, some parents assume an adversarial role with the juvenile justice system, hoping to protect their children from prosecution. By the 1990s, in response to

rising juvenile crime rates, communities and states passed stronger laws about parental responsibility. Several states enacted laws making parents criminally responsible for their children's crimes.

In "From Columbine to Kazaa: Parental Liability in a New World" (*University of Illinois Law Review*, 2005), Amy L. Tomaszewski reports that advocates of parental liability believe the laws motivate adults to become better parents to avoid serious penalties, including jail terms. According to Tomaszewski, even though parental liability laws are not new, states have established a broader range of civil and criminal penalties for parents who do not control their children. However, research shows that juvenile crime rates started declining before most parental liability laws were enacted. For example, between 1994 and 2001 the arrest rates for juvenile murder, rape, robbery, and aggravated assault dropped by 44%.

Furthermore, legislators find it very difficult to determine the age when parents are no longer responsible for their children's actions. Parents might be legitimately responsible for a small child's behavior, but teenagers are more independent, so it is more difficult to decide whether teenage crimes are really the result of poor parenting.

JUVENILES IN RESIDENTIAL PLACEMENT

Accused juveniles, delinquency offenders, and status offenders may be housed in residential placement facilities. These institutions may be under the administration of the state or be operated by private nonprofit or for-profit corporations or organizations and staffed by employees of the corporation or organization.

Every two to three years the OJJDP conducts the Census of Juveniles in Residential Placement (CJRP), a one-day count of the juvenile offenders who are held nationwide. The data collected include juvenile offender demographics, such as gender, race, ethnicity, and most serious offense. As of February 2011, the most recently published CJRP data were from the 2008 census; however, these data include only state-by-state counts, not detailed demographic information. The latter are available from the 2006 census.

In *Juveniles in Residential Placement, 1997–2008* (February 2010, http://www.ncjrs.gov/pdffiles1/ojjdp/229379.pdf), Sickmund notes that juvenile residential placement facilities are also known as "detention centers, juvenile halls, shelters, reception and diagnostic centers, group homes, wilderness camps, ranches, farms, youth development centers, residential treatment centers, training or reform schools, and juvenile correctional institutions." Fewer than 81,000 juvenile offenders were housed in public and private residential placement facilities around the country in 2008. This was down 26% from 2000, when the number of juveniles housed in residential placement facilities peaked at nearly 109,000. According to Sickmund, nearly half (46%) of the juvenile offenders in residential placement in 2008 were housed in six states: California, Florida, New York, Ohio, Pennsylvania, and Texas.

Demographic data from the 2006 census were published by the BJS in *Sourcebook of Criminal Justice Statistics Online* (October 16, 2008, http://www.albany.edu/sourcebook/pdf/t6122006.pdf). There were 92,854 juveniles in residential custody facilities in 2006, including 64,163 (69.1%) juveniles who were in public facilities.

Males accounted for the largest portion (78,911 or 85%) of those in residential placement. The racial and ethnic breakdown was 37,337 (40.2%) non-Hispanic African-Americans, 32,495 (35%) non-Hispanic whites, 19,027 (20.5%) Hispanics, 1,828 (2%) Native Americans, 1,155 (1.2%) Asian-Americans, and 1,012 (1.1%) other races.

The BJS (October 16, 2008, http://www.albany.edu/sourcebook/pdf/t6102006.pdf) provides a breakdown by race and ethnicity for the most serious offense for which juveniles had been placed in residential custody facilities in 2008. The vast majority of the offenses (88,137 or 94.9%) were delinquency offenses. The remaining 5.1% were status offenses. The racial and ethnic breakdown of the juveniles held for delinquency offenses was 35,766 (40.6%) non-Hispanic African-American offenders, 30,133 (34.2%) non-Hispanic white offenders, 18,636 (21.1%) Hispanic offenders, 1,603 (1.8%) Native American offenders, 1,109 (1.3%) Asian-American offenders, and 890 (1%) offenders of other races.

There were 31,704 juvenile offenders in residential custody facilities who had committed violent crimes and 23,177 who had committed property offenses. Additional numbers were held for technical violations (15,316 juveniles), public-order offenses (9,944 juveniles), and drug offenses (7,996 juveniles).

The BJS (October 16, 2008, http://www.albany.edu/sourcebook/pdf/t6112006.pdf) also provides a breakdown of the juveniles in residential custody facilities by age and sex in 2006. The largest contingent (24,646 or 27% of the total) were 16 years old. In descending order, the remaining contingents were 17 years old (23,761 or 26% of the total), 15 years old (17,574 or 19% of the total), 18 years and older (13,115 or 14% of the total), 14 years old (9,127 or 10% of the total), 13 years old (3,424 or 4% of the total), and juveniles less than 13 years old (1,207 or 1% of the total).

The largest proportions of males (26% each) in 2006 were 16 and 17 years old. Together, they accounted for more than half of the males in residential custody facilities. Other age groups made up smaller proportions of males: 15 years old (18% of total males), 18 years and older (15% of total males), 14 years old (9% of total males), 13 years old (3% of total males), and juveniles less than 13 years old (1% of total males). The largest contingents of females were 16 years old (28% of total females), 17 years old (23% of total females), and 15 years old (23% of total females). A breakdown of the other age groups is 14 years old (13% of total females), 18 years and older (7% of total females), 13 years old (5% of total females), and less than 13 years old (1% of total females).

Sexual Victimization of Juvenile Inmates

As noted in Chapter 8, the Prison Rape Elimination Act (PREA) of 2003 requires the BJS to collect data on the incidence and prevalence of sexual assault within correctional facilities. As of February 2011, the most recent report on sexual violence involving juvenile inmates was by Allen J. Beck, Paige M. Harrison, and Paul Guerino of the BJS in *Sexual Victimization in Juvenile Facilities Reported by Youth, 2008–09* (January 2010, http://bjs.ojp.usdoj.gov/content/pub/pdf/svjfry09.pdf). The researchers note that the BJS conducted its first National Survey of Youth in Custody between June 2008 and April 2009. The survey covered 195 public and private juvenile facilities that held adjudicated juveniles for at least 90 days. Overall, 12% of the youths reported experiencing sexual victimization by another youth (2.6%) or by a facility staff person (10.3%) within the previous 12 months or since their time of admission if admission occurred less than 12 months prior to the time of the survey. Nearly all (95%) of the youths reporting sexual victimization by a facility staff person said the staff person was female.

JUVENILE BOOT CAMPS

Boot camps are specialized residential facilities for midrange offenders—those who have failed with lesser sanctions such as probation but are not yet considered hardened criminals. First proposed during the 1980s, juvenile boot camps typically share the 90- to 120-day duration of military boot camps. They employ military customs and have correctional officers acting as uniformed drill instructors who use intense verbal tactics that are designed to break down inmates' resistance. Boot camps emphasize vigorous physical activity, drill and ceremony, and manual labor. The offenders have little free time, and strictly enforced rules govern all aspects of conduct and appearance. Because of state-mandated education rules, programs spend a minimum of three hours daily on academic education. Most programs also include some vocational education, work-skills training, or job preparation.

The first boot camp for juvenile offenders in the United States was established in Orleans Parish, Louisiana, in 1985. Within a decade similar facilities were operating in about 30 states. Despite great hopes for the boot camps to reduce recidivism (repeat offenses) they began to lose favor during the first decade of the 21st century. In *Correctional Boot Camps: Lessons from a Decade of Research* (June 2003, http://www.ncjrs.gov/pdffiles1/nij/197018.pdf), the DOJ states that "participants reported positive short-term changes in attitudes and behaviors; they also had better problem-solving and coping skills.... With few exceptions, these positive changes did not lead to reduced recidivism. The boot camps that did produce lower recidivism rates offered more treatment services, had longer sessions, and included more intensive postrelease supervision. However, not all programs with these features had successful results.... Under a narrow set of conditions, boot camps can lead to small relative reductions in prison populations and correctional costs."

JUVENILE DELINQUENCY PREVENTION

The criminal justice system also focuses resources on preventing juveniles from becoming delinquents in the first place and on helping delinquents to reform. In accordance with the Juvenile Justice and Delinquency Prevention Act of 1974, as amended, the OJJDP provides funding for state programs that are devoted to delinquency prevention. These programs typically provide a variety of services to youths, such as mentoring, substance abuse education and treatment, and educational support. For example, the Florida Department of Juvenile Justice describes in "OJJDP Funded Prevention Programs, FY 2007–08" (March 5, 2008, http://www.djj.state.fl.us/JJDP/Grants/FY0708_Grants.pdf) dozens of programs that together received more than $2 million in OJJDP funding during fiscal years 2007 and 2008. One example is Liberty County's Friends for the Future Program. One of its stated goals is to "reduce early persistent defiant and anti-social behavior." It provides after-school activities, mentoring, substance abuse prevention, and similar programs for at-risk youths.

JUVENILES IN THE ADULT JUSTICE SYSTEM

According to Benjamin Adams and Sean Addie of the OJJDP, in *Delinquency Cases Waived to Criminal Court, 2007* (June 2010, http://www.ncjrs.gov/pdffiles1/ojjdp/230167.pdf), 8,500 juvenile cases were waived to adult criminal court in 2007. This number was down substantially from the mid-1990s, when more than 12,000 waivers were issued per year. The researchers indicate that this decline was driven by an overall drop in the juvenile violent crime rate as well as by more widespread use of nonjudicial transfer laws. These laws allow prosecutors to file charges against juveniles in adult criminal court rather than in juvenile court. As of February 2011, no more recent data than those provided by Adams and Addie were available on the number of juveniles that are handled under nonjudicial transfer laws. However, the BJS explains in "2009 Survey of Juveniles Charged in Adult Criminal Courts Solicitation" (April

2010, http://bjs.ojp.usdoj.gov/content/pub/pdf/sjcacc09sol.pdf) that in early 2010 it was preparing to conduct a nationwide survey to collect data on this subject.

Until 2005 convicted criminals could be executed for crimes they committed as juveniles. Victor L. Streib of Ohio Northern University reports in *The Juvenile Death Penalty Today: Death Sentences and Executions for Juvenile Crimes, January 1, 1973–February 28, 2005* (October 7, 2005, http://www.law.onu.edu/faculty_staff/faculty_profiles/coursematerials/streib/juvdeath.pdf) that between 1973 and 2005, 22 offenders were executed for crimes they committed when they were younger than 18 years old. The U.S. Supreme Court has considered many cases that address the practice of executing offenders for crimes they committed as juveniles. For example, in *Eddings v. Oklahoma* (455 U.S. 104 [1982]), the court found that a juvenile's mental and emotional development should be considered as a mitigating factor when deciding whether to apply the death penalty, noting that adolescents are less mature and responsible than adults and not as able to consider long-range consequences of their actions. In this case, the court reversed the death sentence of a 16-year-old who had been tried as an adult.

Subsequent Supreme Court rulings have further limited the application of the death penalty in cases involving juveniles. In *Thompson v. Oklahoma* (487 U.S. 815 [1988]), the court found that applying the death sentence to an offender who had been 15 years old at the time of the murder was cruel and unusual punishment, concluding that the death penalty could not be applied to offenders who were younger than 16 years old. The following year the court found in *Stanford v. Kentucky* (492 U.S. 361 [1989]) that applying the death penalty to offenders who were aged 16 or 17 years at the time of the crime was not cruel and unusual punishment.

The court was asked to reconsider this decision in 2005. In *Roper v. Simmons* (543 U.S. 551), the court set aside the death sentence of Christopher Simmons by a vote of 5–4, concluding that the "Eighth and Fourteenth Amendments forbid imposition of the death penalty on offenders who were under the age of 18 when their crimes were committed." Snyder and Sickmund note in *Juvenile Offenders and Victims: 2006 National Report* that few states applied death penalty provisions to juveniles at the time of the *Roper* decision, even though 20 states allowed juveniles to be sentenced to death under the law.

After the 2005 *Roper* ruling, the most severe punishment for juveniles convicted of committing serious crimes was a sentence of life in prison without the possibility for parole. However, this sentence has also been challenged on constitutional grounds. In May 2010 the Supreme Court ruled 6–3 in *Graham v. Florida* (560 U.S. ___) that juveniles convicted of crimes in which nobody is killed cannot be sentenced to life in prison without the possibility for parole. The case involved Terrance Graham, a Florida juvenile who was convicted of several armed robberies when he was 16 and 17 years old. In 2005 Graham was sentenced to life in prison. As explained in Chapter 9, Florida does not offer parole to felons convicted after October 1, 1983. Thus, Graham was effectively given a life sentence with no possibility for parole.

In "Justices Limit Life Sentences for Juveniles" (*New York Times*, May 17, 2010), Adam Liptak reports that as of May 2010 only 129 juveniles around the country were believed to be serving life sentences without the chance of parole for nonhomicide crimes. The vast majority (77) of them were in Florida. A far greater number of juveniles nationwide (around 2,000) were believed to be serving life sentences without the chance of parole for committing homicides. It remains to be seen if legal challenges will be raised about the constitutionality of their sentences.

IMPORTANT NAMES
AND ADDRESSES

American Bar Association
321 N. Clark St.
Chicago, IL 60654-7598
(312) 988-5000
E-mail: service@americanbar.org
URL: http://www.abanet.org/

American Civil Liberties Union
125 Broad St., 18th Floor
New York, NY 10004
(212) 549-2500
URL: http://www.aclu.org/

American Correctional Association
206 N. Washington St., Ste. 200
Alexandria, VA 22314
(703) 224-0000
1-800-222-5656
FAX: (703) 224-0179
URL: http://www.aca.org/

American Jail Association
1135 Professional Ct.
Hagerstown, MD 21740-5853
(301) 790-3930
URL: http://www.aja.org/

Anti-Defamation League
1100 Connecticut Ave. NW, Ste. 1020
Washington, DC 20036
(202) 452-8310
FAX: (202) 296-2371
URL: http://www.adl.org/

**Bureau of Alcohol, Tobacco, Firearms,
and Explosives**
Office of Public and Governmental Affairs
99 New York Ave. NE, Rm. 5S 144
Washington, DC 20226
(202) 648-8500
E-mail: atfmail@atf.gov
URL: http://www.atf.gov/

Bureau of Engraving and Printing
U.S. Department of the Treasury
14th St. and C St. SW
Washington, DC 20228
(202) 874-2330
1-877-874-4114

E-mail: moneyfactory.info@bep.gov
URL: http://www.moneyfactory.gov/

Bureau of Justice Statistics
U.S. Department of Justice
810 Seventh St. NW
Washington, DC 20531
(202) 307-0765
E-mail: askbjs@usdoj.gov
URL: http://www.ojp.usdoj.gov/bjs/

Congressional Research Service
Library of Congress
101 Independence Ave. SE
Washington, DC 20540
(202) 707-5000
URL: http://www.loc.gov/crsinfo/

**Federal Bureau
of Investigation**
J. Edgar Hoover Bldg.
935 Pennsylvania Ave. NW
Washington, DC 20535-0001
(202) 324-3000
URL: http://www.fbi.gov/

Federal Bureau of Prisons
320 First St. NW
Washington, DC 20534
(202) 307-3198
URL: http://www.bop.gov/

Federal Trade Commission
600 Pennsylvania Ave. NW
Washington, DC 20580
(202) 326-2222
URL: http://www.ftc.gov/

**Internal Revenue Service Criminal
Investigation Division**
1111 Constitution Ave. NW, Rm. 2501
Washington, DC 20224
URL: http://www.irs.gov/irs/article/
0,,id=98398,00.html

National Center for Victims of Crime
2000 M St. NW, Ste. 480
Washington, DC 20036
(202) 467-8700
FAX: (202) 467-8701
URL: http://www.ncvc.org/

**National Conference of
State Legislatures**
7700 E. First Place
Denver, CO 80230
(303) 364-7700
FAX: (303) 364-7800
URL: http://www.ncsl.org/

National Consumers League
1701 K St. NW, Ste. 1200
Washington, DC 20006
(202) 835-3323
FAX: (202) 835-0747
URL: http://www.nclnet.org/

**National Correctional
Industries Association**
1202 N. Charles St.
Baltimore, MD 21201
(410) 230-3972
FAX: (410) 230-3981
E-mail: info@nationalcia.org
URL: http://www.nationalcia.org/

National Crime Prevention Council
2001 Jefferson Davis
Highway, Ste. 901
Arlington, VA 22202
(202) 466-6272
URL: http://www.ncpc.org/

**National Criminal
Justice Association**
720 Seventh St. NW
Washington, DC 20001
(202) 628-8550
FAX: (202) 448-1723
URL: http://www.ncja.org/

**National Criminal Justice
Reference Service**
PO Box 6000
Rockville, MD 20849-6000
(301) 519-5500
1-800-851-3420
FAX: (301) 519-5212
URL: http://www.ncjrs.gov/

**National Gang Center
Institute for Intergovernmental Research**
PO Box 12729
Tallahassee, FL 32317
(850) 385-0600
FAX: (850) 386-5356
E-mail:
information@nationalgangcenter.gov
URL: http://www.nationalgangcenter.gov/

National Institute of Corrections
320 First St. NW
Washington, DC 20534
(202) 307-3106
1-800-995-6423
URL: http://www.nicic.org/

National Institute of Justice
810 Seventh St. NW
Washington, DC 20531
(202) 307-2942
FAX: (202) 307-6394
URL: http://www.ojp.usdoj.gov/nij/

**National Legal Aid and
Defender Association**
1140 Connecticut Ave. NW, Ste. 900
Washington, DC 20036
(202) 452-0620
FAX: (202) 872-1031
E-mail: info@nlada.org
URL: http://www.nlada.org/

**National Organization for
Victim Assistance**
510 King St., Ste. 424
Alexandria, VA 22314-3132
(703) 535-6682
1-800-879-6682 (information hotline)
FAX: (703) 535-5500
URL: http://www.trynova.org/

National White Collar Crime Center
10900 Nuckols Rd., Ste. 325
Glen Allen, VA 23060-9288

(804) 967-6200
URL: http://www.nw3c.org/

**Office for Victims of Crime
U.S. Department of Justice**
810 Seventh St. NW, Eighth Floor
Washington, DC 20531
(202) 307-5983
FAX: (202) 514-6383
URL: http://www.ojp.usdoj.gov/ovc/

**Office of Juvenile Justice and
Delinquency Prevention**
810 Seventh St. NW
Washington, DC 20531
(202) 307-5911
URL: http://www.ojjdp.ncjrs.org/

**Office of National Drug Control Policy
Drug Policy Information Clearinghouse**
PO Box 6000
Rockville, MD 20849-6000
1-800-666-3332
FAX: (301) 519-5212
URL: http://www.whitehou
sedrugpolicy.gov/

Sentencing Project
1705 DeSales St. NW, Eighth Floor
Washington, DC 20036
(202) 628-0871
FAX: (202) 628-1091
E-mail: staff@sentencingproject.org
URL: http://www.sentencingproject.org/

Southern Poverty Law Center
400 Washington Ave.
Montgomery, AL 36104
(334) 956-8200
URL: http://www.splcenter.org/

**Substance Abuse and Mental Health
Services Administration**
PO Box 2345
Rockville, MD 20847-2345
1-877-726-4727
FAX: (240) 221-4292
E-mail: SAMHSAInfo@samhsa.hhs.gov
URL: http://www.samhsa.gov/

Supreme Court of the United States
One First St. NE
Washington, DC 20543
(202) 479-3000
URL: http://www.supremecourtus.gov/

**UNICOR
Federal Prison Industries, Inc.**
(203) 746-6515
1-800-827-3168
URL: http://www.unicor.gov/

Urban Institute
2100 M St. NW
Washington, DC 20037
(202) 833-7200
URL: http://urban.org/

U.S. Census Bureau
4600 Silver Hill Rd.
Washington, DC 20233
(301) 763-4636
1-800-923-8282
URL: http://www.census.gov/

U.S. Department of Justice
950 Pennsylvania Ave. NW
Washington, DC 20530-0001
(202) 514-2000
E-mail: askdoj@usdoj.gov
URL: http://www.usdoj.gov/

**U.S. Drug Enforcement Administration
U.S. Department of Justice**
8701 Morrissette Dr.
Springfield, VA 22152
(202) 307-1000
URL: http://www.usdoj.gov/dea/index.htm

U.S. Parole Commission
5550 Friendship Blvd., Ste. 420
Chevy Chase, MD 20815-7286
(301) 492-5990
URL: http://www.justice.gov/uspc/

U.S. Securities and Exchange Commission
100 F St. NE
Washington, DC 20549
(202) 942-8088
E-mail: help@sec.gov
URL: http://www.sec.gov/

U.S. Sentencing Commission
Office of Public Affairs
One Columbus Circle NE, Ste. 2-500
Washington, DC 20002-8002
(202) 502-4500
E-mail: pubaffairs@ussc.gov
URL: http://www.ussc.gov/

RESOURCES

The various agencies of the U.S. Department of Justice (DOJ) are the major sources of crime and justice data in the United States. The Bureau of Justice Statistics (BJS) compiles statistics on virtually every area of crime and reports those data in a number of publications. The annual BJS *Sourcebook of Criminal Justice Statistics*, prepared by the Hindelang Criminal Justice Research Center, University at Albany, State University of New York, is a comprehensive compilation of criminal justice statistics. The annual BJS National Crime Victimization Survey provides data for several studies, the most important of which is *Criminal Victimization in the United States*. The BJS also publishes data about the nation's corrections systems, including detailed counts and information about facilities and inmates, courts and sentencing, types of crime, and justice system employment and expenditures.

The Federal Bureau of Investigation (FBI) collects crime data from state and local law enforcement agencies through its Uniform Crime Reports Program. The FBI annual *Crime in the United States* is the most important source of information on crime that is reported to law enforcement agencies. The FBI also publishes the annual *Financial Crimes Report to the Public*, which provides statistical data regarding white-collar crime. Other major resources for white-collar crime information include the National White Collar Crime Center, the DOJ's Computer Crime and Intellectual Property Section, and the Federal Trade Commission's Identity Theft Clearinghouse.

The Office of Juvenile Justice and Delinquency Prevention within the DOJ publishes numerous helpful resources about juvenile crime and justice issues, particularly its annual series *Juvenile Arrests*, *Juvenile Court Statistics*, and *Juvenile Offenders and Victims*.

The FBI's annual report *Hate Crime Statistics* provided valuable data about hate crimes, as did private organizations, such as the Anti-Defamation League and the Southern Poverty Law Center.

Other important government resources included the U.S. Sentencing Commission's *2010 Federal Sentencing Guidelines Manual and Supplement* (November 2010); the Office of National Drug Control Policy of the Executive Office of the President; the Substance Abuse and Mental Health Services Administration of the U.S. Department of Health and Human Services; the U.S. Drug Enforcement Administration; the Federal Interagency Forum on Child and Family Statistics; and the Congressional Research Service.

Key information was also acquired from polling results reported by the Gallup Organization.

INDEX